THE LIBRARY OF CHRISTIAN CLASSICS

THE LIBRARY OF CHRISTIAN CLASSICS

VOLUME XII

WESTERN ASCETICISM

THE LIBRARY OF CHRISTIAN CLASSICS

Volume XII

WESTERN ASCETICISM

*Selected Translations with
Introductions and Notes by*

OWEN CHADWICK

PHILADELPHIA

THE WESTMINSTER PRESS

Published simultaneously in Great Britain and the United States of America
by the SCM Press, Ltd., London, and The Westminster Press, Philadelphia.

First published MCMLVIII

Library of Congress Catalog Card No. : 58-8713

Typeset in Great Britain
Printed in the United States of America

GENERAL EDITORS' PREFACE

GENERAL EDITORS' PREFACE

The Christian Church possesses in its literature an abundant and incomparable treasure. But it is an inheritance that must be reclaimed by each generation. THE LIBRARY OF CHRISTIAN CLASSICS is designed to present in the English language, and in twenty-six volumes of convenient size, a selection of the most indispensable Christian treatises written prior to the end of the sixteenth century.

The practice of giving circulation to writings selected for superior worth or special interest was adopted at the beginning of Christian history. The canonical Scriptures were themselves a selection from a much wider literature. In the Patristic era there began to appear a class of works of compilation (often designed for ready reference in controversy) of the opinions of well-reputed predecessors, and in the Middle Ages many such works were produced. These medieval anthologies actually preserve some noteworthy materials from works otherwise lost.

In modern times, with the increasing inability even of those trained in universities and theological colleges to read Latin and Greek texts with ease and familiarity, the translation of selected portions of earlier Christian literature into modern languages has become more necessary than ever; while the wide range of distinguished books written in vernaculars such as English makes selection there also needful. The efforts that have been made to meet this need are too numerous to be noted here, but none of these collections serves the purpose of the reader who desires a library of representative treatises spanning the Christian centuries as a whole. Most of them embrace only the age of the Church Fathers, and some of them have long been out of print. A fresh translation of a work already translated may shed much new light upon its meaning. This is true even of Bible translations despite the work of many experts through the centuries. In some instances old translations have been adopted in this series, but wherever necessary or desirable, new ones have been made. Notes have been supplied where these were needed to explain the author's meaning. The introductions provided for the several treatises and extracts will, we believe, furnish welcome guidance.

JOHN BAILLIE
JOHN T. MCNEILL
HENRY P. VAN DUSEN

CONTENTS

General Introduction

The monks always looked back to the apostolic Church as the source of their way of life. Medieval monks supposed that their corporate societies were successors, in a continuous line, of that primitive group of disciples which possessed all things in common. To support the texts of the Acts they used a treatise of Philo which described a group of contemplatives contemporary with the apostolic age, a group now believed to be Jewish but then thought to be Christian. From Philo's treatise St Jerome deduced that "the earliest members of the Christian Church lived in the way in which the monks of today try earnestly to live."

Though a stronger sense of history discarded this faith, it contained more truth than the nineteenth century suspected. The little primitive Church was puritan. Its moral standards were lofty, its discipline rigorous, its demands upon the faithful exacting. The monks were the puritans of a Church which in capturing society had partially jettisoned its puritanism. They were the successors of at least one facet, an important facet, of primitive Christianity.

When in the first age Christian evangelists preached the gospel to the Gentiles, they published the coming of the Kingdom, the otherworldly and apocalyptic message which the gospel contained. The circumstances in which they first preached the gospel naturally led them to seize upon those texts and those ideas which looked to another world. They expected the end of the world soon: the sense of detachment from the stuff of this mortal life was sometimes overwhelming. St Paul was not the only writer to use the imminent approach of the end as a ground for advising freedom from the cares of marriage. The earnest waited for the end in continence, prayer, faith. Here and there this expectation of the end persisted for centuries: and among the many in whom it became weaker, the feeling of detachment and otherworldly expectation was

13

maintained in other ways. The government was hostile. In the spasms of persecution the Christian was in hourly danger from the mob or from arrest. In the Apocalypse we see how the suffering of persecution and the awaiting of death were mingled with the expectation of the Lord's Second Coming—"Come ye out and be separate." They believed the Church to be a society set apart from and antagonistic to earthly society with its cruelty and immorality. Every martyr fortified this sense of antagonism. The blood of the martyrs not only propagated the gospel: it ensured that the kind of gospel propagated was that which showed the Christians as strangers and pilgrims upon earth, that their life was in another and a heavenly Zion.

The Christian sources of the second century already show groups of virgins or ascetics in the Christian congregations. By the end of that century the existence of celibates was one of the first facts which enquiring pagans noticed when they examined the institutions of Christianity.

In the New Testament the demand for *ascesis*, self-discipline, possessed many other aspects besides the advice about continence. The cardinal demand, from the Sermon on the Mount downwards, was the demand for detachment: and towards detachment it was believed that continence could be a useful aid. But already in the second century virginity was beginning to appear to be the act of asceticism *par excellence*, the necessary foundation to the earnest and disciplined life.

Many critics have found in the oriental depreciation of the body the source of this concentration upon a particular element in the detachment advocated in the gospel. This view has been found to be an inadequate historical explanation. It can hardly be doubted, indeed, that throughout the history of Christian asceticism from the second to the fifth century and beyond, the eastern suspicion of the body and certain pagan concepts of *ascesis* did in divers times and divers persons reinforce an already existing trend. It cannot be doubted that during the second century the Christian leaders were forced to fight a strenuous battle against a lack of balance in *ascesis*. Groups which not all contemporary Christians would have regarded as heretical exalted continence beyond the limits suggested by the New Testament. The apocryphal writings represent the level to which popular religion tended. Some Gnostics and quasi-Gnostics—Cerdo and others—exacted continence as a condition of membership. Marcion refused to baptize any married person who would not agree to dissolve his marriage.

One saintly bishop who asked for abstinence from sexual union as a necessary element in Christian living was criticized as rigoristic rather than heretical. But a religion based upon the Incarnation could not succumb to any theory that the body was evil. Theologians like Irenaeus and Justin Martyr fought for the Biblical doctrine of Creation and Incarnation. When the struggle was passed, the ascetic life was admitted to be an honourable, earnest and devout way of serving the Lord; and the ideals of the ascetics had come to dominate the Christian conceptions of holiness. But marriage was also honourable: the married Christian could also, in his different way, serve the Lord.

Meanwhile, the work of the congregations, in the narrower sense of "work," needed to be performed. The sick must be visited, the widows shepherded, prayers must be said, alms must be distributed. Apocalyptic feeling and the sense of antagonism to society prevented much idea that one could serve the Lord effectively by the performance of a secular vocation. Some of the professions most useful to society—like magistrates or schoolmasters—were disliked by earnest Christians because their functions were often entangled with pagan ritual. "Serving the Lord" most naturally meant what the modern age has called "church work." It was patently true that if to serve the Lord one must engage in a life of "church work," of prayer, almsgiving, and holy acts in the congregation, then the married woman could not serve the Lord like the virgin or widow: and what was obviously true of females might be held to be true, if less obviously, of males.

These primitive ascetics possessed no more than the most rudimentary form of organization. They were groups of persons who lived in continence, distributed their goods for the benefit of the Church and the poor, kept particular hours of prayer. They did not live in a community: they retained their private means and were not sharers in a common purse: they wore no special garb, though if they appeared in elegant or fashionable clothes they were criticized. By the beginning of the third century Tertullian was acclaiming their numbers. And all through that century the place of the ascetics in the congregation was becoming more important and more honourable. The ascetical idea of gospel holiness was sovereign in moral thought. At the end of the century the virtue of continence has rarely received such panegyric as in the *Symposium* of Methodius in praise of virginity.

To transform these primitive ascetics into monks two developments were necessary: (1) withdrawal from the congregation, (2) common discipline and rule. Already in the third century the need for these developments was becoming urgent.

In Tertullian the Christians are described as numerous, in Origen they are to be found everywhere. The Church was becoming popular. The ascetics slowly found that this popularity forced them to seek some kind of retirement. They were enabled to share the life of the primitive congregation without disrupting it, and without interrupting their own "recollectedness", because the primitive congregation was small, ardent, and puritan. As the congregations swelled, and the standards of morality and of worship were inevitably lowered, the contrast between the ascetic groups and the normal congregation became more manifest and their relations more uncomfortable. Every difference in practice, every extra form of worship, widened the gap between the earnest and the rest. The ascetics often joined in prayer at times like the third, sixth and ninth hours, when the normal working man could not be expected to join with them: and such customs, though still extra-liturgical, were accustoming the ascetics to the idea of worshipping apart from the worship of the congregation as a whole. Perhaps social conditions exacted a certain withdrawal for women. The contemporary standards of modesty separated them further from the everyday life of the congregation. And since they could perform pastoral duties in the church less freely than men, they naturally devoted themselves more to such work as intercession for which withdrawal was helpful. We seem to find "communities" for virgins accepted as normal before communities for male ascetics had become normal. But already at the end of the third century and the beginning of the fourth, there is evidence (from Syria and Egypt) of male societies.

These societies, with their growing sense of separation from the congregation and increasingly distinct customs of worship, were nevertheless engaged to some extent in the "church work" of the congregation. The group about which we know most was probably Syrian. They had adopted their manner of life in pursuit of holiness. They seem to have been withdrawn from any particular congregation. But they worked zealously for the congregations around them. They interceded for the ministers, the sick, and other needs. They went round the villages preaching, praying, reading the Bible, visiting orphans and widows and sick, exorcising demons.

One of the motives for withdrawal was the need for discipline. Even at the beginning of the third century we find cases of indiscipline and error among the ascetics; and a hundred years later the need for organizing communities under some strict rule was more obvious. No satisfactory society could be achieved without a reasonable kind of discipline. It was soon to be plain that a common discipline could only be achieved by sharing a common life and obeying a common rule.

We do not know enough of this intermediate stage whereby groups of ascetics in or round a congregation were becoming societies of ascetics separate from any congregation. One corpus of writings, though late in time, does show how easily and naturally the change occurred—the ascetical writings of St Basil of Caesarea in Cappadocia, probably composed at different periods between 357 and 378. By this time Egypt had begotten those new ascetical ideas which were to influence so momentously the course of the movement. St Basil had once paid a short visit to Egypt. It is possible that he had been influenced a little by the new ideal of community life advocated in Egypt by St Pachomius. But the ruling notion of most Egyptians—the superiority of the hermit life to community life—he rejected. His work is best understood not as an offshoot of Egyptian monasticism but as a continuation and extension of the idea of the primitive ascetic society. (His main teacher was no Egyptian but Eustathius of Sebaste, who was organizing ascetic groups in Asia Minor.) Basil never used the technical terms of the new monasticism. He thought of his societies as "brotherhoods." He demanded from them a common life in retirement from worldly life, a retirement marked by a distinctive dress, a stringent rule of obedience, and common rules for eating, fasting and mortification. But though his groups were withdrawn from the normal congregation, their quest for holiness issued in pastoral work for the congregation. The society of ascetic brothers in Caesarea ran his new hospital and leper settlement, visited the sick, educated children, distributed relief. There is an easy step from the ascetic groups of Tertullian's day to the brothers of St Basil. They were groups existing essentially for the same purpose, but in the later period brought together in a common life so that their pursuit of perfection should be unhindered by worldly distraction, and placed under a stern rule of obedience to ensure the discipline and the training in holiness which a rightly administered rule provided.

We gain some clues to the transition period from the lives of the pious ladies in the city of Rome under the direction of St Jerome towards the end of the fourth century. These ladies, so long as they remained retired in Rome for prayer and good works, were the imitators of the virgins of the third and second century. But the letters of St Jerome also show how the new ideas and vocabulary of monasticism were turning the ascetics to that extra step of retirement which would change them into monks and nuns.

*   *   *   *

In Egypt men began to take this new step: not only withdrawal from the ordinary ways of life but complete separation from the local congregation.

The example of a few individuals appears to have begun the movement into the desert. The most celebrated of these, St Antony, is known to us in the *Life* by St Athanasius, written (perhaps) soon after Antony's death. In this document it is possible to see how a young man became an ascetic of the normal kind and then passed further into the desert to inaugurate the new kind of life, the solitary or "monastic" life.

Antony was the son of rich parents who died when he was only eighteen or twenty years old and bequeathed him the property. He heard in church the text: "If thou wilt be perfect, go sell all that thou hast, and give to the poor; and come, follow me and thou shalt have treasure in heaven." Moved to obey the precept, he placed his young sister in a society of virgins, and began to live the ascetic life near his home. After a time he studied under a holy man who lived in the next village and then visited other ascetics to be edified by them in particular ascetic practices or virtues.

So far, there was nothing new or original. Antony had become an ascetic in the same way as other men and women for more than a century. But after a time he felt the need to withdraw altogether from the neighbourhood of human beings. He retreated to some tombs where he was locked in and remained inaccessible. It is difficult to be certain of the reason. Athanasius describes a succession of temptations by the devil, the chief being the temptation to fornication. The *Life* describes his long battles with demons in the solitudes of the tombs of the deserts.

The second of the Egyptian originators, St Pachomius, came to frame his way of life through a similar series of progressive stages. When a conscript in the army he was imprisoned with his group, during a halt on a journey, in order to prevent desertion. The Christians brought help to the prisoners: and this experience seems to have converted Pachomius to the Christian life. On release he retired to the village of Schenesit, began to lead an ascetic life, helped the poor and sick of the village and the travellers who passed through. Finding that the crowd which resorted to him hindered his practice of holiness, he retired to a senior ascetic Palamon, who lived a little way outside the village, and put himself under his tutelage. After a time he retired further, to the abandoned village of Tabennisi. There he was joined by pupils and began to construct his system for the common life. This community itself became progressively withdrawn from the neighbouring villages. At first the monks, though they lived and worshipped together, earned their livelihood by working in groups for the local farmers. The splitting of the society for these labours encouraged indiscipline: and later Pachomius arranged that the work should be work for the society and not the work of casual employment.

In the lives of Antony and Pachomius we see how the ascetics were gradually moving further away, mentally as well as geographically, from the primitive ascetic in the congregation. Both began their ascetic life in a village: both moved outside the village to join a senior ascetic rather more withdrawn: and both then moved still further away in order to preserve their freedom in the pursuit of holiness. There are many other instances of such a progress. And this gradualness is, on the whole, characteristic of the Egyptian movement. Economically the inhabitants of the solitudes could only survive if they were within reasonable distance of a market for their produce and a place to buy food. The first stages were usually a society of monks gathered in a community outside a town or village but economically associated with it. As the numbers of monks swelled rapidly, the movement was always outwards, away from towns and villages. Cells which earlier hermits inhabited with success, later became unusable on the ground that they were now too near to civilization.

To explain the physical ease with which the ascetic changed into a monk does not explain the religious ideas which the new way of life demanded. As always in Christian history there was interaction between doctrine and practice: and it is never possible to determine precisely how far doctrine created the new way of life and how far the new way of life exacted a certain development in doctrine to account for it. But it is possible to trace, tentatively, certain lines of doctrinal influence.

In what does sanctity, perfection, holiness consist? What
fruits are expected of the holy man? In the fourth century the
Christian reply to these questions was governed by the memory
of the martyrs.

The early Christians believed that they must imitate their
Lord in charity and self-denial. Since the Lord had consum-
mated his life on a Cross, the obedience even to death was an
inevitable climax to the demand to take up the Cross. This
obedience to death was no remote demand. The persecutions
forced many Christians into the choice between death and
apostasy. In conditions of persecution, the virtues to which the
Christians looked as supreme, were the virtues demanded of the
martyr—faith; capacity to bear suffering for Christ's sake; other-
worldliness, and contempt for the goods of this world; longing
for heaven. How near are these qualities to the qualities demanded of the monk two hundred years later, may be seen from
such a document as Tertullian's *Exhortation to the Martyrs*.
Tertullian was trying to encourage an imprisoned group in their
expectation of death. And the prison cell in Tertullian's eyes is
extremely like the desert cell of the Egyptian monk two hundred
years later. It is the place to which the martyr goes to trample
the demons underfoot: it is the place where the martyr can sever
himself from the clutching ties of the world, from his family and
his friends: the world, rather than the cell, is the true prison:
and out of it the martyr passes into the liberty of his confine-
ment. The cell takes him from the stains of lust, the temptations
of pagan holidays and circuses:

> "The prison does for the Christian what the desert did for the
> prophet. . . . Let us drop the name of prison, and call it a
> place of retirement. Though the body is shut in, all doors are
> open to the spirit."

And whatever is hard in their bodily circumstances is to be
counted discipline, like the athlete's training, as the soul
prepares itself for heaven.

Long before the age of persecution was past, the word
martyr is applied to anyone who lives a truly self-sacrificing life.[1]
Tertullian could write of a martyrdom of will "perfect without
suffering," Cyprian of the "martyrdom of virginity": and it was
natural for the ascetical writers of the later fourth century to use

[1] e.g. Clement of Alexandria, *Stromateis* 4, 4; Tertullian, *Scorpiace* 8; Cyprian,
de habitu virginum 21; and cf. E. E. Malone, *The Monk and the Martyr*, in
Antonius Magnus Eremita, ed. B. Steidle (Rome 1956), pp. 201 ff.

the word "martyrdom" in these loose and general senses. It was equally natural, with this memory of persecution stamped upon the mind of the Church, that Christians looked to find the especial virtues of the martyr in the man who obeyed the command to be perfect.

Christian thinkers were beginning more and more to stress the personal and individual element in the idea of sanctity. Plainly sanctity can only exist in individuals, though inseparable from the individual's behaviour to his fellows and perhaps from their behaviour to him. The primitive congregations were little groups of "the saints": and sanctity was a sharing in the gift of the Spirit which dwelt in the Body of Christ and in each member of it. During the third and early fourth centuries the idea of sanctity was becoming less corporate and more individualistic. This issued largely from the growth of the Church. From 313 the Church was becoming ever more "established" and all-embracing. An established Church, which normally expects to contain the majority of the population, is less conscious of its distinctiveness, its separation from the world. It was easier for Christians to feel their common Christianity when anti-Christians were powerful. And when congregations included men and women whose conduct was lax, it was less natural to think of the inspiration of the Spirit among all the members of the Body than to think of the inspiration of certain individuals. Already, before the monastic ideal was widely known, the ascetical writers were beginning to be more individualistic in their emphasis. Here is a hymn sung by virgins about A.D. 300:

"Virgins, a trump has sounded from heaven that wakes the dead, bidding us all to meet the Bridegroom in white robes, and with torches towards the east. Arise, before the King enters within the gates.

I keep myself pure for thee, O Bridegroom, and holding a lighted torch I go to meet thee.

Fleeing from the sorrowful happiness of mortals, and despising the luxuriant delights of life and its love, I desire to be protected under thy life-giving arms, and to behold thy beauty for ever, O blessed one.

I keep myself pure for thee, O Bridegroom, and holding a lighted torch I go to meet thee. . . .

I forget my own country, O Lord, through desire of thy grace. I forget also the company of virgins, my fellows, the desire even of mother and kindred, for thou, O Christ, art all things to me.

I keep myself pure for thee, O Bridegroom, and holding a lighted torch I go to meet thee. . . ."[2]

All this is fully compatible with the Christian doctrine of the Church. Yet there is a running stream of feeling that the soul is so seeking its perfection face to face with God that everything except God and the soul sink into a secondary place. The Church was there to contain: the ascetic group was there to encourage. But in the last resort the soul must work out its own salvation with fear and trembling.

What was the hermit to do in his hermitage? The answer for most was simple—pray, endure, wait for the end. So a hermit answered the enquiry of Melania—"From dawn to three o'clock I pray, and at the same time spin flax. During the remaining hours I think upon the holy patriarchs, prophets, apostles and martyrs. Then after supper I spend my time patiently waiting for the end in cheerfulness and hope." For many, this was all that was necessary. But others needed to provide more intellectual analysis of the *raison d'être* of their life. We must beware of reading into the whole movement ideas which were mainly the food of an intelligent Greek minority. Many sources besides the *Life of Antony* show the primary work of the hermit to be the fight with demons, the cultivation of virtues, the practice of fasting and mortification, praying and reading the Bible. But among the educated groups of Greek monks some thinkers began to construct a theological theory which would account satisfactorily for the nature and purpose and ascetical methods of the hermit life.

The Greek monks adapted an already existing theology to serve the purposes of desert spirituality. In the third century, the school of Alexandria, led by Clement and then Origen, had couched their moral and ascetical thought in terms partially borrowed from the vocabulary of Greek philosophy. The end of life was the vision of God. The training of the body, the conquest of sin, the fight with the demons, the practice of virtue, were all destined to the one great end—contemplation of God by pure mind. This language, utilized as it was by two profound thinkers both of whom were deeply Christian, suited the needs of those monks who theorized upon the purpose of the solitary life: and with certain adaptations educated monks in Egypt used this vocabulary and these ideas to explain their own practice. They supplied the most sensitive, discerning and sober

[2] Methodius, *Symposium* XI, 2, tr. Ante-Nicene Library.

instruction to be found in the Egyptian movement: and their influence is to be seen everywhere, even among those ascetics who came in time to resent it. The spiritual ideal thus proffered may be seen at its wisest and noblest in the work of John Cassian, seven of whose *Conferences* are translated in this volume. It influenced many of the narrative sources like the *Lausiac History* of Palladius, an illuminating account of the movement during its springtime of freshness and promise.

The object of the solitary's life was contemplation, the unceasing concentration upon God in prayer: and the text "Pray without ceasing" was given a new interpretation. Human society was distracting, visitors diverted the mind. Hence physical solitude was a necessary condition for contemplation. The kinds of work selected were those which enabled a monk to sit continuously in his cell and were mechanical and undistracting. Only the virtuous man who had conquered temptations could contemplate in purity of heart. Therefore they undertook the quest for virtue as a preparatory stage in the path to pure contemplation.

It will be observed that this theory was giving a new nuance to the Christian doctrines of worship and perfection. In the less intellectualized tradition virtue was perfection, and faithful prayer was part of the content of the virtuous life. Now the virtuous life is coming to be the preliminary for the highest form of prayer. Worship is becoming an act of the mind. It is not always thought to be worship, in the highest sense, to live a good life in imitation of Christ, a life whose offering is focused in prayer and sacraments. The living of the good life is now the necessary preparation for the highest form of worship.

By 375 the monks had already peopled the deserts round the Nile valley: monks living a common life in a community (*coenobium*): monks living in isolated cells but joining together for worship, for buying and selling, for a rudimentary form of discipline: sightseers visiting the famous cells: enquirers travelling round the various societies, seeking instruction and edification. The dominant ideal through the land was the hermit ideal of the followers of St Antony. Life in solitude needed more endurance, offered more chance of mortification, allowed the opportunity for ceaseless and undistracted contemplation. With all its faults—faults patent to any reader of the sources—a man could find sanctity in the desert communities. The ideal was appealing for utter renunciation of the self: the appeal was answered. In Syria and Asia Minor ascetics had taken up the same ideals: in Rome and Italy the ascetics were becoming interested in the new practices and new theories. Soon a copy of the *Life of Antony* was being read as far away as Trèves in Gaul.

There were also risks.

If the ascetics of the third century had begun to need discipline the solitaries of the desert incurred a still graver danger. Not everyone possessed the strength of Antony. The demons did not always lose their battle. The loneliness of the solitary's life increased the chance of abnormality, eccentricity, even madness. The admiration of visitors could turn weaker heads. The man whose capital fault was pride or lust or gluttony did not find that he had cured himself by escaping from his friends and family. The ordinary aids of the Church—the sacraments, corporate worship—were less accessible. The solitary sometimes lacked wise guidance in *ascesis* and prayer. The call to self-denial could easily become the exaltation of suffering: *ascesis* could become an end instead of a means. The movement needed wise organization, wise discipline, wise instruction.

The leaders met this need by grouping the solitaries in loose organizations. They prayed their offices at common hours, they consulted each other on questions of *ascesis* and prayer, they joined in corporate worship at the church of their group on Saturday and Sunday, they accepted (as a necessary step on the road to holiness) obedience to a senior monk or council of senior monks. And it became the standard teaching of the Antonian leaders that no one should be allowed to attempt the solitary life until he had served a long probation in a community. This ban was sometimes defied. It was difficult to restrain an ardent soul longing for what everyone told him was the higher ideal. But on the whole the teaching was accepted. A renunciant might remain twenty years or more in a community before venturing to join a hermit group—in the endeavour to learn the first steps in conquering self-will by obeying a superior; to train his patience and his charity by accepting the necessary frictions of common life; to become disciplined in regular worship, regular prayer, regular reading or memorization of the Bible; and to have his spiritual development watched and guided by experienced men.

The quest for discipline and sane guidance led some thinkers to reject the ideals of the solitaries altogether. In Upper Egypt Pachomius organized a row of monasteries on the principle of the common life: and, though there was a certain coming and going, these communities were not regarded as preparatory schools for hermits but as houses where the individual might best fulfil the life of sanctity. Basil of Cappadocia on the other hand knew the hermit spirituality and rejected its claim that the solitary life was the loftiest form of ascetic practice.

*   *   *   *

Athanasius, during his western exiles, had introduced the news of the Egyptian movement to the ascetics and religious leaders of Rome and the west. At least two Latin translations of the *Life of Antony* were circulating by 379. The groups of ascetics and virgins in Rome were soon hankering after ways of life more akin to the eastern pattern: and from 386 a little group of Latins, under the leadership of St Jerome, was living in Palestine and proclaiming the new form of the call to the ascetic life. In spite of the contempt and the hostility which puritans usually have to face, the movement quickly captured the minds of Latin Christian leaders. The influence of Augustine in Africa and Ambrose in Milan was perhaps more akin to the old asceticism than the new monasticism. In Gaul, St Martin of Tours, who died in 397, set forth a life obviously adapted from Egyptian models. By 430, when Augustine died, the monastic ideals were sweeping all before them in every country of the west but Spain, where the ascetic leader, Priscillian, became tinged with dualistic heresy in his language and brought a disaster and disrepute which temporarily slowed the rate of advance.

The capital of western monasticism in its first period of flourishing, the fifth century, was the coast of Provence. Here the islands attracted numerous solitaries, and communities were founded like that of St Honoratus (who died in 429) on the island of Lérins. The main channel of Egyptian influence upon these societies was John Cassian. Cassian had spent a few years in a community at Bethlehem, and then ten years or more studying under the solitaries of Egypt. The accidents of exile brought him to Marseilles, where he founded a community of monks and another of nuns. His writings—the *Institutes* and the *Conferences*—gave the west a sane and balanced view of the aims and ideals of the Antonian movement and the Greek theories of ascetical spirituality.

*   *   *   *

St Benedict, of Nursia in central Italy, published his Rule at some uncertain date between 510 and 580. The monastic ideal still commanded the allegiance of the most generous and self-denying Christians—it was to command it for another five centuries or more. But in Benedict's time its practice was suffering: and suffering from the old defect, absence of discipline. One reason was the rapid break-up of western society and the inauguration of the barbarian kingdoms. The stability of society as a whole usually assists the stability of monasteries, and society was often anarchic. The west had received the Antonian ideal as the highest ideal for the perfect. It was true that St Jerome had published a Latin translation of the Rule of St Pachomius (a translation which now seems to be the extant version nearest to the original). It was true that Rufinus had published a Latin translation (with free alterations) of the Longer and Shorter Rules of St Basil. Nevertheless Latin monasteries looked to Cassian and his tradition to supply them with rules as well as with spiritual advice.

Benedict did not intend his communities to "serve" secular society. The communities were retired from the world to work out their salvation in prayer and holy living. Any incidental effects that might accrue (like the copying of manuscripts) were as much outside Benedict's purpose as they were outside that of the Egyptians. But the two weaknesses of the older monasticism sprang in part from this belief in the superiority of the hermit life. For, first, this belief made discipline difficult to administer. The expectation that a monk ought (if he progressed favourably) to move from community to hermitage made stability accidental rather than essential: and without stability it was hard to organize a community effectively. A second weakness arose as the obverse of the greatest strength of the Egyptian tradition. The Antonians held before the eyes of the aspiring monk the supreme ideal of utter self-denial. And because they were exhorting to personal sacrifice, they often talked as though they expected success. This goal can be reached, this renunciation achieved. The reader of this volume will notice the moralism of *The Sayings of the Fathers* and of Cassian's *Conferences*; will see how naturally the monastic leaders exhorted their disciples to a human effort and how naturally they encouraged them by representing the goal as within reach. The early ascetics did not deny that the grace of God must assist every stage in the Christian life: and one of the sanest of them, Cassian, though an opponent of the Augustinian theories of grace, had himself been influenced in his theology by St Augustine. But the practical effect was moral exhortation after moral exhortation.

The sensitive reader of the Benedictine Rule will perceive behind the impersonal regulations a quality in the author which penetrates his book—the spirit of humility. It is, he feels, not at all an advanced kind of rule: it is a minimum, a little rule for beginners in the spiritual life. He knows that monks are called to a lofty ideal: yet he also knows human nature, its weaknesses as well as its potentialities. Benedict thought disobedience very wrong: but he knew that monks are men and was not surprised that they are sometimes disobedient. He was prepared to face the possibility that the whole community shall have fallen into wrong. Putting the contrast in an exaggerated form—in face of the Lord's cry "Be ye perfect," the Egyptian replied: "You can do it and if you try God will give you the necessary help"; and Benedict replied: "God help my weakness." He put himself on a level with his own monks. When he preached to his monks he was preaching to himself among them.

This humility and concern for the weakest of his brothers led him to put no emphasis upon the sterner varieties of *ascesis* or mortification. He confessed that the Rule did not intend to inflict anything "rough or burdensome" upon the monks. The life was a hard life: but it was no harder than the lot of the normal man who lived simply in that age. For the person in need, the sick, the old and the young, the abbot had full powers to relax the ordinary rules of moderate diet. The *ascesis* which he recommended was spiritual—the *ascesis* of obedience, humility, patience.

In the same spirit he expected monks to remain within communities. He recommended to his monks the reading of Cassian and the lives of the desert fathers, with all their stress on solitude, as well as the Rules of St Basil with their condemnation of solitude. There is no word in the Rule to condemn the solitary life. He did not claim that the community life was the only satisfactory form of the life of renunciation. But the assumptions of the rule about stability and discipline make it plain that he expected his monks to continue in community until death. And these assumptions about stability combined with the wise legislation and the ideals of abbatial government which he set forth, to give the monastic organization a new strength and permanence.

The Rule is remarkable for the strange kind of originality which it possesses. Benedict frankly took and adapted phrases of other writers, chief of whom was Cassian. Most of the Rule is reminiscent of some of his monastic predecessors. It now seems possible (the debate among scholars is still proceeding) that he took not merely phrases but many paragraphs from a rule existing before his time, the *Regula Magistri*. But whether this is true or not, nothing can affect the status of the Rule as one of the classical documents of Christian history.

In view of the later developments of Benedictinism it is important to have some kind of picture of the community as he designed it. Its members were drawn from all classes of society; they were nearly all laymen, apart from the occasional priest who joined the community or the occasional monk ordained from the community in order to provide the sacraments. They were governed by an abbot with an authority limited only by the portrait of the ideal and fatherly abbot contained in the Rule and by the necessity for consulting the brethren before taking any decision. Each community was independent of every other community. Their daily life was thus organized (there were variations between summer and winter, and there is still some dispute about the exact meaning of certain details of the Rule): they rose very early, usually about 2 a.m., having had a reasonable period of eight hours' sleep, and celebrated the night office in Church. After an interval for the reading of Scripture or for prayer, they celebrated Lauds at dawn and Prime at sunrise. Between Prime and dinner (held at noon or at 3 p.m., according to the time of year) they worked, mainly in the fields, or read books, and went to church for the offices of Terce, Sext and None at the proper hours. In the afternoon they worked and read again until Vespers. In summer they then had a light supper, and just before dark attended church again for Compline, after which they retired to bed. It is probable that the division of the day, allowing for differences in seasons, amounted to three hours and a half for the office; four hours and a half for reading or meditation; an hour for food; eight hours and a half for sleep; and six hours and a half for work in the fields. The books to be read were either the Bible or books of spiritual reading. There is no provision in the Rule for works of learning, for the reading of non-Christian authors, for the copying of manuscripts.

The Rule did not quickly win acceptance. Monks under the influence of traditional Egyptian thought probably believed it to be lukewarm because it demanded so little physical mortification. The political troubles of Italy prevented steady growth. Benedict had first practised the monastic life during a period of comparative stability, the rule of the Ostrogoths in Italy. But in the second quarter of the sixth century the wars in Italy were endemic: and the new Lombard invasions, beginning in 568, ravaged and impoverished Italy. Benedict's common life at Monte Cassino ended in flames some time before 590, when Lombard raiders sacked the monastery. The monks took refuge in Rome and were installed in a house by the Lateran Church. It is not certain when the discretion and moderation of the Rule began to attract the common sense of the religious leaders in Rome. Gregory the Great, who became Pope in 590, had earlier founded a monastery in his house on the Coelian Hill and himself retired to it: and it is possible that he utilized the Rule of St Benedict.

Meanwhile there were rivals. Many rules used in this period are still extant, and there must have existed many more. Some houses in France and Italy used variations or combinations of the rules recommended by Basil or Cassian. On the whole the modified Egyptian tradition was perpetuating itself: and it received a new impetus from 590 with the landing of Columbanus of Ireland in France. The sources do not allow more than an obscure knowledge of the way in which the monastic ideal passed into Ireland. It must have passed from Gaul in the late fourth or early fifth century: and it is possible (the evidence is doubtful) that St Patrick was himself trained at Lérins off the coast of Provence and took with him to Ireland the ideas of Honoratus and Cassian. The reputation of Martin of Tours appears to have increased rapidly in Ireland: and in these ways the Egyptian tradition was established there. Isolated from the continent, the Irish monks put their ideas in a way which cannot be otherwise paralleled, in the sphere of organization and discipline. Above all they accepted a stern standard of physical mortification. When Columbanus and his fellows landed in France, they appeared men of iron to the Franks and won from them that reverence which was so often given to physical self-sacrifice. For a time it looked as though the Rule of Columbanus would conquer Frankish monasticism. And when Columbanus retired from France to found the house of Bobbio in northern Italy, he began to exercise a powerful influence upon the Italian ideas of asceticism.

During the seventh century the Benedictine Rule began to be adopted by some few monasteries in France. Monasteries had often drawn customs from various sources, and at first they adopted the Rule of Benedict without excluding other customs. Some houses adopted a strange combination, the Rule of

Columbanus and the Rule of Benedict; and though this joining
of severe to gentle might seem a prodigy, it was often the houses
already under Celtic influence who looked towards St Benedict
—for the reason that the Celts were interested in the Roman
see, and the Rule of St Benedict was coming to be the Rule
peculiarly associated with the Roman see. Gregory the Great
had in his *Dialogues*—a book of Italian miracle stories, which
soon achieved an immense popularity—aspired to show the
world the person of St Benedict and devoted to him and his
miracles the whole of the second book. As a result of the
Dialogues, the *Rule*, which was already winning its way on its
own merits, was supported by the reputation of its author for
sanctity. Meanwhile Gregory and his successors had set out to
win the Anglo-Saxons to the Christian faith. With the missionaries went the knowledge of Benedictinism: and during the
seventh century English monasteries received the Rule as part
of the whole movement whereby England adopted Christianity
according to its Roman methods of organization. A century
later Anglo-Saxon missionaries were returning into France and
Germany to reform and evangelize: and it was this which finally
secured the triumph of the Rule in France. From 817 the ob-
servance of the Rule of St Benedict was obligatory in every
monastery of the Frankish Empire.

*   *   *   *

In a volume devoted to early western monasticism it may
appear surprising that so great a bulk of translation is given to
documents describing the teaching of the Egyptian fathers.
Many other documents might with reason have been suggested
as classical in the monastic history of the early west. If we ask
which were the chief documents to which the author of the Rule
looked back, there were many: the Rule of Pachomius, the
Rules of St Basil, perhaps the Rule of Caesarius, perhaps some
of the letters of St Jerome, perhaps the little hagiographies
written by St Jerome, the Life of St Antony by Athanasius in
one of its Latin versions. But certainly one of the most important
documents was *The Sayings of the Fathers* of the Egyptian desert,
which were probably put into their earliest Latin dress in the
middle of the sixth century. (The Greek is lost, though there
are numerous parallels in Greek.) It is possible that St Benedict
did not know this collection, and some scholars hold that the
Rule is earlier than this great Latin collection of *The Sayings
of the Fathers*. I think it more probable that the author of

the Rule knew this Latin collection: but whether he did or not, he knew something of this kind: and this Latin document, translated in the sixth century, effectively and authentically represents the Egyptian tradition in its influence upon Latin monasticism, its enchantment for Latin monks and their moral ideals. With whatever reserves this collection of the old Greek *Apophthegmata* must be used as a source for the history of Egyptian monasticism in the fourth or early fifth centuries (and in spite of these reserves the *Apophthegmata* must remain one of the most significant and rewarding of all the sources, since it contains so much of the "raw material" of history), there can be no doubt of its power in the history of western spirituality.

Secondly, Benedict used Cassian more, probably, than any other author. The *Conferences* of Cassian represent a tradition of spirituality, of ascetical and moral thought, for which Benedict's Rule was intended to provide a suitable and (in Benedict's eyes) an elementary framework.

*　　*　　*　　*

An endemic trial to all translators of early monastic documents is the problem of deciding how to translate "abba." I have translated it as *abba* in *The Sayings of the Fathers* and as *abbot* in *The Rule of St Benedict*; and in Cassian, as befits an intermediary, I have translated it as *abba* when I thought its primary sense was a title of honour for an individual elder, and as *abbot* when I thought its primary sense was the head of a monastic community.

The numbers of the Psalms in the text are the numbers as these authors knew them, the numbers of the Vulgate Version. The numbers of the Psalms in the footnotes are the numbers of the Authorized Version.

I

The Sayings of the Fathers

INTRODUCTION

FROM THE MIDDLE OF THE FIFTH CENTURY, AND probably from the late fourth century,[1] collections of sayings from the hermits of the Egyptian desert began to be circulated. Smaller collections were gradually assembled into larger, some of which were arranged in alphabetical order of the supposed speakers: other collections appeared where the sayings were arranged, more usefully and intelligently, according to the subject. The known collections have different sayings (*apophthegmata*) as well as a different arrangement, but often overlap, sometimes with an obvious literary connexion, sometimes dependent on two versions of an oral tradition. Sometimes a conscious extract, from a translation or précis of a written source, can be shown to have been inserted into the collection. Latin collections, for example, contain Latin translations of a Greek précis or translation of the known Latin text of Cassian.

The historical character and authenticity of the substance of these collections is undoubted. In so great and haphazard a collection, it was easy for a saying, originating no one knew where, to be put into the mouth of a famous speaker: it was easy for later material for sermons or conferences, which had grown a little out of the desire to edify, to be incorporated. But no one who knows the other sources for Egyptian monastic history can doubt that these sayings are in the main the authentic representatives of Egyptian monastic spirituality in the fourth and fifth centuries. This is the raw material of history: here we find ourselves close to the men who founded the monastic movement, for we are not seeing the desert through the

---

[1] Cf. Socrates, *Hist. Eccles.*, IV, 23: and Cuthbert Butler, *The Lausiac History of Palladius*, i, p. 211.

33

spectacles of an individual (like Cassian or Jerome or Palladius
or Sulpicius Severus) with a particular and unifying interest.

Within the collection of *apophthegmata*, different varieties of
saying have been distinguished.[2]

The saying, in its "naked" form, is a delivery of the spirit-
filled man, of the man endowed with particular gifts of wisdom
and discernment from on high. The young man goes to the
aged father and asks him, "Speak to me a word, that I may
live." The sentences are not only collections of moral and pro-
verbial sayings, easy to memorize and therefore handed down
as part of the lore of the desert tradition. There was believed to
be a prophetic quality about what was being said, a quality
dependent in part on moral experience and endeavour, but
not to be gained by human enquiry or the wisdom of the world.
It is the desert form of spiritual direction, the "tradition" of the
fathers which Cassian was so anxious to set forth as the guide to
the moral heights and the curb upon indiscretion, individualism
and eccentricity. The hermit received his "saying": he meditated upon it in his cell until he could put it into practice: he
took it to church at the end of the week, exchanged such sayings
with his brother hermits there—and so the wisdom was handed
on, often taken out of its personal and particular context and
transformed into a pronouncement of general truth and validity.

But other kinds of saying were interwoven with these moral
pronouncements. There are mere requests for help in making
a decision where to build, or how to spend a legacy: puzzles
about the interpretation of different texts of Scripture, or how to
understand a virtue or a vice. There are sayings which are not
authentic *mots* of the desert, but simply quotations from an
ascetic treatise, or extracts from a sermon, or summaries of
edifying incidents in the life of a holy man, anecdotes of the
miraculous or of supernatural apparitions.

The material is often moralistic, sententious, platitudinous,
sometimes tiresome and sometimes trivial. But it always possesses the purity of the best kind of simplicity, the clear vision
of an unimpeded moral integrity, that earnest or smiling discernment which they cultivated as among the supreme virtues.

Soon translations into other languages were circulating,
particularly into Syriac, Coptic and Latin. Our versions for
these three collections date from an earlier period than any
of the extant Greek collections. The most complete of these

[2] Cf. J. C. Guy, "Remarques sur le texte des *Apophtegmata Patrum*" in
Recherches de Science religieuse, 43 (1955), 252–8.

Latin collections is that of which a large part is here given in translation. This collection was translated, from a lost Greek source, as early as the middle of the sixth century, probably by two Roman clerics, the deacon Pelagius and the sub-deacon John, who may possibly (as "tradition" suggested) have been those who later became Popes Pelagius and John. This collection was known (almost certainly) to St Benedict when he wrote his *Rule* (for he appears to quote it), and was the most influential of all the collections upon the history of monasticism in the west. For western monasticism lost neither its memory of the origins of the newcomers in Egypt, nor its consciousness of the flowering of desert spirituality. Whether you read of Peter Damian and the Italian revival of the eleventh century, or of the origins of the great medieval orders like the Cistercians or the Carthusians, the memory of Egypt will be found to be among the sources of the ideas which were there proclaimed.

The standard and celebrated edition of this collection is that printed by the Jesuit Heribert Rosweyde at Antwerp in 1615 (and at Lyons in 1617; revised edition of 1628). Rosweyde, keeping to the pattern of early monastic collections which he had inherited from the later Middle Ages, printed the collection as Books V and VI of *Vitae Patrum*, and this was reprinted by Migne in *Patrologia Latina*, vol. 73, col. 855–1022. Though the work is thus divided into two books, according to the probable Latin translators, and although there are manuscripts of the twelfth century (Troyes 716: Bodleian Douce 351, etc.) already with this division, the collection is a single book, and the division is fortuitous.

I have therefore translated Parts I–XVII of Rosweyde's edition of *The Sayings of the Fathers* (the proper title, found in most early manuscripts, is *Adhortationes Patrum*: but *Verba Seniorum* has become traditional and is appropriate). I have translated this version, partly because it seems to have been the earliest of the western collections: partly because it forms a coherent group, in the early history of western monasticism, with Cassian and Benedict, whose writings are also translated in this volume: and partly because it was probably the most influential of the collections in western monastic history.

The translation of *The Sayings of the Fathers* has this difficulty. Rosweyde appears to have known only two manuscripts of first-class importance, and he was very cautious in his use of them. I have therefore gone to the pre-Carolingian manuscripts to secure that the translation shall represent, so far as is

possible in the present state of knowledge, the authentic text.
I have not attempted to provide a full apparatus: but in the
Appendix will be found sufficient readings to offer some justi-
fication for the many passages where the translation is found to
diverge significantly from Rosweyde's text.[3] The appendix is
intended for use with Rosweyde's text.

Of translations, much parallel material from the Syriac was
translated by E. A. Wallis Budge, *The Paradise of the Fathers*
(1904), a version the text of which is not negligible for the text
history of the Latin version. Charles Kingsley tried his romantic
hand in *The Hermits*. In *The Desert Fathers* (1936) Miss Helen
Waddell, one of the most remarkable translators of our time,
gave an enchanting and incomparable English rendering of a
select number of the sayings. There is also an English incuna-
bulum which translated (from the French) many of these sayings—a fine 1495 edition attributed to "St Jerome," translated
by William Caxton, who finished the translation on the last day
of his life, and printed at Westminster by Wynkyn de Worde
with charming woodcuts.

[3] The Greek original is lost. The Patriarch Photius of Constantinople, in
the ninth century, possessed it, or something very like it, as we know from
his summary. In the Bibliothèque Nationale is a manuscript (MS. grec
1598) written at the monastery of St Sabas in 993, which offers a text
related to the original of the Latin collection. One of the Greek alphabetical collections was printed by Cotelier in the first volume of his
Ecclesiae graecae Monumenta (pp. 338–713) of 1677, and reprinted by
Migne in *Patrologia Graeca*, vol. 65, 71–440.

A small number of other Greek collections have been printed or
analysed (List in J. C. Guy, *art. cit.*, p. 252). A still bigger alphabetical
collection is in the British Museum, Burney MS. 50 (Addit. MSS. 22508).
The history of the text is best studied in A. Wilmart, *Revue Bénédictine*, 34
(1922), pp. 185–98, and A. Siegmund, *Die Uberlieferung der griech. Christl.
Literatur in der Lat. Kirche* (Munich 1949), pp. 136–8. Much remains to be
done. I owe thanks to the learned Bollandist Fr F. Halkin, for advice
upon this question.

The Sayings of the Fathers

THE TEXT

PART I

Of the progress of the fathers in perfection

1. Someone asked Abba Antony: "What rules shall I keep to please God?" The old man replied: "Keep my instructions, and they are these: Wherever you go, recollect God in your mind's eye. Whatever you do, do it after the example of Holy Scripture. And wherever you stay, be in no hurry to move. If you keep these three rules, you will be safe."

2. Abba Pambo asked Abba Antony: "What shall I do?" The old man replied: "Trust not in your own righteousness. Be not penitent for a deed that is past and gone. And keep your tongue and your belly under control."

3. St Gregory said: "God demands three things from a man who is baptized. To hold the true faith with all his soul and strength: to restrain his tongue: to be chaste in body."

4. Abba Evagrius said: "Some of the fathers used to say that a dry and regular diet, combined with charity, will quickly bring the monk to the harbour where the storms of passion do not enter."

5. The same said: "A certain monk was told that his father had died. He said to the messenger 'Stop blaspheming. My father cannot die.' "

6. Abba Macarius said to Abba Zacharias: "Tell me, what makes a monk?" He said: "Is it not wrong that you should be asking me?" And Abba Macarius said to him: "I am sure I ought to ask of you, my son, Zacharias. I have one who urges me on to ask you." Zacharias said to him: "As far as I can tell, Father, I think that whoever controls and forces himself to be content with necessities and nothing more, that man is a monk."

7. They used to say about Abba Theodore (surnamed of

37

Pherme) that he kept these three rules beyond many others—poverty, abstinence, and running from the company of men.

8. Abba John the Short said: "I would make up a man out of all the virtues. Rise at dawn every morning, take the beginning of each virtue, and keep God's commandment—in great patience; fear; long-suffering; in the love of God; with a firm purpose of soul and body; in deep humility; in patience; in trouble of heart and earnestness of practice; in long prayer, with sorrow of heart; in purity of tongue, and guard of the eyes; in suffering injury without anger; peaceful, and not rendering evil for evil; not looking out for the faults of others, nor puffing up the self; meekly subject to every creature; renouncing material property and the things of the flesh; in crucifixion, struggle, lowliness of spirit, in good will and spiritual abstinence; in fasting, in penitence, in weeping, in the fight against evil; wise and discreet in the judgement; chaste in mind; receiving good with tranquillity; in working with your own hands; in watching in the night; in hunger and thirst, in cold and nakedness, in labours; burying yourself in a tomb as though you were already dead, and every day feeling that death is upon you."

9. Abba Joseph of Thebes said: "Three things are honoured in the sight of God. First, when a man is weak, and then temptations come upon him, and yet he accepts them thankfully. The second is when a man's every action is pure before God, mixed with no human motive. The third is when a man remains obedient to a spiritual father, and renounces all his self-will."

10. Abba Cassian related this story of one Abba John, who ruled over a community because he was great in his way of life. When he was dying, cheerfully, and with his mind set upon the Lord, his brothers stood around him and asked for a sentence which would sum the way to salvation, and which he could bestow on them as a legacy by which they might mount to the perfection which is in Christ. With a sigh he said: "I never obeyed my own will, and I never taught anyone to do anything which I did not first do myself." [1]

11. A brother asked an old man: "What thing is so good that I may do it and live by it?" And the old man said: "God alone knows what is good. Yet I have heard that one of the fathers asked the great Abba Nesteros, who was a friend of Abba Antony, and said to him, 'What good work shall I do?' And Antony replied, 'Cannot all works please God equally?

[1] Cassian, *Institutes*, V, 28.

Scripture says, Abraham was hospitable and God was with him. And Elijah loved quiet, and God was with him. And David was humble and God was with him. So whatever you find your soul wills in following God's will, do it, and keep your heart.' "

12. Abba Poemen said: "To keep guard—to meditate on itself—to judge with discernment—these are the three functions of the soul."

13. A brother asked him: "How ought we to live?" The old man replied: "We have seen the example of Daniel. They made no charge against him, except that he rendered service to his God."

14. The same old man said: "Poverty, tribulation and wise discernment—these are the three parts of the hermit's life. It is written that there were these three, Noah, Job and Daniel. Noah is the type of those who own nothing, Job of those in tribulation, Daniel of those who judge wisely. If a man has these three qualities, God dwells in him."

15. Abba Poemen said: "If a monk will hate two things, he can be free of this world." And a brother said: "What are they?" And the old man said: "Bodily comfort and vain-glory."

16. They used to tell of Abba Pambo that in the hour of his death he said to the holy men standing round: "From the time that I came into this lonely place, and built my cell and lived in it, I do not remember having eaten anything which my hands had not worked for, nor repenting of a word spoken until now. And so I go to the Lord, as one who has not yet made a beginning of serving God."

17. Said Abba Sisois: "Be despised: put your self-will behind your back: be free of secular worries—and you shall have rest."

18. When Abba Chame was dying, he said to his sons: "Do not live with heretics. Do not take notice of judges. And let not your hands be open to acquire, let them be stretched out to give."

19. Said a brother to an old man: "How does the fear of God come into the soul?" And the old man said: "If a man has humility and poverty, and will not judge another, then the fear of God comes into him."

20. An old man said: "Let fear, and humility, and want of food, and lamentation, abide in you."

21. Some of the old men used to say: "Whatever you hate, do it not to another. If you hate being evil spoken to, do not speak evil to another. If you hate being slandered, do not slander another. If you hate him who tries to make you despised, or wrongs you, or takes away what is yours, or any such

thing, do not do any such thing to him. If a man can keep this saying, it is enough for his salvation."

22. An old man said: "This is the life of a monk: work, obedience, meditation, not to judge others, not to speak evil, not to murmur. For it is written 'You who love God, hate evil.' [2]

This is the life of the monk: not to go in with the unrighteous, not to see evil, not to be inquisitive, not to be curious, not to hear gossip: not to use the hands for taking, but for giving: not to be proud in heart or wicked in thought: not to fill the belly: in everything to judge wisely.

That is where you find a monk."

23. An old man said: "Ask God to give you heartfelt grief and humility. Look ever on your sins, and judge not another's. Be subject to all. Be not friends with a woman, or a boy, or a heretic. Be not confident. Control your tongue and belly, and drink no wine. If anyone speaks to you on a matter of controversy, do not argue with him. If he speaks well, say 'Yes.' If he speaks ill, say 'I am ignorant in the matter.' But argue not with what he has said, and then your mind will be at peace."

PART II
Of quiet

1. Abba Antony said: "Fish die if they are long out of water. So monks who dally long outside their cell or with men of the world, lose their will to solitude. As a fish can only live in the sea, so we must run back to our cells. Perhaps, if we dallied outside, we might lose our inner guard." [3]

2. He also said: "The man who abides in solitude and is quiet, is delivered from fighting three battles—those of hearing, speech and sight. Then he will have but one battle to fight—the battle of the heart."

3. When Abba Arsenius was still at the palace, he prayed the Lord saying: "Lord, show me the way to salvation." And a voice came to him: "Arsenius, run from men and you shall be saved." He went to become a monk, and again prayed in the same words. And he heard a voice saying: "Arsenius, be solitary: be silent: be at rest. These are the roots of a life without sin."

4. Once Theophilus the archbishop of blessed memory came to Abba Arsenius with a judge. And the archbishop, wishing to

[2] Ps. 97:10.
[3] Cf. *Vita Antonii*, 85.

hear him talk, asked questions. For a short time the old man was silent. Then he replied: "If I tell you anything, will you obey it?" They promised they would obey it. And the old man said to them: "Wheresoever you hear of Arsenius, do not come nigh him."

Another time, the archbishop wanted to see him, but first sent to see if he would open to him. And Arsenius sent a message to him, saying: "If you come, I will open to you. But if I open to you, I open to everyone: and then I shall not abide here any more." When the archbishop heard this, he said: "If I go to persecute the holy man, I shall go to him no more."

5. Once Abba Arsenius came to a place where was a bed of reeds, and the reeds were shaken with the wind. And the old man said to the brothers: "What is this rustling?" And they said: "It is the wind in the reeds." The old man said to them: "Truly, if a man sits in silence and hears the cry of a bird, he will no longer have the same quiet in his heart. How much less can we attain quiet while we listen to the rustle of these reeds?"

6. They used to say about him that his cell was thirty-two miles away, and that he seldom left it, and his needs were served by others. When all the monks were driven from the place called Scete, he went out weeping, and saying: "The world has lost Rome, and the monks have lost Scete."

7. Once when Abba Arsenius was staying at Canopus, there came a virgin lady from Rome to see him, very rich and God-fearing. Theophilus, the archbishop, received her. She asked him to arrange with the old man for her to see him. Theophilus went to Arsenius and asked, saying: "A lady has come from Rome, and wants to see you." The old man would not allow her to come to him. When the lady heard of the refusal, she ordered her beasts to be saddled, and said: "I believe through God's help I shall see him. In my city of Rome there are many inhabitants: but I have come here to see prophets." And when she reached the old man's cell, by God's providence he was found outside it. When the lady saw him, she fell at his feet. He helped her up indignantly, and looking at her said: "If you want to see my face, look close: here it is." But for shame she did not dare to lift her eyes to his face. And the old man said to her: "Have you not heard what I do? A man's actions are what you should try to look at. Why have you dared to come all this way across the sea? Do you not know that you are a woman, and ought not to go out at all? Or have you done it to go back to Rome and say to the other women: 'I have seen Arsenius'?—

then you will turn the sea into a highroad for women coming to see me?"

She said: "If God will that I return to Rome, I will not let any other woman come here. But pray for me, and ever remember me."

He replied: "I pray God that he will blot the memory of you from my heart."

When she heard that, she went away troubled. And when she came to Alexandria, she began in her sorrow to be ill of a fever. And the archbishop was told that she was ill, and came to comfort her. And he asked her what was the, matter. She said: "I would I had never come here. I said to the old man, remember me: and he said: 'I pray God that your memory may be blotted from my heart'—and now I am dying of sorrow." And the archbishop said to her: "Do you not realize that you are a woman, and the enemy uses women to attack holy men? That is why the old man said what he said. He prays for your soul all the time."

And so her mind was healed, and she went away happily to her home.

8. Abba Evagrius said: "Cut out of your heart the desire for many things, and so prevent the mind being disturbed, and the quiet wasted."

9. In Scete a brother went to Abba Moses to ask a word. And the old man said to him: "Go and sit in your cell, and your cell will teach you everything."

10. Said Abba Moses: "A man who avoids men is like a ripe grape. A man who companies with men is like a sour grape."

11. Said Abba Nilus: "The arrows of the enemy cannot touch him who loves quiet. But he who moves in a crowd will be often wounded."

12. Abba Poemen said: "The beginning of evil is to spread the mind."

He said also: "It is good to fly from the things of the body. When a man is engaged in conflict over the body, he is like a man standing on the very edge of a deep pool, into which his enemy can knock him the moment he sees him. But when he has put aside bodily things, he is like a man standing a long way from the pool, where, if the enemy drags him along to throw him in, God will help him while he is being dragged."

13. Once Abraham, the disciple of Abba Sisois, said to him: "Father, you have grown old. Let us go into the world for a short time." Abba Sisois said to him: "Yes, provided that we

go where there are no women." The disciple said: "But where is there a place without women, except in the desert?" The old man said: "Then take me to the desert."

14. Said the abbess Matrona: "Many people living secluded lives on the mountain have perished by living like people in the world. It is better to live in a crowd and want to live a solitary life than to live a solitary life but all the time be longing for company."

15. Said an old man: "A monk ought to buy himself quiet, and so be able to despise any bodily expense which may happen."

16. This story was told.

There were three friends, earnest men, who became monks. One of them chose to make peace between men engaged in controversy, as it is written: "Blessed are the peace-makers." The second chose to visit the sick. The third chose to be quiet in solitude.

Then the first, struggling with quarrelling opponents, found that he could not heal everyone. And worn out, he came to the second who was ministering to the sick, and found him flagging in spirit, and unable to fulfil his purpose. And the two agreed, and went away to see the third who had become a hermit, and told him their troubles. And they asked him to tell them what progress he had made. And he was silent for a little, and poured water into a cup. And he said: "Look at the water." And it was cloudy. And after a little he said again: "Now look, see how clear the water has become." And when they leant over the water, they saw their faces as in a glass. And then he said to them: "So it is with the man who lives among men. He does not see his own sins because of the turmoil. But when he is at rest, especially in the desert, then he sees his sins."

PART III

Of compunction

1. It was said of Abba Arsenius that all his life, whenever he worked with his hands, he kept a handkerchief in his breast because tears fell so often from his eyes.

2. A brother asked Abba Ammon, saying: "Speak to me a word." The old man said to him: "Go, and meditate like the criminals in prison. For they keep asking, where is the judge, and when will he come? And because they await him they lament their punishment. The monk ought always to be awaiting

his trial, and to chide his soul, saying: 'Woe is me, how shall I stand before the judgement seat of Christ? How shall I give an account of my actions?' If you always meditate like this, you will be saved.''

3. Abba Evagrius said: "While you sit in your cell, draw in your mind, and remember the day of your death. And then you will see your body mortifying. Think on the loss, feel the pain. Shrink from the vanity of the world outside. Be retiring, and careful to keep your vow of quiet, and you will not weaken. Remember the souls in hell. Meditate within on their condition, the bitter silence and the moaning, the fear and the strife, the waiting and the pain without relief, the tears that cannot cease to flow.

Remember too the day of resurrection, imagine God's terrible and awful judgement. Bring into your sight the confusion of sinners before God and his Christ, before angels and archangels and powers, and all the human race: punishment, everlasting fire, the worm that never dies, the darkness of Tartarus—and above them all the sound of the gnashing of teeth, fearfulness and torments.

Bring before your eyes the good laid up for the righteous, their confidence before God the Father and Christ his Son, before angels and archangels and the powers, and all the people: the kingdom of heaven and its gifts, joy and rest.

All this remember. Weep and lament for the judgement of sinners, bring to life the grief they suffer; be afraid that you are hurrying towards the same condemnation. Rejoice and exult at the good laid up for the righteous. Aim at enjoying the one, and being far from the other. Do not forget it, whether you are in your cell or abroad. Keep these memories in your mind and so cast out of it the sordid thoughts which harm you.''

4. Said Abba Elias: "I fear three things: the first, the time just before my soul goes out from my body: the second, the time just before I meet God face to face: the third, the time just before he pronounces his sentence upon me.''

5. When archbishop Theophilus of holy memory was dying, he said: "Abba Arsenius, you are a man blessed of God, because you have always kept this moment before your eyes.''

6. There was a story that once when some brothers were eating together at a love-feast, one of the brothers at the table laughed. When Abba John saw it, he wept, and said: "What do you think that brother has in his heart, that he laughed, when he ought rather to weep because he is eating up charity?''

7. Abba Jacob said: "Like a lantern lighting a dark little room, the fear of God comes into a man's heart and lightens it, and teaches him all goodness and the commandments of God."

8. Some of the fathers asked Abba Macarius of Egypt: "Why is your body dry, whether you eat or fast?" And the old man said to them: "A wooden poker in a man's hand which turns over and over the brushwood on the fire, is itself being slowly burnt away. So if a man cleanses his mind in the fear of God, the fear of God also consumes his bones."

9. Once some old men of Mount Nitria sent to Scete, to ask Abba Macarius the Great to come to them. They sent a message that if he would not come to them, the whole crowd of them would go to him, since they wanted to see him before he passed on to the Lord. When Macarius came to Nitria, the whole congregation assembled in his presence. The elders asked him to speak a word to the brothers. But he shed tears and said: "Let us pray and weep, my brothers, before we go hence to the place where our tears consume our bodies." And they all wept, and fell on their faces, saying: "Father, pray for us."

10. In Egypt once Abba Poemen passed by and saw a woman sitting on a grave and weeping bitterly. And he said: "If all the delights of this world should come, they would not bring her soul out of sorrow. Even so the monk should ever be sorrowful within his heart."

11. Another time, he went with Abba Anub to the country of Diolcos. Coming among the tombs they saw a woman striking herself much and weeping bitterly. They stopped and went to her. And when they walked a little further, they met a man and Abba Poemen asked him: "What is the matter with the woman yonder, that she weeps so bitterly?" He said: "Her husband is dead, and her son, and her brother." And Abba Poemen said to Abba Anub: "I tell you that unless a man mortifies all his self-will and possesses this grief, he cannot be a monk. The whole life and mind of that woman is wrapt up in grief."

12. Abba Poemen said also: "Grief is twofold: it works good, and it keeps out evil."

13. A brother asked him: "What shall I do?" And he said: "When Abraham entered the land of promise, he built for himself a grave, and bought the land as a burying-place for his posterity." And the brother said to him: "What burying-place is meant?" And the old man said: "A place of weeping and sorrowing."

14. Athanasius of holy memory asked Abba Pambo to come down from the desert to Alexandria. When he arrived, he saw a woman that was an actress, and wept. And the bystanders asked him why he wept. And he said: "Two things grieved me. The first was her damnation: the second, that I take less trouble about pleasing God than she takes about pleasing the dregs of mankind."

15. Abba Silvanus was sitting one day among the brethren, and was seized into a rapture of mind, and fell upon his face. And after a while he rose up and lamented. And the brothers asked him: "What is the matter, Father?" But he was silent and wept. When they pressed him for an answer, he said to them: "I was taken before the judgement seat, and I saw many of our cloth going down to torment, and many of the world going into the kingdom." And the old man grieved and would not thereafter leave his cell: and if he was forced to go out, he covered his face with his shawl and said: "Why should I have to see the light of this world, wherein nothing is profitable?"

16. Syncletice of holy memory said: "Men endure sore travail and conflict when they are first converted to the Lord, but later they have joy unspeakable. They are like men trying to light a fire, the smoke gets into their eyes, their eyes begin to drop tears—but they succeed in what they want. It is written: 'Our God is a consuming fire' [4]: and so we must kindle the fire of God with tears and trouble."

17. Said Abba Hyperichius: "The wakeful monk toils night and day to pray continually: but if he pierces his heart, and lets tears drop, that calls God down from heaven to have mercy."

18. The brothers went to Abba Felix, who had with him some men of the world, and asked him to give them a word. But the old man said nothing. When they went on asking, he said to them: "Do you want to hear a word?" They replied: "Yes, Father." So the old man said: "I have no word for you now. When an elder is asked to speak, and the brothers do what he tells them, God gives the elder something to say. But now there are brothers who ask for a word, but do not obey the word they hear: and then God takes away his grace from the elder, and he has nothing to say: for he who gives it is not there." When the brothers heard this, they sighed, and said: "Pray for us, Father."

19. It was said of Abba Hor and Abba Theodore, that they were once putting a goatskin over a cell: and then they said to

4 Heb. 12:29.

each other: "If God visits us now, what shall we do?" And sadly they left the place in a hurry and went away to their own cells.

20. An old man told this story. A brother wanted to become a monk, and his mother forbade him. But he did not rest from his purpose, and said: "I want my soul to be saved." She opposed him for a long time. But when she found that she could not stop him, she at last let him go. He went away and became a monk but spent his life carelessly.

It happened that his mother died: and a short time after he fell sick of a grievous illness. And in an ecstasy of mind, he found himself taken before the judgement seat, and there he found his mother among the people being judged. When she saw him she was aghast, and said: "How is this, my son? Are you condemned like me to this place? What about the words you used to say: 'I want my soul to be saved'?"

He was confused at her words and made stupid by his sorrow, and stood without being able to say a word to her in reply. But after this vision, he was recovered by God's mercy from his dangerous illness and restored to health. He meditated on God's purpose in visiting him. He retired into himself, cut himself off from all company, considered his own salvation, and lamented his earlier neglect in penitence. His purpose was so fixed that many people asked him to spare himself a little, for he might hurt himself by these immoderate lamentations. But he would not be consoled and said: "If I was ashamed by my mother's taunts, what sort of shame shall I have when Christ and his holy angels look upon me in the day of judgement to condemn me?"

21. An old man said: "If the souls of men could die of fear at the coming of God after the resurrection, all the world would perish of terror. What shall it be to see the heavens opened, and God revealed in wrath and fury, and the innumerable companies of angels, gazing upon the whole human race gathered together? Therefore we ought to live our lives as men who must render an account of each action to God."

22. A brother asked an old man: "Why is my heart hard, and I do not fear God?" The old man said to him: "I think that if a man has reproach in his heart, he will possess fear." The brother said to him: "What is reproach?" The old man said: "To reprove your soul in all things, saying to it—'Remember that you have to meet God.' Say also to your soul, 'What do I want with man?' I think that if anyone abides in these, the fear of God will come to him."

23. An old man saw a man laughing, and said to him: "We have to render an account of our whole life before heaven and earth—and you laugh?"

24. An old man said: "As the shadow goes everywhere with the body, so we ought to carry penitence and lamentation with us wherever we go."

25. A brother asked an old man: "Abba, speak to me a word." The old man said to him: "When God struck Egypt, there was not a house that did not mourn."

26. A brother asked another old man: "What must I do?" The old man said to him: "We ought ever to lament."

Once one of the elders died, and after several hours recovered consciousness. We asked him: "What did you see there, Abba?" And he told us with sorrow: "I heard there a voice of sadness saying over and over again, 'Woe is me, woe is me.' That is what we should ever be saying."

27. A brother asked an old man: "I hear the old men weeping, and my soul longs for tears: but they do not come, and my soul is troubled." And the elder said: "The children of Israel entered the promised land after forty years in the wilderness. Tears are like the promised land. If you have reached them already you will no longer be afraid of the conflict. For thus God wills that the soul be afflicted, that it may ever long to enter that country."

PART IV
Of self-control

1. Some brothers from Scete wanted to visit Abba Antony, and embarked in a ship to go there. In the ship they found an old man who also wanted to go to Antony, but they did not know him. During the voyage they talked about the sayings of the Fathers, and the Scriptures, and then the work of their hands. But the old man was silent through it all. When they came to the landing-place, they saw that the old man also was preparing to go up to Abba Antony. When they arrived, Abba Antony said to them: "You found good company on your journey in this old man." And he said to the old man: "You found good companions in these brothers." The old man said: "Yes, they are good, but their house has no door. Whoever wants, goes into the stable and steals the donkey." He said this because they uttered the first thing that came into their heads.

2. Abba Daniel said of Abba Arsenius that he used to spend all night watching. He would stay awake all night, and about

dawn when nature seemed to force him into sleep, he would say to sleep: "Come, you wicked servant," and he would snatch a little sleep still sitting: and at once rose up.

3. Abba Arsenius said: "An hour's sleep is enough for a monk: that is, if he is a fighter."

4. Abba Daniel said of him: "All the years he stayed with us, we gave him a little enough measure of food for the year. And every time we came to visit him, he shared it with us."

5. He said also, that he only changed the water for the palm-leaves once a year; otherwise he added to it. He would make a plait of the palm-leaves,[5] and weave it till noon. So the elders asked him why he would not change the water for the palm-leaves, which was stinking. And he said to them: "When I was in the world I used incense and sweet-smelling ointments, so now I must profit from this stink."

6. He also said this. When he heard that all the apples were ripe, he said: "Bring them to me." And he took one little mouthful of each kind, giving thanks to God.

7. They said of Abba Agatho that for three years he kept a pebble in his mouth, to teach himself silence.

8. Once Abba Agatho was going a journey with his disciples. And one of them found a tiny bag of green peas on the road, and said to the old man: "Father, if you command, I will take it." The old man gazed at him in astonishment, and said: "Did you put it there?" The brother replied: "No." And the old man said: "How is it that you want to take something which you did not put there?"

9. Once an old man came to Abba Achillas, and saw blood dripping from his mouth: and he asked him: "What is the matter, Father?" And the old man said: "A brother came and spoke a word which grieved me, yet I have been trying with all my might to nurse that grievance. And I prayed God that he would take it away, and the word turned into blood in my mouth. Look, I have spat it out, and am now at rest, and have forgotten my grievance."

10. Once Abba Achillas came to the cell of Abba Isaiah in Scete, and found him eating. He had put salt and water in his vessel. Seeing that he hid the vessel behind the plaits of palm-leaves, Abba Achillas said: "Tell me what you were eating." And he answered: "Forgive me, Abba; but I was cutting palms and began to be on fire with thirst. And so I dipped a piece of bread in the salt, and put it in my mouth. But my mouth was

---

[5] Cf. Cassian, *Conferences*, XVIII, 15.

parched, and I could not swallow the bread, so I was forced to pour a little water on the salt and then I could swallow it. But forgive me." And Abba Achillas used to say: "Come and see Isaiah eating broth in Scete. If you want to eat broth, go to Egypt."

11. They said of Abba Ammoi that though he was on a bed of sickness for several years, he never relaxed his discipline; and never went into the store-cupboard at the back of his cell to see what he had. Many people brought him presents because he was sick. But even when his disciple, John, went in and out, he shut his eyes so as not to see what he was doing. He knew what it means to be a faithful monk.

12. Abba Benjamin, who was presbyter in Cellia, said that some brothers went to an old man in Scete and wanted to give him a measure of oil. But the old man said: "Look, there is the little vessel of oil which you brought three years ago. It has stayed there, where you put it." And Abba Benjamin said: "When we heard it, we marvelled at the old man's devotion."

13. They told a story of Abba Dioscorus of Namisias,[6] that his bread was made of barley, and his gruel of lentils. And every year he made one particular resolution: not to meet anyone for a year, or not to speak, or not to taste cooked food, or not to eat any fruit, or not to eat vegetables. This was his system in everything. He made himself master of one thing, and then started on another, and so on each year.

14. Abba Evagrius said that an old man said: "I cut away my fleshly pleasures, to remove the opportunities of anger. For I know that it is because of pleasure that I have to struggle with anger, and trouble my mind, and throw away my understanding."

15. Once Epiphanius the bishop from Cyprus sent a message to Abba Hilarion, and asked him: "Come, that I may see you before I die." And when they had met and greeted each other, part of a fowl was set before them. The bishop took it and gave it to Abba Hilarion. And the old man said to him: "Forgive me, Father. From the time I took my habit, I have eaten nothing that has been killed." And Epiphanius said to him: "From the time I took my habit, I have let none go to sleep who still had something against me, and I have never gone to sleep with an enemy in the world." And the old man said to him: "Forgive me. Your devotion is greater than mine."

16. They said of Abba Helladius that he lived twenty years

6 Wallis Budge, *Paradise*, ii, no. 76, p. 18.

in Cellia, and did not once lift his eyes upward to see the roof of the church.[7]

17. Once Abba Zeno was walking in Palestine; and when he had finished his work, he sat down to eat near a cucumber plant. And his soul tried to persuade him, saying: "Pick one of those cucumbers for yourself, and eat it. What does it matter?" And he replied to his temptation: "Thieves go down to torment. Test yourself then to see whether you can bear torment." So he rose and stood in the sun for five days, without drinking, and dried himself in the heat. And his soul (so to say) spoke to him: "I cannot bear torment." So he said to his soul: "If you cannot bear torment, do not steal to get a meal."

18. Abba Theodore said: "The monk's body grows weak with eating little bread." But another elder said: "It grows weaker with watching in the night."

19. Abba John the Short said: "If a king wants to take a city whose citizens are hostile, he first captures the food and water of the inhabitants of the city, and when they are starving subdues them. So it is with gluttony. If a man is earnest in fasting and hunger, the enemies which trouble his soul will grow weak."

20. He also said: "As I was climbing up the road which leads to Scete, carrying plaits of palms, I saw a camel-driver who talked to me and annoyed me. And I dropped what I was carrying, and ran away."

21. Said Abba Isaac the presbyter of Cellia: "I know a brother who was harvesting and wanted to eat an ear of wheat. And he said to the owner of the field: 'Will you let me eat one ear?' And when he heard it, he wondered, and said: 'The whole field is yours, Father, why do you ask me?' So scrupulous was that brother."

22. One of the brothers asked Abba Isidore the priest of Scete: "Why are the demons so violently afraid of you?" And the old man said: "Ever since I became a monk, I have been trying not to let anger rise as far as my mouth."

23. He said also that though he felt in his mind impulses towards the sins of concupiscence or anger, he had not consented to them for forty years.

24. Abba Cassian [8] told a story of an Abba John who went to

---

[7] Cf. Wallis Budge, *Paradise*, ii, no. 254, p. 58, which attributes it to Hor: and cf. *Paradise*, vol. ii, no. 355, p. 224.

[8] *Institutes*, V, 27. The apophthegmatist or his copyist has variations of detail. So has Sulpicius Severus, *Dialogues*, i, 12. It looks probable

see Abba Paesius who had lived for forty years in the deep desert. And because he had much charity towards him, he asked him with the confidence born of charity: "You have been isolated so long, and cannot easily suffer any trouble from man—tell me, what progress have you made?" And he said: "From the time I began to be a solitary, the sun has never seen me eating." And Abba John said to him: "Nor me angry."

25. He said also: [9] "Abba Moses told us what Abba Serapion said to him: 'While I was still a lad, I was staying with Abba Theonas; and after each meal I was moved by some demon and stole one of the rolls of bread, and secretly ate it, Theonas knowing nothing of the matter. For some time I went on with this, until the sin began to dominate my mind, and I could not stop myself. Only my conscience judged me, for I was ashamed to say anything to the old man. But by God's mercy it happened that some visitors came to the old man in search of profit to their soul, and they asked him about their own thoughts. The old man replied: "Nothing harms the monk so much, and gives such happiness to the demons, as when he conceals his thoughts from his fathers in the spirit." And he also talked to them about self-control. And while he was speaking, I thought to myself that God had revealed to him what I had done. Stricken in my heart, I began to weep: then I pulled the roll of bread out of my dress, threw myself on the floor, and begged forgiveness for what I had done, and for prayer that I might be helped not to do it again.

Then the old man said: "My son, you are freed from your captivity though I have said nothing. You are freed by your own confession. The demon which by your silence you let dwell in your heart, has been killed because you confessed your sin. You let him rule you because you never said him nay, never rebuked him. Henceforth he shall never make a home in you, because you have thrown him out of doors into the open air." The old man had not finished speaking, when his words were visibly fulfilled—something like a flame shot out of my breast and so filled the house with its stench, that the people present

that Cassian's version is nearest to the primitive story. The detailed differences between the texts of Cassian and *Verba Seniorum* are remarkable, and may be accounted for only on the supposition that Pelagius knew no text of Cassian, but was translating the unknown Greek text taken by the apophthegmatist from a Greek translation of Cassian; or (more probably) a Greek epitome.

[9] *Conferences*, II, 11.

thought it was burning sulphur. And the old man said: "My son, see the sign, whereby the Lord has proved that I have spoken truly and you are free." ' "

26. They said of Abba Macarius that if he was called among the brothers, he made a rule for himself thus: if wine could be had, he used to drink it for the brothers' sake: and then, for one cup of wine he would go without water for a whole day. And the brothers, wanting to refresh him, used to give him wine. And the old man took it with joy, so as later to crucify himself. But his disciple, knowing the reason, said to the brothers: "For God's sake, I beg you, do not give it him. In the cell afterwards he tames himself with torments." When the brothers knew it, they gave him no more wine.

27. Abba Macarius the Great said to the brothers in Scete after service in church: "Flee, my brothers." And one of the brothers said to him: "Father, where have we to flee beyond this desert?" And he put his finger upon his lips and said: "I tell you, this you must flee." And so he entered his cell, and shut the door, and dwelt alone.

28. Abba Macarius said also: "If when you want to reprove someone you are stirred to anger, you are pandering to your own passion. Lose not yourself to save another."

29. Said Abba Poemen: "Unless Nebuzaradan the captain of the guard had come, the temple of the Lord would not have been burnt.[10] And unless greed brought idleness into the soul, the mind would not fail in its fight against the enemy."

30. They said of Abba Poemen that when he was invited to eat and did not want to go, he went weeping, and praying that he might obey his brothers and not sadden them.

31. They told Abba Poemen that a certain monk did not drink wine. And he said to them: "Wine is not for monks at all."

31A. Abbe Poemen also said: "All rest of the body is an abomination to the Lord."

31B. Abba Poemen also said: "The only way to humble the soul is by eating less bread."

31C. He also said that if a man remembered the word of Scripture "out of thy mouth thou shalt be justified and out of thy mouth shalt thou be condemned"[11] he would more and more choose not to speak.

31D. He also said that a monk asked Abba Pambo if it is

[10] II Kings 25:8-9.
[11] Matt. 12:37: the logion is attributed to Alonius in Budge, *Paradise of the fathers*, vol. ii, no. 44.

good to praise your neighbour. And he answered: "It is a greater good to hold your peace."

31E. A monk asked Abba Poemen: "How should I behave in my common life among the brothers?" The old man said to him: "He who lives among the brothers ought to regard them as though they were but one person, and to keep guard over his mouth and eyes; and so he will be able to win peace of mind."

32. Abba Poemen also said: "They smoke out bees to steal away their honey. And so idleness drives the fear of God from the soul, and steals away good works."

33. One of the old men told this story of Abba Poemen and his brothers, who lived in Egypt. Their mother wanted to see them, and could not. So she looked out for her chance, and presented herself in front of them as they were going to church. The moment they saw her, they turned, went to their cell, and shut the door in her face. But she stood at the door and screamed and besought them in her misery. Abba Anub, hearing her, went to Abba Poemen and said: "What shall we do about the little old woman who is crying outside the door?" Abba Poemen rose up, and went to the door, and stood just inside and heard her beseeching them miserably. And he said: "What are you screaming for, old woman?" When she heard his voice, she cried out the more and implored them: "I want to see you, my sons. Why should I not see you? Am I not your mother? Have I not given you milk at the breast, and now every hair of my head is grey? When I hear your voice, I am in distress." The old man said to her: "Do you want to see us in this world or the next?" She said to him: "If I do not see you in this world, shall I see you in the next, my sons?" He said: "If you can suffer, with a calm spirit, not to see us here, you shall see us there." And so the woman went away happy, and saying: "If I shall truly see you there, I do not want to see you here."

34. They said of Abba Pior that he ate while walking about. And when someone asked him why he ate in this manner, he replied that he did it casually, as if there were no need of it. But when someone else asked the same question, he replied: "So that my soul does not receive bodily pleasure from eating."

35. They said of Abba Peter, named Pyonius, who was in Cellia, that he did not drink wine. And when he grew old, they asked him to take a little wine. When he refused, they warmed some water, and offered it to him. And he said: "Believe me, my sons, I drink it as though it was spiced wine." And he declared that he was content with warm water.

36. Once they celebrated a great service on the mountain of Abba Antony, and a little wine was found there. One of the elders took a small cup, and carried it to Abba Sisois, and gave it him. And he drank it. And a second time Abba Sisois received it, and drank it. And the elder offered it a third time. But he did not receive it, and said: "Stay, brother, do you not know that Satan still exists?"

37. A brother asked Abba Sisois: "What am I to do? When I go to church, out of charity the brothers often make me stay to the meal afterwards." The old man said to him: "That is burdensome."

So Abraham his disciple said to him: "If in the meeting at church on Saturday and Sunday, a brother drinks three cups, is it much?" And the old man said: "If there were no Satan, it would not be much."

38. Often the disciple used to say to Abba Sisois: "Rise, Abba, let us eat." And he would say: "Have we not eaten already, my son?" And the disciple would reply: "No, Father." The old man used to say: "If we have not eaten yet, bring the food, let us eat."

39. Abba Sisois once said with confidence: "Believe me, for thirty years I have not been in the habit of praying to God about sin. But when I pray, I say this: 'Lord Jesus Christ, protect me from my tongue.' And even now, it causes me to fall every day."

40. Once Abba Silvanus and his disciple Zacharias came to a monastery. And the monks made them sup a little before they went on their way. And when they departed, the disciple found a pool by the wayside and wanted to drink. Abba Silvanus said: "Zacharias, today is a fast." And Zacharias said: "Have we not already eaten today, Father?" The old man said to him: "To eat that meal was charity: but as for us, let us keep our fast, my son."

41. The holy Syncletice said: "We who have chosen this holy way ought above all to keep chastity. Even among men of the world chastity is regarded. But in the world they are also stupid about it, and sin with their other senses. For they peep indecently, and laugh immoderately."

42. She said also: "Animal's poison is cured by still stronger antidotes. So fasting and prayer drive sordid temptation from the soul."

43. She also said: "The pleasures of the wealthy world must not seduce you, as if those pleasures were useful. Because of this

pleasure they honour the art of cooking. But by rigorous fasting, you should trample on those pleasures. Never be sated with bread, nor want wine."

44. Abba Sisois said: "Our form of pilgrimage is keeping the mouth shut."

45. Said Abba Hyperichius: "Donkeys are terrified of lions. So temptations to concupiscence are terrified of a proved monk."

46. He also said: "Fasting is the monk's rein over sin. The man who stops fasting is like a stallion who lusts the moment he sees a mare."

47. He also said: "When the monk's body is dried up with fasting, it lifts his soul from the depths. Fasting dries up the channels down which worldly pleasures flow."

48. He also said: "The chaste monk shall be honoured on earth, and in heaven shall be crowned in the presence of the Most Highest."

49. He also said: "The monk who cannot control his tongue when he is angry, will not control his passions at other times."

50. He also said: "Let not thy mouth speak an evil word: the vine does not bear thorns."

51. He also said: "It is better to eat flesh and drink wine than to eat the flesh of the brothers by disparaging them."

52. He also said: "The serpent murmured to Eve and cast her out of paradise. The man who rails against his neighbour is like the serpent. He loses the soul of him that listens to him, and he does not save his own."

53. Once there was a feast in Scete, and they gave a cup of wine to an old man. He threw it down, saying: "Take that death away from me." When the others who were eating with him saw this, they also did not drink.

54. Another time a vessel of wine was brought there from the first fruits of the vintage, so that a cup of it could be given to each of the brothers. And a brother came in and saw that they were drinking wine, and fled up on a roof, and the roof fell in. And when they heard the noise, they ran and found the brother lying half-dead. And they began to abuse him, saying: "It has served you right, for you were guilty of vainglory." But an abba embraced him, and said: "Leave my son alone, he has done a good work. By the living Lord, this roof shall not be rebuilt in my time, as a reminder to the world that a roof fell in Scete because of a cup of wine."

55. Once a priest from Scete went up to see the bishop of

Alexandria. And when he came back to Scete the brothers asked him: "How goes the city?" But he said to them: "Believe me, brethren, I saw no man's face but the bishop alone." And when they heard this, they wondered, and said: "What do you think has happened to all the population?" They hesitated to believe him. But he cheered them by saying: "I have wrestled with my soul, not to look upon the face of a man." And so the brothers were edified, and kept themselves from lifting up their eyes.

56. Once an old man came to another old man. And the second said to his disciple: "Make us a little lentil broth, my son." And he made it. "Dip the bread in it for us." And he dipped it. And they went on with their godly discourse till noon next day. Then the old man said to his disciple: "Make us a little lentil broth, my son." He replied: "I made it yesterday." And so they rose and ate their food.

57. An old man came to a father, who cooked a few lentils and said: "Let us worship God and eat afterwards." One of them recited the whole psalter. The other read and meditated upon two of the greater prophets. And in the morning the old man went away, and they forgot to eat their food.

58. A brother felt hungry at dawn, and struggled with his soul not to eat till 9 o'clock. And when 9 o'clock came, he extracted from himself a resolution to wait till noon. At noon he dipped his bread and sat down to eat—but then rose up again, saying: "I will wait till three." And at 3 o'clock he prayed, and saw the devil's work going out of him like smoke; and his hunger ceased.

59. One of the old men was ill, and for many days could not eat. His disciple asked him to take something and restore his strength. So the disciple went away and made some lentil cake. A jar was hanging in the cell containing a little honey: and there was another jar with evil-smelling linseed oil only used for the lamp. The brother took the wrong jar in error and put grease instead of honey into the mixture. The old man tasted it, and said nothing, but quietly ate the mouthful. The disciple forced him to take a second mouthful. The old man tortured himself and ate it. Yet a third time the disciple pressed it upon him. But he did not want to eat, and said: "Truly, my son, I cannot." But his disciple encouraged him, and said: "It is good, Abba; look, I keep you company." When the disciple tasted it and saw what he had done, he fell flat on his face, and said: "Alas, Father! I have killed you, and you have laid this sin upon me because you did not speak." And the old man said to him.

"Be not sad, my son. If God had willed that I should eat honey you would have been given the honey to mix in those buns."

60. They said of one old man that he sometimes longed to eat cucumber. So he took it and hung it in front of him where he could see it. And he was not conquered by his longing, and did not eat it, but tamed himself, and did penitence that he wanted it at all.

61. Once a brother went to visit his sister who was ill in a nunnery. She was a person full of faith. She herself did not consent to see a man: nor did she want to give her brother occasion to come into the midst of women. So she commanded him thus: "Go, my brother, pray for me. For by Christ's grace I shall see you in the kingdom of heaven."

62. On a journey a monk met some nuns and when he saw them he turned aside off the road. The abbess said to him: "If you had been a perfect monk, you would not have looked so closely as to see that we were women."

63. Once some brothers went to Alexandria, invited by Archbishop Theophilus to be present when after prayer he destroyed a pagan temple. And while they were supping with the archbishop, they were served with veal, and ate it without realizing it. And the archbishop took a piece of meat, and gave it to the old man who was reclining next to him, and said: "Look, here is a good piece of meat. Eat it, Abba." But they answered him: "Till now, we thought we were eating vegetables. If this is meat, we do not eat it." And not one of them would take another mouthful.

64. A brother brought some new bread to Cellia and invited his elders to taste. And when they had each eaten two rolls of bread, they stopped. But the brother knew how austere was their abstinence, and humbly began to beg them: "For God's sake eat today until you are filled." And they ate another two rolls. See how these true and self-disciplined monks ate much more than they needed, for God's sake.

65. Once one of the old men lay gravely ill, and was losing a lot of blood from his bowels. And a brother brought him some dry fruit, and made gruel, and offered them to the old man, and asked him: "Eat; perhaps it is good for you." The old man looked at him for a long time, and said: "In truth, I tell you that I have wanted God to leave me in my sickness for thirty years more." And in his weakness he absolutely refused to take even a little food; so the brother took away what he had brought, and returned to his cell.

66. Another old man had lived in the desert for a long time. And it happened that a brother came to him and found him sickening. He washed his face, and made a meal for him out of what he had brought. And when the old man saw it, he said: "Truly, brother, I had forgotten that men found comfort in food." And he offered him a cup of wine as well. And when he saw it, he wept, saying: "I hoped I would never drink wine until I died."

67. An old man made a resolution not to drink for forty days. And if ever he thirsted he washed a vessel and filled it with water and hung it in front of his eyes. And when the brothers asked him why he was doing this, he replied: "So that if I do not taste what I long for and can see, my devotion will be greater and I shall be granted a greater reward by the Lord."

68. On a journey, one brother had with him his mother, who had now grown old. They came to a river, and the old woman could not get across. Her son took off his cloak, and wrapt it round his hands, so as not to touch his mother's body, and carried her across the river. His mother said to him: "Why did you wrap your hands like that, my son?" He said: "Because a woman's body is fire. Simply because I was touching you, the memory of other women came into my soul."

69. One of the fathers said that he knew a brother who fasted in his cell the whole of Easter week. And when at last he came to mass on Saturday, he ran away as soon as he had communicated, to prevent the other brothers forcing him to join in the dinner in the church. In his own cell he only ate a few boiled beetroots, with salt but without bread.

70. At a meeting of the brothers in Scete, they were eating dates. And one of them, who was ill from excessive fasting, brought up some phlegm in a fit of coughing, and unintentionally it fell on another of the brothers. This brother was tempted by an evil thought and driven to say: "Be quiet, and do not spit on me." So to tame himself and restrain his own angry thought he picked up what had been spat and put it in his mouth and swallowed it. And then he began to say to himself: "If you say to your brother what will sadden him, you will have to eat what nauseates you."

PART V

Of lust

1. Abba Antony said: "I reckon that the body has a natural movement within itself, which obeys the behest of the soul, a

kind of passionless movement of which the body's actions are
but symptoms. And there is a second movement in the body,
caused by eating and drinking, whereby the blood is heated and
excited. That is why Paul said: 'Be not drunk with wine, wherein is excess,' and again the Lord commanded his disciples in the
Gospel: 'See that your hearts be not overcharged with surfeiting
and drunkenness.' 12 And there is another movement which
comes from the craft and envy of demons upon men who are
striving to live a good life. Thus it is a help to know that there
are three bodily movements—from nature, from plenty of food,
and from demons."

2. Abba Gerontius of Petra said: "Many people who are
tempted by bodily delights, do not sin with the body but lust
with the mind: they keep their bodily virginity but lust in the
soul. It is good then, my beloved, to do what is written: 'Let
everyone keep a close guard upon his heart.' " 13

2A. Abba John the Short said: "The man who eats his fill or
talks with a child has already lusted in his mind."

3. Abba Cassian said: 14 "Abba Moses told us: 'It is good not
to hide the thoughts but to disclose them to discreet and devout
old men; but not to men who are old merely in years, for many
have found final despair instead of comfort by confessing to men
whom they saw to be aged, but who in fact were inexperienced.' "

4. There was once a brother exceeding careful about seeking
goodness.15 And being sore troubled by the demon of lust, he
came to an old man and told him his thoughts. The old man
was inexperienced: and when he heard, he was indignant, and
said he was a wicked brother, unworthy of his monk's habit,
because he conceived thoughts like that. When the brother
heard this, he despaired of himself, and left his cell, and started
on his way back to the world. But by God's providence, Abba
Apollos met him. And seeing him disturbed and melancholy,
he asked him: "Son, why are you so sad?" The brother, much
embarrassed, at first said not a word. But when the old man
pressed him to say what was happening to him, he confessed,
and said: "It is because lustful thoughts trouble me. I confessed
them to that old man, and he says I now have no hope of salvation. So I am desperate at myself, and am on my way back

12 Eph. 5:18; Luke 21:34.
13 Prov. 4:23.
14 *Conferences*, II, 10.
15 *Conferences*, II, 13.

to the world." When Father Apollos heard this, he went on asking questions like a wise doctor, and advised him thus: "Do not be cast down, son, nor despair of yourself. Even at my age and experience of the spiritual life, I am still sorely troubled by thoughts like yours. Do not fail at this point, because this trouble cannot be cured by our efforts, but only by God's mercy. Grant me what I ask, just today, and go back to your cell."

The brother obeyed him. But Abba Apollos went away to the cell of the old man who had made him desperate. He stood outside the cell, and prayed the Lord with tears, and said: "Lord, who allowest men to be tempted for their good, transfer the war which that brother is suffering to this old man: let him learn by experience in his old age what many years have not taught him, and so let him find out how to sympathize with people undergoing this kind of temptation." And as soon as he ended his prayer, he saw a negro standing by the cell firing arrows at the old man. As though stricken, he began to totter and lurch like a drunken man. And when he could bear it no longer, he came out of his cell, and set out on the same road by which the young man started to return to the world. Abba Apollos understood what had happened, and met him. He approached him, and said: "Where are you going? And why are you so troubled within?" The old man, seeing that the holy Apollos understood what had happened, was ashamed and said nothing. But Abba Apollos said to him: "Return to your cell, and see your own weakness in another, and keep your own heart. For either you were ignorant of the devil in spite of your age, or you were contemptuous, and did not deserve to struggle for strength with the devil as all other men must. But *struggle* is not the right word, when you could not stand up to his attack for one day. This has happened to you because of the young man. He came to you because he was being attacked by the common enemy of us all. You ought to have given him words of consolation to help him against the devil's attack. But instead you drove him to despair. You did not remember the wise man's saying, whereby we are ordered to deliver the men who are drawn towards death, and not forbear to redeem men ready to be killed. You did not remember our Saviour's parable: 'You should not break the bruised reed, nor quench the smoking flax.' Not a single person could endure the enemy's clever attack, nor quench, nor control the leaping fire natural to the body, unless God's grace preserved us in our weakness. In all our prayers we should pray for his grace to save us, so that he may turn aside the scourge aimed even at you. For he makes a man to grieve, and then lifts him up to salvation: he strikes, and his hand heals: he humbles and exalts, mortifies and enlivens: leads to hell and brings back from hell." [16]

So saying, Abba Apollos prayed again, and at once the old man was freed from his inner war. Abba Apollos urged him to ask God to give him the tongue of the learned, to know the time when it is best to speak.

5. When Abba Cyrus of Alexandria was asked about the temptation of lust, he said: "If you are not tempted, you have no hope: if you are not tempted, it is because you are used to sinning. The man who does not fight sin at the stage of temptation, sins in his body. And the man who sins in his body has no trouble from temptation."

6. An old man asked a brother: "Do you often talk with a woman?" And the brother said: "No." And he went on: "My temptations come from painters old and new, memories of mine which trouble me with their pictures of women." But the old man said to him: "Fear not the dead, but flee the living—flee from assenting to sin or committing sin, and take a longer time over your prayers."

7. Abba Mathois used to say that a brother came and declared that the slanderer was worse than the fornicator. And he replied: "This is a hard saying." Then the brother said to him: "How do you want to reckon the matter?" And the old man said: "Slander is bad, but it is curable quickly; the slanderer can do penitence and say 'I have spoken ill,' and it is over. But lust is essential death."

8. Abba Poemen said: "As a bodyguard is always standing by to protect the Emperor, so the soul ought ever to be ready for the demon of lust."

9. A brother once came to Abba Poemen, and said to him: "What am I to do, Father? I am wretched with lust. And I went to Abba Hybistion, and he told me: 'You ought not to let it dwell in you longer.'" Abba Poemen said to him: "Abba Hybistion lives like the angels above, and he knows not these things. But you and I are in lust. If the monk controls his stomach and his tongue, and stays in solitude, he can trust that he is not dying."

10. They said of the Abbess Sarah that for thirteen years she was fiercely attacked by the demon of lust. And she never

16 Prov. 24:11; Matt. 12:20; I Sam. 2:6.

prayed that the battle should be stayed. But she used to say only this: "Lord, grant me strength."

11. They also said of her that the same demon of lust was once attacking her menacingly, and tempting her with vain thought of the world. But she kept fearing God in her soul and maintained the rigour of her fasting. And once when she climbed up on the roof to pray, the spirit of lust appeared to her in a bodily form and said to her: "You have beaten me, Sarah." But she replied: "It is not I who have beaten you, but my Lord the Christ."

12. A brother was goaded by lust and the lust was like a fire burning day and night in his heart. But he struggled on, not coming to meet his temptation nor consenting to it. And after a long time, the goad left him, annihilated by his perseverance. And at once light appeared in his heart.

13. Another brother was goaded by lust. He rose up in the night and went to tell his temptations to an old man, and the old man consoled him. So he returned, comforted to his cell. But again the spirit of lust tempted him. And a second time he went to the old man. This happened several times. The old man did not reproach him, but spoke words to his profit: "Yield not to the devil, and guard your soul. Whenever the demon troubles you, come to me, and rebuke him, and so he will go away. Nothing troubles the demon of lust more than disclosure of his pricks. Nothing pleases him more than the concealment of the temptation."

Eleven times the brother went to the old man, and blamed himself for his imaginings. And then the brother said to the old man: "Of thy charity, Abba, speak to me a word." The old man said to him: "Believe me, my son, if God allowed the imaginings which goad me to be passed to you, you would not bear them but would be utterly destroyed." And so by his words and deep humility, that brother found rest from the goad of lust.

14. Another brother was goaded by lust. He began to struggle and prolong his fast, and for fourteen years he guarded himself against temptation and did not consent. Afterwards he came to church and disclosed to the whole congregation what he was suffering. And a decree was made, and for a week they all afflicted themselves on his behalf, praying God continually; and so his goad was stayed.

15. An old hermit said about the temptation to lust: "Sloth, do you want to be saved? Go, and discipline yourself, go, 'seek,

and ye shall find': watch, 'Knock and it shall be opened to you.'
In the world there are boxers who are hard hit and yet stand
firm and receive crowns. Sometimes one is set upon by two, and
their blows lend him strength so that he overcomes them. Have
you seen what strength exercise brings? Do you also stand, and
be strong: and the Lord defeats your enemy for you."

16. On this same temptation, another old man said: "You
should be like a man walking along the street past an inn, and
sniffing the smell of meat frying or roasting. Anyone who likes
goes in and eats. People who do not want it, pass by and only
sniff the smell. So you ought to put the smell away from you;
rise, and pray 'Lord, Son of God, help me.' Do this against
other temptations. We cannot make temptations vanish, but
we can struggle against them."

17. Another old man said: "We suffer this through negligence. If we remember that God dwells in us, we shall never
bring into ourselves a vessel that is not his. The Lord Christ
abides in us and with us, and watches our life. And because we
bear him with us and contemplate him, we ought not to be
negligent but ought to make ourselves holy as he is holy. If we
stand upon a rock, the wicked one will be broken. Do not be
afraid, and he will do nothing against you. And pray with
courage this psalm: 'They that trust in the Lord are like
Mount Sion; they that dwell in Jerusalem shall stand fast for
ever.' "[17]

18. A brother asked an old man: "If a monk falls to sin, he
is punished like a person who has fallen from a higher state to
a lower, and is in travail until he rises again. But he who comes
from the world, is like a beginner advancing to a higher state."
And the old man replied: "A monk falling into temptation is
like a collapsing house. If he is a serious and sober person, he
rebuilds the ruined house. He finds the right materials for building, lays foundations, and collects stone and sand, and all the
other needful things, and so his building rapidly grows higher.
But the builder who did not dig or lay foundations, and has
none of the right materials, goes away hoping that some day the
house will be built. So if the monk falls into temptation, and
turns to the Lord, he has the best equipment—meditation on
the law of God, psalmody, work with his hands, prayer, and the
others—foundations of his building. The novice will find himself low down on the ladder of religion until he learns all these."

17 Ps. 125 : 1.

19. A brother, held in the grip of lust, went to a great old man and asked him: "Of your charity, pray for me: for I am troubled by lust." The old man prayed to the Lord. And he came a second time to the old man and said the same: and again the old man was careful to beseech the Lord on his behalf, and said: "Lord, show me why the devil is doing this work in that brother. I prayed to you, but he has not yet found rest." And the Lord revealed to him what was happening to that brother. And he saw the brother sitting down, and the spirit of lust near him and, so to speak, playing with him: and an angel was standing near to help him and was frowning upon that brother because he did not throw himself upon God, but took a pleasure in his thoughts, and turned his mind towards them. And the old man saw that the chief cause was in the brother himself. And he said to him: "You are dallying with your thought." And he taught him how to resist thoughts like this. And the brother's soul revived under the old man's teaching and prayer, and he found rest from his temptation.

20. Once the disciple of a great old man was tempted by lust. When the old man saw him struggling, he said: "Do you want me to ask the Lord to release you from your trouble?" But he said: "Abba, I see that although it is a painful struggle, I am profiting from having to carry the burden. But ask God in your prayers, that he will give me long-suffering, to enable me to endure." Then his Abba said to him: "Now I know that you are far advanced, my son, and beyond me."

21. They said of an old man that he went down to Scete taking his infant son with him. The boy, being brought up among the monks, did not know what women were. When he became a man, the demons showed him visions of women at night. And he told his father, and he wondered. And once they both went into Egypt and saw women. And the son said: "Abba, there are the people who came to me during the night in Scete." And his father said: "These are monks from the world, my son. They use one kind of dress, and hermits another." And the old man marvelled that the demons should show him visions of women in Scete, and they both went straight back to their cell.

22. A brother was tested by temptation in Scete. And the enemy sent to his soul the memory of a fair woman, and troubled him sorely. And by God's providence it chanced that another brother came down from Egypt and arrived in Scete. And when they met to talk, he told him that his wife was dead (she was the woman about whom he was being disturbed).

When he heard the news, he put on his cloak in the night and went to the place where he had heard she was buried. And he dug the place, and wiped the blood of her corpse on his cloak, and kept it in his cell when he returned. And when it smelt too much, he put it in front of him and hurriedly said to his temptation: "Look, this is what you desire. You have it now, fill yourself." And so he chastised himself with the smell until his passions died down.

23. A man once came to Scete to become a monk. And he brought with him his infant son, who had been lately weaned. When the child grew to be a young man, the demons began to attack him and trouble him. And he said to his father: "I am going back to the world, because I cannot bear these bodily passions." His father comforted him: but the youth said: "I cannot endure any longer, father. Let me go back to the world." His father said to him: "Listen just this once to me, my son. Take forty loaves, and palm leaves for forty days, and go to the inner desert, and stay there forty days—and God's will be done." He obeyed his father, and rose and went into the desert, and remained there, making plaits from the dry palm leaves and eating dry bread. And after he had been there twenty days, he saw the demon coming against him. There stood before him a person like a negro woman, ill-smelling and ugly. He could not bear her smell and thrust her from him. And she said to him: "I am she who seems sweet in the hearts of men. But because of your obedience and travail, God has not let me seduce you, but has shown you my ill-favour." He rose, and thanked God, and came to his father, and said: "Now I do not want to go to the world, father. I have seen the devil's work, and his foulness." But his father also knew what had happened, and said: "If you had stayed there forty days, and kept my command right to the end, you would have seen still greater things."

24. An old man was once living far out in the desert. A woman of his kinsfolk wanted to see him after so many years, and enquired where he was living, and rose and came on the road to that desert. And finding camel-drivers, she joined them and came with them into the desert. For she was being drawn onward by the devil. When she reached the old man's door, she began to knock and say who she was—"I am your kin;" and she stayed with him.

But another monk was living nearer to Egypt. He filled his vessel with water at his supper time. And suddenly the vessel was upset, and the water spilt. And by God's inspiration he said to himself: "I will go to the desert, and tell the elders what happened to this water." And he rose and went. And at evening he slept in a heathen temple by the roadside, and during the night he heard demons saying: "Tonight we have driven yonder monk to lust." And when he heard this, he was saddened. And he came to the old man, and found him sad, and said to him: "What am I to do, Abba? I filled my jug with water, and at supper-time it was spilt." And the old man said to him: "You have come to ask me why your vessel was upset. But what am I to do?—for last night I fell to lusting." And he replied: "I knew it." And the old man said: "How did you know?" And he said: "I was sleeping in a temple, and I heard demons talking about you." And the old man said: "Look, I am going to the world." But he besought him, "Do not go, father, stay here in your cell. But send the woman away. This has happened because the enemy attacked you." When the old man heard this, he endured and made his way of life more penitential and sorrowful, until he returned to his earlier state.

25. An old man said: "Chastity is born of serenity, and silence, and secret meditation."

26. A brother asked an old man: "If a man happens to fall into temptation, what becomes of those who are led to stumble by it?" And the old man told this story. "In a monastery in Egypt was a deacon. And an official, persecuted by a judge, came with all his family to that monastery. And by the devil's instigation, that deacon came in to his wife, and all the brothers were disturbed. But he went away to an old man, and told him what had happened. Now the old man had a secret inner room to his cell. When the deacon saw this, he said: 'Bury me alive here, and tell no one.' And he hid in that inner room, and there did true penitence.

But a long time after, it happened that the Nile failed to flood. And when they were all making litanies, it was revealed to one of those holy men that unless the deacon who had hidden with such and such a monk, should return, the water would not rise. When they heard this, they marvelled, and they came and hurriedly brought him out of his hiding-place. And he prayed, and the water rose. And the men who had before been scandalized at him, were now edified by his penitence, and glorified God."

27. Two brothers went to a town to sell what they had made. In the town they separated, and one of them fell into fornication. Afterwards the other brother said: "Let us go back

to our cell, brother." But he replied: "I am not coming." And the other asked him: "Why, brother?" And he replied: "Because when you left me, I met temptation, and was guilty of fornication." The other, wanting to help him, said: "It happened also to me: after I left you, I also fell into fornication. Let us go together, and do penance with all our might, and God will pardon us sinners." When they returned to their cell, they told the elders what had happened to them, and were instructed what penance they should do. But the one did penance not for himself, but for the other, as though he himself had sinned. God, seeing his earnestness and his charity, disclosed to one of the elders, a few days later, that he had forgiven the fornicator because of the charity of the brother who had not sinned. Truly, this was to lay down his soul for his brother.

28. Once a brother came to an old man and said: "My brother keeps leaving me, and goes travelling everywhere: and I am suffering for it." And the old man besought him: "Bear it calmly, brother. And God will see your earnestness and endurance, and will bring him back to you. It is not possible for a man to be recalled from his purpose by harshness and severity— demon cannot drive out demon: you will bring him back to you better by kindness. That is how God acts for our good, and draws us to himself."

And he told him this story: "In the Thebaid were two brothers. And when one of them began to lust, he said to the other: 'I am going back to the world.' The other wept and said: 'I am not letting you go away, my brother, to lose your toil and your chastity.' But he refused and said: 'I am not staying here: I am going. Either come with me, and I will return with you, or let me go, and let me remain in the world.' The brothers came and told this to a great old man. And the old man said to him: 'Go with him, and because of your effort, God will not let him perish.' So he rose and went with him to the world. And when they came to a village, God looked on the efforts of him who followed his brother out of charity and need, and took away that brother's passion. And he said to his brother: 'Let us go back to the desert, my brother. Look, I imagine that I have already sinned with a woman. And what gain have I from that?' And they returned to their cell unharmed."

29. A brother, being tempted by a demon, went to an old man and said: "Those two monks over there who live together, live wickedly." But the old man knew that a demon was playing with him, and he sent and called them to him. And at

evening he put a mat for them, and covered them with a single blanket, and said: "They are sons of God, and holy persons." But he said to his disciple: "Shut this slandering brother up in a cell by himself: he is suffering from the passions of which he accuses them."

30. A brother said to an old man: "What am I to do, for these foul thoughts are killing me?" The old man said to him: "When a mother wants to wean her baby, she smears something bitter on her breasts: and when the infant comes as usual to suckle, he tastes the bitterness and is repelled. So you ought to put a bitterness into your thought." The brother said to him: "What bitterness is this?" The old man said to him: "The thought of death and torment, which is prepared in the next world for sinners."

31. A brother asked an old man about thoughts of this kind. And the old man said: "I have never been goaded by it." And the brother was scandalized at him, and went to a second old man and said: "Look, that old man said this to me and has scandalized me, because it is unnatural." The old man said to him: "The meaning of the words of that man of God is not upon the surface. Rise up, go and be penitent to him, and he will disclose to you the power in his words." So the brother rose and came to the old man, and was penitent to him. And he said: "Forgive me, father, that I was a fool, and did not bid you goodbye when I left. But I beg you, explain to me how it is that you are untroubled by lust." The old man said to him: "It is because, ever since I became a monk, I have never taken my fill of bread, or water, or sleep; and because I am tormented by desire for food, I cannot feel the pricks of lust." And the brother went away, taking profit from the words of the old man.

32. A brother asked an old man: "What am I to do? My mind is ever thinking about fornication; and lets me not rest even for an hour, and my soul is suffering." But the old man said to him: "When the demons sow thoughts in your heart, and you feel this, do not hold converse with your soul, for that is the demons' suggestion. Though the demons are careful to send in thoughts, they do not force you. It is yours to receive or reject. Do you know what the Midianites did? They adorned their daughters, and set them where the Israelites could see them: yet they did not force them to intermingle, but as each one wished. But others were wrathful and uttered threats, and avenged the act of whoredom with the death of those who had

dared it. This is what should be done with the lust that rises in the mind." But the brother replied: "And what am I to do, in that I am frail, and this passion masters me?" And the old man said: "Be earnest in this way. When they start to speak in your heart, do not answer them. But rise up, pray, do penance, and say 'Son of God, have mercy upon me.' " But the brother said to him: "Look, Abba, I meditate, and there is no penitence in my heart, for I do not know the meaning of the words on which I meditate." And the old man said: "Yet, go on meditating. I have heard that Abba Poemen and other fathers said this: 'The snake-charmer knows not the meaning of his words: but the snake hears them, and knows their meaning, and obeys the charmer, and lies down. So though we know not the meaning of what we say, the demons hear, and are fearful, and flee.' "

33. An old man used to say: "A lustful thought is brittle like papyrus. If it is thrust into us, and we do not accept it but cast it from us, it is broken easily. If it casts its sweetness over us and we dally with it, it is as difficult to break as iron. So we need a discrimination of mind, to know that men who consent lose their hopes of salvation: and for men who do not consent, a crown is laid up."

34. Two brothers, who were attacked by lust, went away and married wives. Afterwards they said to each other: "What have we gained that we have ceased to live like angels, and have come to impurity, and later will come to fire and torment? Let us go back to the desert, and do penance for our fault." And they came to the desert, and asked the fathers to accept them as penitents, and confessed what they had done. And the elders shut them up for a whole year, and gave them each an equal measure of bread and water. Now they were alike in appearance. And at the end of the year's penance, they came out. And the fathers saw that one looked pale and melancholy, the other looked strong and bright. And they were astonished, for each had had the same quantity of food and drink. And they asked the man who was sad and troubled: "What were you doing with your thoughts in that cell?" And he said: "I was turning over in my mind the punishment I shall incur for the evil I have done, and I was so afraid that my bones cleaved to my flesh." And they asked the other: "What were you thinking about in your cell?" And he said: "I was thanking God that he had delivered me from the pollution of this world and the punishment of the next, and has called me back to live here like the angels: and as I thought continually upon my God, I was

glad." And the old men said: "The penitence of both men is equal before God."

35. In Scete there was an old man who became gravely ill, and was nursed by the brothers. When the old man saw how much they did for him, he said: "I am going to Egypt, and then I shall not be a trouble to these brothers." And Abba Moses said to him: "Don't go: you will run into lust." But the old man was vexed, and said: "My body is dead. How can you say that to me?" So he rose and went to Egypt.

When the surrounding inhabitants in Egypt heard that he had arrived, they brought him many gifts. And a devout maiden came to him, wishing to minister to him because he was sick. And after a short time he recovered somewhat from the illness which had gripped him, and he came to her, and she conceived. And when her neighbours asked her, who was the father, she said: "This old man." But they did not believe her. Then the old man said: "It is I who am the father. Keep for me the baby when it is born." And when the baby had been weaned, the old man carried it on his shoulders, and arrived at Scete on a feast day, and went into church in front of the whole congregation. When they saw him, they wept. And he said to the brothers: "Do you see this baby? He is the child of disobedience. Beware, my brothers, remember what I have done though I am old, and pray for me." And going to his cell, he returned to his earlier way of life.

36. A brother was grievously tempted by the demons of fornication. Four demons appeared before him like beautiful women, and attacked him continuously for forty days. But he fought like a man, and was unconquered. And God, seeing his good struggle, granted that he should no more suffer the sting of bodily passion.

37. In lower Egypt there was a very famous hermit, who lived alone in his cell. And it happened that by Satan's wiles a harlot heard of him, and said to the young men: "What will you give me, if I ruin that hermit?" They agreed to give her a present. At evening she went out and came to his cell like a person who had lost her way. When she knocked at his door, he came out. And seeing her, he was troubled, and said: "How have you come here?" She pretended to weep, and said: "I lost my way." He felt truly sorry for her, and led her into the little courtyard of his cell, and himself went to the inner room of his cell and shut the door. And she cried aloud in woe: "Abba, the beasts will eat me here." Again he was troubled, and afraid of

the judgement of God; and he said: "Why has God's wrath come upon me thus?" And he opened the door and brought her inside.

Then the devil began to goad his heart to want her. He knew that it was the devil's goading, and said silently: "The ways of the enemy are darkness: but the Son of God is light." He rose, and lit the lamp. And when he began to burn with desire, he said: "People who do things like this go into torment. Test yourself, and see whether you can bear a fire which is ever-lasting." And he put his finger in the flame of the lamp. And he burnt it: but he did not feel the pain because of the fire of passion within him. And so, until the dawn came he burnt his fingers one after the other.

The wretched woman saw what he was doing, and in her fear lay still as a stone. And at dawn the young men came to the monk and said: "Did a woman come here yesterday evening?" He said: "Yes, she is asleep over there." And they went in, and found her dead. And they said: "Abba, she is dead." Then he turned back the cloak which he was wearing, and showed them his hands, and said: "Look what that child of the devil has done to me. She has cost me every finger I possess." And he told what had happened, and said: "It is written, Render not evil for evil." And he prayed, and raised her up. She was converted, and lived chastely for the rest of her days.

38. A brother was assailed by lust. By chance he came to a village in Egypt, and saw the daughter of the heathen priest there, and greatly loved her. And he said to her father: "Give her to be my wife." He answered: "I cannot give her to you until I have besought my god." And he went to the demon whom he served and said: "Here is a monk wanting to marry my daughter. Do I give her to him?" The demon answered: "Ask him if he denies his God, and his baptism, and his monastic vow." And the priest came and said to the monk: "If you deny your God, and your baptism, and your monastic vow, I will give you my daughter." The monk agreed. And at once he saw something like a dove fly out of his mouth and up into the sky. Then the priest went to the demon and said: "He has promised to do the three things you said." Then the devil answered: "Do not give your daughter to be his wife, for his God has not left him, but will yet help him." And the priest went back and said to the monk: "I cannot give her to you, because your God is still helping you, and has not left you."

When the monk heard this, he said in himself: "If God has

shown me such kindness, though like a wretch I have denied him, and my baptism and my monastic vow, if God is so good that he still helps me though I am wicked, why am I running away from him?" And he was restored to his right and sober mind, and came into the desert to a great old man, and told him what had happened. And the old man replied: "Stay with me in this cave, and fast for three weeks, and I will pray God for you." And the old man travailed on behalf of the brother, and prayed God thus: "I beseech thee, O Lord, grant me this soul, and accept its penitence."

And God heard his prayer. At the end of the first week, the old man came to the brother and asked: "Have you seen any thing?" And the brother replied: "Yes, I saw a dove above in the sky over my head." And the old man answered: "Look to your heart, and pray God earnestly." After the second week the old man came again to the brother, and asked him: "Have you seen anything?" And he replied: "I have seen a dove coming down by my head." and the old man charged him: "Pray, and pray seriously." And at the end of the third week, the old man came again and asked him: "Have you seen anything else?" And he answered: "I saw a dove and it came and sat on my head, and I stretched out my hand to catch it, and it entered my mouth."

And the older man thanked God, and said to the brother: "Look, God has accepted your penitence. In future be careful, and on your guard." And the brother answered: "See, I will stay with you now, until I die."

39. One of the old men in the Thebaid used to say that he was the son of a heathen priest, and that as a little boy he had often seen his father go into the temple and sacrifice to the idol. And once, when he had crept in secretly, he had seen Satan on his throne, and his host standing around: and one of his chief-tains came and adored him. And the devil said: "Where have you come from?" And he answered: "I was in such and such a province, and there I stirred wars and riots, and much blood was spilt, and I have come to tell you." And the devil asked him: "How long did it take you?" And he answered: "A month." Then the devil said: "Did you take so long over it?" and ordered him to be beaten.

Then a second came to adore him. And the devil said to him: "Where have you been?" And the demon replied: "I was in the sea, and I raised storms, and sunk ships, and drowned many, and have come to tell you." And the devil said: "How long did it take you?" And he answered: "Twenty days." And the devil said: "Why did you take so long over this one task?" and ordered him also to be flogged.

Then a third came and adored him. And the devil said to him: "Where have you been?" And he answered: "I was in such and such a city: and during a wedding I stirred up quarrelling until the parties came to bloody blows, and in the end even the husband was killed, and I have come to tell you." And the devil said: "How long did it take you?" And he answered: "Ten days." The devil commanded him also to be flogged because he had been idle.

Another came to adore him, and he said: "Where have you been?" And he answered: "I was in the desert: and for forty years I have been attacking one monk. And at last in the night, I prevailed, to make him lust." When the devil heard this, he rose, and kissed him. And taking off his own crown, he put it on his head, and made him sit with him on a throne, and said: "You have been brave, and done a great deed."

"When I heard and saw this, I said within myself: 'Great indeed is the discipline of the monks'. And so it pleased God to grant me salvation: and I went out, and became a holy monk."

40. They said this of a father, that he had been a man who lived in the world, and had turned to God, but was still goaded by desire for his wife; and he told this to the fathers. When they saw him to be a true labourer, one who did more than his duty, they laid on him a course of discipline which so weakened his body that he could not stand up. By God's providence a father came to visit Scete. And when he came to this man's cell, he saw it open, and he passed on, surprised that no one came to meet him. But then he thought that perhaps the brother inside was ill, and returned, and knocked on the door. And after knocking, he went in, and found the monk gravely ill. And he said: "What's the matter, father?" And he told him: "I was living in the world, and the enemy still troubles me because of my wife. And I told the fathers, and they laid upon me various burdens to discipline my life. And in trying to carry them out obediently, I have fallen ill—and yet the goad is worse." When the old man heard this, he was vexed, and said: "The fathers are powerful men, and did well in laying these burdens upon you. But if you will listen to me who am but a child in these matters, stop all this discipline, take a little food at the proper times, recover your strength, join in the worship of God for a little, and turn your mind to the Lord—for this is a thing you

cannot conquer by your own efforts. The human body is like a coat. If you treat it carefully, it will last a long time. If you neglect it, it will fall into tatters."

The sick man did as he was told, and in a few days the incitement to lust vanished.

41. A very old hermit, of saintly life, lived on a mountain near Antinoë, and helped many people towards sanctity by his teaching and example—so I have been told by well-known monks. And because he was saintly, the devil was stirred to envy him, as he envies all men of true goodness. And the devil sent into his heart the thought that if he was really the man he wanted to be, he ought not to let others minister to his needs, but himself ought to be ministering to them: or at least, if he could not minister to the needs of others, he ought to minister to his own needs. So he said: "Go to the town and sell the baskets you are making, and buy what you need, and come back to your cell, and so be a burden to no one." But the devil suggested this because he envied his quietness and his opportunity of leisure to hear God, and the good which he did to so many people. All round him the enemy was scurrying, hurling at him, trying to capture him.

He assented to what he believed a good thought, and came down from his hermitage. And everyone admired him and recognized him when they saw him, but did not know that he was entangled in the devil's net. And after a long time he saw a woman. And because he was being careless, he was overthrown, and came to her. And he went into a desert place, with the devil at his heels, and fell down by a river. And he thought that the enemy rejoiced at his ruin, and wanted to despair, because he had sorely grieved the Spirit of God, and the holy angels, and the venerable fathers, many of whom had overcome the devil though they lived in towns. And because he could not become like them, he was utterly downcast; and he forgot that God is a God who gives strength to them who devoutly turn to him. Blinded, and not seeing how to cure his sin, he wanted to throw himself in the river, and fill the enemy's cup to overflowing. In the agony of his soul, his body began to sicken. And unless God in his mercy had helped him, he would have died impenitent, to the perfect satisfaction of the enemy.

But at the last moment he found his right mind again. He resolved to inflict a severe penance upon himself, and pray to God in sorrow and grief: and in this mind he went back to his cell. He marked the door of his cell in the usual way to show that the man inside was dead, and so he wept and prayed to God. He fasted, and watched, and became thin with his austerity; and still he did not think he had made fit penance or satisfaction. When the brothers came to him to be taught, and knocked at the door, he said that he could not open it—"I am bound by an oath to do penance for a whole year devoutly. Pray for me." When they heard this, they were scandalized, because they believed him to be truly honourable and great: but he found no means of explaining himself to them.

For a whole year he fasted rigidly, and did penance. On Easter Eve, he took a new lamp and put it on a new pot, and covered it with a lid. At evening he stood up to pray, and said: "Merciful, pitying Lord, who willest that barbarians be saved and come to the knowledge of the truth: I flee to thee, the Saviour of the faithful. Have mercy upon me that I moved thee to anger, that I made the enemy happy: here am I, dead, but obedient to thee. Thou, Lord, who pitiest even the wicked, even the pitiless, thou who commanded us to show mercy to our neighbours, have mercy upon me humbled before thee. With thee nothing is impossible: for in the mouth of hell my soul was scattered like dust. Have pity on thy creation because thou art kind and merciful, thou who wilt on the day of the resurrection raise up even bodies that are not. Hear me, O Lord, for my spirit has failed, and my soul is wretched. I have polluted my body, and now I cannot live, because I did not believe. Look at my penitence and forgive my sin, a sin that was double because I despaired. Send life into me, for I am contrite: and light this lamp with thy fire. So I may be enabled to receive confidence in thy mercy and pardon, to keep thy commandments, to remain in thy fear, to serve thee more faithfully than before, for the rest of the span of life which thou hast allotted to me."

On the night of Easter Eve he prayed thus and wept. And he rose to see if the lamp were lit. When he took off the lid, he saw that it was unlit. And again he fell on his face and besought God: "I know, O God, that when I struggled for my crown, I did not stand on my feet, but rather chose the pleasures of the body and so the punishment of the wicked. Spare me then, Lord. Here am I: again I confess my disgrace to thee, who art goodness, and in the presence of thy angels, and of all just men, I would confess it to all mankind, if I should not cause them thereby to stumble. Lord, have mercy upon me, and I will teach others: Lord, send life into me."

When he had prayed three times, God heard his prayer. He

rose up and found the lamp burning brightly. And his heart leapt with hope, and happiness, and he worshipped God's grace who had thus forgiven his sins, and answered his soul's prayer. And he said: "I thank thee, O Lord, that thou hast pitied me who am unworthy to live in this world, and hast given me confidence by this great new sign of thy power; thou art merciful to spare the souls which thou createst."

He was still praying thus when the dawn came. And forgetting his need for food, he rejoiced in the Lord. All his life he kept that lamp alight, pouring in oil from the top to prevent it going out. And so, once again, God's Spirit dwelt within him, and he was famous among all the monks, and showed humility and joy in his praise and thanksgiving to God. A few days before his death it was revealed to him how he should pass to another life.

PART VI

That a monk should possess nothing

1. A brother was renouncing the world, and in giving his goods to the poor, he kept a little for his own support. And he came to Abba Antony. When the old man knew what he had done, he said: "If you would be a monk, go to the village yonder and buy some meat, and hang it about your naked body, and come back here." And when the brother did so, dogs and birds tore at his body. He came back to the old man, who asked him if he had done what he was told. He showed St Antony his torn body. Then said St Antony: "People who renounce the world but want to keep their money, are attacked like that by demons and torn in pieces."

2. Abba Daniel told this story about Abba Arsenius. An official once came bringing the will of a kinsman, who was a senator, and had left Arsenius a very great bequest. Arsenius took the will into his hands and wanted to tear it up. But the official fell at his feet, and said: "Please do not tear it; the blame will be on my head." And Abba Arsenius said to him: "I died before he did. Now that he is dead, how can he make me his heir?" And he gave back the will, and would accept nothing.

3. Once Abba Arsenius fell ill in Scete, and in his plight needed just one penny. And he could not find one, so he accepted it as alms from someone, and said: "I thank thee, O God, that for thy name's sake thou hast made me worthy to come to this, that I should have to ask for alms."

4. They told this story of Abba Agatho. He and his disciples spent a long time in building his cell. After they had finished it, he began to live there; and in the first week he saw a vision harmful to himself. And he said to his disciples what the Lord said to his apostles: "Rise, let us go hence." [18] But the disciples were exceedingly vexed, and said: "If you meant the whole time to move from here, why did we have to work so hard and spend so long in building you a cell? People will begin to be scandalized at us, and say: 'Look, they are moving again, they are restless and never settle.' " But when he saw that they were afraid of what people would say, he said: "Although some may be scandalized, there are others who will be edified and say: 'Blessed are they, for they have moved their abode for God's sake, and despised all their property.' Yet I say to you, whoever wants to come, let him come, because I at any rate am going." They threw themselves on the ground before him, and begged to be allowed to go with him.

5. Abba Evagrius [19] said that there was a brother who had no possessions but a Gospel, and sold it to feed the poor. And he said a word which is worth remembering: "I have even sold the word which commands me to sell all and give to the poor."

6. Abba Theodore, surnamed Pherme, had three good books. And going to Abba Macarius, he said to him: "I have three good books, and I am helped by reading them. But other monks also want to read them, and they are helped by them. Tell me, what am I to do?" And the old man said: "Reading books is good, but possessing nothing is more than all." When he heard this, he went away and sold the books, and gave the money to the poor.

7. One of the fathers told a story of John the Persian, how from manifold virtue he attained to a deep simplicity and innocence. He dwelt in the part of Arabia that lies near to Egypt. And once he borrowed from a monk a shilling and bought linen with which to make things. And a brother came and asked him: "Abba, give me a little linen, and I will make myself a vest to wear." John gave it gladly. Then another came and asked him for a little linen, so that he could make himself a coat. And he gave it. When many others came he gave it simply and with pleasure. Later the owner of the borrowed shilling arrived and asked for his money back. And the old man said to him: "I will fetch it for you." And when he could

18 John 14:31.
19 Cf. Socrates, *H.E.*, iv, 23, for the Greek from Evagrius *Practice*.

not find the wherewithal to pay, he went to Abba Jacob the steward, and asked him for a shilling. On the way he found a shilling lying on the ground. He did not touch it, but said a prayer, and went back to his cell. And again came the owner of the shilling and began to speak harshly to him for his money. And John said: "I will give it back to you." And again the old man went away, and found the shilling lying as before on the ground, and said a prayer, and went back to his cell. Then the owner began again to be troublesome: and the old man said: "Wait for me just once more, and I will bring you your shilling." And he rose, and came to that place where he found the shilling on the ground. He said a prayer, and fetched it up, and came to Abba Jacob and said: "Abba, on my way here I found this shilling on the ground. Of your charity make proclamation among the neighbours, to see if anyone has lost it." And the Abba summoned them and announced the find, but they could discover none who had lost it. Then John said to the Abba Jacob: "If no one has lost it, give it to that monk there, because I owe him a shilling." And Abba Jacob was surprised that John, being pressed to pay his debt, had not at once picked the shilling up when he found it, and used it to pay.

There was another remarkable thing about Abba John. If anyone came to borrow something from him, he did not take it in his own hands and lend it, but said: "Come in, take what you need." And when a borrower brought anything back, John used to say: "Put it back where you found it." But if a man borrowed something and did not bring it back, the old man said nothing about it to him.

8. Some of the fathers said that a monk once came to the congregation at Cellia, and appeared before Abba Isaac in a small hood. And the old man rebuked him, and said: "This is where monks live. You are a man of the world, and cannot stay here."

9. Abba Isaac said to the brothers: "Abba Pambo and our fathers used to wear ancient and much-patched clothes. You wear expensive clothes. Go away, you have abandoned this place." When they were starting out for the harvest, he said: "Now I shall give you no more orders, for you never obey me."

10. Abba Cassian said [20] that one Syncleticus renounced the world, and divided his property among the poor. But he kept some for his own use, and was unwilling to accept either the poverty of those who renounced everything or the normal rule

20 *Institutes*, VII, 19.

of monasteries. Basil of blessed memory said to him: "You have stopped being a senator, but you have not become a monk."

11. A brother said to Abba Pistamon: "What am I to do? I find it painful to sell what I make." Abba Pistamon replied: "Abba Sisois and others used to sell what they made. There is no harm in this. When you sell anything, say straight out the price of the goods. If you want to lower the price a little, you may—and so you will find rest." The brother said: "I have enough for my needs from other sources, do you think I need worry about making things to sell?" The old man answered: "However much you have, do not stop making things, do as much as you can provided that the soul is undisturbed."

12. A brother asked Abba Serapion: "Speak to me a word." The old man said: "What can I say to you? You have taken what belongs to widows and orphans and put it on your window-ledge." He saw that the window-ledge was full of books.

13. Syncletice of blessed memory was asked:" Is absolute poverty perfect goodness?" And she said: "It is a great good for those who can. Even those who cannot bear it find rest to their souls though they suffer bodily anxiety. As sturdy clothes are laundered pure white by being turned and trodden under-foot in water, a sturdy soul is strengthened by freely accepting poverty."

14. Abba Hyperichius said: "Freely to accept poverty is the monk's treasury. Therefore, my brother, lay up treasure in heaven, where there will be endless time for rest."

15. One of the holy men named Philagrius lived in Jerusalem and laboured to earn himself enough to eat. And when he was standing in the market-square trying to sell what he had made, by chance a bag fell on the ground near him, containing a great many shillings. The old man found it, and stood there thinking, "The loser must soon come here." And soon the man who had lost it came lamenting. So Philagrius took him apart and gave him back his bag. The owner asked him to accept some of the shillings, but the old man would have nothing. Then the owner began to shout and call: "Come and see what the man of God has done." But the old man fled away un-perceived, and went out of the town, so that they should not know what he had done, nor pay him honour.

16. A brother asked an old man: "What must I do to be saved?" He took off his clothes, and put a girdle about his loins, and stretched out his hands and said: "Thus ought the monk to

be naked of everything worldly, and crucify himself against temptation and the world's struggles."

17. Someone asked an old man to accept money for his future needs. But he refused, because the produce of his labour was enough for him. But when the man persisted, and begged him to take it for the needs of the poor, the old man replied: "My disgrace is twofold. I do not need, yet I accept: and I give to others, and so will suffer from vanity."

18. Some Greeks once came to give alms in the city of Ostracine: and they sought out the stewards of the church to show them who was most in need. The stewards led them to a leper to whom they gave money. But he did not want it, and said: "Look, I have a few palm leaves to work, and I make plaits of them, and so get enough to eat." Then the stewards led them to the house of a widow who lived with her daughters. When they knocked on the door, one of the daughters ran to open it though she was naked. Her mother had gone out to work as a laundress. They gave the daughter clothing and money. But she refused to accept it, and said that her mother had told her: "Trust in God's will. Today I have found work to supply us with a livelihood." And when the mother came back, they asked her to accept it. But she refused, saying: "I have my God to care for me. Do you want to take him away from me today?" They perceived her faith, and glorified God.

19. A great man came from far to Scete carrying gold, and he asked the presbyter of the desert to distribute it among the brothers. But the presbyter said to him: "The brothers do not need it." And he was very pressing, and would not give way, and put a basket of money in the church porch. And the presbyter said: "Whoever is in need may take money from it." No one touched it, some did not even look at it. And the old man said: "God has accepted your offering to him. Go away, and give it to the poor." And he went away much edified.

20. Someone brought an old man money and said: "Take this to spend, for you are old and ill": he was a leper. But the old man replied: "Are you coming to take me away from him who has fed me for sixty years? I have been infirm the whole of that time, and have needed nothing because God has fed me and given me what I need." And he refused to accept it.

21. The old men told of a working gardener who gave away all his profit in alms, and kept for himself only enough to live on. But later Satan enticed his heart and said: "Store up a little money, as a provision to spend when you are old and infirm."

And he made a store of coins in a big pot. It happened that he fell ill, and his foot became gangrenous; and he spent all his coins on doctors, but grew no better. And an experienced doctor told him: "Unless you amputate your foot, the gangrene will spread through your whole body." And they decided to amputate. But the night before the operation, he recovered his right mind, and did penance for what he had done, and groaned and wept saying: "Lord, remember my earlier good works, when I worked in the garden and ministered to the poor." And when he said this, an angel of the Lord stood before him and said: "Where is your store of coins? Where is your hope in them gone?" Then he understood, and said: "I have sinned, Lord. Forgive me, I will not do it again." Then the angel touched his foot, and it was healed at once.

And he rose at dawn, and went to the field to work. And at the appointed time the surgeon came with his instruments to amputate the foot. And people told him: "He went out at dawn to work in the fields." Then the doctor, astonished, went out to the field where he was working. And he saw him digging, and glorified God that he had restored his health.

22. A brother asked an old man: "Would you have me save two shillings for myself, in case I fall ill?" The old man, seeing into his heart that he wanted to save them, said: "Yes." And the brother went into his cell, and was worn down by his thoughts, saying to himself: "Do you think the old man spoke the truth to me or not?" He got up and went back to the old man, did penance, and asked: "For the Lord's sake speak the truth to me, for I am troubled in my thoughts about those two shillings." The old man said to him: "I told you to save them because I saw you intended to save them. But it is not good to save more than the body needs. If you keep two shillings, you will put your hope in them. And if by chance they are destroyed, God is then no longer thinking of our needs. Let us cast our thought upon the Lord: it is for him to care for us."

PART VII

Of patience, or fortitude

1. Once when the holy Abba Antony was living in the desert, his soul was troubled by boredom and irritation. And he said to God: "Lord, I want to be made whole and my thoughts do not let me. What am I to do in this trouble, how shall I be made whole?" And rising up after a little while, he began to go

outside. And he saw someone like himself sitting down and at work; then standing up to pray; then sitting down again to make a plait of palm leaves, and again standing up to pray. It was an angel of the Lord sent to correct Antony and make him careful. And he heard the voice of the angel saying: "Do this and you will be made whole." When he heard it he was very glad and recovered his confidence. And he did what the angel had done, and found the salvation which he was seeking.

2. A brother asked Abba Agatho: "I have been instructed to go somewhere, and I have a grievous struggle in the place where I have been told to go. I want to obey the order, yet I am frightened of the inner struggle which will ensue." The old man said: "Agatho was like that. He obeyed orders, and so won the battle."

3. Abba Ammonas said that for fourteen years he had prayed God in Scete night and day to give him power to control his temper.

4. Abba Bessarion said that for forty nights he had stood up among the thorns, and had not slept.

5. A hermit who was troubled in mind went to Abba Theodore of Pherme and told him so. The old man said to him: "Go, make your mind humble, put yourself in subjection, and go to live with others." So he went to a mountain, and there lived with a community. Later he returned to the old man and said: "Not even when I lived with other men did I find rest." And the old man said to him: "If you are not at rest when a hermit, nor when in community, why did you want to be a monk? Was it not that you might suffer? Tell me, how many years have you been a monk?" And he said: "Eight." And the old man said: "Believe me, I have been a monk for seventy years, and I have not been able to get a single day's peace. And do you want to have peace after eight years?"

6. A brother asked Abba Theodore: "If you suddenly hear the sound of falling masonry, are you frightened, Abba?" And the old man said: "If the heaven fell down on the earth, Theodore would not be afraid." For he had prayed to God that fear might be taken from him, and that was why the brother asked him.

7. They said of Abba Theodore and Abba Lucius from the region of Alexandria, that they lived fifty years enticing their souls onwards thus. They said: "When this winter is past, we will move from here." And in the summer time they said: "At the end of the summer let us move from here." And so those memorable fathers lived their whole lives in devotion.

8. Abba Poemen said of Abba John the Short that he prayed the Lord to take away his passions. And so he was made tranquil in heart, and came to an old man and said: "I find that I am at rest, with no war of flesh and spirit." And the old man said to him: "Go, ask the Lord to stir a new war in you. Fighting is good for the soul." And when the war revived in him, he no longer prayed for it to be taken away, but said: "Lord, grant me long-suffering to endure this war."

9. Abba Macarius the Great came to Abba Antony on the mountain. And when he knocked at the door, Antony went out to him and said: "Who are you?" And he said: "I am Macarius." And Antony went in and shut the door, and left Macarius outside. And afterwards, when he saw how patiently he waited, he opened the door to him. And he welcomed him, saying: "I have heard of you, and for a long time I have wanted to see you." And he was hospitable to him and refreshed him; for Macarius was tired with his endeavours. In the evening Abba Antony put out a few palm leaves for himself. And Abba Macarius said to him: "Give me some, so that I can work at them." Antony said: "I have no more." So he made a pile of what he had, and they sat late, talking to the profit of their souls, and made a plaited rope, and the rope hung out of the window in the cave. And at dawn Antony went in and saw the plaits which Abba Macarius had made, and he wondered at them and kissed his hand, saying: "There is much virtue in those plaits."

10. This Macarius once went down from Scete to a place named Terenuthis, and he climbed into an old pagan cemetery to sleep. And he put one of the bodies under his head as a pillow. The demons hated him when they saw his assurance, and tried to frighten him by calling out "Lady, come with us to bathe." And another demon answered, from underneath Macarius, as though he were the dead woman: "I have a pilgrim on top of me, and cannot move." The old man was not frightened, but confidently thumped the body, saying: "Get up, go if you can." When the demons heard it, they cried with a loud voice and said: "You have beaten us." And they fled in confusion.

11. Abba Mathois said: "I want to find some easy but continual work, rather than a heavy work that is quickly finished."

12. They said of Abba Milidus, that while he was living on the frontiers of Persia with two disciples, two sons of the emperor came on their usual hunting expedition, and put nets

over an area of forty miles, and speared whatever they trapped. And they found the old man and his disciples within the area. And when they saw his hairy and forbidding face, they were surprised and said: "Are you a man or a Spirit?" And he said: "I am a sinful man, and I have come out here to lament my sins; and I worship Jesus Christ the Son of the living God." They said to him: "There is no God but the sun, and the fire and the water. Worship them and sacrifice to them." And he replied: "You are wrong: these are but creatures. I beseech you, be converted—recognize the true God who made these and all things else." But they mocked him and said: "Are you saying that the true God is a condemned and crucified man?" "Yes," said Milidus, "I say that the true God is he who crucified sin and killed death."

So they tortured him and his two monks to force them to sacrifice. And after much torture they beheaded the two monks, but they went on torturing the old man day after day. But afterwards they fastened him in one place and fired arrows into him, one in front and one behind, so that he looked like a signpost. The old man said to them: "Since you have conspired to shed innocent blood, tomorrow, at this very moment of the day, your mother shall be bereaved of her children and your affection for her, and you will spill each other's blood by your own arrows." They thought his words were silly: and next day went out again to hunt. It happened that a stag escaped from their net, and they jumped on their horses and chased him. And each fired an arrow which hit the heart of the other: and so they died as the old man had foretold.

13. Abba Poemen said: "The mark of the true monk only appears under temptation."

14. Another saying of his was this. Isidore the presbyter in Scete once addressed a congregation of monks and said: "My brothers, is not work the reason why we are here? And now I see that there is no work here. So I am taking my cloak and going where there is work, and there I shall find rest."

15. Saint Syncletice said: "If you live in a monastic community, do not wander from place to place: if you do, it will harm you. If a hen stops sitting on the eggs she will hatch no chickens: and the monk or nun who moves from place to place grows cold and dead in faith."

16. She also said: "When the devil does not use the goads of poverty to tempt, he uses wealth for the purpose. When he cannot win by scorn and mockery, he tries praise and flattery.

If he cannot win by providing health, he tries illness: if he cannot win by comfort, he tries to ruin the soul by vexations which lead a person to act against the monastic vow. He inflicts severe sicknesses on people whom he wants to tempt, and so makes them weak, and thereby shakes the charity which they feel towards God. But although the body is shattered and running high temperatures and thirsting unbearably—yet you who endure all this are a sinner, and remember the punishments of the next world, and the everlasting fire, and the torments of the judgement. So you will not fail in the sufferings of this present time; indeed you should rejoice because God has visited you. Keep saying the famous text: 'The Lord hath chastened and corrected me: but he hath not given me over unto death.' [21] Iron is cleaned of rust by fire. If you are righteous and suffer, you grow to a yet higher sanctity. Gold is tested by fire. A messenger from Satan is given to you to be a thorn in your flesh. Lift up your heart, for you see that you have received a gift like that of St Paul. If you suffer from fever and cold, remember the text of Scripture, 'We went through fire and water,'—and then 'thou broughtest us out into a place of rest.' If you have won the suffering, you may expect the place of rest, provided you are following what is good. Cry aloud the prophet's words, 'I am poor and destitute and in misery'—for threefold suffering like this shall make you perfect. He said also, 'Thou hast set me at liberty when I was in trouble.' [22]

Thus, let us test our souls by this kind of self-discipline, for we have our enemy before our eyes."

17. Saint Syncletice also said: "If you are troubled by illness, do not be melancholy, even if you are so ill that you cannot stand to pray or use your voice to say psalms. We need these tribulations to destroy the desires of our body—in this they serve the same purpose as fasting and austerity. If your senses are dulled by illness, you do not need to fast. In the same way that a powerful medicine cures an illness, so illness itself is a medicine to cure passion. And there is much profit of soul in bearing illness quietly and giving thanks to God. If we go blind, let us not be disturbed. We have lost a means to excellence, yet we can contemplate the glory of God with the inward eyes of the soul. If we go deaf, let us remember that we shall no longer hear a lot of silly talk. If suffering has weakened the strength of

21 Ps. 118:18.
22 Ps. 66:12; Ps. 4:1.

your hands, you still have an inner strength against the enemy's attacks. If the whole body is afflicted by disease, the health of the inner man is still increasing."

18. She also said: "People in the world who commit crime are thrown into prison against their will. For our sins, let us put ourselves under guard, and by willingly accepting it now we shall avoid punishment in the future. If you fast, you should avoid saying that by weakening your frame you have fallen ill, for people who do not fast, fall ill in the same way. If you have begun some good work, you should not be turned from it by the enemy's attempts to hinder you, indeed your endurance will conquer the enemy. Seamen beginning a voyage set the sails and look for a favourable wind—and later they meet a contrary wind. Just because the wind has turned, they do not throw the cargo overboard or abandon ship: they wait a little and battle against the storm until they can again set a direct course. And when we run into headwinds, let us put up the cross for our sail, and we shall voyage through the world in safety."

19. They said of Abbess Sarah of blessed memory, that for sixty years she lived on the bank of a river, and never looked down to see the water.

20. Abba Hyperichius said: "Keep praising God with hymnody, and meditate continually, and so lift the burden of the temptations that come upon you. A traveller carrying a heavy burden stops from time to time to take deep breaths, and so makes the journey easier and the burden lighter."

21. He also said: "Temptations come to us in all kinds of ways. We ought to be armed at all points, and then we shall appear to them to be tried warriors when they come against us."

22. An old man said: "If a man is tempted, sufferings crowd round him on all sides, and he becomes timid and begins to grumble." And the old man told this story. A temptation came to a brother who lived at Cellia. And if anyone saw him, they did not wish him well, nor did they welcome him into their cells. If he was short of bread, no one lent him any. If he was on his way back from harvesting, no one followed the usual custom of inviting him in for refreshment. Once he had been reaping, and he became very thirsty, and had no bread in his cell. But in all these tribulations he kept thanking God. And God seeing his patience, took away his inner struggle and gave him rest. And immediately there was a knock on his door, and a man from Egypt was outside leading a camel laden with

bread. When the brother saw it, he began to weep, and said: "Lord, I am not worthy of even a little suffering." And now that his trial was over, the brothers welcomed him in their cells and in the church, and refreshed him.

23. An old man said: "We do not make progress because we do not know what we can do; we lose heart in the work we have begun; and we want to be good without trying to be good."

24.[23] A brother asked an old man: "What am I to do? My thoughts will not let me sit alone in my cell even for an hour." The old man said: "My son, go back and stay in your cell, wash your hands, pray God continually, and cast your thoughts upon God: and let no one persuade you to go out of your cell." And he said: "A lad who was living in the world with his father, decided to become a monk. But though he begged his father to allow it, the father kept refusing: until in the end, at the request of some devout friends, he consented with an ill grace. And the lad left home and entered a monastery. As soon as he was a monk, he began to keep the monastic rule perfectly, and to fast every day. He even began to go without food for two days and to eat a proper meal only once a week. His Abba saw him and marvelled, and blessed God for his self-discipline.

After a short time it happened that the monk began to beg his Abba: 'Please let me go into the desert.' The Abba said: 'My son, do not think of it. You cannot endure austerity like that, or the skill and temptation of the devil. When you are tempted in the desert, there is no one to comfort you in the troubles which the devil stirs up.' But the monk began the more to ask him to let him go. And his Abba, seeing that he could not hold him, said a prayer and let him go. Then he said to his Abba: 'Please give me guides to show me the right way.' And the Abba selected two monks from that monastery to go with him.

For two days they walked through the desert, and then were exhausted with the heat. So they lay down and slept for a little. While they were asleep, an eagle swooped down and beat at them with its wings, and then flew off a little and alighted. They woke up and saw the eagle, and said: 'Here's your angel: rise and follow him.' The brother rose and bid the brothers good-bye, and followed the eagle, which flew a little and then alighted, and on his approach flew a little further; this went on for three hours. Then the eagle flew off to the right of the pursuing monk, and did not reappear. Nevertheless the

[23] Omitted from all the early manuscripts.

monk went that way, and saw three palm-trees, and a spring, and a little cave. He said: 'Here's the place that God has made ready for me.'

He went into the cave and stayed there, eating dates and drinking the water from the spring; for six years he lived there alone and saw no man. But one day the devil came to him disguised as an elder, with a fierce expression on his face. The brother saw him and was frightened, and fell down to pray. And when he rose again, the devil said to him: 'Let us pray again, brother.' And when they rose again, the devil said: 'How long have you been here?' He answered: 'Six years.' And the devil said: 'This is remarkable. I have had you as my neighbour, and I did not find out until four days ago. I have a hermitage not far from here, and this is the first day in eleven years that I have left it, because I discovered that you were living near me. And I considered the matter and said, Shall I go to this man of God, and consult him for the good of my soul? I tell you, brother, we do no good sitting like this in our cells. We cannot receive the body and blood of Christ, and I am afraid that he will cast us away if we separate ourselves from that sacrament. But I tell you, brother, three miles from here is a monastery with a presbyter. Let us go there every Sunday, or every other Sunday, and receive the body and blood of Christ, and return to our cells.'

The brother was pleased and persuaded by the devil's suggestion. On Sunday the devil came and said: 'Come, it is time to go.' They went out and came to the monastery where the presbyter was, entered the church and fell to prayer. When the monk ended his prayer, he could not see his guide anywhere, and said: 'Where do you think he has gone? Has he had to go out?' He waited some time; but his guide did not return. He went out of the church and looked round for him, but could not find him. So he asked the monks of the place: 'Where is the Abba who came to church with me?' They said: 'We saw no one else but you.'

Then the brother knew he was a demon, and said: 'See the skill with which the devil has winkled me out of my cell. Yet he cannot touch me, because I have come here for a good reason. I shall receive the body and blood of Christ, and go back to my cell.' After mass in the church, the brother wanted to go back to his cell. But the abbot of the monastery kept him, saying: 'Unless you dine with us, we shall not let you go back.' So he shared their dinner, and went back to his cell.

Then the devil came again, this time in the likeness of a young man of the world, and began to look him up and down from head to foot and say: 'Is this the man? It is not.' And he began to stare at him. The brother said to him: 'Why are you gazing at me?' And the devil said: 'I think you do not know who I am. How should you know after so long a time? I am the son of your father's neighbour. Is not your father's name this, and your mother's that, and your sister's that, and your name that? Are not your two serving girls called such and such? But your mother and sister died three years ago. Now your father has died, and left his property to you, saying: "My son, who in holiness left the world and followed God, is the only heir left to me, so I will leave him everything. If anyone is a prophet of the Lord and knows where he is, let him speak. Then my son, can come and take my wealth and give it away to the poor for the benefit of my soul and his soul." And many people went seeking you but could not find you. I was brought here accidentally by some work and recognized you. Do not delay, but come; sell it all and do what your father wanted.'

The brother answered: 'I have no need to go back to the world.' The devil said: 'If you do not come and your wealth vanishes you will have to give an account of it before God. Surely I am saying nothing wicked in telling you to come and give money to the poor and needy like a good and generous man, and so prevent money left to the poor from being misappropriated by evil men and women? What is the trouble in coming to give alms as your father wanted for the good of your soul, and then returning to your cell?'

So he persuaded the brother to return to the world. He went with him as far as the town and left him. The brother was making to enter his father's house, as the house of a dead man, when his father came out alive and well. He did not recognize his son, but said: 'Who are you?' The monk in his surprise could not say a word. His father began again to ask him who he was and whence he came. Then, in his confusion, he said: 'I am your son.' His father said: 'Why have you come back?' He was ashamed to say why he had come, so he said: 'My love made me return; I wanted to see you.' And he stayed at home. And soon he fell into lust, and was severely punished by his father, and was wretched and did no penance but remained in the world.

So I tell you, my brothers, that a monk never ought to let himself be persuaded by anyone to leave his cell."

25. In the desert some people came to a great old man and

said: "How is it you are happy here in this severe life?" And the old man said: "All the severity of my life here cannot compare with the day of torment prepared for sinners in the next world."

26. An old man said: "The ancients were reluctant to move from place to place—except perhaps for three reasons: first, if a man was vexed against them and no amount of satisfaction would propitiate him: secondly, if many people praised them: and thirdly, if they were tempted to lust."

27. A brother said to Abba Arsenius: "What am I to do, Abba? My thought troubles me, telling me 'You cannot fast, nor work, nor visit the sick, because even these things are selfish.' " The old man saw that the devil had sown the thought and said: "Go, eat and drink and sleep, only do not leave your cell; remember that staying in the cell is what keeps a monk on his proper path." He did it for three days and then suffered from accidie. So he found a few palm leaves and split them; the next day he began to make a plait from them. When he grew hungry, he said to himself: "Here are a few more palm-leaves. I shall lay them out before I eat." And after he had finished, he said: "I shall read a little before I eat." And after he had finished, he said: "I shall say a few psalms, and then I shall eat with an untroubled mind."

So step by step he made progress with God's help, until he came back to the right way. And when he had received confidence against evil thoughts, he overcame them.

28. An old man was asked by a brother why, when he stayed in his cell, he suffered accidie. The old man answered: "You have not yet seen the resurrection for which we hope, nor the torment of fire. If you had seen these, then you would bear your cell without accidie even if it was filled with worms and you were standing in them up to your neck."

29. The brothers asked an old man to rest from his great labour. He answered: "Believe me, my sons, if Abraham was penitent when he saw God's glorious gifts, should we not struggle the more in our labour?"

30. A brother asked an old man and said: "My thoughts wander, and I am troubled." He answered: "Go on sitting in your cell, and your thoughts will come back from their wanderings. If a she-ass is tethered, her foal skips and gambols all round her but always comes back to the mother. So will it be with the man who for God's sake sits patiently in his cell. Though his thoughts wander for a time, they will come again."

31. An old man lived in the desert twelve miles from the

nearest water. Once, on his way to draw water, he felt exhausted. So he said: "What need to suffer this? I will come and live by the spring." As soon as he said this, he turned round and saw a man following him and counting his steps. He asked the man, "Who are you?" And he said: "I am an angel of the Lord, sent to count your steps and reward you." When the old man heard this, his mind was strengthened, and he moved his cell five miles further from the spring.

32. The fathers used to say: "If you are tempted where you are, do not leave the place at a time of temptation. If you do leave it, you will find the temptation which you are fleeing wherever you next place your cell. Be patient till the temptation is past; then your departure will scandalize no one and bring no trouble to the other people who live there."

33. A brother was restless in the community and often moved to anger. So he said: "I will go, and live somewhere by myself. And since I shall be able to talk or listen to no one, I shall be tranquil, and my passionate anger will cease." He went out and lived alone in a cave. But one day he filled his jug with water and put it on the ground. It happened suddenly to fall over. He filled it again, and again it fell. And this happened a third time. And in a rage he snatched up the jug and broke it. Returning to his right mind, he knew that the demon of anger had mocked him, and he said: "Here am I by myself, and he has beaten me. I will return to the community. Wherever you live, you need effort and patience and above all God's help." And he rose up, and went back.

34. A brother asked an old man: "What am I to do, father? I do nothing like a monk. I eat, drink and sleep as I like, I am much troubled by vile thoughts, I shift from task to task, and my mind wanders everywhere." The old man answered: "Stay in your cell, and do what you can without trouble of mind. It is only a little that you do now, yet it is even as when Abba Antony did mighty things in the desert. I trust God that whoever stays in his cell for God's sake, and guards his conscience, will be found where Antony is."

35. An old man was asked how a watchful monk should not be scandalized when he sees others returning to the world. And he replied: "A monk ought to look at hounds when they are hunting a hare. One of them glimpses the hare and gives chase: the others merely see a hound running, run some way with him, then they get tired and go back on their tracks. Only the leading hound keeps up the chase until he catches

the hare. He is not deterred by the others who give up; he thinks nothing of cliffs or thickets or brambles; he is often pricked and scratched by thorns; yet he keeps on until he catches the hare. And so the man who searches for the Lord Jesus, aims unceasingly at the cross, and leaps through every obstacle in his way until he comes to the Crucified."

36. An old man said: "A tree cannot bear fruit if it is often transplanted. So it is with the monk."

37. When a brother was troubled by thoughts of leaving the monastery, he told this to his abbot. And he said: "Go and sit down, and entrust your body to your cell as a man puts a precious possession into a safe, and do not go out. Then let your thoughts go where they will. Let your mind think what it likes, so long as it does not drive your body out of the cell."

38. An old man said: "The monk's cell is the furnace in Babylon in which the three children found the Son of God. It is the pillar of cloud out of which God spoke to Moses."

39. For nine years a brother was assailed by temptations to leave his community. Every day he picked up his cloak to go, the cloak in which he wrapped himself at night. At evening he would say: "I will go away tomorrow." And at dawn he would think: "I ought to bear this torment and stay here just today for the Lord's sake." He did this every day for nine years, until the Lord took away temptation.

40. A brother fell into temptation, and in his suffering he stopped keeping the monastic rule. When he later tried to start keeping the fundamentals of the rule, he was hampered by his suffering; and he said to himself: "When shall I be as I once was?" And in this gloomy state of soul he could not make himself begin the monastic office. So he went to an old man and told him what had been happening. When the old man heard of his sufferings, he told him this story by way of example.

"A man had a plot of land. And through his carelessness brambles sprang up and it became a wilderness of thistles and thorns. Then he decided to cultivate it. So he said to his son: 'Go and clear that ground.' So the son went to clear it, and saw that the thistles and thorns had multiplied. So his spirit weakened, and he said: 'How much time shall I need to clear and weed all this?' And he lay on the ground and went to sleep. He did this day after day. Later his father came to see what he had done, and found him doing nothing. And he said to him: 'Why have you done nothing till now?' And the lad said to his father: 'I was just coming to work, father, when I saw this

wilderness of thorn and thistle, and I was deterred from starting, and so I lay on the ground and went to sleep.' Then his
father said to him: 'Son, if you had cleared each day the area
on which you lay down, your work would have advanced
slowly and you would not have lost heart.' So the lad did what
his father said, and in a short time the plot was cultivated.

So you, brother, do a little work and do not faint, and God
will give you grace and bring you back to your proper way of
life."

The brother went away and patiently did what the old man
had told him. And he found peace of mind, and made progress
with the help of the Lord Christ.

41. There was an old man who was often ill. But one year
he did not fall ill. And he was grievously troubled and wept,
saying: "The Lord has left me, and has not visited me."

42. An old man said that a brother was goaded by his
thoughts for nine years to despair of his salvation. He judged
himself and said: "I have ruined my soul. And because I have
perished already, I will go to the world." On his journey he
heard a voice saying: "Those temptations which you endured
for nine years were your crowns. Go back to your cell, and I
will take from you these evil thoughts." Thereupon he realized
that it is not good to despair of oneself because of the temptations
that come. If we use these thoughts well they will give us a
crown.

43. An old man was living in a cave in the Thebaid with one
well-tested disciple. It was usual for the old man to teach the
disciple during the evening and show him how the soul should
progress: and after the address, he prayed and sent him away
to sleep.

Some devout laymen who knew the old man's ascetic life
happened to visit him. He gave them consolation, and they went
away. Then the old man sat down after the evening offices as
usual to address and instruct the brother. But while he was
talking, sleep overcame him. The brother waited for the old
man to wake and end with the usual prayer. But the old man
went on sleeping, and the brother went on sitting for a long time:
and in the end the disciple, with greatly troubled mind, was
forced to go away to sleep. But he tormented himself, and resisted the temptation, and went back to sit by the old man. A
second time he was forced up by the longing for sleep, but sat
down again. This happened seven times, and still he went on
resisting his soul.

In the middle of the night the old man awoke, and found him sitting nearby and said: "Are you not gone away yet?" And he said: "No, you did not dismiss me, father." The old man said: "Why did you not wake me up?" He answered: "I did not dare to nudge you for fear of disturbing you."

They both stood up and began to say mattins. After mattins the old man dismissed his disciple. And while the old man was sitting alone, he was rapt and was shown a vision of a glorious place, and a throne in it, and on the throne seven crowns. And he asked the angel who showed the vision: "Whose are those?" And he said: "They are the crowns of your disciple: God has given him this place and throne because of his goodness: tonight he has been granted these seven crowns."

The old man marvelled, and tremblingly called his disciple to him and said: "Tell me what you did last night." He answered: "Forgive me, father, I did nothing." The old man judged that he was being humble and concealing something, and said: "Believe me, I cannot rest until you tell me what you did and thought last night." But the brother was not aware that he had done anything and could not say a word. But he said to the old man: "Forgive me, father, I did nothing—except only this, that seven times I was driven by wandering thoughts to go away and sleep; but you had not dismissed me as you usually do, so I did not go."

Then the old man at once understood that every time he resisted the temptation, God bestowed a crown on him. To the disciple he said nothing, thinking it best for his soul: but he told other directors of souls, to teach us how God can bestow crowns upon us even for resisting little temptations. It is good that a man discipline his whole self for God's sake. As it is written: "The kingdom of heaven suffereth violence, and the violent take it by force." [24]

44. Once a hermit fell ill. Because he had no one to look after him, he rose and ate whatever he found in his cell. Though this happened for several days, no one came to visit him. Even after a month no one had come. And the Lord sent his angel to minister to him. After the angel had ministered to him for a week, the fathers remembered him and said to each other: "Let us go and see whether the old man is ill." They went to his cell: and the moment they knocked on the door, the angel departed from him. The old man inside shouted: "Go away, my brothers." But they lifted the door off its hinge and went in,

[24] Matt. 11:12.

and asked him why he shouted. And he said: "For a month I was ill and no one visited me. Now for a week an angel of the Lord has ministered to me, but he went away the moment you arrived." And with these words, he peacefully died. The brothers marvelled, and glorified God, saying: "The Lord does not leave them who trust in him."

45. An old man said: "If you fall ill, do not be a weakling. If the Lord God has willed that your body be feeble, who are you to bear it with grief? Does he not look after you in all you need? Surely you do not live without him. Be patient in your illness, and ask him to give you what is right—that is, that you may do his will, and abide in patience, and in charity eat what you have."

46. One of the fathers said: "When I was in Oxyrhynchus, the poor came on Friday evening to eat the agape. And while they were asleep afterwards, there was one only with a mat. He put half the mat underneath him and the other half on top, but he was still very cold. And when he went to relieve himself, I heard him grumbling and moaning about the cold: and he consoled himself thus: 'I thank thee, Lord. How many wealthy men are in prison, sitting on iron or with shackled feet, so that they cannot even go out and relieve themselves freely. But I am like an emperor—I can stretch my legs and walk wherever I like.' I was standing there and heard what he said: and I went in and told the brothers, and they were much edified to hear it."

47. A brother asked an old man: "If I were somewhere where there was no one whom I could consult in a suffering which afflicted me, no one to show me the passion of my soul, what should I do?" The old man said: "Believe in God, for he will send his grace, and will himself be your consolation, if you ask him in charity." And he added: "I have heard a story like this from Scete. There was a man enduring temptation, and he had no confidence in any of the confessors and so he got his bundle ready to go away. But during the night he saw a vision of God's grace in the form of a maiden, who asked him: 'Do not go: stay here with me, for no ill will happen to you from what you have heard.' He believed her words, and stayed in his cell, and at once was healed in his heart."

PART VIII

That nothing should be done for show

1. Abba Antony once heard this about a young monk and the piece of show he wrought on a journey. He saw some old men

wearily walking along the road, and he ordered donkeys up to carry them until they reached home. When the old men told this to Abba Antony, he said: "I think that monk is like a ship laden with a rich cargo but not yet certain of reaching port in safety." And shortly afterwards, Abba Antony began to weep, and pull his hair, and groan. When his disciples saw it, they said: "Why are you weeping, Abba?" And the old man answered: "A great pillar of the church has just fallen." He said this about the young monk, and added: "Come, walk over to him, and see what has happened." So his disciples went, and found the monk sitting on his mat and weeping for the sin which he had committed. When he saw Abba Antony's disciples, he said: "Tell the old man to pray God to give me an armistice for only ten days, and I hope to be able to satisfy him." Within five days he was dead.

2. The monks praised a brother to Abba Antony. But Antony went to him and tested whether he could endure abuse. And when he perceived that he could not bear it, he said: "You are like a house with a highly decorated façade, where burglars have stolen all the furniture out of the back door."

3. They said of Abba Arsenius and Abba Theodore of Pherme that they hated reputation and praise above everything. Abba Arsenius avoided people likely to praise him. Abba Theodore did not avoid them, but their words were like daggers to him.

4. Archbishop John had a disciple named Eulogius. Eulogius was a presbyter who fasted for two days at a time, and sometimes ate nothing but bread and salt for a whole week: wherefore he had a high reputation. He came to Abba Joseph at Panephysis because he believed he would find harder discipline under him. The old man welcomed him, and of his charity made ready what he had to eat. But the disciples of Eulogius said: "The presbyter only eats bread and salt." Abba Joseph silently began to eat. They spent three days in silence, hearing not even the sound of psalm or prayer (for they said the office secretly): and then Eulogius and his disciples went away, nothing edified.

But by God's providence a mist came over the plain: and they wandered in a circle and came back in error to the old man Joseph's cell. Before they knocked on the door, they heard the singing of psalms within: and they waited a long while outside, listening. Then they knocked on the door, and the old man welcomed them again. Eulogius was thirsty: and his disciples picked up a jug of water and gave it to him to drink. But the jug had sea-water mixed with fresh, and he could not drink it.

Eulogius considered this in his mind, and then began to ask the old man to show him his system, saying: "How is it, Abba, that first you did not sing any psalms, and then you began after we had gone away? And why was the water salt when I tried to drink it?" The old man said: "My disciple is away at work and I made a mistake and put sea-water in." But Eulogius went on asking the old man, wanting to know the truth. And the old man told him: "That little chalice is for wine which we use in charity to guests. This is for the water which the brethren drink every day."

With these words he taught him to have mental discretion, and drove out of him the merely human motives: and he became like other people, and in future ate what was put before him. And he learnt to be severe in secret, and said to the old man: "Truly, yours is a labour of love."

5. Abba Zeno (the disciple of Abba Silvanus) said: "Never stay in a well-known place nor sit with a famous man, nor lay a foundation on which you might sometime build yourself a cell."

6. Once a brother came to Abba Theodore of Pherme, and spent three days asking him for a word. But the Abba did not answer, and he went away sadly. So Abba Theodore's disciple asked him: "Abba, why did you not speak to him? Look, he has gone away sad." And the old man said: "Believe me, I said nothing to him because his business is getting credit by retailing what others have said to him."

7. Another brother asked Abba Theodore: "Would you like me to eat no bread for several days?" And the old man said: "You would do well. I have sometimes done that." And the brother said: "Should I take a few peas to the mill and make vegetable meal?" And Abba Theodore said: "If you go to the mill, make yourself bread. What need is there of this carrying to and fro?"

8. Another brother asked the same old Abba Theodore, and he began to talk and enquire about matters of which he had no experience. And the old man said to him: "You have not yet found a ship to sail in, nor put your luggage aboard, nor put out to sea, and are you already in the city which you mean to reach? If you make some attempt at a thing you are discussing, you will discuss it as it truly is."

9. Abba Cassian [25] said that a brother came to Abba Sera-

[25] *Conferences*, XVIII, 11: *Apophthegmata* Serapion 4. Cf. this translation p. 271.

pion. And the old man encouraged him in the usual way to
offer prayer. But he said that he was a sinner, and unworthy of
the monk's habit, and so refused. Serapion wanted to wash his
feet, but he used the same words and would not allow it.
Serapion gave him supper, and then began to exhort him in
charity, saying: "Son, if you want to make progress, stay in your
cell, keep a watch upon yourself and attend to the work of your
hands. Nothing is more profitable to you than staying in your
cell." But when the brother heard him, he was bitterly angry,
and the old man could not help seeing the change in his face.
So Abba Serapion said to him: "Just now you were saying 'I am
a sinner' and accusing yourself of living like an unworthy monk.
Then why were you angry when I warned you charitably? If
you truly would be humble, learn to carry like a man the
burdens which others lay upon you, and do not shower terms of
abuse over yourself." When the brother heard this, he did
penance before the old man, and went away with much profit.

10. Once a provincial judge heard of Abba Moses and went
to Scete to see him. They told the old man that he was on his
way, and he rose up to flee into a marsh. The judge and his
train met him, and asked: "Tell me, old man, where is the cell
of Abba Moses?" And the old man said: "Why do you want to
see him? He is a fool and a heretic."

The judge came to the church, and said to the clergy: "I
heard of Abba Moses and came to see him. But an old man on
his way to Egypt met me, and I asked him where was the cell
of Abba Moses. And he said: 'Why are you looking for him? He
is a fool and a heretic.' " And the clergy were distressed and
said: "What sort of person was your old man who told you this
about the holy man?" And they said: "He was an old man, tall
and dark, wearing the oldest possible clothes." And the clergy
said: "That was Abba Moses. And he told you this about himself because he did not want you to see him." And the judge
went away much edified.

11. A brother asked Abba Mathois: "If I go to live in such-
and-such a place, what would you have me do there?" The old
man said: "If you live there, do not try to make a reputation
for yourself on some pretext—like saying: 'Either I will not
join the congregation or I will not eat this and that.' This is the
sort of thing that creates a bubble reputation, and afterwards
you will suffer from crowds. When people hear that sort of thing
they flock there."

12. Abba Nesteros the Great was walking in the desert with

a brother when they saw a dragon and ran away. The brother said: "Are you afraid, father?" The old man answered: "I am not afraid, my son. But it was good to run away from the dragon, for otherwise I should have had to run away from vanity."

13. A provincial judge once wanted to see Abba Poemen and the old man would not allow it. The judge arrested his sister's son as a criminal and imprisoned him, saying: "If the old man comes to ask for him, I will release him." And the lad's mother came to Abba Poemen her brother and began to weep outside the door of his cell. Stricken with grief, she began to reproach him, saying: "You may have a heart of cold steel, you may be pitiless, but at least have mercy on your kin and relent." But he told her: "Poemen is the father of no children." And she went away. When the judge heard this he sent a messenger to say: "You have only to order his release and I will release him." The old man sent back the messenger with this message: "Try his case legally. If he ought to die, let him die. If he is innocent, do as you say."

14. Abba Poemen also said: "Teach your heart to keep what your tongue teaches others."

He also said: "Men try to appear excellent in their preaching; they are less excellent in practising what they preach."

15. Once Abba Adelphius, who was bishop of Nilopolis, came to Abba Sisois on the mountain of Abba Antony. When he was just leaving, he made him eat at dawn—but it was a fast day. And when they brought the table, some brothers knocked at the door. The old man said to his disciple: "Give them a few buns, because they are weary." And Abba Adelphius said to him: "Dismiss them for a time, or they will say 'Abba Sisois ate at dawn.' " And Abba Sisois looked at him, and said to the brother: "Go, give them some."

So when they saw the cooked food they said: "Have you got visitors? Is even the old man eating with you?" And the brother said: "Yes." Then they began to be sad and say: "God forgive you, that you have let the old man eat at this hour. Do you not know that he has gone into a severe discipline for a great many days?"

When the bishop heard this, he began to do penance before the old man and said: "Forgive me, Abba, my thought was human, you did what is of God." And Abba Sisois said to him: "Unless God glorifies man, man's glory cannot last."

16. Abba Ammon (of the place called Raythu) brought this enquiry to Abba Sisois: "When I read the Scripture, I am

tempted to make elaborate comments and so prepare myself to answer questions on it." The old man said: "There is no need. It is better to speak the word simply, with a good conscience and a pure mind."

17. Once a provincial magistrate came to see Abba Simon. And Abba Simon took the leather belt which he wore and climbed a palm-tree to clean it with the palm leaves. When the judge's party came up, they said: "Where is the old hermit of this wilderness?" And he answered: "There is no hermit hereabouts." So the judge went away.

18. Another time a magistrate came to see him. And the clergy who went in front said to him: "Abba, be ready: for the judge has heard of you and is coming to be blessed by you." And he covered himself with his sackcloth and took bread and cheese in his hand, and sat down in his doorway and began to eat it. The magistrate arrived with his retinue. And when they saw the old man, they were contemptuous of him and said: "Is this the hermit about whom we heard such great things?" And they turned round and went straight home.

19. Saint Syncletice said: "An open treasury is quickly spent. And any virtue will be annihilated if it is published abroad and becomes famous. If you put wax in front of a fire it melts; and if you pour vain praises on the soul, it goes soft and weak in seeking goodness."

20. She also said: "The same thing cannot at once be seed and full grown bush. So men with a worldly reputation cannot bear heaven's fruit."

21. Once at a feast day in Cellia, the brothers were eating their meal in church. But one of them said to the server: "I eat nothing cooked, but salt." And the serving monk called to another brother in front of the whole crowd: "This brother does not eat what is cooked, bring him the salt." But one of the old men stood up and told him: "Today it would have been better for you to eat meat in your cell than to have heard this said in front of so many brothers."

22. A man was being abstinent and not eating bread, and he went to visit an old man. By chance some other pilgrims arrived there and the old man made them a little vegetable soup. When they sat down to eat, the fasting brother took a single pea which he dipped in the soup and chewed it. When they rose from the table, the old man took him to one side and said: "Brother, if you visit someone, do not display to him your manner of life. If you want to keep your own rules, stay in your

cell and never go out." The brother accepted the advice, and thenceforth behaved like other people and ate what was put before him.

23. An old man said: "If a man takes thought for the morrow, it cuts away his fertility of spirit and leaves him dry."

24. An old man said: "Make yourself in many things a fool in fleeing the company of men, or in mocking the world and the men of the world."

PART IX

That we should judge no man

1. A brother in the community of Abba Elias was once tempted. And being expelled from the community, he went away to the mountain to Abba Antony. And when he had stayed there with him for some time, Antony sent him back to his old community. But when they saw him, they drove him out again. Again he went to Abba Antony and said: "They will not have me, father." So the old man sent a message to them, saying: "A ship was wrecked in the ocean and lost its cargo, and with great difficulty the lightened ship was brought to land. Do you want to run a rescued ship aground and sink it?" They saw that Abba Antony had sent him back, and at once accepted him.

2. A brother sinned, and the presbyter ordered him to go out of church. But Abba Bessarion rose up and went out with him, saying: "I too am a sinner."

3. Abba Isaac of the Thebaid came to a community and saw one of the brothers to be blameworthy, and sentenced him. But when he had gone out to the desert, the angel of the Lord came and stood in front of the door of his cell, and said: "I will not let you go in." He asked: "Why not?" And the angel of the Lord answered: "God sent me to say this to you: 'Where do you command me to send that blameworthy brother whom you sentenced?' " And at once Abba Isaac did penance, saying: "I have sinned, forgive me." And the angel said: "Arise, God forgives you. But in future take care you judge no man before God has judged him."

4. In Scete a brother was once found guilty. They assembled the elders, and sent a message to Abba Moses telling him to come. But he would not come. Then the presbyter sent, saying: "Come, for a meeting of monks is waiting for you." Moses rose up and went. He took with him an old basket which he filled with sand and carried on his back. The people who went

to meet him said: "What is this, father?" The old man said to
them: "My sins are chasing me, and I do not see them—have I
come today to judge the sins of someone else?" They listened to
him, and said nothing to the erring brother, but pardoned him.

5. Abba Joseph asked Abba Poemen: "Tell me how to become a monk." The old man said: "If you want to find rest in
this life and the next, say at every turn 'Who am I?' and judge
no man."

6. A brother asked Abba Poemen: "If I see my brother sin,
is it good to tell no one about it?" The old man said: "Whenever we cover our brother's sin, God will cover our sin. Whenever we tell people about our brother's guilt, God will do the
same with ours."

7. Once a brother in a community stumbled. In the same
region there lived a hermit who for a long time had not gone out
of his cell. The abbot of the community went to the hermit and
told him of the monk's offence. The hermit said: "Expel him."

So the monk was expelled from the community, and flung
himself in a ditch and wept. Some other monks happened to
pass that way to see Abba Poemen, and they heard him groan-
ing in the ditch. They climbed down and found him in desperate grief: and they asked him to go to the old hermit. But he
refused, saying: "I shall die here." The brothers went to Abba
Poemen and told him about it. He asked them to go back to the
monk and say: "Abba Poemen summons you." They did what
he said, and the monk came to Abba Poemen. The old man
saw how he was suffering, and rose up and kissed him, and
hospitably invited him to take supper.

But Abba Poemen sent one of his brothers to the hermit
with this message: "I have heard of you, and for many years
have wanted to meet you, but we were both too lazy to arrange
a meeting. But now, by God's will and this opportunity, make
the tiring journey so that we can meet." For Poemen was under
a rule of not going out of his cell. When the hermit heard the
message, he said: "He would not have sent to me unless God
had inspired him to it." And he rose up and went.

They greeted each other with pleasure and sat down. Abba
Poemen said to him: "There were two men in one place, and
they were each mourning for a dead man. But one left his own
dead, and went away to weep for the other's." And the old
hermit was stricken at the saying, and remembered what he
had done. And he said: "Poemen is up in heaven, I am down on
earth."

8. A brother asked Abba Poemen: "What am I to do, for I become a weakling just by sitting in my cell?" The old man said: "Despise no one: condemn no one: abuse no one: and God will give you quietness, and you will sit tranquil in your cell."

9. Once there was a meeting of monks in Scete, and the fathers discussed the case of a guilty brother. But Abba Pior said nothing. Afterwards he rose up and went out; he took a sack, filled it with sand, and carried it on his shoulders. And he put a little more sand in a basket, and carried it in front of him. The fathers asked him: "What are you doing?" He answered: "The sack with a lot of sand is my sins: they are many, so I put them on my back and then I shall not weep for them. The basket with a little sand is the sins of our brother; and they are in front of me, and I see them and judge them. This is not right. I ought to have my own sins in front of me, and think about them, and ask God to forgive me."

When the fathers heard this, they said: "Truly this is the way of salvation." 26

10. An old man said: "Judge not the adulterer if you are chaste—or you will break the law of God likewise. For he who said 'Do not commit adultery' also said 'Judge not.' "

11. The presbyter of a church came to a hermit to consecrate the offering for him to communicate. But another man came to the hermit and made accusations against that presbyter. The next time that the presbyter came to consecrate as usual, the hermit was scandalized and would not let him in. The presbyter saw it and went away. And then the hermit heard a voice saying: "Men have taken my judgement into their own hands." And he was rapt, and saw a vision of a well of gold and a bucket of gold, and a rope of gold, and plenty of drinking water. And he saw a leper emptying and refilling the bucket: and he wanted to drink himself, but did not because the leper had emptied it. Then the voice came a second time to him and said: "Why do you not drink this water? What does it matter who fills it? For he only fills it, and pours it out again."

Then the hermit came back to his normal mind, and understood what the vision had meant. He called the presbyter and made him consecrate the offering as before.

12. Two brothers in a community lived a saintly life, and had made such progress that they could see the grace of God in each other. It happened that one of them went out of the

26 Notice the doublet with section 4 of this part: cf. the version in *Vitae Patrum*, III, 136.

monastery on a Friday and saw a man eating, though it was morning. He said to him: "Are you eating at this hour on a Friday?" On the Saturday the usual celebration of mass was held. And his brother saw that the grace which had been given him had departed from him, and he was distressed. He went to the cell and said: "What have you done, brother? I did not see the grace of God in you as I used to do." And he said: "I am not aware of having sinned, either in deed or thought." His brother said: "Did you say an idle word to someone?" And he remembered, and said: "Yes. Yesterday I saw someone eating food in the morning, and I said to him: 'Are you eating at this hour on a Friday?' That is my sin. Be severe with me for a fortnight and we will beg God to forgive me." They did so. And after a fortnight the brother saw the grace of God again coming upon his brother. And they were comforted, and gave thanks to God who alone is good.

12A. A holy man wept bitterly when he saw someone sinning, and said: "He today: I tomorrow." However grave a sin is brought to your notice, you must not judge the culprit, but believe yourself to be a worse sinner than he.

PART X
On discretion

1. Abba Antony said: "Some wear down their bodies by fasting. But because they have no discretion, it puts them further from God."

2. Some brothers came to Abba Antony to tell him their dreams and discover whether they were true or were the illusions of demons. They had with them a donkey, who died on the journey. When they arrived at the old man, he said (before they told him): "Why did your donkey die on the journey?" And they said: "How do you know, father?" And he said: "The demons showed me." They said to him: "Indeed we came to ask you on the subject. We have seen dreams which have often come true: and we did not want to go astray." The old man satisfied them, taking his example from the donkey, and showing them that these dreams are caused by demons.

A hunter happened to come through the brush and saw Abba Antony talking gladly with the brothers, and was displeased. The old man wanted to show him how we should sometimes be less austere for the sake of the brethren, and said to him: "Put an arrow in your bow, and draw it." He did so. And he said: "Draw it further:" and he drew it. He said again: "Draw it yet further:" and he drew it. The hunter said to him: "If I draw it too far, the bow will snap." Abba Antony answered: "So it is with God's work. If we go to excess, the brothers quickly become exhausted. It is sometimes best not to be rigid." The hunter was penitent when he heard this, and profited much from it. And the brothers, thus strengthened, went home.

3. A brother said to Abba Antony: "Pray for me." And the old man answered: "Neither I nor God will have mercy on you unless you take trouble about yourself and ask God's help."

4. Abba Antony also said: "God does not let inner wars be stirred in this generation, because he knows that they are too weak to bear it."

5. Abba Evagrius once said to Abba Arsenius: "How is it that we educated and learned men have no virtue, and Egyptian peasants have a great deal?" Abba Arsenius answered: "We have nothing because we go chasing worldly knowledge. These Egyptian peasants have acquired virtues by hard work."

6. Abba Arsenius of blessed memory said: "A foreign monk not living in his native province will be half-hearted in nothing, and so will be at rest."

7. Abba Mark asked Abba Arsenius: "Is it good not to have any comfort in one's cell? I saw a brother who had a few cabbages, and he was rooting them out." And Abba Arsenius said: "It is good. But each man should do what is right for his own discipline. If he has not strength to endure that, he will plant them again."

8. Abba Peter, the disciple of Abba Lot, told this story. "I was once in the cell of Abba Agatho, when a brother came to him and said: 'I want to live with the monks; tell me how to live with them.' The old man said: 'From the first day you join them, remember you are a pilgrim all the days of your life, and do not be too confident.' Abba Macarius said to him: 'What does confidence do?' The old man said: 'It is like a fierce drought. When it is so dry, everyone flees the land because it destroys even the fruit on the trees.' Abba Macarius said: 'Is bad confidence like that?' Abba Agatho said: 'No passion is worse than confidence—it is the mother of all passion. It is best for the monk's progress that he should not be confident, even when he is alone in his cell.' "

9. Abba Daniel said: "When Abba Arsenius was dying, he charged us thus: 'Do not make a love-offering for me. For if I

have made any love-offering for myself during my life, I shall find it.' "

10. They said of Abba Agatho that some people went to him because they heard he was a man of much discretion. And wanting to test whether he was irritable, they said to him: "Are you Agatho? We have heard of you that you are an adulterer and an arrogant man." And he answered: "It is true." And they said to him: "Are you that Agatho who gossips and slanders?" And he answered: "I am." And they asked him: "Are you Agatho the heretic?" And he answered: "I am no heretic."

And they asked him: "Tell us, why did you patiently endure us when we so abused you, but did not endure when we said you were a heretic?" And he answered: "I assented to the first charges against myself—it is for the good of my soul. But I did not agree when you said I was a heretic because that is to be separated from God, and I do not want to be separated from God." They admired his discretion, and went away edified.

11. Abba Agatho was asked: "Which is more difficult, bodily discipline, or the guard over the inner man?" The Abba said: "Man is like a tree. His bodily discipline is like the leaves of the tree, his guard over the inner man is like the fruit. Scripture says that 'every tree which bringeth not forth good fruit is hewn down and cast into the fire.' [27] So we ought to take every precaution about guarding the mind, because that is our fruit. Yet we need to be covered and beautiful with leaves, the bodily discipline."

Abba Agatho was wise in understanding, earnest in discipline, armed at all points, careful about keeping up his manual work, sparing in food and clothing.

12. In Scete there was a meeting to discuss a matter; and after the decision was taken, Abba Agatho came and said: "You have not made a good decision." They said to him: "Who are you, that say this?" And he answered: "The son of man. For it is written, 'If ye truly speak righteousness, judge ye the thing that is right, O ye sons of men.' " [28]

13. Abba Agatho said: "If an angry man raises the dead, God is still displeased with his anger."

14. Three old men came to Abba Achillas, and one of them had a bad reputation. The first old man said: "Abba, make me a fishing-net." And he said: "I will not." And the second said

[27] Matt. 3:10.
[28] Cf. Ps. 58:1.

to him: "Will you give us a memento of yourself to keep in our community?" And he answered: "I have no time." Then the third, who had the bad reputation, said to him: "Make me a fishing-net, and so I shall have a blessing from your hands, Abba." And at once he answered: "I will do it."

But the first two, whom he had refused, said privately to him: "Why did you refuse our requests and consent to his?" The old man answered: "I said to you that I would not do it because I had no time, and you were not vexed. But if I did not do it for this man, he would say 'the old man has heard my reputation and for that reason has refused to make me a net.' So immediately I set to work with the string, to soothe his soul and prevent him being sad."

15. They said of one old man that for fifty years he ate no bread and drank little water. And he said: "I have destroyed lust and greed and vanity." When Abba Abraham heard that he had said this, he came to him and said: "Was it you who said this?" And he answered: "Yes." And Abba Abraham said to him: "Supposing you go into your cell and find a woman on your mat, could you not think she was a woman?" And he said: "No: but I attack my thought, so as not to touch her." Abba Abraham said: "Then you have not killed lust, but the passion is still alive; you have imprisoned it. Suppose you were walking along a road and saw stones on one side and gold in jars on the other, could you think the gold and the stones of the same value?" And he answered: "No: but I resist my thought, so as not to pick it up." And Abba Abraham said to him: "Then the passion still lives but you have imprisoned it." And he went on: "If you heard that one brother loved you and spoke well of you, and another brother hated you and slandered you, and they both came to visit you, would you give them both the same welcome?" And he said "No: but I torture my soul, to treat him who hates me just as well as him who loves me." And Abba Abraham said to him: "Then passions are alive: only in some measure holy men have got them chained."

16. One of the fathers said that an old man was working earnestly in his cell, wrapt in his mat. He went to visit Abba Ammon, who saw him using his mat, and said to him: "This is not good for you." And the old man said: "Three thoughts trouble me. One tries to drive me to live somewhere else in the desert: the second that I should go out and find a foreign country where no one knows me: the third, that I should shut myself in my cell, see no one, and eat every other day." Abba

Ammon said to him: "None of these three would profit you. Stay in your cell, and eat a little every day, keeping always in your heart the words of the publican in the Gospel,[29] and you can be saved."

17. Abba Daniel said: "If the body is strong, the soul withers. If the body withers, the soul is strong."

He also said: "If the body is fat, the soul grows lean: if the body is lean, the soul grows fat."

18. Abba Daniel also said that when Abba Arsenius was in Scete, there was a monk who stole the property of the old men. Abba Arsenius, wanting to do him good and free the old men from being troubled, took him to his cell and said: "If you will stop stealing, I will give you whatever you want." And he gave him gold, money and trinkets, and everything he found in his bag.

But the monk stole again. The old man, seeing that he was always troubling them, expelled him, and said: "If you find a brother committing crime through bodily infirmity, you must bear with him. But if he does not stop after being warned, expel him. He hurts his own soul, and also disturbs everyone who lives there."

19. Soon after Abba Evagrius had become a monk, he went to an old man and said: "Abba, speak to me a word by which I may be saved." He said: "If you would be saved, when you go to visit a man, do not speak until he asks you a question." Evagrius was stricken by this word, and did penance before the old man, and satisfied him, saying: "Believe me, I have read many books, and never found such learning." And he went away much profited.

20. Abba Evagrius said: "A wandering mind is strengthened by reading, and prayer. Passion is dampened down by hunger and work and solitude. Anger is repressed by psalmody, and long-suffering, and mercy. But all these should be at the proper times and in due measure. If they are used at the wrong times and to excess, they are useful for a short time. But what is only useful for a short time, is harmful in the long run."

21. Abba Ephraem was passing by when a harlot (she was someone's agent) began to make every effort to attract him to unlawful intercourse: or, if she failed in this, at least to stir him to anger. For no one had ever seen him angry or brawling. He said to her: "Follow me." When they came to a crowded place, he said to her: "Come now, I will lie with you as you wanted."

29 "God be merciful to me a sinner," Luke 18:13.

She looked round at the crowd and said: "How can we do it here, with all these people standing round? We should be ashamed." He said: "If you blush before men, should you not blush the more before God, who discloses the hidden things of darkness?" And she went away without her pleasure, confused and nonplussed.

22. Some brothers once came to Abba Zeno and asked him: "What is meant by the text in the book of Job 'Heaven is not pure in God's sight'?"[30] The old man answered: "These brothers have left their sins, and search the heavenly places. The meaning of that text is that since God alone is pure, it may be said that not even heaven is pure in his sight."

23. Abba Theodore of Pherme said: "If a friend of yours is tempted by lust, give him a helping hand if you can and pull him back. But if he falls into heresy, and persists in spite of your efforts, go away quickly, cut off his friendship. For if you dally with him, you might be dragged with him into the deeps."

24. Once Abba Theodore came to Abba John, who had been born a eunuch. While they were talking, Abba Theodore said: "When I was in Scete, I devoted myself to the soul's work, and treated the body's work, so to speak, as a side-issue. But now it is vice versa: I treat the soul's work as though it was the side-issue."

25. Once one of the fathers came to Abba Theodore and said: "Look, that brother has gone back to the world." And Abba Theodore said to him: "Do not be surprised at that. Be surprised when you hear that a man has been able to escape the jaws of the enemy."

26. Abba Theodore said: "Many choose the repose of this world before God gives them his rest."

27. They said of Abba John the Short that he once said to his elder brother: "I wanted to be free of trouble as the angels are free, labouring not, and serving God unceasingly." He stripped himself of his clothes and went into the desert. After a week there, he went back to his brother. And when he knocked on the door, his brother answered without opening it, and said: "Who's there?" He said: "I am John." And his brother answered: "John has become an angel, and is no longer among men." But he went on knocking and saying: "It is I." And his brother did not open the door, but left him out till morning as a punishment. At last he opened the door and said: "If you are a

[30] Job 15:15.

man, you need to work again in order to live. If you are an
angel, why do you want to come into my cell?" And he did
penance, and said: "Forgive me my sin, brother."

28. Once some old men came to Scete, and Abba John the
Short was with them. During supper, an eminent presbyter rose
to give them each a little cup of water to drink. No one except
John the Short accepted it. The others were surprised, and said:
"How is it that you, the least of all, dared to accept the ministry
of a great old man?" And he said: "When I get up to give the
water round, I am glad if everyone takes it, because I have been
able to do them a service and will have a reward. That is why I
took it just now, to let the minister have his reward; perhaps he
would have been sad if no one had accepted it." And they all
admired his discretion.

29. Abba Poemen once asked Abba Joseph, saying: "What
am I to do, when temptations approach me? Do I resist them,
or let them come in?" The old man said: "Let them come in,
and then fight them."

So he went back to his cell at Scete. And it happened that
a man from the Thebaid told the brothers in Scete that he had
asked Abba Joseph the question: "When temptation approaches, do I resist it, or do I let it come in?" And he said to
him: "On no account let it come in, but cut it straight off."

When Abba Poemen heard that Abba Joseph had said this
to the man from the Thebaid, he rose and went back to Abba
Joseph at Panephysis and said to him: "Abba, I entrusted my
thoughts to your care: and you said one thing to me, and the
opposite to a monk from the Thebaid." And the old man said:
"You know that I love you?" And he answered: "Yes." And
he said: "Did you not tell me to say what I thought as though I
was talking for my own good? If temptations come in, and you
deal with them there, they will prove you. I said this to you as I
should say it to myself. But there are other men whom it is bad
that passions should come near, and they should cut them
straight off."

30. Abba Poemen said: "In Lower Heracleon I once came
to Abba Joseph, and he had in his monastery a very beautiful
mulberry tree. In the morning he said to me: 'Go fetch yourself
some mulberries, and eat.' It was Friday. So I did not eat, as it
was a fast day. And I asked: 'For the Lord's sake, tell me why
you said to me "go, eat." I did not go because it was a fast day,
but I was ashamed to disobey your command: for I think you
had some reason for it.' But he replied: 'Elders do not at first

speak straightly to brothers, but say some very twisted things. And if they see that the brothers do these twisted things, then they only speak what is good for them, because they know that the brothers will obey them in everything.' "

31. A brother asked Abba Joseph: "What shall I do? I cannot bear to be troubled, nor to work, nor to give alms." And the old man said to him: "If you cannot do any of these, at least keep your conscience from every sin against your neighbour, and you will be saved: for God seeks the soul that does not sin."

32. Abba Isaac from the Thebaid said to his brothers: "Do not bring children here. Children were the reason why four churches in Scete were deserted."

33. Abba Longinus asked Abba Lucius: "I have three ideas, the first is to go on a pilgrimage." And the old man answered: "If you do not control your tongue whensoever you travel, you will be no pilgrim. But control your tongue here, and you will be a pilgrim without travelling." Abba Longinus said: "My second idea is to fast two days together." And Abba Lucius answered: "The prophet Isaiah said: 'Even if you bend your neck to the ground, your fast will not so be accepted': [31] you should rather guard your mind from evil thoughts." And Abba Longinus said: "My third idea is to avoid the sight of men." And Abba Lucius answered: "Unless you first correct your sin by living among men you will not be able to correct yourself when you live alone."

34. Abba Macarius said: "If we remember the ill which men have done us, we cut off from our minds the power of recollecting God. But if we remember the ill which the devils raise, we shall be undisturbed." [32]

35. Abba Mathois said: "Satan knows not which passion will seduce the soul, and so he scatters his tares in it without direction. At one time he throws in the seeds of lust, at another the seeds of slander, and the rest in the same way. And wheresoever he sees a soul drawn towards one of the passions, he ministers to that soul. If he knew what was most tempting to a soul, he would not scatter such a variety of temptations."

36. They told this story of Abba Nathyra, who was the disciple of Abba Silvanus. When he was living in his cell on Mount Sinai, he regulated his life with moderation and allowed himself what his body needed. But after he was made bishop in

31 Cf. Isa. 58:5.
32 A fuller version is *Verba Seniorum* (Paschasius), VII, 37, 4.

Pharan, he sorely afflicted his spirit with severe austerities. And his disciple said to him: "Abba, when we were in the desert, you were not wont to torment yourself like this." And the old man said to him: "My son, there we had solitude, and quiet, and poverty: and so I wanted to discipline my body in such a way that I did not fall sick. For if I had fallen sick, I would have needed assistance which I could not have upon Mount Sinai. But now we are in the world; and there are many opportunities of sin. And if I fall ill, there are friends who will help me, and prevent me from falling away from a monk's purpose."

37. A brother asked Abba Poemen: "I am troubled in spirit, and want to leave this place." And the old man said: "Why?" And he said: "I have heard unedifying stories about one of the brothers." And the old man said: "Are the stories true?" And he said: "Yes, Father. The brother who told me is a man of trust." And the old man answered: "The brother who told you is not a man of trust. For if he was so, he would not have told you these stories. When God heard the cry of the men of Sodom, he did not believe it until he had gone down and seen with his own eyes." And the brother said: "I too have seen it with my own eyes."

When the old man heard this, he looked down and picked off the ground a wisp of straw: and he said: "What is this?" And he answered: "Straw." Then the old man reached up and touched the roof of the cell, and said: "What is this?" And he answered: "It is the beam that holds up the roof."

And the old man said: "Take it into your heart, that your sins are like this beam: and that brother's sins are like this wisp of straw."

When Abba Sisois heard this saying, he marvelled, and said: "How shall I bless you, Abba Poemen? Your words are like a precious jewel, full of grace and glory."

38. Some neighbouring priests once came to the monastery of Abba Poemen. Abba Anub went in and said to him: "Let us invite these priests to receive the gifts of God here in charity." But Abba Poemen stood in silence for a long time, and made no reply: and Abba Anub went out sadly. The men sitting round said to Abba Poemen: "Why did you not answer him?" And Abba Poemen said to them: "I have no reason to do so: for already I am dead. Dead men do not speak. Do not blame me, that I am here in your company."

39. A brother once went out on a pilgrimage from the monastery of Abba Poemen, and came to a hermit, who lived

in charity towards all and received many visitors. The brother told the hermit stories of Abba Poemen. And when he heard of Poemen's strength of character, he longed to see him.

The brother returned to Egypt. And after some little time, the hermit rose and went from his country to Egypt to see the brother who had visited him: for he had told him where he lived. When the brother saw the hermit, he was astonished, and very glad. The hermit said to him: "Of your charity towards me, take me to Abba Poemen." And the brother raised him up and showed him the way to the old man.

And the brother told Abba Poemen this about the hermit, "A great man of much charity, and particular honour in his own province, has come here wanting to see you." So the old man received him kindly. And after they had exchanged greetings, they sat down.

But the hermit began to talk of the Holy Scripture, and of the things of the spirit and of heaven. But Abba Poemen turned his face away, and answered nothing. When the hermit saw that he would not speak with him, he was distressed and went out: and he said to the brother who had brought him there: "My journey was useless. I went to the old man and he does not deign to speak to me."

The brother went to Abba Poemen, and said: "Abba, it was to talk with you that this great man came here, a man of much honour in his own land. Why did you not speak to him?" The old man answered: "He is from above, and speaks of the things of heaven. I am from below, and speak of the things of earth. If he had spoken with me on the soul's passions, I would willingly have replied to him. But if he speaks of the things of the spirit, I know nothing about them."

So the brother went out and told the hermit: "The reason is that the old man does not easily discuss Scripture. But if anyone talks to him about the soul's passions, he answers."

Then the hermit was stricken with penitence, and went to the old man and said: "What shall I do, Abba? My passions rule me." And the old man gazed at him with gladness and said: "Now you are welcome: you have only to ask and I will speak with understanding." And the hermit was much strengthened by their discourse, and said: "Truly, this is the way of charity." And he thanked God that he had been able to see so holy a man, and returned to his own country.

40. A brother asked Abba Poemen and said: "I have committed a great sin, and I would do penance for three years."

But Abba Poemen said to him: "That is a long time." And the brother said: "Do you order me one year's penance?" And again the old man said: "That is a long time." Some of the people who were nearby said: "A penance of forty days?" Again the old man said: "That is a long time." And he added: "I think that if a man is penitent with his whole heart, and determined not to sin that sin again, God will accept a penance of even three days."

41. Abba Ammon questioned him on the subject of the impure thoughts bred within a man's heart, and on the subject of vain desire. And Abba Poemen said: "Shall the axe boast unless the woodman wield it? [33] Do not reach out your hands for these things, and they shall do you no harm."

42. Abba Isaiah asked him about the same subject. Abba Poemen said: "Clothes, left too long in a chest, become rotten. If our bodies do not bring those thoughts forward, then at length they will rot or be destroyed."

43. Abba Joseph asked him about the same subject. And Abba Poemen said: "If you shut a snake or a scorpion in a box, in the end it will die. And the wicked thoughts, which the demons scatter, slowly lose their power if the victim has endurance."

44. Abba Joseph asked Abba Poemen: "How should we fast?" And Abba Poemen said: "I would have everyone eat a little less than he wants, every day." Abba Joseph said to him: "When you were a young man, did you not fast for two days on end?" And the old man said to him: "Believe me, I used to fast three days on end, even for a week. But the great elders have tested all these things, and they found that it is good to eat something every day, but on some days a little less. And they have shown us that this is the king's highway, for it is easy and light."

45. Abba Poemen said: "Do not live in a place where some are jealous of you: you will make no progress there."

46. A brother came to Abba Poemen, and said to him: "I sow seed in my field, and make a love-feast with the crop." The old man said: "You do a good work." And he went away with purpose, and invited more to the love-feast which he was making.

When Abba Anub heard this, he said to Abba Poemen: "Are you not afraid of God that you spoke so to the brother?" And the old man said nothing. But two days later Abba Poemen sent

[33] Cf. Isa. 10:15.

to the brother and called him to his cell. And he said to him, in the hearing of Abba Anub: "What did you ask me the other day? My mind was elsewhere." The brother said: "I sow my field, and make a love-feast with the crop." And Abba Poemen said to him: "I thought you were talking about your brother, who is a layman. What you are doing is not a monk's work." The brother was sad when he heard this, and said: "This is the only kind of work that I can do or know: I cannot stop sowing seed in my field."

When he had gone away, Abba Anub began to do penance before Abba Poemen, and said: "Forgive me." Abba Poemen said to him: "Look, I knew from the beginning that it was not a monk's work. But I spoke to his soul's need, and stirred his soul to an increase of charity; and now he has gone away melancholy, yet he will go on with the same work."

47. A brother asked Abba Poemen: "What is the meaning of the text 'Whoever is angry with his brother without a cause'?" [34] And he answered: "It is if you are angry with your brother for any trouble whatsoever that he tries to lay upon you—that is anger without a cause, and it is better to pluck out your right eye and cast it from you. But if anyone wants to separate you from God, be angry with him."

48. Abba Poemen said: "If a man sins and denies it, saying 'I have not sinned'—do not blame him, or you will break his purpose to amend. If you say: 'Do not be cast down, my brother, but keep a watch on it in future,' you stir his heart to be penitent."

49. The same father said: "Experience is good. By experience men are tested."

50. He also said: "If a man preaches but does not practise what he preaches, he is like a well of water where everyone can quench their thirst and wash their dirt, but which cannot clean away the filth and dung that is around it."

51. He also said: "He who knows himself is a man."

He also said: "One man seems silent of speech, but is condemning other people within his heart—he is really talking incessantly. Another man seems to talk all day, yet keeps his silence: for he always speaks in a way that is useful to his hearers."

52. He also said: "Suppose there are three men living together. One lives a good life in quietness, the second is ill but gives thanks to God, the third ministers to their needs with

[34] Matt. 5:22, according to many ancient authorities.

sincerity. These three men are alike; it is as if they were all doing one work."

53. He also said: "Wickedness cannot drive out wickedness. If anyone hurts you, do him good: and so by your good work you will destroy his wickedness."

54. He also said: "The grumbler is no monk. The man who gives evil for evil is no monk: the irritable man is no monk."

55. A brother came to Abba Poemen and said to him: "Many thoughts come into my head and put me in peril." And the old man drove him out into the open air, and said: "Open your lungs and hold your breath." And he answered: "I cannot do it." And the old man said to him: "Just as you cannot stop air coming into your breast, you cannot stop thoughts coming into your mind. Your part is to resist them."

56. A brother asked him: "I have been left a fortune, what am I to do with it?" And Abba Poemen said to him: "Go, and come back in three days, and I will tell you." The brother came back as he was told, and the old man said: "What can I tell you, brother? If I say, Give it the church, they will dine off it. If I say, Give it to your relations, you will have no profit. If I say, Give it to the poor, you will be safe. So go and do what you like with it, I can give you no reasons for choosing."

57. Abba Poemen also said: "If a thought about your bodily needs comes to you, and you put it aside; and then it comes again, and you put it aside, what will happen? If it comes a third time, you will not heed it, and it will do you no harm."

58. A brother said to Abba Poemen: "If I see something, do you want me to tell you?" The old man said to him: "It is written, 'If a man answers before he has heard, it is foolishness to him and discredit.' [35] If you are asked, speak: if not, say nothing."

59. Abba Poemen told a saying of Abba Ammon: "One man carries an axe all his life but cannot cut down a tree: another knows how to use it, and cuts down the tree with a few strokes." He used to say that the axe was discretion.

60. He also said: "The will of a man is a brazen wall, and a stone hurled between himself and God. If he puts it aside, he can say the words of the psalm: 'In my God I shall go over a wall' and, 'as for my God, his way is undefiled.' [36] If righteousness helps the will, then a man does good."

61. A brother asked Abba Poemen: "I am suffering the loss

[35] Cf. Ecclesiasticus 11:8.
[36] Ps. 18:29-30.

of my soul by being with my abba. What do you order me? Should I continue to stay with him?" And Abba Poemen knew that his soul was being harmed by his abba, and was astonished that he asked whether he ought to stay with him. And he said to him: "If you want to stay, do so." And the brother went away and stayed with his abba.

But he came a second time to Abba Poemen, and said: "I am burdening my soul." And Abba Poemen did not say to him: "Leave the abba." He came a third time, and said: "Believe me, henceforth I shall no longer stay with him." And the old man said: "Now you are saved: come, and stay with him no longer." And he went on: "A man who sees his soul being harmed, has no need to ask. A man ought to ask about his secret thoughts, to get them tested by the elders. But there is no need to ask about obvious sins: they must at once be cut off."

62. Abba Abraham, who was a disciple of Abba Agatho, once asked Abba Poemen: "Why do the demons attack me?" And Abba Poemen said to him: "Do the demons attack you? The demons do not attack us when we follow our self-wills, because then our wills become demons and themselves trouble us to obey them. If you want to know the kind of people with whom the demons fight, it is Moses and men like him."

63. Abba Poemen said that a brother asked Abba Moses: "How does a man mortify himself? Is it by his neighbour?" And he answered: "Unless a man has it in his heart that he has been shut in a tomb for three years, he cannot attain to mortification."

64. A brother asked Abba Poemen and said: "How ought a brother to sit in his cell?" And the old man said: "To sit in the cell is, externally, to work with the hands, eat once a day, keep silence and meditate; and, internally, to make progress by carrying a reproach wheresoever you may be, and keeping the hours of prayer, and keeping a watch on the secret thoughts of the heart. If it is time to stop working with the hands, fall to prayer and finish it in tranquillity. The end of it all is to keep company with men of good life, and avoid the company of the wicked."

65. Two brothers once came to Abba Pambo. And one of them asked him: "Abba, I fast for two days, and then eat two large buns. Do you think I am saving my soul, or losing it?" And the other said: "With my hands I make two vegetable stews every day, and I keep a little for food, and give the rest away in alms: do you think I shall be saved or lost?" And al-

though they pressed him for an answer he did not reply. After four days they were on the point of going. And the clergy said to them: "Do not be distressed, God will reward you. This is always the way of the old man, he does not talk easily, unless God gives him something to say." So they went in to the old man and said: "Abba, pray for us." And he said to them: "Do you want to go away?" And they said: "Yes." And he gazed at them; and supposing himself in their place, he wrote upon the ground and said: "Pambo fasts for two days and eats two large buns: do you think this makes him a monk? No." Then he said: "And Pambo makes two vegetable stews every day and gives them away to the poor: do you think this makes him a monk? Not yet." He was silent for a little, and then said: "These works are good. But if you act conscientiously to your neighbour, that is the way to be saved."

And so the brothers were edified, and went away joyfully.

66. A brother asked Abba Pambo: "Why do the spirits prevent me doing good to my neighbour?" The old man said: "Do not talk like that, or you will make God a liar. Say 'I do not at all want to be kind.' For God came down and said: 'I have given you the power of treading upon scorpions and snakes, and over all the might of the enemy.' [37] Why then do you not trample on the unclean spirits?"

67. Abba Palladius said: "The soul which is being trained according to the will of Christ should either be earnest in learning what it does not know, or should publicly teach what it knows. If it wants to do neither, though it could, it is mad. The first step on the road away from God is contempt for teaching, when it has no desire for the foods of the soul which truly loves God." [38]

68. A brother said to Abba Sisois: "Why do my passions not leave me?" And the old man said to him: "Because the vessels of those passions are within you. Give them a pledge and they will go away."

69. A brother came to Abba Silvanus on Mount Sinai. And when he saw the brothers working, he said to the old man: "Labour not for the meat which perisheth": and "Mary hath chosen the best part." [39] And the old man said to his disciple: "Call Zacharias, and put this brother in a cell where there is

[37] Luke 10:19.
[38] From the letter of Palladius to Lausus: cf. the Greek in C. Butler, *The Lausiac History of Palladius*, vol. ii, p. 7.
[39] John 6:27; Luke 10:42.

nothing." And when three o'clock came, he kept looking at the door, to see when they would send someone and summon him to eat. But no one spoke to him. So he rose and went to the old man and said: "Abba, do not the brethren eat today?" And the old man said: "Yes, they have eaten already." And the brother said: "Why did you not call me?" And the old man answered: "You are a spiritual person and do not need food. We are earthy, and since we want to eat, we work with our hands. But you have chosen the good part, reading all day, and not wanting to take earthly food." When the brother heard this he prostrated himself in penitence and said: "Forgive me, Abba." And the old man said: "I think Mary always needs Martha, and by Martha's help Mary is praised."

70. Saint Syncletice said: "Merchants toil in search of riches and are in danger of their lives from shipwreck: the more wealth they win, the more they want; and they think of no worth what they have already, but bend their whole mind to what they have not yet. But we have nothing, even of what we ought to seek, and we do not even want to possess what we need, because we fear God."

71. She also said: "There is a useful sorrow, and a destructive sorrow. Sorrow is useful when we weep for sin, and for our neighbour's ignorance, and so that we may not relax our purpose to attain to true goodness: these are the true kinds of sorrow. Our enemy adds something to this. For he sends sorrow without reason, which is something called accidie. We ought always to drive out a spirit like this with prayer and psalmody."

71A. She also said: "It is good not to be angry. If it happens, do not give way to it for as much as one day."

71B. She said: " 'Let not the sun go down upon your wrath.' But you wait until the sun is going down on your life; you do not know how to say: 'Sufficient unto the day is the evil thereof.' Why do you hate the man who has harmed you? It is not he who has harmed you but the devil. You ought to hate the sickness, not the sick man."

71C. She also said: "It is dangerous for a man to try teaching before he is trained in the good life. A man whose house is about to fall down may invite travellers inside to refresh them, but instead they are hurt in the collapse of the house. It is the same with teachers who have not carefully trained themselves in the good life: they ruin their hearers as well as themselves. Their mouth invites to salvation, their way of life leads to ruin."

72. She also said: "The devil sometimes sends a severe fast, too

prolonged—the devil's disciples do this as well as holy men. How do we distinguish the fasting of our God and King from the fasting of that tyrant the devil? Clearly by its moderation. Throughout your life, then, you ought to keep an unvarying rule of fasting. Do you fast four or five days on end and then lose your spiritual strength by eating a feast? That gladdens the devil. Everything which is extreme is destructive. So do not suddenly throw away your armour, or you may be found unarmed in the battle and made an easy prisoner. Our body is like armour, our soul like the warrior. Take care of both, and you will be ready for what comes."

73. Two old men came from the Pelusium country to the Abbess Sarah. On their way they said to each other: "Let us humble this old woman." And they said to her: "Take care that your soul be not puffed up, and that you do not say: 'Look, some hermits have come to me, a woman!'" And the Abbess Sarah said to them: "I am a woman in sex, but not in spirit."

74. Abbess Sarah also said: "If I asked God that all men should be edified in me, I should be doing penance at the door of everyone. I pray rather that my heart should be pure in all things."

75. Abba Hyperichius said: "The man who teaches men by his life and not his speech is the true wise man."

76. There once came from the city of Rome a monk who had held a high place in the palace. He lived near the church in Scete, and had with him a servant who ministered to him. The priest of the church saw that he was infirm and knew that he was accustomed to comfort: and so he passed to him whatever the Lord gave him or was given to the church. After he had lived in Scete for twenty-five years, he became celebrated as a contemplative with the spirit of prophecy.

One of the great Egyptian monks heard of his reputation and came to see him in the hope that he would find a more austere way of life. He came into the cell and greeted him: and after they had prayed they sat down. But the Egyptian saw his soft clothing, and a bed of reeds, and a blanket under him, and a little pillow under his head, and his clean feet with sandals on them; and he was inwardly scandalized. In Scete they never used to live like this, but practised a sterner abstinence.

But the old Roman, with his gift of contemplation and second sight, saw that the Egyptian monk was inwardly scandalized. And he said to his servant: "Make us a good meal today, for this abba who has come." And he cooked the few vegetables which he had, and they rose and ate at the proper hour: and he had a little wine by reason of his infirmity, and they drank that. And at evening they said twelve psalms, and went to sleep afterwards: and the same in the night. But at dawn the Egyptian rose, and saying: "Pray for me," he went away, not edified at him.

And when he had gone a little way off, the old Roman wanted to heal his mind, and sent after him and called him back. And he said: "What is your province?" And he answered: "I am an Egyptian." And he said: "Of what city?" And he answered: "Of no city, I never lived in a city." And he said: "Before you were a monk, how did you earn your living?" And he answered: "I was a herdsman." And he said to him: "Where did you sleep?" He answered: "In the fields." And he said: "Had you any mattress?" And he answered: "How should I have a mattress for sleeping in a field?" And he said: "And how did you sleep?" He answered: "On the ground." And he said: "What did you eat when you were in the fields? And what wine did you drink?" And he answered: "What kind of food and drink do you find in a field?" And he said: "How then did you live?" He answered: "I ate dry bread, and salt fish if there were any, and I drank water." And the old man said: "A hard life." And he said: "Was there a bath on the farm where you worked?" And the Egyptian said: "No: I washed in the river, when I wanted."

And when the old man had extracted these answers, and knew how he lived and worked before he became a monk, he wanted to help him: and so he described his own past life in the world. "This wretch in front of you came from the great city of Rome, where I had an important post at the palace in the Emperor's service." And when the Egyptian heard this first sentence, he was stricken, and began to listen attentively. And he went on: "So I left Rome, and came into this desert." And he said: "I, whom you see, had great houses and wealth: and I scorned them, and came to this little cell." And he said: "I, whom you see, had beds ornamented with gold, with costly coverings: and instead of them God gave me this bed of reeds and this blanket. My clothes were rich and expensive: and instead of them I wear these tatters." And he said: "On my dinner-table I used to spend much money: and instead of it he has given me these few vegetables and this little cup of wine. Many servants used to wait upon me, and instead the Lord has given this one man alone a spirit penitent enough to look after me. Instead of a bath I dip my feet in a little bowl of water, and I use sandals because of my infirmity. For the pipe and the lyre and all the varieties of music which used to delight me at dinner, I say twelve psalms in the day, and twelve psalms in the night. But for the sins which once I committed, I now offer this poor and useless service to God in quietness.

See then, Abba, do not be scandalized at my infirmity."

And when the Egyptian heard it, he came to himself and said: "I am a wretch. I came from a hard life of labour to be at rest in the monk's way of life: and now I have what I did not have before. But you have come of your own accord to this hard life, and have left the comforts of the world: you came from honour and wealth to loneliness and poverty."

And he went away with much profit; and he became his friend, and used to go to the old man for his soul's good, for he was a man of discerning, and was full of the fragrance of the Holy Spirit.

77. An old man said: "All this talking is unnecessary. Nowadays everyone talks: and what is needed is action. That is what God wants, not useless talking."

78. A brother asked some of the fathers whether a man suffered pollution if he thought on vileness. When they were asked this question, some said: "Yes": and some said: "No: for if he were polluted we ordinary people could not be saved. If we think of vile actions but do them not, this brings salvation."

The questioner was discontented with the fathers' diverse answers, and he went to an experienced old man and asked him. And the old man replied: "Everyone is required to do according to his capacity." Then the brother asked the old man: "For the Lord's sake, explain this saying to me." And the old man said: "Look, suppose there was a jug of value. And two brothers came in, one of whom had a great capacity for a disciplined life, and the other a small capacity. Suppose that the mind of the more disciplined man were moved at the sight of the jug and he said inwardly 'I would like to own that jug'—but the thought does not remain, and he quickly drives away the desire—then he would not be polluted. But if the less disciplined man coveted the jug and was strongly moved by an impulse to take it, and yet did not take it, he would not be polluted."

79. An old man said: "If a man lives in a place but does not harvest the crops of that place, the place drives him out because he has not done the work of that place."

80. An old man said: "If a man does anything according to his self-will, and not according to God's will, he can afterwards return to the Lord's way, if he did it in ignorance. But the man who obeys his self-will and not God's, and will not listen to admonition, but thinks he knows, will hardly be able to come to the Lord's way."

81. An old man was asked: "What is meant by the text 'Narrow and strait is the way'?" And the old man answered: "Narrow and strait is the way by which a man does violence to his thoughts and for God's sake breaks down his self-will. This is what was written of the apostles, 'Lo, we have left all, and followed thee.'"[40]

82. An old man said: "As the order of monks is more honourable than that of men of the world, so the travelling monk ought to be in every way a mirror for the monks of the places where he stays."

83. One of the fathers said: "If a labourer remains where there are no other labourers, he can make no progress. The true labourer struggles that the work may not deteriorate. If an idle man works with a labourer the idle man becomes less idle; and if he does not make progress, at least he does not get idler by seeing someone working."

84. An old man said: "If a man has words but no works, he is like a tree with leaves but no fruit. Just as a tree laden with fruit is also leafy, the man of good works will also have good words."

85. An old man said that a man once committed a grave sin. Stricken with penitence, he went to confess to an old man. He did not tell him what he had done, but put it in the form of a question: "If such a thought rose in a man's mind, would he be saved?" The old man, who had no discretion, answered: "You have lost your soul."

When the brother heard this, he said: "Well, if I perish, I will go to the world." But on his way he considered the matter and decided to tell his temptations to Abba Silvanus, who possessed great discretion in these matters. The brother went to him and did not tell him what he had done, but again put it in the form of the question: "If such a thought arose in a man's mind, would he be saved?" Silvanus began to speak to him with texts from Scripture, and said: "That judgement does not fall on people *tempted* to sin." The brother perceived the force of the saying, and took hope, and told him what he had done. When

40 Matt. 7:14; 19:27.

Abba Silvanus learnt what he had done, he acted like a skilled physician and put on his soul a poultice made of texts from Scripture, showing him that repentance is available for them who in truth and in charity turn to God. After some years Abba Silvanus met the old man who had driven the brother to despair, and told him what had happened, and said: "That brother, who despaired because of your words, and had gone back to the world, is now a bright star among the brothers." He told him this so that we may know how perilous it is when a man confesses his thoughts or sins to people without discretion.

86. An old man said: "We are not condemned if ill thoughts enter us, but only if we use them ill. Through our thoughts we may suffer shipwreck, through our thoughts we may attain a crown."

87. An old man said: "Do not give to or receive from men of the world. Take no notice of a woman. Do not have confidence for long in a boy."

88. A brother asked an old man: "What shall I do, for I am troubled by many temptations, and know not how to repel them?" The old man said: "Do not fight against them all, but against one of them. All the temptations of monks have a single head. You must consider what it is, what kind of temptation, and fight it. And in this way all the other temptations will be defeated."

89. An old man said against evil thoughts: "I beg you, my brothers, control your thoughts as you control your sins."

90. An old man said: "Anyone who wants to live in the desert ought to be a teacher and not a learner. If he still needs teaching, he will suffer harm."

91. An old man was asked by a brother: "How do I find God? With fasts, or labour, or watchings, or works of mercy?" The old man replied: "In all that you have said, and in discretion. I tell you that many have afflicted their body, but have gained no profit because they did it without discretion. Even if our mouths stink with fasting, and we have learnt all the Scriptures, and memorized the whole Psalter, we still lack what God wants—humility and charity."

92. A brother asked an old man: "Abba, look: I ask my elders questions, and they speak to me for the salvation of my soul, and I can remember nothing that they say. Is it any use asking questions when I profit nothing? I am deep in impurity."

There were two empty vessels nearby. And the old man said: "Go, and take one of those vessels away and put oil in it, and rinse it, and pour out the oil, and put the vessel back." And he did so. And he said: "Do it again." And he did it. And after he had done it several times, the old man said: "Now, take both vessels and see which is the cleaner." And he answered: "The one into which I put oil." The old man said: "So it is with the soul which asks questions. Although it remembers nothing that it hears, it will be cleaner than the soul which never asks questions."

93. A brother was sitting quietly in his cell, and demons wanted to seduce him in the guise of angels. And they stirred him up to go out to the congregation in church, and they showed him a light. But he went to an old man and said: "Abba, angels come to me with light, and stir me to go to the congregation." And the old man said to him: "Heed them not, my son: they are demons. When they come to stir you out, say: 'I go when I want, and do not listen to you.' " He accepted the command and returned to his cell. On the next night the demons came again as usual to stir him. He answered as he had been told: "I go when I want, and do not listen to you." And they said to him: "That wicked old man has trapped you. A brother came to him to borrow money; and, although he had some, he lied and said that he had none, and would give him nothing; that shows you he is a deceiver."

At dawn the brother rose and came to the old man and told him what had happened. The old man said to him: "It is true. I had money, and I did not give to the brother who wanted to borrow some. I knew that if I gave it to him, I should be harming his soul. I thought it better to transgress one commandment than ten. If he had received money from me, we should have come into trouble on his account. So do not listen to the demons who want to seduce you."

And the brother went back to his cell, much comforted by the words of the older man.

94. Three brothers once came to an old man in Scete. One of them asked him: "Abba, I have memorized the Old and New Testaments." And the old man answered: "You have filled the air with words." And the second asked him: "I have written the Old and New Testaments with my own hand." But the old man said: "And you have filled the window-ledge with manuscripts." And the third said: "The grass is growing up my chimney." And the old man answered: "And you have driven away hospitality."

95. Some of the fathers told this story of a great old man. If

anyone came to ask a word of him, he used to say with great confidence: "Look, I am acting in place of God and sitting in his judgement seat: what do you want me to do for you? If you say to me, 'Have mercy upon me,' God says to you, 'If you want me to have mercy on you, you must have mercy on your brothers and then I will have mercy on you. If you want me to forgive you, you must forgive your neighbour.'

Then is God the cause of guilt? God forbid. It is in our power, if we do not want to be saved."

96. They said of an old man in Cellia that he was a great worker. While he was at a work, a holy man happened to come to his cell; and when he was outside the door, he heard the old man within battling with his thoughts, and saying: "Am I to lose everything because of a single word?" The man outside thought that he was quarrelling with someone else, and knocked on the door to go in and make peace between them. But when he went in and saw no one else there, he had faith in the old man, and said: "With whom were you quarrelling, Abba?" He replied: "With my thoughts. I have memorized fourteen books; and when I was outside I heard one little word. And when I came to say the divine office, I had forgotten all fourteen books and could remember only the one word which I heard outside. And that is why I am quarrelling with my thoughts."

97. Some brothers from a monastery came into the desert to see a hermit: and he received them gladly. And as is the way of hermits, he saw that they were tired with their journey and made a meal for them, though it was not the proper time for a meal, and so refreshed them with what he had in his cell. And in the evening they said twelve psalms, and twelve more in the night. While the old man was keeping watch, he heard them saying: "Hermits have more rest in the desert than do monks in the monastery."

In the morning they were departing to visit a neighbouring hermit. And he said to them: "Greet him for me, and tell him: 'Do not water the vegetables.'" The neighbouring hermit understood the message, and kept them working until evening without any food. And at evening he prolonged the divine office to great length, and then said: "Let us rest a little for your sakes. You are tired after your labours." And he said: "We do not usually eat today, but let us eat a little for your sake." And he brought them dry bread and salt, and said: "Look, we have a feast today because you have come": and he added a little sour wine to the mixture. And they rose, and began to sing psalms until dawn. And he said: "Because you travellers are here, you must rest a little, and that prevents us keeping the rule." And at daybreak, they wanted to go hastily. But he asked them to stay, and said: "Spend a little time with me: or at least, for the commandment's sake, keep the hermit's way of life with me for three days."

But when they saw that he was not letting them rest, they stole away in secret.

98. A brother asked one of the fathers: "If by chance I oversleep, and am late for the hour of prayer, I am ashamed that others will hear me praying so late, and so I become reluctant to keep the rule of prayer." And the old man said: "If ever you oversleep the dawn, rise when you wake, shut the door and the windows, and say your office. For it is written 'The day is thine and the night is thine.' [41] God is glorified whatever time it is."

99. An old man said: "One man eats a lot and is still hungry. Another eats a little and has had enough. The man who eats a lot and is still hungry has more merit than the man who eats a little but enough for him."

100. An old man said: "If some distressing controversy rises between you and another, and the other denies it and says: 'I said no such thing,' do not argue with him or say: 'You did say it.' For he will be exasperated, and will say: 'Very well: I did say it.' "

101. A brother asked an old man: "My sister is poor. If I give her alms, am I giving alms to the poor?" The old man said: "No." The brother said: "Why, Abba?" And the old man replied: "Because your kinship draws you a little towards her."

102. An old man said: "A monk ought not to listen to disparagement: he ought not to be disparaged: and he ought not to be scandalized."

103. An old man said: "Do not be pleased at everything which is said, and do not agree with everything that is said. Be slow to believe, and quick to say what is true."

103A. An old man said that even though holy men had to endure much in the desert they had already received some portion of the heavenly rest. But he meant it for those who are free from worldly cares.

103B. An old man said: "If a monk knows a person with

41 Ps. 74:16.

whom he would make progress, but in a place where the life would be hard, he is an atheist if he does not go there."

103c. A brother asked a boy monk: "Is it good to speak or keep silence?" The boy said to him: "If the words are idle, leave them unsaid. If good, find room for them and speak. But even if the words are good, do not prolong what you say but cut it short: and so you will have peace of mind."

104. An old man said: "Sometimes a text enters the heart of a brother as he is sitting in his cell: and the brother, meditating inwardly upon the text, cannot understand its meaning and is not drawn by God to true understanding. Then demons come to his help, and show him whatever meaning suits them."

105. One of the old men said: "When first we used to meet each other in the assembly and talk of what was helpful to our souls, we became ever more withdrawn from the things of sense, and mounted to the heavenly places. But now we meet, and spend our time in gossip, and each drags the other downwards."

106. Another of the fathers said: "If our inner man behaves with seriousness, it can control the outer man: but if the inner man does not, what other means is there of controlling the tongue?"

107. He also said: "We need to labour in praise of God because we have come into the desert. If we are not labouring with our body, we may labour mightily in God's praise."

108. Another father said: "A man ought always to be working at something in his cell. If he is busy with the divine office, the devil comes to him day after day, but finds no resting-place there. And if he succeeds in conquering him and taking him prisoner, God's spirit often comes again. But if we are sinners and do not let God's spirit come to us, he goes away."

109. Some Egyptian monks once went down to Scete to see the elders of that place. And they saw them famished with a long fast and so wolfing their food: and they were scandalized at them. But the priest saw it and wanted to heal their minds and send them away edified. And he preached to the people in the church, saying: "My brothers, prolong your fast yet further." The Egyptian visitors wanted to leave, but he kept them. When they had fasted one day and then a second, they were much weakened; for he had made them fast for two days without a break. (But in Scete the monks fast for a week.)

On Saturday the Egyptians sat down to eat with the old men. And they reached voraciously for their food. And one of the old men checked their hands, and said: "Eat like monks, in a disciplined way."

One of the Egyptians threw off his restraining hand, and said: "Leave go. I am dying, I have not eaten cooked food all the week." And the old man said to him: "If you are so weak at a meal after a fast of only two days, why were you scandalized at brothers who always keep their abstinence for a week at a time?"

And they did penance before them, and went away gladly, edified at their abstinence.

110. A brother who renounced the world and took the monk's habit, immediately shut himself up in a hermitage, saying: "I am a solitary." When the neighbouring elders heard of it, they came and threw him out of his cell, and made him go round the cells of the brothers and do penance before them, and say: "Forgive me. I am no solitary but have only lately begun to be a monk."

111. Some old men said: "If you see a young man climbing up to heaven by his own will, catch him by the foot and pull him down to earth: it is not good for him."

112. A brother said to a great old man: "Abba, I wanted to find an old man after my own heart, and die with him." And the old man said: "Your search is good, my Lord." The brother reiterated his desire, not understanding the irony of the old man. But when the old man saw that he thought this was a good idea, he said to him: "If you find an old man after your own heart, you want to live with him?" And the brother said: "Yes. I wholeheartedly want this, if I can find one according to my mind." Then the old man said to him: "You do not want to follow the will of an old man: you want to follow yours, and so you will be comfortable with him."

But the brother saw the sense of what he said, and rose and prostrated himself in penitence, saying: "Forgive me. I was very proud of myself for saying something good, when in truth there was nothing good about me."

113. Two earthly-minded brothers renounced the world. The younger was the first to begin the converted life. One of the fathers came to stay with them, and they brought a basin of water for him to wash. And the younger came to wash the feet of the old man. But the old man took his hand and motioned him away, and made the elder do it: it is the custom for the first men in a monastery to do this. But the brothers standing near said: "Abba, the elder brother is the younger in religion." The old man answered: "And I take away the first place from the younger, and give it to him who is older in years."

114. An old man said: "The prophets wrote books. Our fathers came after them, and worked much at them, and then their successors memorized them. But this generation has come, and it copies them on papyrus and parchment and leaves them unused on the window-ledge."

115. An old man said: "The cowl we use is the symbol of innocence. The amice which covers neck and shoulders is the symbol of a cross: the girdle, the symbol of courage. Let us live our lives in the virtues symbolized by our habit. If we do everything with earnestness, we shall not fail."

PART XI

That it is right to live soberly

1. A brother asked Abba Arsenius to speak a word to him. The old man said to him: "As far as you can, strive to make your inner progress as God would have it, and by it conquer the passions of the outer man."

He also said: "If we seek God, he will appear to us: if we hold him, he will stay with us."

2. Abba Agatho said: "A monk ought not to let his conscience accuse him about anything."

When this Abba Agatho was on his death-bed, he remained motionless for three days with his eyes open. The brothers shook him, saying: "Abba, where are you?" And he said: "I am standing in the presence of God's judgement." They said to him: "Are you afraid?" And he said: "Mostly I have worked as much as I could to keep the commandments of God. But I am a man, and I do not know whether my works will be pleasing in God's sight." The brothers said to him: "Do you not trust in your works? For they were obedient to God's will." And the old man said: "I do not presume, except I come before God: for the judgements of God are not the judgements of men."

When they still wished to ask him to speak, he said to them: "Of your charity do not talk to me, for I am busy." And at the words, he breathed forth his spirit with joy. And they saw him welcoming his spirit as a man greets his dear friends. In everything Abba Agatho kept a careful guard, and he used to say: "There is no virtue which a man can acquire without taking guard."

3. They said of Abba Ammoi that when he went to church, he did not let his disciple walk with him, but made him follow a long way behind. And if the disciple drew near to ask him

something, he gave him a rapid answer and drove him back at once, saying: "I am afraid that while we are talking for the soul's good, some irrelevant words will be spoken: and that is why I do not let you walk by my side."

4. Abba Ammoi began by saying to Abba Aesius: "How do you see me now?" And he said: "Like an angel, father." And later he said again: "Now how do you see me?" And he said: "Like Satan: for even if you speak a good word, it is like a sword to me."

5. Abba Allois said: "Unless a man say in his heart, Only I and God are in the world, he shall not find rest."

6. He also said: "If a man wills, in one day he can come by the evening to a measure of divinity."

7. Abba Bessarion said when he was dying: "A monk ought to be all eye, like the Cherubim and Seraphim."

8. Abba Daniel and Abba Ammoi were once on a journey together. Abba Ammoi said: "Do you think sometime we shall rest in a cell, father?" Abba Daniel said to him: "Who can take God away from us? God is abroad in the world, and he is in the cell likewise."

9. Abba Evagrius said: "It is a great thing to pray without hindrance. It is a greater, to sing psalms without hindrance."

10. He also said: "If you always remember your death and do not forget the eternal judgement, there will be no sin in your soul."

11. Abba Theodore of the ninth region of Alexandria said: "If God reckons to us the carelessness of our times of prayer, and the captivity of our minds to other things during our psalmody, we cannot be saved."

12. Abba Theonas said: "Our mind is hindered and held back from contemplating God, because we are imprisoned in our bodily passions."

13. Some of the brothers once came to tempt Abba John the Short, for he never let his mind wander among worldly thoughts, and he never spoke for the world's sake. They said to him: "Thanks be to God, it has rained hard this year, and the palm-trees have had enough water to begin to bear; and so the brothers who are engaged in bodily labour will find fruit from their labour." So Abba John said to them: "So it is when the Holy Spirit comes down into the hearts of saintly men. They grow green and fresh, and in the fear of God put forth leaves."

14. They said of this Abba John that he once made enough

material for two baskets, and twisted it all into one basket, but did not see what he was doing until he tried to hang them on the wall. For his mind was occupied in the contemplation of God.

14A. Abba John the Short also said: "I am like a man sitting in the shade of a tall tree, who sees wild beasts and snakes coming at him and knows his danger and rushes to climb the tree to safety. I sit in my cell, and see temptations coming at me: and when I cannot stand up to them I rush to pray God, and so I find safety from the enemy's attack."

15. There was an old man in Scete, with a reasonable rule of bodily life, but not at all careful in remembering what he heard. So he went to Abba John the Short to ask him about forgetfulness. He listened to Abba John, went back to his cell. and forgot what he had been told. He came a second time and asked him, listened, went back, and forgot what he had heard the moment he had reached his cell. Many times he went backwards and forwards, but could never remember.

He happened to meet the old man and said: "Do you know, father, that I again forgot what you told me? I did not wish to trouble you, so I did not come again." Abba John said to him: "Go, light a lamp." And he lit it. And he said: "Bring more lamps and light them from the first." And he did so. And Abba John said to the old man: "Was the first lamp harmed, because you used it to light others?" And he said: "No." "So John is not harmed: even if all the monks of Scete should come to me, it does not keep me from God's love. So come to me whenever you want, and do not hesitate."

And so, by patience on both sides, God cured the forgetfulness of the old man. This was the work of the men of Scete, to strengthen those who were attacked by passion; their own experience in the moral struggle enabled them to help others along the road.

16. A brother asked Abba John: "What am I to do? A brother keeps coming and takes me away to help with the work which he is doing: but I am wretched and sick, and am too weak for it. How then am I to obey God's commandment?" The old man answered him: "Caleb the son of Jephunneh said to Joshua the son of Nun [42] 'I was forty years old when Moses the servant of the Lord sent me with you to that country: and now I am eighty-five. Then I was strong: and I am still just as capable of beginning and ending a battle.' And so do you go,

[42] Josh. 14:6 and 10–11 inaccurately.

if you can finish the work as well as you begin it. If you cannot, sit in your cell and lament your sins. And if they find you weeping when they come, they will not force you to go out with them."

17. Abba Isidore, who was the priest in Scete, said: "When I was a young man and stayed in my cell, I made no limit to the number of psalms which I used in the service of God. Night and day alike were spent in psalmody."

18. Abba Cassian told a story of an old man, living in the desert, who asked God to grant that he never fell into a doze when the conversation was edifying: but that, if anyone spoke with back-biting or hate, he should immediately fall asleep, and so he would not listen to the poisonous words. He said that the devil strove earnestly to make men speak idle words, and assailed all spiritual teaching.

In this connexion he gave the following example: "When once I was talking to some brothers for the good of their souls, they fell into a drowsiness so deep that they could not even keep their eyelids open. I wanted to show them that this was the devil's work, so I started gossiping: and at once they lost all drowsiness and began to enjoy what I was saying. But I said sorrowfully: 'We were talking of the heavenly till just now, and your eyes were drooping into heavy slumber: but the moment the talk is frivolous, you all begin to listen avidly. I beg you then, dear brothers, since you know that this is the work of an evil demon, to look to yourselves, and beware of sleep whenever you are doing or hearing the things of the spirit.' " [43]

19. When Abba Poemen was a young man, he once went to an old man to ask him three questions. When he arrived at the old man's cell he forgot one of his three questions, and went back to his own cell. And he was just stretching out his hand for the key of his cell when he remembered the question which he had forgotten. He left the key lying there, and returned to the old man. The old man said to him: "You have travelled fast to get here, my brother." And Poemen told him: "When I was stretching out my hand for the key, I remembered the question: so I did not open my cell door, but immediately returned to you."

The distance between the cells was very great. The old man

43 Cassian, *Institutes*, V, 29 and 31. *Verba Seniorum* has, again, translated from a Greek translation of Cassian's Latin text, but it was a full translation and not an epitome. Cassian himself attributed the first story to an old man named Machetes.

said to him: "Truly you are Poemen,[44] shepherd of sheep: for your name shall be renowned in all Egypt."

20. Abba Ammon came to Abba Poemen, and said to him: "If I go to my neighbour's cell, or if he comes to mine, we are both frightened of unsuitable conversation, which may harm our monastic purpose." And the old man said to him: "You are right. Young men need to be on their guard." Abba Ammon said to him: "What about old men?" And Abba Poemen said to him: "Old men who make progress, and are stable, do not find these unsuitable words in their mouths and so they do not say them." And Abba Ammon said: "If I need to talk with my neighbour, do you think I should talk to him about the Scriptures, or about the sayings and judgements of the elders?" And the old man said to him: "If you cannot keep silence, it is much better to talk about the sayings of the elders than about the Scriptures. For the danger is no small one."

21. Abba Poemen was asked about pollutions. He replied: "If we strengthen our moral life and make earnest efforts, we shall not find pollutions in ourselves."

22. They used to say of Abba Poemen that when he was soon to go out for the divine office, he first sat by himself for an hour in self-examination, and then went out.

23. Abba Poemen said that a man asked Abba Paysio this question: "What am I to do to my soul? It has become incapable of feeling and does not fear God." And he said to him: "Go, and put yourself under a man who does fear God: and when you live with him, you will learn to fear God also."

24. He also said: "The beginning and the end is the fear of the Lord. For thus it is written, 'The fear of the Lord is the beginning of wisdom': and, when Abraham built an altar the Lord said to him: 'Now I know that thou fearest God.' "[45]

24A. He also said: "If a man makes a new heaven and a new earth, he still cannot be safe from temptation."

25. He also said: "Depart from any man who is always scornful in his conversation."

26. He also said: "I once asked Abba Peter, the disciple of Abba Lot: 'When I am in my cell, my soul is at peace. But if some brother arrives and tells me what is being said outside, my soul is troubled?' And Abba Peter told me that Abba Lot said: 'Your key has opened my door.'

[44] *Poemen* is Greek for shepherd. Some of the Latin translators turned his name into *Pastor*.
[45] Ps. 111:10, *et al.*; Gen. 22:9 and 12.

And I said: 'What does that mean?' And he said: 'If someone comes to visit you, you ask him: How are you? Where do you come from? How are such-and-such brothers faring, did they receive you or not? Then you are opening the door for your brother to talk, and you hear words which you do not want to hear.' And I said to him: 'That is so. But what shall a man do otherwise, when a brother visits him?' And the old man said: 'True teaching is always in sorrow. Where sorrow is not, you cannot keep a watch on the mind.'

And I said to him: 'When I am in my cell, sorrow is with me. But when anyone visits me, or when I go out of my cell, I am sorrowful no longer.' And the old man said: 'You are not yet stable in sorrow, you use it as a transitory and expedient feeling.' And I said: 'What does that mean?' And he said to me: 'If a man labours for something as vigorously as he can, he finds it ready to hand whenever he needs it for his spiritual profit.' "

27. A brother asked Abba Sisois: "I long to guard my heart." The old man said to him: "And how can we guard the heart if our tongue leaves the door of the fortress open?"

28. Abba Silvanus was once living on Mount Sinai. His disciple, who was about to go off on some necessary task, said to the old man: "Bring water, and water the garden." The old man went to draw water: and he covered his face with his cowl, so that he could see only his feet. By chance a visitor arrived to see him at that moment: and looking at him from a distance, marvelled at the sight. And he went up to him and said: "Tell me, Abba, why did you cover your face with your hood, and so water the garden?" And the old man said to him: "So that my eyes should not see the trees, and my mind should not be disturbed from its work by the sight."

29. Abba Moses asked Abba Silvanus: "Can a man live every day as though it were the first day of his religious life?" Abba Silvanus answered: "If a man is a labourer, he can live every day, nay every hour, as though it were the first day or hour of his religious life."

30. Some brothers once asked Abba Silvanus: "What way of life did you practise to be endowed with such prudence?" And he answered: "I never let any embittering thought remain in my heart."

31. Abba Serapion said: "The imperial guards while on duty in the emperor's presence must keep their eyes to the front and not turn their heads to one side or the other. And the monk, in God's presence, must keep his attention all the time upon

the fear of God and so none of the enemy's wickednesses can affright him."

31A. Saint Syncletice said: "My sons, we all know the way to be saved, and fail to travel it because we do not care."

32. Saint Syncletice said: "Let us live soberly. For through our bodily senses, willy-nilly, robbers come in. The inside of the house is sure to be blackened when the smoke that is climbing up the outer walls finds the windows open."

33. She also said: "We ought to be armed at all points against the demons. They come at us from outside; and are invited by the inner man if the soul is weak. Sometimes a ship is crushed by the battering of heavy seas; sometimes it is sunk because the bilge water steadily rises within. And in the same way we are sometimes condemned because we have committed wicked acts, and sometimes because the inner thoughts are evil. So we must watch for the assaults of unclean spirits, and cleanse the thoughts of the heart."

34. She also said: "We have no security in this world. The Apostle said: 'Let him that standeth, take heed lest he fall.'[46] We are sailing on uncharted seas; as the Psalmist David said: 'Our life is like a sea.' Yet some seas have dangerous reefs, some are full of sharks, some seas are calm. We seem to be sailing in calm waters, while men of the world are sailing in rough weather. And we are sailing in daylight, led by the Sun of righteousness, while they are being driven along in the night time—the night of ignorance. Yet it often happens that worldly men, sailing in darkness and through storms, are so afraid of the danger that they save the ship, by calling upon God and by watchfulness: while we, in our calm waters, become negligent, get off the proper course of righteousness, and are sunk."

35. Abba Hyperichius said: "Let your mind be ever upon the kingdom of heaven, and you will soon win its inheritance."

36. He also said: "The life of a monk should be like that of the angels, in burning up sin."

37. Abba Orsisius said: "I think that unless a man has a good watch on his heart, he will become forgetful and careless in his conversation. And so the enemy gets a footing in him and overthrows him. A lamp will give light if it has oil and a trimmed wick. But if the oil is forgotten, it goes slowly out and little by little the shadows creep in upon it. If a mouse comes to it and tries to eat the wick before it is quite out, it is thwarted by the heat of the dying flame. But when it sees that the light

[46] I Cor. 10:12.

is gone and the wick is cool, it knocks the lamp to the floor. If the lamp is earthenware, it is smashed, if it is brass, it is reparable.

If the soul is negligent, the Holy Spirit goes from it little by little, until it has grown quite cold: and then the enemy devours the soul's purpose, and wickedness puts an end to it. If a man through his Godward affection is a good man and has merely been caught in temporary negligence, the merciful God stirs the mind to remember the punishment waiting for sinners in the next life; and henceforth the mind takes trouble to be earnest and watches itself carefully, until the time of its visitation."

38. An old man visited another old man. In their conversation one said: "I am dead to the world." And the other said: "Do not be self-confident until you die. You may say about yourself that you are dead: but Satan is not dead."

39. An old man said: "A monk ought every day to examine himself morning and evening, how far he has kept the Lord's will. He ought to be leading a penitential life all his days. That was the way Abba Arsenius lived."

40. An old man said: "If you lose gold or silver, you can find something as good as you lost. But the man who loses time can never make up what he has lost."

41. An old man said: "Before soldiers or hunters start on expeditions, they do not consider whether some will be wounded and others unhurt. Each one fights for himself alone. That is how the monk should be."

42. An old man said: "No one can harm the man at the emperor's side: and Satan cannot harm us if our souls are fixed upon God: as it is written, 'Draw nigh to me, and I shall draw nigh unto you.' [47] But because we are so often puffed up with pride, it is easy for the enemy to snatch away our wretched soul to carnal passion and its ignominy."

42A. An old man said: "A man must work so that his work does not perish. However much he does, it is no use if it is impermanent. It is work that is little and lasting which shall stand."

42B. An old man said: "Sometimes I do a great work, sometimes a little. And I have regard to the results in my thoughts and deeds."

42C. An old man said: "Waking or sleeping, whatever you do, you will not fear the devil if God be before your eyes. Even

[47] Zech. 1:3.

if temptation stays with a man, so does God's power stay with him."

42D. An old man said: "When you wake in the morning, tell yourself this: 'Work, my body, for your food. Be earnest, my soul, to win your inheritance.' "

43. A brother said to an old man: "I see no battle in my heart." And the old man said: "You are like double doors: anyone who likes can go inside, and come out again when he likes, and you are unaware of what is happening. If you had a door and shut it, you would not let wicked thoughts come in, and then you would see them standing outside the door and fighting against you."

44. They said of an old man that his thoughts suggested to him: "Let be today; tomorrow you shall do penance." And he contradicted them thus: "No, I do penance today, and to-morrow the Lord's will be done."

45. An old man said: "Unless the inner man live soberly, the outer man is uncontrollable."

46. An old man said: "Satan has three powers, which lead to all the sins. The first is forgetfulness, the second negligence, the third concupiscence. If forgetfulness comes, it begets negligence: negligence is the mother of concupiscence: and by concupiscence a man falls. If the mind is serious, it repels forgetfulness, negligence does not come, concupiscence finds no entry—and so with help from Christ's grace, he shall never fall."

47. An old man said: "Take care to be silent. Empty the mind. Attend to your meditation, in the fear of God, whether you are resting in bed or at work. If you do this, you will not fear the assaults of demons."

48. An old man said to a brother: "The devil is like a hostile neighbour and you are like a house. The enemy continually throws into you all the dirt that he can find. It is your business not to neglect to throw out whatever he throws in. If you neglect to do this, your house will be so full of mud that you will not be able to walk inside. From the moment he begins to throw, put it out again, bit by bit: and so by Christ's grace your house shall remain clean."

49. An old man said: "When the donkey's eyes are covered, it walks round the mill-wheel. If you uncover its eyes, it will not go on walking in the circle. And if the devil succeeds in covering a man's eyes, he lowers him into every kind of sin. But if man's eyes are uncovered, he can more easily escape."

50. The old men used to say that on the mountain of Abba Antony, seven monks took turns at the time of the grape harvest to drive away the birds from the fruit. One old man among them, on the day when it was his turn to guard the grapes, used to shout: "Go away—ill thoughts within, birds without."

51. A brother collected palm-leaves in his cell. And as soon as he sat down to plait them, his mind suggested to him that he should go visit one of the old men. He meditated on it, and said: "I will go in a few days." And then his mind suggested: "Suppose he dies during the next few days, what will you do?" "I will go now and talk with him, because it is summer time." And again he thought: "No, it is not the proper time yet." Then he said: "It will be time when you have cut the reeds for the mats." And he said: "I will spread out these palm-leaves and then go." Then he said: "But today it is fine weather."

So he rose, left his pile of palms, took his cloak, and went out. But nearby was another old man, a man of prophetic vision. When he saw the brother hurrying out, he called to him: "Prisoner, prisoner, where are you running to? Come here to me." He came: and the old man said to him: "Go back to your cell." The brother described to him the ups and downs and indecisions of his mind, and then went back to his cell. And as soon as he entered it, he fell down and did penance. And suddenly the demons shrieked aloud: "You have conquered us, monk, you have conquered us." And the mat on which he lay was singed as though by fire, and the demons vanished away like smoke; and so the brother learnt their wiles.

52. They told a story of an old man who was dying in Scete. The brothers stood round his bed, and clothed him, and began to weep. But he opened his eyes and began to laugh; it happened three times. So the brothers asked him: "Tell us, Abba, why do you laugh at our weeping?" And he told them: "I laughed the first time because you fear death; I laughed the second time because you are not ready for death; I laughed the third time, because I am passing from labour to rest, and yet you weep." And so saying, he closed his eyes and died.

53. A brother who was living in his cell once came to one of the fathers and said that he was grievously troubled by his thoughts. And the old man said: "You have thrown on the ground a mighty weapon, which is the fear of God, and taken in your hand a stick made of reeds, which is wicked thoughts. You must take to yourself the fire which is the fear of God.

And when the wicked thought approaches you, the fear of God will destroy it as a fire burns reeds. Wickedness cannot overcome men who fear God."

54. One of the fathers said: "Unless you first hate, you cannot love. Unless you hate sin, you cannot live righteously. As it is written: 'Eschew evil and do good.'[48] But mental purpose is needed for all this. Adam, though in Paradise, disobeyed God's command: Job, living in a dung-hill, kept it. It seems that God requires from man a good purpose, the purpose of fearing him always."

PART XII

That we ought to pray earnestly and unceasingly

1. They said of Abba Arsenius that on Saturday evening he put his back to the setting sun and stretched out his hands towards heaven, and prayed, until at dawn on Sunday the rising sun lit up his face: and then he sat down again.

2. The brothers asked Abba Agatho: "Father, which virtue in our way of life needs most effort to acquire?" And he said to them: "Forgive me, I think nothing needs so much effort as prayer to God. If a man is wanting to pray, the demons infest him in the attempt to interrupt the prayer, for they know that prayer is the only thing that hinders them. All the other efforts of a religious life, whether they are made vehemently or gently, have room for a measure of rest. But we need to pray till we breathe out our dying breath. That is the great struggle."

3. Abba Dulas, the disciple of Abba Bessarion, said: "I once went into the cell of my abba, and found him standing in prayer, with his hands stretched towards heaven. He stayed like that for fourteen days. At the end he called me and said: "Follow me." We went out and took our way through the desert. I grew thirsty, and said to him: "Abba, I am thirsty." He took off his cloak, and went away a stone's throw: and he prayed, and brought me the cloak full of water. And we went to the city of Lycus, and came to Abba John, and greeted him, and prayed. Then they sat down and began to talk about a vision which they had seen. Abba Bessarion said: "The Lord has given a commandment that the temples be destroyed." And so it was done. They were destroyed.

4. Abba Evagrius said: "If your soul grows weak, pray. As

[48] Ps. 37:27.

it is written,[49] pray in fear and trembling, earnestly and watchfully. We ought to pray like that, especially because our unseen and wicked enemies are vehemently trying to hinder us."

5. He also said: "When a contrary thought enters the heart, do not cast around here and there in your prayer, but be simply penitent—and so you will sharpen your sword against your assailant."

6. Epiphanius, of holy memory, the bishop from Cyprus, was told this by the abbot of his monastery in Palestine. "By your prayers we have kept our rule; we carefully observe the offices of terce, sext, none and vespers." But Epiphanius rebuked him and said: "Then you are surely failing to pray at other times. The true monk ought to pray without ceasing, ought always to be singing psalms in his heart."

7. Abba Isaiah said: "A priest at Pelusium was holding a love-feast: and while the brothers in church were eating and conversing, he rebuked them thus: 'Be silent, my brothers. I know of one brother who is supping among you, and his prayer mounts in the sight of God like a darting flame.' "

8. Abba Lot went to Abba Joseph and said: "Abba, as far as I can, I keep a moderate rule, with a little fasting, and prayer, and meditation, and quiet: and as far as I can I try to cleanse my heart of evil thoughts. What else should I do?" Then the old man rose, and spread out his hands to heaven, and his fingers shone like ten candles: and he said: "If you will, you could become a living flame."

9. Some monks called Euchites,[50] or "men of prayer," once came to Abba Lucius in the ninth region of Alexandria. And the old man asked them: "What work do you do with your hands?" And they said: "We do not work with our hands. We obey St Paul's command and pray without ceasing." The old man said to them: "Do you not eat?" They said: "Yes, we eat." And the old man said to them: "When you are eating, who prays for you?" Again, he asked them: "Do you not sleep?" They said: "We sleep." And the old man said: "Who prays for you while you are asleep?" They would not answer him.

---

[49] Later copyists removed "As it is written."

[50] These are members of the celebrated heretical sect, otherwise known as Messalians: for the best account see Hans Lietzmann, *The Era of the Church Fathers* (ET. 1951), pp. 168 ff. For recent bibliography upon a much debated question, see A. Kemmer, "Gregor von Nyssa und Ps. Makarius: Der Messalianismus im Lichte ostlicher Herzenmystik," in *Antonius Magnus Eremita* (edited by B. Steidle, O.S.B.), Rome 1956, pp. 268–82.

And he said to them: "Forgive me, brothers, but you do not practise what you say. I will show you how I pray without ceasing though I work with my hands. With God's help, I sit and collect a few palm-leaves, and plait them, and say: 'Have mercy upon me, O God, after thy great mercy: and according to the multitude of thy mercies do away with mine iniquity.' "[51] And he said to them: "Is that prayer, or is it not?" They said: "It is prayer."

And he said: "When I stay all day working and praying in my heart, I make about sixteen pence. Two of these I put outside the door, and with the rest I buy food. And he who receives the two pennies outside the door, prays for me while I am eating and sleeping: and so by God's grace I fulfil the text: 'Pray without ceasing.' "

10. Some brothers asked Abba Macarius: "How should we pray?" And the old man said: "There is no need to talk much in prayer. Spread out your hands often, and say: 'Lord, have mercy upon me, as thou wilt and as thou knowest.' But if war presses into the soul, say: 'Lord, help me.' He knows what is best for us, and has mercy."

11. They said of Abba Sisois that unless he soon lowered his hands when he stood up to pray, his mind was snatched up into the heavenly places. So if he happened to be praying with another brother, he quickly lowered his hands and ended the prayer, so that his mind should not be rapt or remain in prayer too long for his brother.

12. An old man used to say: "Constant prayer soon cures the mind."

13. One of the fathers said: "No one can see his face reflected in muddy water: and the soul cannot pray to God with contemplation unless first cleansed of harmful thoughts."

14. An old man once visited Mount Sinai. And when he was going away, a brother met him by the path, and groaned, and said: "Abba, we are afflicted by drought. There has been no rain." And the old man said: "Why do you not pray and ask God?" And he said: "We have been praying and asking God constantly, and still there is no rain." And the old man said: "I believe you are not praying intently enough. Shall we try whether it is so? Come, let us stand and pray together." He stretched out his hands to heaven and prayed; and at once the rain fell. The brother was afraid at the sight, and fell down and worshipped him. But the old man fled away from that place.

[51] Ps. 51:1.

15. The brothers told this story. "We once visited some old men, and after the usual prayer we exchanged greetings and sat down. And after we had talked together, we made ready to go, and asked once again for prayer to be made. But one of the old men said to us: 'What, have you not prayed already?' And we said: 'Yes, father, when we came in, we prayed, and since then we have been talking.' And he said: 'Forgive me, brothers; one brother, while he was sitting and talking with you, offered a hundred and three prayers.' And with these words he prayed, and sent us away."

PART XIII

That we ought to be hospitable and show mercy with cheerfulness

1. Some of the fathers once came to Abba Joseph in Panephysis, to ask him if they should break their fast when they received brothers as guests, and so could celebrate their coming. And before they asked their question, the old man said to his disciple: "Meditate on what I am going to do today." And he put two seats, made of reeds, tied in bundles, one on his left and the other on his right, and said: "Sit down." Then he went into his cell and put on rags; and he came out, and walked past them, and then went in again and put on his ordinary clothes.

The visitors were astonished, and asked him what it meant. He said to them: "Did you see what I did?" They said: "Yes." And he said: "Did the rags change me for the better?" They said: "No." He said: "Did the good garment change me for the worse?" They said: "No." And he said: "So I am myself whether I wear good clothes or rags. I was not changed for better or worse because I changed my clothes. That is what we ought to do in receiving guests. It is written in the Holy Gospel, 'Render unto Caesar the things that are Caesar's; and unto God the things that are God's.' So when visitors come, we ought to welcome them and celebrate with them. When we are by ourselves, we need to be sorrowful."

When they heard it, they were astonished that he knew what they intended to ask him, and they glorified God.

2. Abba Cassian said: [52] "We came from Palestine to Egypt, and visited one of the fathers. After he had offered us hospitality, we asked him: 'Why, when you receive guests, do you not keep the fast? In Palestine they keep it.' He answered: 'Fasting is ever with me. I cannot keep you here for ever. Fasting is

[52] *Institutes*, V, 24.

useful and necessary, but we can choose to fast or not fast. God's law demands from us perfect charity. In you I receive Christ: and so I must do all I can to show you the offices of charity. When I have bidden you farewell, I can return and make up my rule of fasting. The sons of the bridegroom cannot fast while the bridegroom is with them: when he is taken from them, then they can fast.' [53] "

3. Abba Cassian also said: [54] "We came to another old man and he invited us to sup, and pressed us, though we had eaten, to eat more. I said that I could not. He answered: 'I have already given meals to six different visitors, and have supped with each of them, and am still hungry. Have you only eaten once and yet are so full that you cannot eat with me now?' "

4. In Scete there once went out an order that they should fast that week, and then celebrate Easter. During the week some brothers happened to come from Egypt to visit Abba Moses, and he cooked a little vegetable stew for them. The nearby hermits saw the smoke, and said to the clergy of the church: "What is that smoke? Moses must be disobeying the order, and cooking stew in his cell." The clergy said: "We will talk to him when he comes." On Saturday the clergy, who knew the greatness of his way of life, said to Abba Moses in front of the whole congregation: "Abba Moses, you have broken a commandment of men: but you have mightily kept the commandments of God."

5. A brother came to Abba Poemen in the second week of Lent and told him his thoughts, and found peace of mind from his answer. Then he said: "I was almost stopped from coming to see you today." And the old man said: "Why?" And he said: "I was afraid that the door would not be opened as it is Lent." And Abba Poemen answered him: "We were not taught to shut wooden doors; the door we need to keep shut is the mouth." [55]

6. A brother said to Abba Poemen: "If I give my brother anything like a piece of bread, the demons pollute the gift; for it makes it seem to be done to please men." And the old man told him: "Even if it is done to please men, we still ought to give our brothers what they need." And he told him this parable: "There were in a town two farmers. One of them sowed seed,

---

[53] Matt. 9:15.
[54] *Institutes*, V, 25.
[55] In Latin a pun—"non januam ligneam [lineam MB.] sed linguae januam." But the Greek had no pun, cf. *Apophthegmata* Poemen 27, PG 65, col. 335.

and gathered a poor harvest: the other was idle and did not sow, and had no harvest to gather. If famine came, which of them would survive?" And the brother answered: "The one who sowed, even if the harvest was poor." And the old man said: "It is so with us. We sow a few seeds, and they are poor— but in a time of famine we shall not die."

7. A brother came to a hermit: and as he was taking his leave, he said: "Forgive me, Abba, for hampering you in keeping your rule." The hermit answered: "My rule is to welcome you with hospitality, and to send you on your way in peace."

8. A hermit, possessed of much virtue, lived not far from a community of monks. Some visitors to the community happened to go to see him and made him eat, though it was not the proper time. Later the monks of the community said to him: "Were you not disturbed, Abba?" And he answered: "I am disturbed when I do my own will."

9. An old man in Syria, they said, lived near the way to the desert: and it was his work faithfully to refresh every monk who came from the desert, at whatever time he came. One day a hermit arrived, and was asked by him to sup. But the hermit refused, saying: "I am fasting." The old man was grieved, and said: "I beseech you, do not pass by your servant, do not scorn me. Come, let us pray together. Look, here is a tree: let us obey him for whom the tree bows down when he kneels and prays." So the hermit knelt and prayed: but nothing happened. Then the old man knelt down, and at once the tree bent its trunk as he did. They rejoiced at the sight, and gave thanks to God who is ever performing marvels.

10. Two brothers once came to an old man, whose custom it was not to eat every day. When he saw them, he greeted them gladly, and said: "A fast has its reward." And "He who sups from a motive of charity, obeys two commandments. He leaves his self-will, and refreshes his brothers."

11. An old man in Egypt lived in a desert place. And far away lived a Manichaean who was a priest, at least was one of those whom Manichaeans call priests. While the Manichaean was on a journey to visit another of that erroneous sect, he was caught by nightfall in the place where lived this orthodox and holy man. He wanted to knock and go in and ask for shelter; but was afraid to do so, for he knew that he would be recognized as a Manichaean, and believed that he would be refused hospitality. But, driven by his plight, he put the thought aside, and knocked.

The old man opened the door and recognized him: and he welcomed him joyfully, made him pray with him, gave him supper and a bed. The Manichaean lay thinking in the night, and marvelling: "Why was he not hostile to me? He is a true servant of God." And at break of day he rose, and fell at his feet, saying: "Henceforth I am orthodox, and shall not leave you." And so he stayed with him.

12. A monk of the Thebaid received from God the grace of ministry, to minister to the poor as they had need. In a village once he happened to be holding a love-feast. And a woman clad in tatters came up to him to receive her share. When he saw the tatters, he meant to take a great handful, so as to give her a big helping: but his hand was kept nearly shut, and he took little. Another, well-dressed, woman came up: and seeing her clothes, he meant to take a little handful for her: but his hand was opened, and he took a big helping. So he made enquiry about the women, and he found that the well-dressed woman had been a lady who had sunk to poverty and clothed herself well because she felt that she had a standard to maintain before her family. But the other had put on tatters so as to receive more.

13. A monk had a poor brother living in the world, to whom he gave all the profit from his work. But the more he gave him, the poorer he became. So the monk went and told an old man what was happening. The old man said to him: "If you take my advice, you will give him nothing more, but will tell him: 'Brother, I have given you what I had. It is yours to work now, and give me of the produce': accept whatever he brings you, and give it to any poor pilgrim or old man whom you find, and ask them to pray for him."

The monk listened to the advice, and did so. When his brother from the world came, he spoke to him as the old man advised, and his brother went away grieved. And then, the next day, he brought the monk a few vegetables from the garden. The monk accepted them, and gave them to some old men, asking them to pray for his brother. He received a blessing from them and returned home. Later his brother brought him vegetables and three loaves of bread: and he accepted it and gave it, and again received a blessing. But the third time his brother brought costly articles, wine and fish. The monk was astonished at the sight, and called in poor men, and fed them. But he said to his brother from the world: "Do you not need all that bread?" And his brother said: "No, Lord. When I used to accept presents from you, it was as though a fire entered into my house and consumed it: but now, while I am receiving nothing from you, I have plenty, and God blesses me."

So the monk went and told the old man what had happened. And the old man said to him: "Do you not know that the monks' work is a fire which consumes wherever it passes? It is best for your brother that he should eke out a pittance from his own effort, and be prayed for by holy men: then he receives God's blessing, and he will have plenty."

14. One of the old men said: "There are some who do good, yet the devil insinuates a mean spirit into their souls, so that they lose the reward of all the good that they do. When I was once living in Oxyrhynchus with a priest who was generous in almsgiving, a widow came to ask him for a little barley. He said to her: 'Go and fetch a measure, and I will weigh you some.' She brought a measure. But he weighed the measure in his hand and said: 'It is too big': and he made the widow ashamed.

After she had gone, I said: 'Priest, did you lend barley to that widow, or what?' He said: 'No; I gave it her.' But I said: 'If you wanted to make her a free gift, why were you so exact about the measure and made her ashamed?' "

15. An old man lived a common life with another brother, and he was an old man with a merciful disposition. Once in a time of famine, people began to come to his door to take part in a love-feast, and the old man ministered bread to everyone who came. But when his brother saw this, he said: "Give me my share of the bread, and do what you like with your share." The old man divided the bread into two, and went on giving away his own share as usual. But a multitude flocked to the old man, hearing that he gave to all comers. And God, seeing his purpose, blessed that bread.

But the brother who had taken his share, gave none away: and he ate up his bread, and said to the old man: "I have only a little of my bread left, Abba: so take me back to a life in common." And the old man said to him: "I will do whatever you want." And again they began to live together and have everything in common. Again, they had plenty of food, and again the needy kept coming to receive a love-feast.

One day the brother happened to go in and see that there was no bread left. And a poor man came, asking for the love-feast. So the old man said to the brother: "Give him some bread." And he said: "There is none left, father." And the old man said: "Go in, and look for some." The brother went in, and saw the bin full of loaves. He was afraid at the sight, and took some and gave to the poor man. And he recognized the faith and goodness of the old man, and glorified God.

PART XIV

Of obedience

1. Abba Arsenius, of blessed memory, once said to Abba Alexander: "When you have finished your palm-leaves, come and have supper with me. But if pilgrims come, eat with them."

Abba Alexander worked away gently and unhurriedly. And at supper-time he had not finished his palm-leaves. Wanting to obey the old man's order, he went on, hungry, until he had finished the palm-leaves. Abba Arsenius saw that he was late, and had his own supper: for he thought that perhaps pilgrims had come, and he was eating with them. Abba Alexander finished his task, and in the evening came to Abba Arsenius. And Abba Arsenius said to him: "Did pilgrims visit you?" And he said: "No." And Abba Arsenius said: "Then why did you not come?" And he answered: "Because you told me, come when your palm-leaves are finished. I kept your word in mind, and did not come, and have only just now finished the work." And the old man admired the exactness of his obedience, and said to him: "You should lay aside your work sooner, so as to make your psalmody, and fetch water for yourself: otherwise your body will soon grow weak."

2. Abba Abraham came to Abba Ares; and while they were sitting together, a brother came and said to Abba Ares: "Tell me, what must I do to be saved?" And the old man said: "Go away, eat bread and salt every evening for a whole year: and come back, and I will talk to you." So the brother went away and did so, and at the end of a year came again to Abba Ares. By chance Abba Abraham was again with him. This time Abba Ares said to the brother: "Go away, fast for a year, and eat every second day."

When he had gone, Abba Abraham said to Abba Ares: "Why, when you put a light yoke on all the brothers, have you laid such a grievous burden on this brother?" And the old man said to him: "Other brothers come to ask questions and go away as they came. But this brother comes to hear a word for God's sake, and he is a mighty labourer of God who takes the greatest trouble to do whatever I tell him. That is why I speak to him the word of God."

3. They told this story of Abba John the Short. He went to an old man from the Thebaid, who was living in the desert of Scete. His abba once took a dead stick and planted it, and told him: "Pour a jug of water over its base every day until it bears fruit." Water was so far from their cell that he went away to fetch it every evening and did not return until dawn. At the end of three years the stick turned green, and bore fruit. The old man picked some of the fruit and took it to church, and said to the brothers: "Take and eat the fruit of obedience." [56]

4. They said of Abba John, the disciple of Abba Paul, that he was a man who possessed the virtue of obedience in great measure. There was a tomb, in which lived a dangerous lioness. The old man saw the dung of the lioness lying round, and said to Abba John: "Go fetch that dung." And Abba John said to him: "And what am I to do, Abba, about the lioness?" The old man smiled and said: "If she comes at you, tie her up and bring her here."

So the brother went there in the evening, and the lioness rushed out at him. He obeyed the old man's word, and ran at her to catch her. The lioness turned and fled: Abba John chased her, shouting: "Wait! My abba told me to tie you up." And he caught her and tied her up.

The old man sat a long time waiting for him, and was greatly troubled in his mind because he was late. But at last he came, and brought the lioness with him, tied. The old man marvelled at the sight. But wanting to humble him, he beat him and said: "You fool, have you brought me a silly dog?" And the old man immediately untied her, and drove her away.

5. They said that Abba Silvanus had a disciple in Scete named Mark, who possessed in great measure the virtue of obedience. He was a copyist of old manuscripts: and the old man loved him for his obedience. He had eleven other disciples, and they were aggrieved that he loved Mark more than them. When the nearby old men heard that he loved Mark above the others, they took it ill. One day they visited him. Abba Silvanus took them with him, and went out of his cell, and began to knock on the door of each of his disciples, saying: "Brothers, come out, I have work for you." And not one of them appeared immediately. Then he came to Mark's cell, and knocked, saying: "Mark." And as soon as Mark heard the voice of the

---

[56] The same story is to be found in Cassian, *Institutes*, IV, 24 and Sulpicius Severus, *Dialogues*, 1, 19. Each tradition of the story appears to be independent of the others.

old man, he came outside; and the old man sent him on some errand.

So Abba Silvanus said to the old men: "Where are the other brothers?" And he went into Mark's cell, and found a book which he had just begun to write, and he was making the letter O. And when he heard the old man's voice, he had not finished the line of the O. And the old men said: "Truly, Abba, we also love the one whom you love; for God too loves him." [57]

6. Once the mother of Mark, with many attendants, came to see him. She said to the old man, when he went out to receive her: "Abba, tell my son to come out to me, so that I can see him." The old man went into Mark's cell, and said to him: "Go out, so that your mother can see you." Mark was clad in a torn piece of sackcloth patched with rags, and his head and face were sooty from smoke of the cooking fire. He came out obediently, but closed his eyes, and so greeted his mother and her attendants, saying: "I hope you are well." And none of them, not even his mother, knew who he was. Again she sent a message to the old man, saying: "Abba, send me my son, so that I may see him." And he said to Mark: "Did I not tell you to go out so that your mother could see you?" And Mark said to him: "I went out as you said, Father. But I beg you, do not give me that order again, for I am afraid of seeming disobedient to you." The old man went out and said to his mother: "Your son is the man who came out and greeted you with 'I hope you are in good health.' " And he comforted her, and sent her on her way.

7. Four monks once came from Scete to Abba Pambo, clothed in tunics of skin. And each described the goodness of one of the others, though not in his presence. One of them fasted much, one of them owned nothing, the third was a man of great charity; and they said of the fourth that he had lived in obedience to the elders for twenty-two years.

Abba Pambo answered: "I tell you, this last is a greater virtue than the others. Each of you others has to use his own will to keep his virtue. But he eradicates his self-will and makes himself the servant of another's will. Men like that, if they persevere till death, are confessors."

8. There once came to Abba Sisois of the Thebaid a man who wanted to become a monk. And the old man asked him: "Have you any ties in the world?" And he said: "I have a son." And the old man said to him: "Go and throw him in the river, and

[57] Cassian knew the story: cf. *Institutes*, IV, 12: and *Rule of St Benedict*, 5.

then you would be a monk." He went away to throw his boy into the river. But the old man sent a monk to stop him. He was already holding his son, ready to throw him in, when the brother said: "Stop! What are you doing?" And he said: "The Abba told me to throw him in." And the brother said: "Now the Abba says, do not throw him in." So he left his son, and came to the old man, and became a monk of high worth, tested through obedience.[58]

9. Saint Syncletice said: "I reckon that for coenobites obedience is a higher virtue than continence, however perfect. Continence carries pride with it, obedience has the promise of due humility."

10. She also said: "We ought to rule our souls with discretion: and to remain in the community, not following our own will, nor seeking our own good. We are like exiles: we have been separated from the things of the world and have given ourselves in faith to the one Father. We need nothing of what we have left behind. There we had reputation and plenty to eat: here we have little to eat and little of everything else."

11. Abba Hyperichius said: "The monk's service is obedience. He who possesses it shall have his prayers answered, and shall stand by the Crucified in confident faith. For that was how the Lord went to his cross, being made obedient even unto death."

12. The old men said: "If a man trusts another man, and makes himself his servant, he ought not to think about God's commandments, but give himself completely to obey the will of his spiritual father. If he obeys him in everything, he will not sin against God."

13. The old men used to say: "God demands this of Christians: to obey the inspired Scriptures, which contain the pattern of what they must say and do, and assent to the teaching of the orthodox bishops and fathers."

14. A brother from Scete was going to harvest: and he turned to a great old man and said: "Tell me, Abba, what am I to do, for I go to harvest?" The old man said to him: "If I tell you, will you do as I say?" The brother answered: "Yes; I will obey you." The old man said: "If you do what I say, you will rise, and give up your harvesting: and come here, and I will tell you what to do."

So the brother abandoned his harvesting, and came to the

---

[58] Cassian knew a different version of the same story: *Institutes*, IV, 27. It was a common piece of desert homiletic.

old man. The old man said: "Go into your cell, and stay there fifty days without a break. Eat bread and salt once a day. At the end I will tell you what to do next." And he did so, and at the end came back to the old man. The old man knew him for an earnest person, and told him what sort of a person he ought to be in his cell. And the brother went down to his cell, and for three days and nights he lay prone upon the ground, in penitence before God. Then the thought came into his mind: "You are exalted, you are a great man," and so he took control of his thoughts, and in humility called his sins to mind, saying: "And where are all the sins I have done?" And if the thought rose in his mind that he had much neglected the commandments of God, he said to himself: "I will offer God a little service, and I believe that he will have mercy upon me." So he conquered the spirits which sent wicked thoughts: and the spirits appeared before him in a visible form, and said: "You are troubling us." He said to them: "Why?" They said: "If we exalt you, you are quick to be humble: if we humble you, you lift yourself on high."

15. The old men used to say: "From those who have not long been converted to the life of a monk, God demands no virtue so much as earnest obedience."

16. An old hermit had a servant, who himself lived on a nearby estate. Once it happened that because the servant did not come, the hermit had not what he needed, neither food to eat nor materials to work. He was troubled at having neither means of work nor means of keeping alive, and said to his disciple: "Do you want to go to the estate, and call here the servant who usually brings what we need?" And he answered: "I will do as you say." But the old man would not yet give him an order to go, for he did not dare to send the monk. After they had suffered for a long time because the servant did not come, the old man again said to his disciple: "Do you want to go to the estate, and bring him here?" And he answered: "I will do what you want." The disciple was afraid that if he went down to the estate, he would cause scandal: but so as not to be disobedient to his father, he consented to go. The old man said: "Go, and believe in the God of your fathers, who will protect you in every temptation": and he prayed, and sent him on his way.

The monk came to the estate, and enquired where the servant lived, and found his house. The servant happened to be away from the estate with all his family except a daughter.

When the monk knocked, the daughter opened the door. And when he asked her where her father was, she urged him to come into the house, and indeed tried to pull him inside. He at first refused to go in, but in the end she pressed him and succeeded in persuading him in. Then she flung herself about him and tried to seduce him to lie with her. He felt lust rising in him, and his mind in a turmoil; and he groaned and called out to God: "Lord, for the prayers of my father, give me liberty now." As soon as he said it, he found himself by the river on the path to the hermitage, and so was restored, unharmed, to his abba.

17. Two men, who were brothers (in the worldly sense) came to live in a monastery. One possessed the virtue of self-control, the other the virtue of obedience, each to a remarkable degree. If the abba said to the second, Do this, he did it: if he said, Sup at dawn, he supped at dawn. And so he gained a reputation in the monastery for his obedient conduct. But the other brother was pricked by the needle of envy against him, and said to himself: "I will test whether he is so obedient." He went to the father of the monastery, and told him: "Send my brother away with me, and we will go somewhere else." The abba sent them on their way.

And the ascetic brother wanted to tempt the obedient brother. They came to a river infested by crocodiles. And he said to him: "Walk down into the river, and cross." He immediately walked into the river and the crocodiles swam to him, and licked his body, but did not hurt him. And when his brother saw what happened, he said: "Come out of the river."

On their journey they found a corpse lying by the wayside. And the ascetic said to his brother: "If we had an old coat, we could put it over the corpse." And he answered: "We had better pray: perhaps he will live again." And when they had stood in earnest prayer, the dead man stood up. The ascetic brother was proud, and said: "This dead man has been raised because I am so self-controlled."

But God revealed what had happened to the abba of the monastery, how he had tempted his brother, how the crocodiles had not hurt him, and how the dead had been raised. And when they came back to the monastery, the abba said to the ascetic: "Why did you do this to your brother? The dead man was raised because he is so obedient."

18. A man of worldly life, who had three sons, renounced the world: and leaving his sons in the city, came to a monastery.

After three years in the monastery, he began to be much troubled in his mind by memories of the three sons, and was very grieved for their sakes: he had not told his abba of their existence. The abba, seeing him to be grieving, said: "Why are you sad?" He told him that he had three sons in the city, and he wanted to bring them to the monastery. The abba told him to bring them.

When he arrived at the city, he found that two of them were already dead, and only one survived. He took him back to the monastery, and looked for the abba but could not find him. He asked the brothers where was the abba, and was told that he had gone to the bakery. He took his child in his arms and went to the bakery. The abba saw him coming, and greeted him. And he took the child, and hugged and kissed him. Then he said to the father: "Do you love him?" He said: "Yes." And he said: "Do you love him with all your heart?" He answered: "Yes." At these words the abba said: "Then, if you love him, pick him up and throw him into the oven, throw him now while it is red-hot." And the father took his son, and threw him into the red-hot oven. And in that moment the oven was transformed and became as cool as the dew. So the father received glory for an act like that of the patriarch Abraham.

19. An old man said: "A brother who entrusts his soul in obedience to a spiritual father has a greater reward than the brother who retires alone to his hermitage." And he said: "One of the fathers saw a vision of four ranks in heaven. The first rank was of men who are sick, yet are grateful to God. The second rank was of men who minister to them with willingness and generosity. The third rank was of men who live in the desert and see no one. The fourth rank was of men who for God's sake put themselves under obedience to spiritual fathers. But the rank of the obedient men had a golden necklace and a crown, and shone more than the others. And I said to the being who showed me the vision: 'How is it that the rank, which is least, shines the most?' And he answered: 'Hospitable men do what they themselves want. Hermits have followed their own will in withdrawing from the world. But the obedient have cast away their self-will, and depend on God and the word of their spiritual father: that is why they shine the most.'

So, my sons, obedience is good, if it is for God's sake. Strive to win at least some trace of this virtue. It is the salvation of the faithful, the mother of virtue, the opening of the kingdom of heaven, the raising of men from heaven to earth. Obedience lives in the house of the angels, is the food of all the saints, who turn to it at their weaning and by its nourishment grow to a perfect life."

Part XV

Of humility

1. Abba Antony was baffled as he meditated upon the depths of God's judgements, and prayed thus: "Lord, how is it that some die young and others grow old and infirm? Why are there some poor and some wealthy? And why are the rich unrighteous and grind the faces of the righteous poor?"

And a voice came to him: "Antony, look to yourself: these are the judgements of God, and it is not good for you to know them."

2. Abba Antony said to Abba Poemen: "Man's great work is to lay his guilt upon himself before God, and to expect to be tempted to the end of his life."

3. Abba Antony also said: "I saw all the devil's traps set upon the earth, and I groaned and said: 'Who do you think can pass through them?' And I heard a voice saying: 'Humility.'"

4. Once some old men came to Abba Antony, and Abba Joseph was with them. Abba Antony, wanting to test them, began to speak about holy Scripture. And he began to ask the younger monks the meaning of text after text, and each of them replied as he was able. And to each the old man said: "You have not yet found it." Then he said to Abba Joseph: "What do you say is the meaning of this word?" He answered: "I do not know." And Abba Antony said: "Truly Abba Joseph alone has found the true way, for he answered that he does not know."

5. Some demons were once standing near Abba Arsenius in his cell, and were troubling him. Then some brothers came, who usually ministered to him. And as they stood outside the cell, they heard him crying aloud to the Lord: "Lord, do not leave me, though I have done nothing good in thy sight. Grant me, Lord, according to thy loving-kindness, at least the very beginning of a good life."

6. They said of Abba Arsenius, that while he was in the Emperor's palace he was the best dressed person there: and while he was leading the religious life, no one was clothed in worse rags.

7. Abba Arsenius was once asking an old Egyptian for advice

about his temptations. And another, who saw this, said: "Abba Arsenius, how is it that you, who are so learned in the Greek and Latin languages, come to be asking that uneducated countryman about your temptations?" He answered: "I have acquired the world's knowledge of Greek and Latin: but I have not yet been able to learn the alphabet of this uneducated man."

8. The old men said that they once gave the brothers in Scete a few figs: but because they had so few, they did not give any to Abba Arsenius, for fear he should be offended. When he heard of this, he did not go out as usual to the divine office with the brothers, and said: "You have excommunicated me, by not giving me the blest food which the Lord sent to the brothers, because I was not worthy to receive it." And they were edified at his humility, and the priest went and took him some of the figs, and brought him back to the congregation happy.

9. They used to say that no one could fathom the depth of his religious life. Once when he was living in Lower Egypt, and suffering from importunate visitors, he decided to leave his cell. He took nothing with him, and said to his disciples Alexander and Zoilus: "Alexander, you board a ship, and you, Zoilus, come with me to the Nile and find for me a little boat that is sailing to Alexandria, and then sail to join your brother." Zoilus was troubled at this, but said nothing, and so they parted.

The old man went down to the country near Alexandria, and there fell gravely ill. But his disciples said to each other: "Do you think one of us has grieved him, and that is why he has separated from us?" They examined themselves, but could not find that they had been ungrateful to him, or that they had ever disobeyed him. When the old man had recovered from his illness, he said to himself: "I will go to my fathers." And so he came to the place called Petra, where were Alexander and Zoilus his servants. While he was by the river-bank, he met an Ethiopian girl, who came up and touched his cloak. The old man rebuked her. But she said: "If you are a monk, go to the mountain."

The old man was stricken in heart at these words, and said to himself: "Arsenius, if you are a monk, go to the mountain." And on the way his disciples Alexander and Zoilus met him, and fell at his feet. And the old man too threw himself on the ground, and they all wept. Then the old man said: "Did you not hear that I fell ill?" They said to him: "Yes, we heard." And he said: "Then why did you not come to see me?" And Alexander said: "We were aggrieved at your parting from us. For many people were vexed at it, and said: 'Unless they had disobeyed the old man, he would surely not have left them.' " And the old man said to them: "Yes, I knew this would be said. But men shall say again: 'The dove found no rest for his feet, and so returned to Noah in the ark.' "

The minds of his disciples were healed by the saying, and they stayed with him to the end of his life. But when he lay dying, they were much distressed. And he said to them: "The hour is not yet come. But I will tell you when it comes. You will be judged with me before the judgement seat of Christ, if you let anyone touch my dead body." And they said: "What then shall we do? We do not know how to clothe or bury a dead body." And the old man said: "Surely you know how to tie a rope to my leg and pull me up the mountain?"

When he was soon to commit his soul to God, they saw him weeping, and said: "Truly, Father, are you afraid, even you, of death?" And he said: "Truly. The fear which possesses me now has been with me since I became a monk: and I am very afraid." So he slept in peace.

Arsenius always used to say this: "Why, you words, did I let you go out? I have often been penitent that I spoke, never that I kept silent."

When Abba Poemen heard that Arsenius had departed this life, he wept, and said: "You are blessed, Abba Arsenius; for you wept for yourself in this world; and he who does not weep for himself in this world, shall lament for ever in the next. We cannot escape lamentation: if we do not lament here of our own will, we shall later be forced to lament against our will."

10. Abba Daniel said of Abba Arsenius that he never wanted to discuss any question about the Scripture, though he was wonderful at expounding it when he wanted: and that he was very slow to write anyone a letter. When from time to time he came to the meeting in church, he sat behind a pillar so that none should see his face and he himself should be undistracted. And like Jacob, he looked like an angel, having white hair, a man lovely to look upon, yet somehow dried up. He had a long beard which reached down to his waist: his eyes were dim with constant weeping: and although he was tall, his body was bent, for he died at the age of ninety-five. He lived for forty years in the palace of the Emperor Theodosius the Great of holy memory, the father of Arcadius and Honorius: then he lived forty years in Scete, ten years in the place called Trohe, above

Babylon, near the city of Memphis, and three years in Canopus near Alexandria. Then he returned to Trohe for two more years, and there ended his life in peace and the fear of God. He was "a good man, full of the Holy Spirit and of faith." [59]

11. Abba John told this story. Abba Anub and Abba Poemen and the others, who were born of the same mother, were monks in Scete. And some savage Mazicae came and sacked Scete. The monks went away, and came to a place called Terenuthis, while they discussed where to live, and stayed a few days there in an old temple. Abba Anub said to Abba Poemen: "Of your charity, let me live apart from you and your brothers, and we shall not see each other for a week." And Abba Poemen said: "Let us do as you wish": and they did so.

In the temple stood a stone statue. And every day at dawn Abba Anub rose and pelted the face of the statue with stones: and every day at evening he said: "Forgive me." Every day for a week he did this: and on Saturday they met again. And Abba Poemen said to Abba Anub: "I saw you, Abba, throwing stones at the face of the statue every day this week, and later doing penance to the statue. A true Christian would not have done that." And the old man answered: "For your sakes I did it. When you saw me throwing stones at the statue's face, did it speak? Was it angry?"

And Abba Poemen said: "No."

And he said: "When I did penance before the statue, was it troubled in heart? Did it say: 'I do not forgive you?'" And Abba Poemen answered: "No."

And he said: "Here we are, seven brothers. If we want to stay together, we must become like this statue, which is untroubled by the injuries I have done it. If you will not become like this statue, see, there are four doors to this temple, and each of us may go in the direction he chooses."

At these words they fell upon the ground before Abba Anub, and said to him: "As you say, Father. We will do what you tell us." And afterwards Abba Poemen described what happened. "We remained together all our lives, doing our work and everything else as the old man directed us. He appointed one of us as a steward, and we ate whatever he put before us; no one could have said: 'Bring something else to eat,' or 'I will not eat that.' And so we passed our lives in quiet and peace."

12. They said of Abba Ammon that some people asked him to arbitrate in their quarrel. But the old man took no notice

[59] Acts 11:24.

of them. And one woman said to another woman standing next to her: "That old man is a fool." And the old man heard what she said; and he called her, and said: "Can you imagine what travail I have endured in different deserts in the effort to acquire this folly? And you are making me lose it all today."

13. There was a bishop of the city of Oxyrhynchus named Affy. They said that while he was a monk, he treated his body very severely. And when he became a bishop, he wanted to continue in his city the austerities which he had practised in the desert, but he could not. So he fell prostrate before God, and said: "Dost thou think, my Lord, that thy grace has left me because I have become a bishop?" And it was revealed to him: "No: in the desert you had no man to help you, and God alone sustained you. But now you are in the world, and have men to help you."

14. Abba Daniel said that in Babylon there was a nobleman's daughter, who had a devil. Her father sought out a monk. And the monk said to him: "No one can cure your daughter except some hermits I know: and if you go to them, they will refuse to do it from motives of humility. Let us do this: when they come, bringing their produce for sale, tell them that you want to buy what they have. And when they come into the house to receive the money, we will ask them to pray, and I believe that your daughter will be healed."

So they went into the street, and found a disciple of the old men, who was sitting there to sell his baskets. They took him back with them to the house, as if to receive the money for his wares. And when the monk had come into the house, the girl, who was troubled with the demon, went up to him and slapped him. And he followed the Lord's commandment, and turned her the other cheek. The demon was forced out, and began to cry: "Violence! The commandment of Jesus Christ is driving me out": and so the girl was in that moment healed. When they came to the old men, they told them what had happened, and glorified God, saying: "The pride of devils cannot but fall before the humble obedience to the commandments of Jesus Christ."

15. Abba Evagrius said: "The beginning of salvation is, to contradict yourself."

16. Abba Serapion said: "I have afflicted my body far more than my son Zacharias, and I cannot equal his humility or his silence."

17. Abba Moses said to the brother Zacharias: "Tell me what to do." And at the words, Zacharias threw himself at his

feet, saying: "Why ask me, Father?" The old man said: "Believe me, my son Zacharias, I saw the Holy Spirit coming upon you, and so I cannot but ask you." Then Zacharias took his cowl from his head, and put it beneath his feet and stamped on it, and said: "Unless a man stamps upon himself like that, he cannot be a monk."

18. Abba Poemen said: "Abba Moses asked the monk Zacharias, who was dying: 'What can you see?' And he said: 'Nothing better than being silent, Father.' And Abba Moses said: 'Truth, my son: keep silent.'"

At the moment of his death Abba Isidore looked up to heaven, and said: "Rejoice, my son Zacharias: for the gates of the kingdom of heaven are opened to you."

19. Theophilus of holy memory, the bishop of Alexandria, once went to the mount of Nitria, and an abba of Nitria came to him. The bishop said: "What have you found upon your way, Father?" And the old man answered: "To blame myself unceasingly." And the bishop said: "This is the only way to follow."

20. When Abba Theodore was supping with the brothers, they received the cups with silent reverence, and did not follow the usual custom of receiving the cup with a "Pardon me." And Abba Theodore said: "The monks have lost their manners and do not say 'Pardon me.'"

21. They said of this Abba Theodore, that after he was ordained deacon in Scete, he refused to minister in services, but escaped to various places to avoid having to do so. And the old men brought him back, and said: "Do not desert your ministry." Abba Theodore said to them: "Let me go, and I will pray to God. If he shows me that I ought to act as a minister, I will do so." And he prayed to God thus: "Show me, Lord, if it be thy will that I minister as a deacon." And there appeared a pillar of fire from earth to heaven, and a voice was heard saying: "If you can become like this pillar, go, and exercise your ministry." When he heard this, he determined never to exercise his ministry. And when he came back to the church, they did penance before him, and said: "If you do not want to take part in the service, at least hold the chalice." But he refused, saying: "If you do not let me go, I will leave this place altogether." And so they left him.

22. Abba John the Short said: "The gateway to God is humility. Our fathers endured much suffering and so entered the city of God with joy."

He also said: "Humility and the fear of God surpass all the other virtues."

23. Abba John of the Thebaid said: "The monk ought above all to be humble. For this is the Saviour's first commandment: 'Blessed are the poor in spirit, for theirs is the Kingdom of heaven.' " [60]

24. The brothers in Scete were once assembled, and began to discuss Melchizedek the priest. But they forgot to call for Abba Copres. Later, they summoned him and asked him what he thought upon the question. He struck his mouth three times and said: "Woe upon you, Copres. You have left undone what God commanded you to do, and you have dared to enquire into things which he did not ask of you." At these words the brothers fled, each to his own cell.

25. Abba Macarius once said of himself: "When I was a young man, and was staying in my cell in Egypt, they caught me, and made me a cleric at a village. And because I did not want to minister, I fled to another place. And a man of the world, but of a devout life, came to me, and took what I made with my hands and ministered to my needs.

It happened that a girl of the village was tempted by the devil and seduced. And when she was seen to be pregnant, she was asked who was the father of the child: and she said: 'It was this hermit, who slept with me.' They came out, arrested me, and brought me back to the village: and they hung dirty pots and jug handles on my neck, and made me walk round the village, beating me as I went, and saying: 'This monk has seduced our girl. Away with him, away with him.' And they beat me until I was almost dead: but one of the old men came and said: 'How long have you been beating that stranger monk?' The man who used to minister to my needs followed behind, ashamed: and they heaped insults on him, saying: 'You bore witness to this hermit, and look what he has done.'

The parents of the girl said that they would not let me go unless I found someone to guarantee her support. I spoke to the man who used to minister to me and asked him to be my guarantor, and he gave a pledge on my behalf. I went back to my cell, and I gave him all the baskets I had, and said: 'Sell them, and give my woman some food.' Then I said to myself: 'Macarius, you have found a woman for yourself; you need to work much harder to support her.' So I worked night and day, and passed her the money which I made.

[60] Matt. 5:3.

When it was time that the unfortunate girl should bear a child, she spent many days in travail, and still did not bring forth the baby. They said to her: 'What's the matter?' She said: 'I know why I am in agony so long.' Her parents asked her why. She said: 'I accused that monk falsely, for he had nothing to do with it: the father is a young man named N.'

The man who ministered to me heard this, and came to me with joy saying: 'The girl could not bear her child, until she confessed that you had nothing to do with it and that she told lies against you. And look—all the villagers want to come to your cell and glorify God, and do penance to you.' When I heard this, I did not want the men to trouble me, so I rose and fled here to Scete: and this was the reason why I began to live here."

26. Abba Macarius was once returning to his cell from the marsh carrying palm-leaves. And the devil met him by the way, with a sickle, and wanted to run him through with the sickle, but could not. The devil said: "Macarius, I suffer much violence from you, for I cannot overcome you. For whatever you do, I do also. If you fast, I eat nothing: if you keep watch, I get no sleep. But it is only one quality in you which overcomes me." And Abba Macarius said to him: "What is that?" The devil answered: "Your humility—that is why I cannot prevail against you."

27. Abba Mathois once went from Raythu to the country of Gebalon, and his brother was with him. And the bishop of Gebalon came to him, and ordained him priest. And at supper the bishop said: "Forgive me, Abba. I know that you did not want to be ordained: but I dared to do it, so that you would give me your blessing." The old man said humbly: "My soul did not much want ordination, it is true. But I am grieved by the fact that I must be divided from my brother who is with me: and by myself I cannot offer all the prayers which together we offer." The bishop said: "If you know that he is a worthy person, I will ordain him too." Abba Mathois said: "Whether he is worthy I do not know: but one thing I do know, that he is better than I am."

So the bishop ordained his brother too: and neither of them, when he died, had offered the sacrifice at the altar. The old man said: "I trust God, that perhaps he will not judge me hardly for my ordination, provided I do not dare to consecrate the offering. For that is the duty of men who live innocently."

28. Abba Mathois said: "The nearer a man comes to God,

the more he sees himself to be a sinner. Isaiah the prophet saw the Lord, and knew himself to be wretched and unclean." [61]

29. They said of Abba Moses that when he was ordained a cleric, they put the pall on his shoulders. And the archbishop said to him: "See, you are clothed in white and ready for your ordination, Abba Moses." He answered: "White outside, Lord Pope, or white inside, do you think?"

The archbishop, wishing to test him, said to the clergy: "When Abba Moses comes to the altar, turn him away: but follow him and listen to what he says." They began to drive him from the church, saying: "Get out, Ethiopian." As he went out, he said: "You thing of dust and ashes, they have done you a good turn. You are not a man, how dare you remain in the company of men?"

30. While Abba Poemen was in a community, he heard of Abba Nesteros and wanted to see him. So he sent a message to his abba to ask him to let Nesteros come to him. But the abba did not wish it, and refused. A few days afterwards the steward of the monastery asked the abba to let him go to Abba Poemen, so that he could tell him his thoughts. His abba, when he was giving him leave, said to him: "Take with you the brother Nesteros whom the old man asked me to send him. I did not dare to let him go alone, and have put off sending him until now." When the steward reached the old man, he talked to him about his thoughts, and the old man healed his mind by his answer. Then the old man turned to the brother and said: "Abba Nesteros, how have you won this virtue, that if there is trouble within the monastery, you do not speak, and remain serene?" The brother had to be pressed by the old man for an answer. In the end he said: "Forgive me, Abba. When I first entered the community, I said to my soul, You and the donkey must be alike. The donkey says nothing when he is beaten. That is what you must do: as you read in the Psalm: 'I am become as a beast before thee: and I am always with thee.' " [62]

31. They told this story of Abba Olympius in Scete. He was a slave, and each year went down to Alexandria carrying what he had earned for his masters. They met him, and greeted him. The old man put water in a basin and brought it to wash his masters' feet. But they said to him: "No, Father, please do not put a burden on us." He answered: "I confess that I am your slave: and I am grateful that you have let me go free to serve

[61] Isa. 6.   [62] Ps. 73:21-2.

God. Yet I wash your feet, and here is what I have earned."
But they refused to accept it. And he said: "Believe me, if you
will not accept my earnings, I shall stay here and be your
servant." But they revered him, and gave him leave to do what
he wanted. And they brought him back to the desert with
honour, and gave him what he needed to make a love-feast on
their behalf; and henceforward was renowned in Scete.

32. Abba Poemen said: "A man ought ever to be absorbing
humility and the fear of God, as the nostrils breathe air in and
out."

33. A brother asked Abba Poemen: "How ought I to behave,
in my cell in the place where I live?" The old man answered:
"Be as prudent as a stranger; and wherever you are, do not
expect your words to be powerful in your presence, and you
will find peace."

34. He also said: "The tools of the soul are these: to cast
oneself down in God's sight; not to lift oneself up; and to put
one's self-will behind one."

35. He also said: "Do not put a value on yourself, but cleave
to the man who is living a good life."

36. He also said: "A brother asked Abba Alonius: 'What is
lowliness?" And the old man said: 'To be lower than brute
beasts; and to know that they are not condemned.' "

37. He also said: "Humility is the ground whereon the Lord
ordered the sacrifice to be offered."

38. He also said: "If a man keeps his own place, he shall not
be troubled."

39. He also said: "Once when the old men were sitting down
to supper, Abba Alonius stood and waited on them: and when
they saw it, they praised him. But he said not a word. So one
of them whispered to him: "Why do you not answer when the
old men praise you?" And Abba Alonius said: "If I answer
them, I shall find pleasure in being praised."

40. Abba Joseph told this story. "Once when we were sitting
with Abba Poemen, he talked of 'Abba' Agatho. We said to
him: 'He is a young man, why do you call him Abba?' And
Abba Poemen said: 'His speech is such that we must call him
Abba.' "

41. They said of Abba Poemen, that he never wanted to cap
the saying of another old man, but always praised what had
been said.

42. Once Theophilus of holy memory, the archbishop of
Alexandria, came to Scete. The brothers assembled there said

to Abba Pambo: "Say a word to the Pope, that his soul may be edified here." And the old man answered: "If my silence does not edify him, my speech certainly will not."

43. A brother named Pystus told this story. "Seven of us, hermits, went to Abba Sisois, who was living in the island of Clysmatus. And when we asked him to give us a word, he answered: 'Forgive me, I am an ignoramus. But I once went to Abba Hor and Abba Athrem: Abba Hor had been ill for eighteen years. And I began to beg them to speak a word to me. And Abba Hor said: "What have I to say to you? Go and do whatever you think right. God is the God of the man who extracts from himself more than he can do, and carries all by violence."

These men, Abba Hor and Abba Athrem, were not of the same province. But there was much grace between them, until they died. Abba Athrem was a man of perfect obedience, Abba Hor of great humility. I spent a few days with them, observing their virtues; and I saw Abba Athrem do a wonderful thing. Someone brought them a little fish, and Abba Athrem wanted to prepare it for his elder, Abba Hor. So Abba Athrem took a knife and cut into the fish: but at that moment Abba Hor called him: "Athrem, Athrem." And he left the knife in the middle of the fish and did not finish the cut but ran to Abba Hor. I was astonished at his obedience, and that he did not say: "Wait until I have cut the fish." So I said to Abba Athrem: "Where did you find this obedience?" And he answered me: "It is not mine: it is that old man's." And he took me and said: "Come and see his obedience." He cooked a piece of fish badly, intentionally so, and put it in front of the old man. Abba Hor ate it without saying a word. Abba Athrem said: "Is it good, Abba?" He answered: "Very good." Then he brought him another piece, very well cooked, and said: "See, I have ruined it, Abba, by cooking it badly." Abba Hor answered: "Yes, you have cooked it rather badly." And Abba Athrem turned to me and said: "Did you see his obedience?" And I left them: and have tried, as far as I could, to practise what I saw.'

All this was told the brothers by Abba Sisois. One of us asked him: 'Of your charity, speak us a word.' And he said: 'The man who has limitless knowledge understands the Scriptures perfectly.'

Another of us asked him: 'What is pilgrimage, Father?' He answered: 'Keep silent: and wherever you go, say "I am at peace with all men": that is pilgrimage.'"

44. A brother once came to Abba Sisois on the mountain of Abba Antony. And in their talk he said to Abba Sisois: "Have you not yet attained the stature of Abba Antony, Father?" And the old man answered: "If I had a single thought like Abba Antony, I should quite leap toward heaven like a flame. But I know myself to be a man who can only with an effort bear his thoughts."

45. The same brother asked him: "Do you think Satan persecuted the men of old as he persecutes us?" And Abba Sisois said: "More: for now his doom has drawn nearer, and he is troubled."

46. Some others came to hear a word from Abba Sisois. And he said nothing to them, but kept repeating: "Forgive me." They saw his baskets, and said to his disciple, Abraham: "What are you doing with those baskets?" And he answered: "We sell them now and then." The old man heard, and said: "And so Sisois eats now and then." They were very edified at his humility, and went away happy.

47. A brother asked Abba Sisois: "I observe my own mind, and I see that it is recollected and intent upon God." And the old man said to him: "This is no great thing that your mind should be with God. The great thing is to see yourself to be lower than every created being. Bodily toil will put it right, and lead you on the way to humility."

48. Syncletice of blessed memory said: "As a ship cannot be built without nails, a man cannot be saved without humility."

49. Abba Hyperichius said: "The tree of life is lofty, and humility climbs it."

50. He also said: "Imitate the publican, to prevent yourself being condemned with the Pharisee. Follow the gentleness of Moses, and hollow out the rocky places of your heart, so that you turn them into springs of water."

51. Abba Orsisius said: [63] "If you put a piece of unbaked tiling in a building with a river nearby, it does not last a day. If it is baked, it is as good as stone. So it is with the man with worldly wisdom, who is not proved by the word of God, as Joseph was proved at his beginning. To live among men is to be tempted often. It is good that a man should know his weakness, and not pick up too heavy a burden at first. But men of strong faith cannot be moved. Take the life of Saint Joseph and see what grievous temptations he suffered, and

[63] In the Syriac (Wallis Budge, *Paradise*, vol. ii, no. 220) of Arsenius.

in a country where there was no trace of the true worship of God. But the God of his fathers was with him, and kept him safe in every tribulation, and he is now with his fathers in the kingdom of heaven. Let us then own our weakness, and so struggle onward. For it is hard for us to escape the judgement of God."

52. There was an old hermit in the desert who said to himself that he was perfectly virtuous. He prayed God and said: "Show me what makes me perfect, and I will perform it." But God wanted to humble him, and said: "Go to that archimandrite, and do what he tells you." God gave a revelation to the archimandrite, before the hermit came, and said: "A hermit is soon coming to see you. Tell him to take a whip, and go and herd your swine." The old man arrived, knocked at the door, and went in to the archimandrite: they greeted each other, and sat down. The hermit said: "Tell me what I must do to be saved." And the archimandrite said: "Will you do what I tell you?" And he said: "Yes." The archimandrite said: "Take this whip, and go herd the swine."

When those who knew the hermit and his reputation, saw that he had gone to be a swineherd, said: "Do you see that hermit who had won so great a reputation? Look what he is doing. He has gone mad, and is troubled by a demon, and is herding swine." But God looked upon his humility, and saw how he bore these insults with patience, and told him to go back to his cell.

53. A demoniac, frothing terribly at the mouth, struck an old hermit on the jaw, and the old man turned him the other cheek. The humility tortured the demon like flames, and drove him out there and then.

54. An old man said to a brother: "When a proud or vain thought enters you, examine your conscience to see if you are keeping God's commandments; if you love your enemies; if you rejoice in your adversary's triumph, and are grieved at his downfall; if you know yourself to be an unprofitable servant, and a sinner beyond all others. But not even then must you think yourself to have corrected all your faults; knowing that this thought alone in you shall undo all the other good you have done."

55. An old man said to a brother: "Do not measure your heart against your brother, saying that you are more serious or more continent or more understanding than he. But be obedient to the grace of God, in the spirit of poverty, and in

charity unfeigned. The efforts of a man swollen with vanity are futile. It is written, 'Let him that thinketh he standeth take heed lest he fall.' Be in your spirit seasoned with salt—and so dependent upon Christ." [64]

56. An old man said: "He who is praised and honoured above his deserts suffers grievous loss. He who receives no honour at all among men, shall be hereafter glorified."

57. A brother asked an old man: "Is it good to be constant in penitence?" And the old man answered: "We have seen Joshua the son of Nun: it was when he was lying prostrate on his face that God appeared to him." [65]

58. An old man, asked why we are troubled by demons, answered: "Because we throw away our armour—humility, poverty, patience and men's scorn."

59. A brother asked an old man: "If a brother brings me talk from the world, Abba, do you want me to tell him not to bring them to me?" And the old man said: "No." The brother said: "Why?" The old man answered: "Because we cannot stop ourselves doing the same. We should find ourselves doing what we are telling our neighbour not to do." And the brother said: "Then what is best?" And the old man answered: "If we would keep silence, that is enough for our neighbour as well."

60. An old man was asked: "What is humility?" He answered: "If you forgive a brother who has wronged you before he is penitent towards you."

61. An old man said: "In every trial do not blame another, but blame yourself, saying: 'This has happened to me because of my sins.' "

62. An old man said: "I never push myself up and walk above my station; and am untroubled when I am put in a low place. For all the time I try to pray God to strip me of unregenerate man."

63. A brother asked an old man: "What is humility?" And the old man answered: "To do good to them that do ill to you." And the brother said: "Suppose a man cannot attain that standard, what is he to do?" The old man answered: "He is to run away, and choose silence."

64. A brother asked an old man: "What is the work of pilgrimage?" And he said: "I know a monk who was on pilgrimage, and came into a church where a love-feast was being held: and he sat down to eat with the monks. But some

[64] I Cor. 10:12; Col. 4:6.   [65] Josh. 5:14.

of them said: 'Who brought that man in here?' And they said
to him: 'Get out of here.' He rose from the table and went out.
But some of the others were grieved that he had been driven
away and went outside and brought him back. Then someone
asked him: 'How do you think you felt in your heart when you
were driven out and then brought back?' And he said: 'I put
it in my heart that I was no better than a dog, and a dog goes
out when he is chased out and comes back when he is called.' "

65. Some people once came to an old man in the Thebaid,
so that he might cure a demoniac whom they brought with
them. After the old man had been importuned for some time,
he said to the demon: "Go out of God's creature." The demon
answered: "I will go: but I ask you a question; tell me, who are
the goats and who are the sheep?" And the old man said: "The
goats are people like myself: who the sheep are, God alone
knows." And the demon shouted aloud at the words, crying:
"See, I go out because of your humility": and he went out at
that moment.

66. An Egyptian monk was living in the suburbs of Constantinople: [66] and when the Emperor Theodosius II passed
that way he left his train of courtiers and came unattended to
the cell. The monk opened the door to his knock, and at once
recognized him to be the Emperor: but he received him as
though he was one of the imperial guards. After he had come
in, they prayed together and sat down. The Emperor began to
ask him: "How are the fathers in Egypt?" He answered: "They
are all praying for your salvation." The Emperor looked round
the cell to see if he had any food, and saw nothing except a
basket with a little bread, and a flagon of water. The monk
said to him: "Will you take a little supper?" And he put the
bread in front of him, and mixed oil and salt, and gave him
to eat and drink.

The Emperor said to him: "Do you know who I am?" And
he said: "God knows you, who you are." The Emperor said:
"I am the Emperor Theodosius." The monk at once fell down
before him and did humble obeisance. The Emperor said:
"Blessed are you, for you have an untroubled life, without
thought of the world. I tell you truly, I was born an emperor,
and I have never enjoyed bread and water as I have today: I
have supped with real pleasure." And he began to do honour
to the monk.

But the old man went out, and fled back to Egypt.

[66] In *Vitae Patrum*, III, 19, the narrator of this story is Poemen.

67. The old men said: "We are the more humbled when we are tempted: for God, knowing our weakness, protects us. But if we boast of our own strength, he takes away his protection, and we are lost."

68. The devil appeared to a monk in the guise of an angel of light, and said to him: "I am the angel Gabriel, and I have been sent to you." But the monk said: "See whether you were not sent to someone else. I am not worthy that an angel should be sent to me." And the devil vanished.

69. The old men said: "If an angel in truth appears to you, do not accept it as a matter of course, but humble yourself, and say: 'I live in my sin and am not worthy to see an angel.' "

70. They said of another old man, that while he was undergoing temptation in his cell, he saw the demons face to face, and was contemptuous of them. The devil, seeing himself overcome, came and showed himself, saying: "I am Christ." The old man looked at him, and then shut his eyes. The devil said: "I am Christ, so why have you shut your eyes?" The old man answered: "I would not see Christ in this life, but in the next." And the devil vanished at the words.

71. The demons, wanting to seduce an old man, said to him: "Would you like to see Christ?" He said: "A curse be upon you and him of whom you speak. I believe my Christ when he said: 'If anyone says to you, Lo, here is Christ, or Lo, there, do not believe him.' " And they vanished at the words.

72. They said of an old man that he went on fasting for seventy weeks, eating a meal only once a week. He asked of God the meaning of a text of the holy Scriptures and God did not reveal it to him. So he said to himself: "Here I am: I have worked so hard, and profited nothing. I will go to my brother and ask him." Just as he had shut his door on the way out, an angel of the Lord was sent to him; and the angel said: "The seventy weeks of your fast have not brought you near to God: but now you are humbled and going to your brother, I have been sent to show you the meaning of the text." And he explained to him what he had asked, and went away.

73. An old man said: "If anyone, in humility and the fear of God, orders a monk to do something, the very word, thus spoken for God's sake, makes the monk ready, and obedient to the command. But if he gives the command because he wants to give a command, if he sets himself up as an authority and seeks power over the monk, and does not give a command in the fear of God, God sees the secrets of the heart and does not

let the monk obey the command. Everyone can see whether the work is done for God, or whether it is an order of self-will and desire for power. An order from God is given with humility and gentleness. An order given from a desire for power is given with anger and trouble of mind, for it is of the devil."

74. An old man said: "I would rather be defeated and humble than win and be proud."

75. An old man said: "Do not think little of your neighbour for you do not know whether God's Spirit is in you or in him. I tell you that your servant is your neighbour."

76. A brother asked an old man: "If I live with other monks, and see something wrong, do you want me to speak out?" The old man said: "If some are older than you, or your contemporaries, you will have more peace of mind in keeping silent. For you will make yourself at peace in the fact that you are putting yourself below the others." The brother said to him: "What then am I to do, father? For the spirits trouble me." The old man said to him: "If you are suffering about the matter, give a piece of advice, once, with humility. If they do not obey you, leave what you have done in God's sight, and he will comfort you. For this is the way the worshipper of God should lay himself before God, and not follow his self-will. But take care that your anxiety be of God. Yet, as far as I see, it is good to be silent, for here silence is humility."

77. A brother asked an old man: "What is man's way of progress?" The old man answered: "Humility. The more a man bends himself to humility, the more he is lifted up to make progress."

78. An old man said: "If anyone says, Forgive me, and humbles himself, he burns up the demons which tempt him."

79. An old man said: "Even if you have succeeded in the habit of keeping silent, you are not to have it in you as though it was a kind of virtue, but say: 'I am not worthy to speak.'"

80. An old man said: "Unless the miller blindfolded the donkey in the treadmill, it would turn round and eat the corn. And God has mercifully blindfolded us, so that we cannot see the good that we do: for then we should perhaps pat ourselves on the back, and lose our reward. That is why we are left for a time with ill thoughts, so that as we see them, we judge and condemn ourselves. Those very thoughts are the cloth which blindfolds and prevents the piece of goodness from being seen. When a man accuses himself, he does not lose his reward."

81. An old man said: "I would learn rather than teach."

He also said: "Do not teach too early, or you will have less understanding during the rest of your life."

82. An old man was asked: "What is humility?" He answered: "Humility is a great work, and a work of God. The way of humility is to undertake bodily labour, and believe yourself a sinner, and make yourself the servant of all." And a brother said: "What does it mean, to be the servant of all?" The old man answered: "To be the servant of all is not to look out for the sins of others, ever to look out for your own sins, and to pray God without ceasing."

83. A brother asked an old man: "Tell me one thing, that I may keep it and live by it." And the old man said: "If you can suffer injury and endure, this is a great thing, above all virtues."

84. An old man said: "He who bears scorn and injury and loss with patience, can be saved."

85. An old man said: "Do not take much notice of your abba, and do not often go to see him: for you will get confidence from it, and start to want yourself to be a leader."

86. A brother [67] so took upon himself any charge that threatened his community, that he even accused himself of fornication. Some of the monks, who did not know the truth about his life, began to murmur against him, saying: "This man does much ill and no work." The abba, knowing the truth, said to the brothers: "I want rather one mat with humility, than all your mats with pride." And to show by God's judgement the kind of person the monk was, he brought all the things which the monks had made, and the mat made by the monk of whom they were complaining. And he brought a lighted brand, and threw it into the pile of mats. All the mats were burnt except the mat of this monk, which was untouched. The brothers were afraid at the sight, and did penance to him, and thenceforth treated him as a father.

87. An old man was asked how it was that some people said they had seen angels. He answered: "Blessed is he who always sees his own sin."

88. A brother learnt that another brother was aggrieved at him, and went to make satisfaction. But the other did not open the door of his cell. So he went to an old man, and told him the circumstances. And the old man said: "See that you have no reason, which looks like a just reason, in your heart for blaming your brother: as though you would accuse him and justify yourself, and so God would not touch his heart to open the door

[67] *Vitae Patrum*, III, 29, gives him the name of Eulalius.

to you. I tell you this: even if he has sinned against you, keep it in your heart that you have sinned against him: justify your brother rather than yourself: and then God will put it into his heart to make peace with you." And he told him the following story:

"There were two devout men, living in the world: and after talking with each other they went out and became monks. Wanting to equal the precept in the Gospel, but not according to knowledge, they castrated themselves, as if it was for the sake of the kingdom of heaven. The archbishop heard of it and ex-communicated them. They believed that they had done right, and were indignant with the archbishop saying: 'Have we castrated ourselves for the kingdom of heaven, and he ex-communicates us? Let us go and persuade the archbishop of Jerusalem against him.' They went and told everything to the archbishop of Jerusalem. And he said: 'And I excommunicate you too.' Further aggrieved, they went to the archbishop of Antioch, and told him everything: and he excommunicated them likewise. So they said: 'Let us go to see the patriarch at Rome, and he will vindicate us from all these others.' So they went to the Pope of Rome and put before him what the other arch-bishops had done, saying: 'We have come to you, as you are the head of all.' But he also said to them: 'I excommunicate you, and you are put out of the Church.'

Then the excommunicated persons had no further excuse, and said to each other: 'These bishops defer to each other, and reach agreement because they meet in synods. Let us go to that holy man of God, Epiphanius, the bishop in Cyprus, for he is a prophet, and takes no account of anyone's rank.' As they were approaching his city, he received a revelation about them, and sent to meet them, saying: 'Do not enter this city.'

Then they recovered their right minds and said: 'Truly, we are rightly blamed: why then do we seek to justify ourselves? Even supposing the archbishops excommunicated us unjustly, that cannot be true of this prophet, for he has received a revela-tion about us.' And they charged themselves with the great guilt of what they had done. So God, who sees men's hearts, revealed to Epiphanius the bishop that they had made them-selves guilty for the truth's sake. And so, of his own initiative, he sent and brought them back, and comforted them, and received them to communion. He wrote to the archbishop of Alexandria about them, saying: 'Receive back your children, for they have done penance in the truth.'

The old man, who told the story, added: 'This is a man's sanity and his obedience to God's will, that he casts himself before God with confession of his sin.' "

At these words the brother obeyed his word, and went and knocked on the other monk's door. As soon as the other learnt who it was, he spoke penitently, and opened the door at once: they kissed each other with sincerity and perfect peace was established.

89. Two monks, brothers in the flesh, lived together, and the devil wanted to cause division between them. The younger once lit a lamp and put it on the lampstand. The demon playing his trick, upset the lampstand and the elder was angry and beat his younger brother. But the younger was penitent, and said: "Be patient with me, brother, and I will light it again." And suddenly the power of the Lord came and tortured that demon until break of day. So the demon told his chief, a pagan priest, what had happened. And the pagan priest went out and became a monk; and from the start of his religious life he held to humility, saying: "Humility breaks the power of the enemy. I know, for I have heard them saying: 'When we trouble the monks, one of them turns to God and is penitent, and so destroys our power.' "

PART XVI
Of patience

1. The brothers said that Abba Gelasius [68] had a parchment book worth eighteen shillings, containing the whole of the Old and New Testament. The book was put in the church, so that any monk who wished could read it. But a travelling monk came to visit the old man: and when he saw the book, he coveted it, stole it, and went away. The old man, though he knew who the thief was, did not give chase or try to catch him.

The thief went to a city and looked for a buyer. He found a man who wanted it, and began by asking him sixteen shillings for it. The man, who wished to beat him down, said: "First give it to me so that I may show it to someone and get advice, and then I will pay your price." So the monk gave him the book for this purpose. He took the book to Abba Gelasius to discover whether it was a good bargain and worth this high price. He told Abba Gelasius the price that the seller was asking. The old

[68] VP, III, 30 attributes this to Anastasius. In Budge, ii, no. 184 it is anonymous.

man said: "Buy it. It is a good bargain, and worth that price."

So he went back to the seller, but instead of doing what the old man had told him, he said: "Look, I showed this book to Abba Gelasius, and he told me it was too highly priced, and not worth what you said." The thief said: "Did the old man tell you nothing else?" He answered: "Nothing." Then the thief said: "Now I do not want to sell the book."

Stricken in heart, he went to the old man, did penance, and asked him to take the book back. The old man did not want to accept it. Then the monk said: "Unless you take it back, I cannot have peace of mind." And the old man said: "If you cannot have peace of mind unless I take it back, I will take it back."

And the brother remained with the old man until his death, and made progress by learning from his patience.

2. At a meeting of the hermits in Cellia, an Abba Evagrius spoke. And the priest there said: "Abba Evagrius, we know that if you were in your own country, perhaps you would already be a bishop, and ruling over many souls. Here you are like a stranger." Evagrius was stricken in heart at the words: but, serenely and without haste, he bent his head, looked at the ground, wrote in the dust with his finger, and said: "Truly, Fathers, it is so. But, as it is written, I have spoken once: and I will no more answer."[69]

3. The brothers surrounded Abba John the Short when he was sitting in front of the church, and each of them asked him about their thoughts. Another old man flared up in envy at the sight, and said: "Abba John, your cup is full of poison." And Abba John answered: "Yes, Father, it is. But you have said this when you can only see the outside—what would you say if you saw the inside?"

4. John the Less of the Thebaid, a disciple of Abba Ammonius, was said to have lived for twelve years ministering to an old man who was ill, and sitting on a mat near him. But the old man was always cross with him; and although John worked a long time for him, he never said: "May it be well with you." But when the old man was on his death-bed, in the presence of the elders of the place, he held John's hand and said: "May it be well with you, may it be well with you." And the old man commended John to the old men, saying: "This is an angel, not a man."

5. They said of Abba Isidore, the priest in Scete, that if

[69] Job 40:5.

anyone had a monk sick, or weak, or insolent, and wanted to drive him out, he would say: "Bring him to me." And he took him, and cured the soul by his patience.

6. Abba Macarius, when in Egypt, found a man who had brought a beast to his cell and was stealing his possessions. As though he was a traveller, who did not live there, he went up to the thief and helped him to load the beast, and peaceably led him on his way, saying to himself: "We brought nothing into this world; [70] but the Lord gave: as he willed, so it is done: blessed be the Lord in all things."

7. At a meeting of monks in Scete, the old men wanted to test Abba Moses. So they poured scorn on him, saying: "Who is this blackamoor that has come among us?" Moses heard them, but said nothing. When the meeting had dispersed, the men who had given the insults, asked him: "Were you not troubled in your heart?" He answered: "I was troubled, and I said nothing."

8. Paysius, the brother of Abba Poemen, loved a monk of his cell. Abba Poemen did not like it. So he rose and fled to Abba Ammonas, and said to him: "My brother Paysius loves some people and I do not like it." Abba Ammonas said to him: "Abba Poemen, are you still alive? Go sit in your cell, and put it in your heart that you have been already a year in your grave."

9. Abba Poemen said: "Whatever travail comes upon you shall be overcome by silence."

10. A brother who was hurt by another brother went to the Theban Abba Sisois and said: "I want to avenge myself on a brother who has hurt me." The old man begged him: "Don't, my son: leave vengeance in the hands of God." But he said: "I cannot rest until I avenge myself." The old man said: "My brother, let us pray." The old man stood up and said: "O God, we have no further need to think of thee, for we take vengeance of ourselves." The brother heard it and fell at the old man's feet, saying: "No longer will I quarrel with my brother: I beg you to forgive me."

11. A man who saw a religious person carrying a corpse on a bed, said: "Are you carrying dead men? Go and carry the living."

12. They said of a monk, that the more bitterly anyone injured or assailed him, the more he was well-disposed to him; for he said: "People like this are a means to cure the faults of serious men. People who make them happy, do their souls harm.

[70] I Tim. 6:7; Job 1:21.

For it is written: 'They that call thee blessed, deceive thee.' "[71]

13. Some robbers once came to the hermitage of an old man and said: "We have come to remove everything in your cell." And he said: "Take what you see, my sons." So they took what they found in the cell, and went away. But they missed a little bag which was hidden in the cell. The old man picked it up, and gave chase, shouting out: "My sons, you missed this—take it." They admired his patience and restored everything, and did penance to him: and said to each other: "Truly this is a man of God."

14. Some brothers came to a holy old man who lived in the desert; and outside the hermitage they found a boy tending the sheep and using ill-mannered words. After they had told the old man their thoughts and profited from his reply, they said: "Abba, why do you allow those boys to be here, and do not order them to stop hurling abuse at each other?" The old man said: "Believe me, my brothers, there are days when I want to order them, but I stop myself; saying, If I cannot put up with this little thing, how shall I put up with a serious temptation, if God ever lets me be so tempted? So I say nothing to them, and try to get a habit of enduring whatever happens."

15. There was a story that an old man had a little boy living with him. And seeing him doing some unsuitable work, he said: "Don't do that." The child disobeyed him. The old man, observing him to be disobedient, washed his hands of his upbringing, and let him do as he liked. But for three days the boy kept shut the door of the room with the bread and let the old man go without food. The old man did not say: "Where are you?" or "What are you doing out there?"

A neighbour of the old man saw that the boy was late in bringing food; he made a little stew, and passed it to him through a hole in the wall of the cell, and asked him to eat. And he said to the old man: "Why is that disciple of yours so long away?" The old man said: "When he has leisure, he will come back."

16. There was a story that some philosophers once came to test the monks. One of the monks came by dressed in a fine robe. The philosophers said to him: "Come here, you." But he was indignant, and insulted them. Then another monk came by, a good person, a Libyan by race. They said to him: "Come here, you wicked old monk." He came to them at once, and they began to hit him: but he turned the other cheek to them. Then

[71] Isa. 3:12.

the philosophers rose and did homage to him, saying: "Here is a monk indeed." And they made him sit down in their midst, and asked him: "What do you do in this desert more than we do? You fast: and we fast also. You chastise your bodies and so do we. Whatever you do, we do the same." The old man answered: "We trust in God's grace, and keep a watch on our minds." They said: "That is what we cannot do." And they were edified, and let him go.

17. An old man, who had a proved disciple, once turned him out in a fit of irritation. The disciple sat down outside to wait: and the old man found him there when he opened the door, and did penance to him, saying: "You are my Father, because your humility and patience have conquered the weakness of my soul. Come inside: now you are the old father, and I am the young disciple: my age must give way to your conduct."

18. One of the old men said that he had heard holy men say that there are young men who show old men how to live: and they told this story.

There was a drunken old man, who wove a mat a day, sold it in the next village, and drank as much as he could with the money. Then a monk came to live with him, and also wove a mat a day. The old man took this mat as well, sold it, bought wine with the price of both, and brought back to the monk only a little bread for the evening meal. Though this went on for three years, the brother said nothing.

At the end of three years the monk said to himself: "Here am I, with little enough bread and nothing else, I will go away." But then he had second thoughts, and said to himself: "Where can I go? I will stay here, and for God's sake continue with this common life." And immediately an angel of the Lord appeared to him, and said: "Don't go away, we shall come for you tomorrow." That day the monk begged the old man: "Don't go anywhere: today they will come to take me away." At the time when the old man usually went out to the village, he said to the monk: "They will not come today, my son: it is already late." The monk used every argument to show that they would come: and even while he was talking, he slept in peace.

The old man wept, and said: "I am sorrowful, my son, that I have lived in neglect for so many years, and you through patience have saved your soul in so short a time." And thenceforward the old man became sober and serious.

19. A brother who lived near a great old man, is said to have entered his cell from time to time and stolen the contents.

Though the old man saw him, he did not abuse him, but struggled to produce more than usual, saying: "I believe that brother is in need." And while he worked harder than usual, he tightened his belt and ate less. When the old man was on his death-bed, the brothers stood round him. And he looked at the thief, and said: "Come here and touch me." And he grasped his hand and kissed it, saying: "I thank these hands of yours, my brother: it is because of them that I go to the kingdom of heaven." The thief was stricken with remorse and did penance: and he became a true monk, and followed the example of that great old man.

[20. [72] There was a harlot named Thais, so beautiful that for her sake many people impoverished themselves. Her lovers used always to be quarrelling, and several young men spilt their blood on her doorstep.

When Abba Paphnutius heard of it, he took a secular dress and a gold shilling, and set out to see her in one of the cities of Egypt. He gave her his gold shilling for the price of her sin; she accepted it, and said: "Let us go into the house." As he was about to lie on the bed, which was strewn with costly coverlets, he beckoned her and said: "If there is an inner room, let us go into it." She said: "There is an inner room. But if you are frightened of men, no one comes into this outer room. If you are frightened of God, you cannot escape his eye anywhere." To this the old man said: "Do you know about God?" She answered: "I know about God, and the kingdom of the next world, and the future torment for sinners." He said: "If you know this, why have you destroyed so many souls, and therefore will have to give account for theirs as well as your own?"

When Thais heard this, she fell down at Paphnutius' feet, weeping: and said: "Lay a penance upon me, father. I trust with your prayers to win forgiveness. Let me have three hours' grace, and I will come wherever you command and do whatever you tell me." When Abba Paphnutius had appointed her a place to meet, she collected all the presents she had won by her sins. She took them into the city square and publicly burnt them, crying: "Come, all you people who have sinned with me, see how I am burning your presents." The value of the pile was forty pounds.

When she had burnt it all, she went to the appointed place. He found for her a hermitage for maidens, and put her in a

[72] A later addition: found in none of the manuscripts.

little cell. He sealed the door, and left a little window through which she could receive food, and told the sisters of the convent to bring her a little bread and water every day. When Paphnutius had sealed the door and was going away, Thais said to him: "Where, father, would you have me pour my water?" And he said: "In the cell, you are worthy." Then she asked him how to pray to God. He said: "You are not worthy to have God's name on your lips, nor to stretch out your hands towards heaven; for your lips are full of wickedness and your hands polluted. You must simply sit down, look towards the east, and say this prayer again and again: 'Thou who hast fashioned me, have mercy upon me.' "

After she had been shut there for three years, Abba Paphnutius was moved with sympathy, and went to see Abba Antony, to ask him whether God had forgiven her sins or not. Abba Antony, learning all the circumstances, summoned his disciples and told them to watch all night, and persevere in earnest prayer that God would declare to one of them the answer for which Abba Paphnutius had come. They all went apart, and prayed continually: and Abba Paul, the chief disciple of Saint Antony, suddenly saw a bed in heaven covered with precious coverlets, and guarded by three maidens whose faces shone. Paul said to himself: "This is the gift of none but my father Antony." And a voice came to him: "It is not the gift of your father Antony, but of the harlot Thais."

Abba Paul told what he had seen: and Abba Paphnutius recognized the will of God, returned to the hermitage where Thais was shut, and broke the seals on the door. She asked him to let her stay shut in. But he opened the door, and said: "Come out, for God has forgiven your sins." She answered: "I call God to witness that from the time I came here I have kept my sins in my mind's eye like a burden, and I have kept weeping at the sight of them." Abba Paphnutius said: "God has forgiven you, not for your penitence, but because you always kept in your mind the thought of your sins." And he brought her out: and she lived for only fifteen days, and died in peace.]

PART XVII
Of charity

1. Abba Antony said: "Now I do not fear God, but I love him: for love casteth out fear." [73]

[73] I John 4:18.

2. He also said: "From our neighbour are life and death. If we do good to our neighbour, we do good to God: if we cause our neighbour to stumble, we sin against Christ."

3. Abba Ammon of Nitria came to Abba Antony, and said to him: "I see that I endure more than you: how is it that your reputation is great among men?" And Abba Antony said: "It is because I love God more than you do."

4. Abba Hilarion once came from Palestine to Abba Antony on the mountain: and Abba Antony said to him: "Welcome, morning star, for you rise at break of day." And Abba Hilarion said: "Peace to you, pillar of light, for you prop up the earth."

5. Abba Mark said to Abba Arsenius: "Why do you run away from us?" The old man said: "God knows I love you. But I cannot be with God and with men. The countless hosts of angels have but a single will, while men have many wills. So I cannot let God go, and come and be with men."

6. Abba Agatho said: "I never went to sleep intentionally while I kept a grudge against anyone. Nor did I let anyone go away to sleep while he had a grievance against me."

7. Once when Abba John was going up from Scete with other monks, their guide missed his way in the night. The brothers said to Abba John: "What are we to do, Abba, to prevent ourselves dying in the desert, now that this brother has missed the way?" The old man said: "If we say anything to him, he will be grieved. Look, I will pretend I am worn out, and say I cannot walk, and will lie here till daylight." And they did so. The others said: "We will not go on, but will stay with you here." They stayed there until daybreak, so that they should not abuse the monk who had wrongly guided them.

8. Before Abba Poemen went to Egypt, there was an old man there with a great reputation. But when Abba Poemen came up from Scete with his monks the people left this old man in favour of Abba Poemen. The old man was jealous, and spoke ill of them. When Poemen heard this, he was sad, and said to his monks: "What shall we do for that old man? These people have made us suffer, by leaving that old man and visiting us who are nobody. How can we heal his mind?" And he said to them: "Make some supper, and take a little jug of wine: we will go and eat with him, perhaps we shall be able to heal his mind." So they took the bread which they had made ready, and went to the old man's cell.

When they knocked, his disciple answered the door, and said: "Who are you?" They said: "Tell the abba that it is Poemen, who wants to be blessed by you." The disciple told the old man, who returned the message: "Go away, I am busy." But they persevered and said: "We will not go away until we have got the old man's blessing." So seeing their perseverance and their humility, the old man was stricken with remorse, and opened the door to them. They entered, and supped with him. While they were having supper, the old man said: "Truly, I have heard less than the truth about you. I see that you do a hundred-fold more than I was told." And he became their friend from that moment.

9. Abba Poemen said: "Try, so far as you can, to do wrong to no man, and keep your heart chaste to every man."

10. He also said: "There is nothing greater in love than that a man should lay down his life for his neighbour. When a man hears a complaining word and struggles against himself, and does not himself begin to complain; when a man bears an injury with patience, and does not look for revenge; that is when a man lays down his life for his neighbour."

11. Abba Pambo happened once to be travelling in Egypt with some monks. He saw some men from the world sitting down, and said to them: "Stand up, and give a greeting, and kiss the monks that you may be blessed. For they often talk with God, and their mouths are holy."

12. Abba Paphnutius is said to have drunk wine seldom. But once on a journey he happened upon a meeting-place of robbers, while they were drinking. The chief of the robber band recognized him and knew that he would not drink wine. He saw that he was tired out. So he filled a cup with wine, held a naked sword in his other hand, and said: "If you do not drink, I will kill you." The old man knew that the robber chieftain was trying to obey the commandment of God: and in his desire to help him, he took the cup and drank.

Then the robber chieftain did penance before him, and said: "Forgive me, Abba, that I grieved you." And the old man said to him: "I believe that because of this cup my God will have mercy upon you in this world and the next." And the robber chieftain answered: "And I believe in God that henceforward I shall harm no one." And the old man won over the whole band of robbers, because for God's sake he let himself fall into their power.

13. Abba Hyperichius said: "Snatch your neighbour from his sins, so far as you can, and refrain from condemning him: for God does not reject those who turn to him. Let no word of

wickedness towards your brother dwell in your heart, so that you can say: 'Forgive us our debts, as we also forgive our debtors.' "

14. Two monks were in Cellia. One of them was an old man, and asked the younger: "Let us stay together, my brother." The other said: "I am a sinner, and cannot stay with you, Abba." But he begged him: "Yes, we can stay together." The old man had a clean heart, and the younger did not want him to know that he sometimes fell to lust. The monk then said: "Let me go away for a week, and we will talk about it again." At the end of the week the old man came back, and the younger, wishing to test him, said: "I succumbed to a great temptation during this week, Abba. When I had gone to a village on an errand, I lay with a woman." The old man said: "Are you penitent?" And the brother said: "Yes." The old man said: "I will carry half the burden of the sin with you." Then the brother said: "Now I know that we can stay together." And they remained together till death parted them.

15. One of the fathers said: "If anyone asks you for something, and you give it to him; even if you are forced to give it, let your heart be in the gift: as it is written: 'If a man forces you to go with him one mile, go with him two': [74] it means, if you are asked for something, give it with a willing heart."

16. A monk is said to have made baskets and put handles on them, when he heard another monk saying nearby: "What am I to do? The trader is soon coming, and I have no handles to put on my baskets." So he took off the handles he had put on his own baskets, and took them to the nearby monk, saying: "I do not need these: take them and put them on your baskets." And he allowed the brother to finish his baskets, but left his own unfinished.

17. They said that an old man in Scete, who was ill, wanted to eat a little new bread. One of the experienced monks heard of it: and he took his cloak, put stale bread into it, went to Egypt, changed the stale bread for new, and brought the new bread back to the old man. When the brothers saw the new bread, they were astonished. The old man did not want to eat it, and said: "It is the blood of this brother." And the old men begged him, saying: "For God's sake eat, so that his sacrifice is not vain." And so he ate it.

18. A brother asked an old man: "There are two monks: one stays quietly in his cell, fasting for six days at a time, and

[74] Matt. 5:41.

laying many austerities upon himself: and the other ministers to the sick. Which of them is more acceptable to God?" The old man answered: "If the brother, who fasts six days, even hung himself up by his nostrils, he could never be the equal of him who ministers to the sick."

19. An old man was asked: "How is it that some struggle away at their religious life, but do not receive grace like the old fathers?" The old man said: "Because then charity ruled, and each one drew his neighbour upward. Now charity is growing cold, and each of us draws his neighbour downward, and so we do not deserve grace."

20. Three monks once went to harvest, and were given a big area to harvest. But the first day one of them fell sick, and returned to his cell. Of the two remaining, one said to the other: "Look, brother, our brother has fallen ill: you work as hard as you can, and I will do what little extra I can, and we will trust God that by our sick brother's prayers we shall harvest his part of the field as well as finishing our own part." So they harvested the whole area which they had been given, and went to receive their pay.

And they summoned their brother, saying: "Come, brother, take your money." He said: "I have not harvested, so I have earned nothing." They said to him: "We finished the harvest through your prayers: come and take your pay." And there was fierce argument between them, the one saying: "I will not take it because I have not earned it," the others refusing to accept their pay unless he would take his share. So they went off to a great old man, to accept his judgement. And the brother who had been sick said to him: "We three went to earn money by harvesting in a man's field. When we came to the place, I fell ill on the first day and returned to my cell, and I could not harvest a single day with them. And now they are forcing me, saying: 'Come, brother, take your pay for work you have not done.'"

But the other two said: "The truth is this. When we arrived at the field, we were given a big area to harvest. If there had been three of us, we might with the greatest difficulty have just finished the work. But by the prayers of this our brother, the pair of us harvested the field more quickly than three of us would have done. So we say to him: 'Come, take your pay,' and he will not."

The old man marvelled to hear them, and said to one of his monks: "Ring the bell in the brothers' cells to gather them here." When they had assembled, he said to them: "Come, brothers, and hear today a just judgement." And the old man told them the whole story, and decided that the brother should receive his pay, and do with it whatever he would. And the brother went away grieved and weeping like a man who has been sentenced.

21. An old man said: "Our fathers had the custom of visiting the cells of new brothers who wanted to lead a solitary life, to see if any of them was tempted by demons and had taken harm from his thoughts. And if they found anyone who had taken harm, they brought him to church. A basin was filled with water. Then, after they had all prayed for the one who was suffering under temptation, all the monks washed their hands in the basin: and then the water was poured upon the tempted brother, and he was at once cleansed."

22. Two old men lived together for many years without a quarrel. One said to the other: "Let us have one quarrel with each other, as is the way of men." And the other answered: "I do not know how a quarrel happens." And the first said: "Look, I put a tile between us, and I say, That's mine. Then you say, No, it's mine. That is how you begin a quarrel."

So they put a tile between them, and one of them said: "That's mine." And the other said: "No; it's mine." And he answered: "Yes, it is yours. Take it away." And they went away unable to argue with each other.

23. A brother asked an old man: "If I see a monk of whom I have heard as guilty of a sin, I cannot persuade my soul to bring him into my cell. But if I see a good monk, I gladly bring him in." And the old man said: "If you do good to a good brother, it is little to him. To the other, give twofold, for it is he who is sick."

24. An old man said: "I never wanted a work to be useful to me while causing loss to my brother: for I have this hope, that what helps my brother will bring fruit to me."

25. There was a brother who served one of the fathers. The old man's body happened to be badly hurt, and evil-smelling pus flowed out of the wound. The serving brother thought to himself: "Get out of here. You cannot bear the smell of the gangrene." To quell the thought, he took a bowl, washed the wound, and kept the water which he used: and whenever he was thirsty, he drank from it. But the thought began to trouble him again, saying to him: "If you will not go away, at least do not drink this pus." The brother struggled away with endurance,

and went on drinking the washing water. And God saw his charity as he ministered to the old man; and God turned the washing water into the purest water, and by some unseen means healed the old man.

* * * *

Part XVIII of the Sayings is of ecstasies and raptures and prophecies and wondrous visions: such as this:

A brother went to the cell of Abba Arsenius in Scete, and looked through the window, and saw him like fire from head to feet. (He was a brother worthy to see such sights.) And when he knocked, the old man came out, and saw the brother standing there in amazement, and said to him: "Have you been knocking long? Did you see anything?" And he answered: "No." And after talking with him, Abba Arsenius sent him on his way.

In the middle of Part XVIII is the division, where it is believed that the deacon Pelagius ceased to translate, and the subdeacon John continued the work.

Part XIX is of the holy men who wrought signs: for example:

A demoniac once came to Scete. Prayer was made for him in the church, and his demon could not be cast out because it was a powerful demon. The clergy said to each other: "What shall we do to this demon? Nobody but Abba Bessarion can cast him out: and if we ask Abba Bessarion, he will not even come to the church. This is what we will do: he will come to the church at daybreak tomorrow before anyone else: and we will make the demoniac sit in Abba Bessarion's seat. And when he comes in, we will stand in prayer, and say: 'Abba, wake up that brother!' " And they did so. When the old man came at daybreak, they stood in prayer, and said: "Abba, wake up that brother!" And the old man said to the sufferer: "Get up and go outside": and at once the demon went out of him, and he was made whole.

Part XX is of the holy life of various men, and contains a miscellany of stories, some of which might from their subject have been included under one of the existing headings. Here is one example (5):

Abba Sisois was once living alone on the mountain of Antony. His servant was slow in coming to him, and for ten months he did not see a single human being. But walking one

day on the mountain, he found a tribesman herding beasts.
The old man said to him: "Where have you come from, and
how long have you been here?" He said: "Abba, I have
been eleven months on this mountain, and you are the first
person I have seen." When he heard this, the old man went
back to his cell, and struck himself, and said: "Look, Sisois,
you thought you had done something: and you have not even
done as much as that man from the world."

And it contains one of the most celebrated of the Macarius stories (17):

Once when Abba Macarius was praying in his cell, he
heard a voice which said: "Macarius, you have not yet
reached the standard of two women in that city." On his
arrival, he found the house and knocked at the door. A
woman opened it, and welcomed him to her house. He sat
down, and called them to sit down with him. Then he said to
them: "It is for you that I have taken this long journey. Tell
me how you live a religious life." They said: "Indeed, how
can we lead a religious life? We were with our husbands last
night." But the old man persuaded them to tell him their way
of life.

Then they said: "We are both foreigners, in the world's
eyes. But we accepted in marriage two brothers. Today we
have been sharing this house for fifteen years. We do not
know whether we have quarrelled or said rude words to each
other; but the whole of this time we have lived peaceably
together. We thought we would enter a convent, and asked
our husbands for permission, but they refused it. So since we
could not get this permission, we have made a covenant
between ourselves and God that a worldly word shall not pass
our lips during the rest of our lives."

When Macarius heard it, he said: "Truly, it is not whether
you are a virgin or a married woman, a monk or a man in the
world: God gives his Holy Spirit to everyone, according to
their earnestness of purpose."

*Part XXI is another miscellany; in some early manuscripts (MP)
there is a Part XXII, of various final sayings (Sententiae Patrum),
but in spite of Dom Wilmart's judgement I do not think they formed part
of the original translation.*

The M manuscript gives at the end this prayer:

"Lord Jesus Christ, whose will all things obey: pardon
what I have done and grant that I, a sinner, may sin no more.

Lord, I believe that though I deserve it not, thou canst cleanse me from all my sins. Lord, I know that man looks upon the face, but thou seest into the heart. Send thy spirit into my inmost being, to take possession of my soul and my body. Without thee I cannot be saved. With thee to protect me I long for thy salvation. And now I ask thee for wisdom. Deign of thy great goodness to help and defend me. Guide my heart, Almighty God, that I may remember thy presence day and night."

II

The Conferences of Cassian

INTRODUCTION

CASSIAN HAD BEGUN HIS CAREER IN A MONASTERY in Bethlehem, though not the monastery presided over by St Jerome. He had then visited Egypt for some uncertain number of years (more than seven, probably ten or twelve), and studied under various Egyptian hermits and coenobites, mainly near the Nile delta and in Scete. Like many others among the more educated Greek-speaking monks, he was concerned in the Origenist controversy of 399–401, which sharply divided the monastic world, and soon found himself with other Origenists seeking the support and patronage of the patriarch John Chrysostom of Constantinople. With the fall of his protector he had to take refuge elsewhere, and like other refugees he found his way to Rome. Whether he ever returned to the east is not known. When the Visigothic leader Alaric sacked Rome in 410, many prominent men fled to Provence: and it is possible that the flowering of monastic life in Provence and its surrounding islands from 410 onwards is connected with the circumstance that Provence seemed a haven for refugees. Cassian was in a monastic house, which he had founded in Marseilles, at least as early as 425 and probably for several years before that. There, as one of the rare persons in the west with expert and first-hand knowledge of the Egyptian monks, he was in demand to instruct, edify and inform the young Gallic monastic houses. Castor, Bishop of the little town of Apt forty miles north of Marseilles, was founding a monastery and asked Cassian to give it both practical arrangement and spiritual ideals, based upon the Egyptian models. The result was the *Institutes*, published about 425–426. These were followed by the *Conferences*, which purport to be the addresses of various ascetics, mainly hermits, whom Cassian interviewed during his stay in Egypt. Just as the Egyptians regarded the coenobium as the training school, for those who could endure, before the monk went out to the higher life of prayer possible in the desert solitudes, so the *Institutes* are designed (like the Rule of St Benedict) for the training school, and the *Conferences* for hermits or those who might be turning from the life in a community to the hermit life.

How far the *Conferences* represent the actual words of the Egyptian abbots, in whose mouths Cassian puts the addresses, is still a matter of debate. Almost everyone allows that Cassian, who had been away from Egypt for a quarter of a century, touched them, gave them his own framework. Many scholars think that each Egyptian father talked upon the subject which Cassian says he talked, and substantially in the sense which Cassian ascribes to him. Others, with whom I agree, think that not even the subjects can safely be attributed to the individual authors whom he mentions, but that the substance of the teaching is certainly Egyptian teaching, seen through Cassian's later perspective. He certainly believed that he was transmitting the authentic doctrine of the Egyptian desert, and there is no adequate reason for supposing him to be mistaken.

The Latin of Cassian is as far apart from the Latin of *The Sayings of the Fathers* as it well could be. The rugged, stark, often ungrammatical, vigorous staccato of the apophthegmatists gives way to the smooth flowing rhetorical periods by a master of fifth-century Latin prose. It is clear, its meaning unmistakable: but its expression has the amplitude—part cloudiness, part exuberance, part delight in patterns and rhythms— acquired from the rhetorical schools. To put the apophthegmatists into English you sometimes need to expand the laconic epigram. To put Cassian into English you need to remember that the epithets of the fifth century have less than their full value, that Cassian's contemporaries constantly used a superlative, or two superlatives, where a simple epithet would have represented the meaning. To translate the jejune aphorisms of the apophthegmatists is like Abba John watering his dead stick until it burst into flower: to translate the urbane reiterations of Cassian, you need a moderate use of the pruning knife, to cut away some of the luxuriant foliage in order to see the fruit. Apart from the partial removal of a few superlatives or the exclusion of what Fowler calls "elegant variation," I have taken one other liberty. Occasionally Cassian reinforces his point

with a string of Scriptural quotations. Had he been writing in a
modern manner, he would have transferred these quotations
to a footnote, which is where they ought to be: for they interrupt the sense of what he is saying, and are armoury to protect
his argument against critics—precisely the function of the
modern footnote. I have therefore transferred a small number
of blocks of texts to footnotes; these footnotes are given in
quotation marks and this will show the reader that these are in
Cassian's original text.

So popular was Cassian as reading matter in the medieval
monasteries that the manuscript tradition is over-abundant,
and work is still needed upon it. But for most practical purposes
the edition of M. Petschenig, published in the Vienna *Corpus*,
volumes 13 and 17 (1886–8) is excellent, and is certainly indispensable. I have followed his text, and departed from it only,
I believe, at one point where his apparatus seemed to provide
the more likely reading.

The Conferences of Cassian

THE TEXT

Preface

To the best of my slender ability, I have now fulfilled the promise which I made to bishop Castor in the preface to the *Institutes* which I wrote (with God's help) about the rules of the monks and the cures for the eight chief sins. I should much like to know what you and he think about the book after a sober examination of it: and whether, in putting into prose (for the first time, I believe) a discussion of a subject so profound and so sublime, I have succeeded in producing a work of value and interest to you and all the brothers in the community.

Bishop Castor was a man who above all others longed for saintliness. And so, in his charity, and oblivious of the difficulty of the task and of my incompetence to fulfil it rightly, he required me to write in the same way these first ten Conferences of the best of all the fathers, the hermits who used to live in the desert of Scete. But he has died, and passed to be with Christ: and therefore I have thought it right to dedicate these Conferences to you two, Bishop Leontius and my brother Helladius. For one of you is Castor's brother, in blood-relationship, in the office of a bishop, and (above all) in love for sacred study, and so has the hereditary right to demand the payment of a debt incurred to Castor. The other has chosen the austere life of a hermit, not (like some) out of personal presumption, but following the lawful tradition of ascetic doctrine, which he began to receive from the inspiration of God's Spirit almost before he began to learn it consciously: rather than search out his own way of life, he has chosen to receive it from the regular teaching of the fathers.

Just as I have taken my little boat into harbour and decided not to write any more, I see an ocean opening out in front of

193

me. It is evidently my duty that I should, however rashly, set down on paper something about the way of life and the teaching of those great Egyptian saints before it is forgotten. And my little boat has now to venture out among the perils of much deeper water than before: for life in a hermitage is a finer life than that in a monastic community, and the contemplation of God (which is the continual aim of the hermits) is a loftier life than the pursuit of the daily virtues which is the purpose of life in a monastic community. It is therefore your duty to help me with your prayers. I am going to treat this sacred subject as faithfully as I can: but I ask you to pray that my boat may not sink amid these deep waters through mere clumsiness or inexperience.

I pass now from the outward and visible life of the monk (the subject of my earlier book) to the invisible life of the inner man; from the vocal prayers of the canonical office to the unceasing prayer which St Paul commanded. If anyone, through reading my earlier work, has won the allegorical name Jacob got for himself by "supplanting" the sins of his flesh, he may now learn the rules of the perfect life and win (if I may so put it) the merit and the name of Israel (which means, the man who sees God); and he will do it by receiving the doctrines of the Fathers—I am not inventing this teaching but simply passing on what I learnt— and by contemplating the purity of God.

God deemed me worthy to see them and learn from them and live with them. I ask you to pray that I may truly remember what they told me and may be given a ready tongue to tell it; that I may be enabled to pass it on with the same completeness, and in the same pious spirit, as I received it: and that I may be enabled to show you the men themselves, who are in a measure inseparable from their way of life, and to transmit their teaching by making them speak in the Latin language.

I want to give the reader of these Conferences, as of the earlier book, an emphatic warning. If perhaps he thinks anything here impossible or very difficult because of his condition or his manner of life or habits, he should not measure it against the limits of his own powers, but against the worth and sanctity of the speakers. He should first consider their earnestness and determination—truly they were dead to the life of this world and had cut every string which tied them to it, even their natural family feeling. Then he ought to remember the kind of place they lived in, how they had their hermitages scattered over a great desert and were far removed from any company of men: and so they found their senses quickened, and saw or uttered what perhaps will seem impossible to the ignorant and the uninitiated who know only their own ordinary manner of life.

But if the reader wants to judge them rightly, and would test whether what they did is possible, let him without further delay resolve to adopt their purpose and their earnestness as his own. Then he will find that what once seemed beyond human capacity is not only possible but most pleasant.

And now, without further preface, I come to their Conferences.

CONFERENCE I

First Conference of Abba Moses

ON THE MONK'S GOAL

1. I was staying in the desert of Scete, where are the hermits of highest repute and spiritual perfection. I had as my companion the holy Abba Germanus, who had been my fellow-warrior since the earliest days of my ascetic life, first in the community at Bethlehem and afterwards in the desert; a friend so close, sharing so intimately the same aims, that people might say there was a single mind and a single spirit in our two bodies. Together we sought out Abba Moses: to find him among the other hermits it was like looking along a bed full of fragrant flowers until we found the flower which smelt the sweetest. As he was so eminent in the practice of virtue and in the art of contemplative prayer, we asked him—with a deep compunction of heart—to give us words which would help us in our spiritual progress. We had heard of his inflexible rule never to give instruction in the spiritual life except to persons who sought it in faith and heartfelt contrition. For he was afraid that if he poured out the water of life indiscriminately to people who had no use for it or were hardly even thirsty, he would cast his pearls before swine and would be liable to the charge either of boasting about his prowess or of betraying his trust.

In the end he consented to our importunities. And this is what he said:

2. "All arts and sciences have some immediate goal or destination (*scopos*); and also an ultimate aim, a *telos*. The earnest student of each art willingly endures the hard work and peril and expense by looking towards the goal which he will ultimately achieve. The farmer in his ploughing suffers heat, or frost and ice, or rocklike soil, and turns the ground again and again to clear it of brambles and weeds and make it as soft and

fine as grains of sand—that is his immediate purpose, his *scopos*. His ultimate purpose is to gather a bumper harvest and so live without fear of starvation and grow wealthy. When his barn is fulfilled he uses some of the crop as manure and is prepared to lessen his present stock in the expectation of future harvest. Merchants are not afraid of storm and tempest because they are carried onward by the hope of gain. Ambitious soldiers think nothing of far journeys, hardships and risk of life in battle, because they have their eyes set upon the goal of power and place, and will endure anything to obtain it.

The hermit, in the same way, has his immediate goal and his ultimate goal: and for this he endures every kind of labour tirelessly, even gratefully. For this he grows not weary of fasting, enjoys the fatigue of watching in the night, is not tired by the continual reading of the Scriptures and meditation upon them, bears even the naked and grinding poverty and loneliness of life in this desert. I have no doubt that this was the goal which has led you on to turn from your family and homeland and scorn the pleasures of this world, and to travel so far to find us, ordinary and ignorant men, living squalidly in this desert."

"Tell me," he said, "what is the purpose which has brought you to bear all this cheerfully?"

3. I tried not to answer. But when he persisted, I said that we bore all this for the sake of the kingdom of heaven.

4. "Yes," said Moses, "that is indeed the ultimate goal. But first you ought to know the immediate goal for which we strive in order to make the ultimate goal possible."

I said simply that I did not know.

"I compared the aims of every art or science," said Moses, "and how each must have its immediate goal on which the mind may concentrate: and unless it does concentrate with care and perseverance, it cannot attain its ultimate goal. The farmer's ultimate goal is to live well with fertile crops, his immediate goal is to eradicate brambles and weeds from the soil, and he knows that this is the only way to be sure of his ultimate end. The trader has to amass goods for sale before he can amass riches: it is vain to yearn for wealth without choosing the path which leads to it. Ambitious men have first to decide what profession they will follow so as to have some reasonable prospect of attaining the honours they desire.

In the same way, the ultimate goal of our life is the kingdom of heaven. But we have to ask what the immediate goal is: for if we do not find it we shall exhaust ourselves in futile efforts.

Travellers who miss their way are still tiring themselves though they are walking no nearer to their destination."

At this remark we stood and gaped. The old man went on:

"The ultimate goal of our way of life is, as I said, the kingdom of God, or kingdom of heaven. The immediate aim is purity of heart. For without purity of heart none can enter into that kingdom. We should fix our gaze on this target, and walk towards it in as straight a line as possible. If our thoughts wander away from it even a little, we should bring back our gaze towards it, and use it as a kind of test, which at once brings all our efforts back onto the one path.

5. When expert archers want to display their prowess before a king, they try to shoot their arrows into little targets which have the prizes painted on them: they know they can only win the prize which is their real goal by shooting straight into the mark which is their immediate goal. But suppose that the target were carried out of sight. They would then have no means of knowing how unskilfully and crookedly they were shooting, but would be shooting their arrows at random into the air without any guide to accurate or inaccurate aim and without the possibility of estimating what correction was needed.

St Paul tells us that the end which we have set before us is eternal life: 'having your fruit unto holiness, and the end everlasting life.'[1] The *scopos* is purity of heart, which he rightly terms 'holiness,' without which eternal life cannot be won. It is as though he said, having your *scopos* in purity of heart, and your *telos* eternal life. And significantly he uses the very word *scopos* to describe it—'forgetting those things which are behind, and reaching forth unto those things which are before, I press forward toward the mark for the prize of the high calling of God.'[2] In Greek the words for 'press forward to the mark' are *kata scopon dioko* and really mean 'press forward according to the mark.' It is as if he said: 'With this aim, whereby I forget what is behind—the sins of the old man—I strive to attain to the prize of heaven.'

Then whatever can guide us towards purity of heart is to be followed with all our power: whatever draws us away from it is to be avoided as hurtful and worse. It is for this end—to keep our hearts continually pure—that we do and endure everything, that we spurn parents and home and position and wealth and comfort and every earthly pleasure. If we do not keep this mark continually before the eyes, all our travail will be futile waste

[1] Rom. 6:22.   [2] Phil. 3:13–14.

that wins nothing, and will stir up in us a chaos of ideas instead of singlemindedness. Unless the mind has some fixed point to which it can keep coming back and to which it tries to fasten itself, it will flutter hither and thither according to the whim of the passing moment and follow whatever immediate and external impression is presented to it.

6. This is the reason why some people, who have given away worldly wealth in gold or silver or lands, are afterwards agitated about a knife, a pencil, a pin or a pen. If they steadily contemplated purity of heart, they would never suffer, over these trivialities, the state of mind which they sought to avoid by giving away their property. Some people guard their books so closely that they refuse to let anyone else touch them or read them for a moment: and so they minister to themselves the irritation which is the death of the prayerful life, in those very times which ought to give them an opportunity for patience and charity. They have given up all their property for the love of Christ; and yet keep their old acquisitive attitude over little things and quickly become upset over them. Then they are as barren of fruit as those who, as St Paul said, lack charity. Prophesying in the spirit, he said: 'Though I give all my goods to feed the poor and though I give my body to be burned, and have not charity, it profiteth me nothing.' [3]

It is clear that you do not attain the perfect life simply by self-denial or simply by throwing away your money or your rank. There must go with it the charity which the apostle described, and which consists in purity of heart alone. For not to be envious, not to be puffed up, not to be angry, not to do wrong, not to seek one's own, not to rejoice in iniquity, not to think evil, and the rest—what is this except the continual offering of a perfect and pure heart to God, a heart which is kept free from every earthly distraction?

7. To this end everything is to be done. Solitude, watches in the night, manual labour, nakedness, reading and the other disciplines—we know that their purpose is to free the heart from injury by bodily passions and to keep it free; they are to be the rungs of a ladder up which it may climb to perfect charity. If by accident some right and needful occupation prevents us from keeping these acts of discipline, we should not be guilty of gloom or annoyance—for the aim of these acts is to drive away these faults. The loss you incur by being irritated outweighs the gain of fasting; dislike of your brother cannot be

[3] I Cor. 13:3.

counterbalanced by reading the Bible. These practices of fasting, watching, withdrawal to the hermitage, meditation on the Scriptures, are all subordinate means to your chief aim which is purity of heart, or charity, and we ought never to allow them to take precedence over charity. Charity will not suffer hurt if some necessary reason prevents us fulfilling our disciplinary rule. None of these practices are of any profit at all if the purpose for which they are undertaken is lost.

A man diligently collects all the tools of his trade. He does not expect to sit in idleness and enjoy possession of the tools but to use them skilfully for the purpose for which they were designed. In the same way fasting, watching, meditation on Scripture, nakedness and poverty are not perfection but the means towards it; not the end of our discipline but the means to that end. The man who is content with these practices as the *summum bonum* and not as means, will use them in vain. He possesses the tools of the trade but has no idea what they are for.

Whatever can trouble our purity and peace of mind, however useful and necessary it seems to be, should be avoided as hurtful. This is the general rule by which we can avoid wandering off the right path and keep in a straight line towards our end.

8. It should be our main effort, the immovable and steadfast purpose of the heart, to cleave with our mind to the things of God and to God himself. Whatever is not this, however important, should be put second, or last, and judged to be hurtful. There is a lovely type of this mental attitude in the Gospel story of Martha and Mary. When Martha was performing her act of holy ministry in serving the Lord and his disciples, Mary was sitting at Jesus' feet, which in faith she had kissed and anointed, and was hanging upon his words as he taught the things of the spirit. The Lord praised Mary above Martha, because she had chosen the better part and that which should not be taken away from her. For when Martha was working away, in a truly religious spirit, and was busy about much serving, she saw that, unaided, she could not serve so many people, and asked the Lord that her sister might help her, saying: 'Carest thou not that my sister has left me to serve alone? bid her therefore that she help me.' She was calling Mary to no lowly task, but to an excellent work of ministry. Yet the Lord replied: 'Martha, Martha, thou art anxious and troubled about many things: we need few things, or even one thing. Mary has chosen the good part, which shall not be taken away from her.' [4]

[4] Luke 10:40–2; a text with no mean manuscript authority to support it.

The Lord, you see, placed the chief good in divine contemplation. All the other virtues, however necessary and useful and good we deem them, must be placed on a lower plane because they are sought for the sake of this one thing. When the Lord said: 'Thou art anxious and troubled about many things, but we need few things or even one thing,' he was putting the supreme good, not in the pursuit of virtue, however excellent and fruitful, but in the pure and simple and singleminded contemplation of himself. When he said that few things were needful, he means, that contemplation which begins with meditation upon a few holy subjects. From the contemplation of these few subjects, the soul in its progress mounts with God's help to one thing, the gazing upon God: the soul passes beyond saintly acts and ministries and attains the true knowledge of God and feeds upon his beauty. 'Mary therefore has chosen the good part, which shall not be taken away from her.' Mark the text. When he says: 'Mary has chosen the good part,' he is silent about Martha and seems in no way to blame her. Yet in praising Mary, he declares the work of Martha to be lower. Again, when he says: 'which shall not be taken away from her,' he shows that Martha's part could be taken away from her. To minister to the body is a transitory work: to listen to his word is the work of eternity."

9. Germanus and I were deeply disturbed at these words. "What," I said, "shall fasts and reading and works of mercy, of righteousness, and of kindness be taken away from us? Surely the Lord promises to these works the reward of the kingdom of heaven, when he says: 'Come ye blessed of my Father, inherit the kingdom prepared for you from the beginning of the world. For I was an hungered, and ye gave me to eat: I was thirsty and ye gave me to drink,' [5] and the rest? How shall we lose these things which open to the doers of them the gates of the kingdom of heaven?"

10. "I did not say," answered Moses, "that the *reward* for good deeds should be taken away. The Lord said: 'Whosoever shall give to one of the least of these a cup of cold water only, in the name of a disciple, verily I say unto you, he shall not lose his reward.' [6] I say that the deed itself, which has to be done because of the needs or temptations of the body or the injustice of the world, will be taken away. The earnest practice of reading or of fasting is only useful to purify the heart and chastise the flesh, so long as 'the flesh lusteth against the spirit.' [7] Sometimes

[5] Matt. 25:34-5.   [6] Matt. 10:42.   [7] Gal. 5:17.

we see that, even in this life, these works are 'taken away'—men, exhausted with austerities or old age, are no longer able to perform them. All the more shall they cease in that future life, when 'this corruptible shall have put on incorruption,' and the body which is now 'a natural body' shall have risen 'a spiritual body' [8], and the flesh has begun to be transformed so that it no longer lusts against the spirit.

St Paul is plainly referring to this when he says: 'bodily exercise is profitable for a little: but godliness' (by which he surely means charity) 'is profitable for all things, having the promise of the life which now is and of the life to come.' [9] What is said to be profitable for a little, cannot be profitable for ever, and cannot (of itself) bring a man to the perfect life.

The phrase 'for a little' might mean one of two things. It might mean 'for a short time,' since these bodily exercises are not going to last as long as the man who practises them. Or it might mean 'only of little profit': corporal austerity brings the first beginnings of progress, but it does not beget that perfect charity which has the promise of this life and the life to come.

We deem these works necessary because without them we cannot climb to charity. For what you call works of godliness and mercy are necessary for this life where inequality prevails among men. But we should not expect to do them unless we found the world full of the needy and destitute and infirm— thanks to the wickedness of greedy men who have seized and kept for their use (though they do not use them) the goods which God created for all in common. So long as injustice prevails in the world, works of mercy are needed and will be useful to the man who practises them, and his godliness and good intention will make him an heir of eternal life.

But in the world to come, when all men are equal, these works will not be needed. There everyone will pass from the multiplicity of different good works to the love of God and the contemplation of the things of God in an unceasing purity of heart. This is the goal which the hermits direct all their efforts to win, even in this world. This is why they study to win the true knowledge of God and to purify their minds. Though still in this corruptible flesh, they seek that state which they will find when they lay aside their corruption, and attain to the promise of our Lord and Saviour: 'Blessed are the pure in heart: for they shall see God.' [10]

[8] I Cor. 15:53 and 44.   [9] I Tim. 4:8.   [10] Matt. 5:8.

11. It is no wonder that these works shall pass away, when St Paul asserts that even the loftier gifts of the spirit will pass away, and declares that charity alone will abide for ever. 'Whether there be prophecies they shall fail: whether there be tongues, they shall cease: whether there be knowledge, it shall vanish away'—but 'charity never faileth.' [11] Every other gift is granted for our temporal needs and use and in the future kingdom will disappear; charity will continue uninterrupted. For charity is not only useful to us in this life: it will abide, yet more excellently, when we have put aside the burden of this flesh, and cleave in spotless purity to God."

12. Germanus: "Is there any frail mortal who can be immovable in contemplation, and never think about a guest arriving, or visiting the sick, or manual labour, or the need to show kindness to pilgrims and travellers? Must he not be interrupted by the need to eat?

We should like to know how the mind is capable of clinging to God, whom men can neither see nor understand."

13. Moses: "You are right. A frail mortal cannot contemplate God in such a way that his mind is never drawn aside. What is important is knowing where we ought to concentrate our mental attention and how to direct the eyes of the soul. When the mind succeeds in this, it can be glad. When it fails—and it fails as often as the mental attention is withdrawn from God—it can be sorry and feel that this is a fall from the supreme good, and think that even a passing lapse in contemplating Christ is a sin like adultery.

Whenever the gaze strays even a little, we should turn back the eyes of the heart into the straight line towards him. Everything depends upon the soul's detachment. If the devil has been driven out and sin no longer reigns, then the kingdom of God is founded in us. As it is written in the Gospel: 'The kingdom of God cometh not with observation, nor shall they say, Lo here, or Lo there: verily I say unto you, that the kingdom of God is within you.' [12] The only thing which can be 'within us' is knowledge of the truth or ignorance of it, and affection for righteousness or affection for sin, whereby we prepare our hearts to be a kingdom either of Christ or the devil. St Paul described the nature of this kingdom thus: 'For the kingdom of God is not meat and drink, but righteousness and peace and joy in the Holy Spirit.' [13] If the kingdom of God is within us and the kingdom of God is righteousness and peace and joy, then the man

[11] I Cor. 13:8 and 10.   [12] Luke 17:20–1.   [13] Rom. 14:17.

who abides in these is surely within the kingdom of God; and the man who abides in unrighteousness, and conflict, and the melancholy that kills the life of the spirit, is already a citizen of the devil's kingdom, of hell and of death. These are the signs whether it is God's kingdom or the devil's.

If we lift up our mind's eye to the condition of heavenly and supernatural virtues which are truly in the kingdom of God, how shall we imagine it to be anything but a state of continual joy? What is so natural in true blessedness as unshakable peace of mind and happiness? This is not a mere guess. You have the sure authority of the Lord when he disclosed the nature of that heavenly kingdom. 'Behold I make a new heaven and a new earth: and the former things shall not be remembered nor come into the heart. But ye shall be glad and rejoice for ever in my creation.' And again: 'Joy and gladness shall be found therein: thanksgiving and the voice of praise, and there shall be month after month, and sabbath after sabbath.' And again: 'They shall have joy and gladness, sorrow and sighing shall flee away.' And, still more clearly, listen to what the Lord himself says of Jerusalem: 'I will make thine officers peace, and thine overseers righteousness. Violence shall no more be heard in thy land, nor desolation nor destruction within thy borders. Salvation shall possess thy walls, and praise shall possess thy gates. The sun shall be no more thy light by day, neither shall the brightness of the moon give light to thee: but the Lord shall be thine ever-lasting light, and thy God thy glory. Thy sun shall no more go down, neither shall thy moon withdraw itself: but the Lord shall be thine everlasting light, and the days of thy mourning shall be ended.' [14]

St Paul does not say simply and without qualification that all joy is the kingdom of God, but selectively and specially, joy in the Holy Spirit. He knew that there was another kind of joy, a joy to be detested. The Scripture refers to this kind of joy in texts like 'The world shall rejoice' or 'Woe unto you that laugh, for you shall mourn.'

The kingdom of heaven, then, may be understood in three ways. First, the heavens shall reign, which means the rule of the saints (as in texts like 'Be thou over five cities, and thou over ten': or the word to the disciples 'Ye shall sit upon twelve thrones judging the twelve tribes of Israel'): second, that Christ begins to reign over the heavens when all creation is subject to God

[14] Isa. 65:17–18; 51:3; 66:23; 35:10; 60:17–20.

and he becomes all in all: or third, that the saints shall reign in heaven with the Lord.[15]

14. Everyone knows that on earth he shares the ministry which the Lord shared during his earthly life. And he doubts not that in the life to come, he will be a companion of the Lord whose servant and friend he has in this life chosen to be. The Lord himself said: 'If anyone serve me, let him follow me: and where I am, there shall my servant also be.'[16]

A man gains the kingdom of the devil by consenting to sin, the kingdom of God by practising goodness in purity of heart and in knowledge of the things of the spirit. Wherever the kingdom of God is, is life eternal: wherever the kingdom of the devil is, is death and hell.

If a man is in death and hell, he cannot praise the Lord: the prophet spake thus: 'The dead shall not praise thee, O Lord: nor shall those who go down into hell' (he means, the hell of sin). 'But we are alive' (he means, alive not to sin nor this world, but to God) 'and shall bless the Lord from this time forth for evermore. For in death no man remembereth God: and who shall confess the Lord in hell?'[17] (again he means the hell of sin). No one—not even though he call himself a Christian or a monk a thousand times over, confesses God while he is sinning, no one remembers God while he allows what the Lord hates: it is like pretending he is a faithful servant while he takes no notice of his master's commands.

St Paul says of a widow: 'She that giveth herself to pleasure is dead while she liveth':[18] and this is the kind of death he means. Many men whose bodies are alive are dead and in hell and cannot praise God. And many whose bodies are dead, bless and praise God together in the spirit—'O ye spirits and souls of the righteous, bless ye the Lord,' and 'let every spirit praise the Lord.'[19] In the Apocalypse the souls of the martyrs are described as praying to God as well as praising him. In the Gospel the Lord said plainly to the Sadducees: 'Have you not read the word which God had spoken to you, "I am the God of Abraham and the God of Isaac and the God of Jacob? He is the God not of the dead but of the living." ' All men live to him. And St Paul says: 'God is not ashamed to be called their God: for he hath prepared for them a city.' After they have parted from their body they can still act and feel, as is evident from the

15 John 16:20; Luke 6:25; Luke 19:17 and 19; Matt. 19:28.
16 John 12:26.   17 Ps. 115:17–18; 6:5.   18 I Tim. 5:6.
19 Dan. 3:86 LXX; Ps. 150:6.

parable of Dives and Lazarus, where the poor man went to Abraham's bosom, the place of bliss, and the other was consumed with the agonizing heat of everlasting fire.

Remember what he said to the thief on the cross: 'Today shalt thou be with me in Paradise.' [20] Surely this means, not only that the original understandings remain in souls, but also that they enjoy a state proportionate to the goodness or otherwise of their deeds? The Lord would never have promised him this if he had known that his soul would after its separation from the body lose all power of perception or be annihilated. It was not his flesh, but his soul, which was to enter Paradise with Christ. The heretics have suggested an ungodly punctuation of the sentence which we should at all costs disallow and detest. Because they do not believe that Christ could be in Paradise on the same day on which he descended into hell, they put the comma after the word 'today,' and read 'Verily I say unto thee today, Thou shalt be with me in Paradise.' The aim of this punctuation is to suggest that the promise was not fulfilled at once, but that it will be fulfilled in the general resurrection. These heretics have appealed to a text which they have misunderstood—the word which he spoke to the Jews who believed that he was tied and bound like themselves in the coils of human frailty, 'No one hath ascended into heaven, but he who came down from heaven, even the Son of man who is in heaven.' [21]

By this text to the penitent thief he shows that the souls of the dead do not lose their senses or their affections like hope and melancholy, joy and fear, and that they begin to experience a foretaste of what they will receive in the Last Judgement: that they are not annihilated as some infidels think, but they enjoy a fuller life and praise God more ardently.

Put aside Scriptural evidence for a moment, and consider the matter a little by the light, admittedly dim, of human reason. Must not the mind be worse than silly—nay, worse than deranged—which can even think it possible for the most precious part of human nature, that part which, St Paul tells us, is formed in the image of God, to lose consciousness in the moment when it puts aside the burden of mortal flesh? This is the part of the human being which contains the whole power of the reasoning faculty, the part which enables the dumb and unperceptive material flesh to perceive and perceive reasonably. It follows logically that when the mind has put off the flesh which blunts its faculties, it will recreate into fresh strength the

[20] Matt. 22:31-2; Heb. 11:16; Luke 23:43.   [21] John 3:13.

intellectual faculties and, so far from losing them, will find them purer and more acute.

St Paul was so vividly aware of this truth that he wished to depart from the flesh and thereby come into closer unity with his Lord: 'I have a desire to be dissolved and to be with Christ, which is far better; for while we are in the body we are absent from the Lord.' And therefore 'We are bold and have our desire always to be absent from the body, and present with the Lord. Wherefore also we strive, whether absent or present, to be pleasing to him.' He believed with an absolute and confident faith that being in the body meant absence from Christ and departure from the body brought presence with Christ. He spoke again, still more openly, about this fuller life of souls in the text: 'But ye are come to Mount Sion, and the city of the living God, the heavenly Jerusalem, and to an innumerable company of angels, and the church of the first born, who are written in heaven, and the spirits of just men made perfect.' And again: 'We have had our earthly fathers and masters, and we revered them; shall we not much more be subject to the Father of spirits and live?' 22

15. In many ways we come to contemplate God. We know him in worshipping his very being which we cannot fathom, the vision which is yet hidden, though it is promised, and for which we may hope. We know him in the majesty of his creation, in regarding his justice, in apprehending the help we receive for our daily lives. We contemplate him when we see what he has wrought with his saints in every generation: when we feel awe at the mighty power which rules creation, the unmeasurable knowledge of his eye which sees into the secrets of every heart; when we remember that he has counted the grains of sand upon the shore and the waves upon the sea and the raindrops, that he sees every day and hour through all the centuries past and future: when we remember his mercy unimaginable—seeing countless sins committed every moment and yet bearing them with inexhaustible long-suffering; when we contemplate that he has called us by reason of no merit which he found in us but simply of his free grace: when we see so many opportunities of salvation offered to those whom he is going to adopt as his sons: how he caused us to be born in circumstances where we might from our cradles receive his grace and the knowledge of his law: how he is working to overcome the enemy in us, simply for the pleasure of his goodness, and is

22 Phil. 1:23; II Cor. 5:6; Heb. 12:22-3 and 9.

rewarding us with everlasting blessedness: and, finally, how for our salvation he was incarnate and made man, and has spread his wonderful mysteries among all nations. There are countless other contemplations of this kind, which arise in our perceptions in proportion to our holiness of life and our purity of heart and through which, if our eyes are clean, we see and grasp God. No man in whom anything of earthly passion remains can keep the vision continually. 'Thou canst not see my face' said the Lord 'for no man shall see me and live' [23]—live to this world and its desires."

16. Germanus: "How is it that idle thoughts creep into our minds when we do not want them or are unaware of them, so that it is quite difficult even to understand them, let alone drive them away? Is it possible for a mind to avoid delusions like this?"

17. Moses: "Thoughts inevitably besiege the mind. But any earnest person has the power to accept or reject them. Their origin is in some ways outside ourselves, but whether to choose them or not lies within us. [24] But because I said it was impossible for thoughts not to come to the mind, you must not put all the blame upon the spirits who assault our integrity. Otherwise the will of man would not be free, and we could make no effort for our own improvement. To a great extent we have the capacity to better the sort of thoughts we receive, to let holy thoughts or secular thoughts grow into our minds. This is the purpose of reading the Bible often and meditating upon it always, to attain a higher state of recollectedness: this is the purpose of singing psalms often, so that feelings of repentance may be continually elicited: this is the purpose of constancy in watchings or fasts or prayer, so that the mind, in its weakened body, may care nothing for the world but may contemplate the things of heaven. If we neglect these, the mind will surely creep back towards squalid sin and fall.

18. This movement of the heart may suitably be compared to a mill wheel spinning round under power from a waterfall. The wheel must revolve so long as the water flows. But the mill owner can decide whether to grind wheat or barley or darnel and the wheel will crush whatever he chooses.

So the mind cannot but move hither and thither under the impetus of external circumstances and the thoughts which pour

[23] Ex. 33:20.
[24] *Reprobatio vel electio* lies in our power—possibly a sentence glancing at St Augustine's theology of grace.

in upon it like a torrent. But which thoughts to reject or accept, an earnest and careful mind will determine. If we are continually meditating upon Holy Scripture and lifting up the mind to desire a perfect life and to hope for a future blessedness, the mind cannot help receiving, and dwelling upon, the thoughts of the spiritual which thereby arise. If sloth and carelessness dominate us, and we spend our time in sinful and idle gossip or are busied unnecessarily with the cares of the world, a variety of tares will infallibly spring up and minister temptations harmful to the heart. As our Lord and Saviour said, where our treasure is—of effort and intention—there will our heart abide.[25]

19. It is important to distinguish three sources of our thoughts: God, the devil, ourselves.

Thoughts are of God when he illuminates our minds with his Holy Spirit, helping us upon our road: or when for our salvation he chastens us, and casts us into a mood of repentance that we have failed and been idle: or when he opens to us the mysteries of heaven, and turns us to choose decisively to amend our lives.[26]

Thoughts are of the devil, when he tries to make us fall by holding before us the pleasure of sin; by making bad appear good, or transforming himself into an angel of light.[27]

Thoughts are of ourselves when, as normally, we remember what we are doing, or have done, or have been told.[28]

[25] Cf. Matt. 6:21.

[26] "Examples from the Bible: When King Ahasuerus was chastened by the Lord, he was stirred to ask for the books of the annals, and so remembered the services of Mordecai, rewarded him with the highest rank, and revoked his bloody order to kill the Jews. The prophet says: 'I will hearken what the Lord God shall speak within me' (Ps. 85:8); another prophet says: 'An angel uttered, speaking within me' (Zech. 1:14); the Son of God promised that he will come with his Father and dwell among us, (cf. John 14:23): 'It is not you that speak, but the spirit of your Father who speaks within you' (Matt. 10:20); and St Paul: 'You seek a proof of Christ, who speaks in me' (II Cor. 13:3)."

[27] "The Evangelist notices it: 'And after supper was ended, when the devil had already put it into the heart of Judas Iscariot, Simon's son, to betray the Lord'; and 'after the sop, Satan entered with him' (John 13:2 and 27). Peter said to Ananias: 'Satan has tempted thee in thy heart, to lie to the Holy Spirit' (Acts 5:3). Compare what we read much earlier in the Gospel, in Eccl. (10:4): 'If the spirit ascend upon thee with power, leave not thy place.' (This description of Ecclesiastes as in evangelio caused much perturbation to the copyists.) In the third book of Kings, it is said to God against Ahab in the character of an unclean spirit—'I will go forth and will be a lying spirit in the mouth of all his prophets' (I Kings 22:22)."

[28] "Examples: David said: 'I thought upon the ancient days, and had in

20. We ought always to remember that thoughts may arise in these three different ways, and try to determine discreetly the source and the author of the thoughts we find. This judgement upon their author enables us to consider how we ought to behave towards them, and so become, what the Lord commanded us to be, 'good money-changers.' [29] The highest skill of a money-changer consists partly in testing when the gold coin is unadulterated and, as they commonly say, 'of true alloy,' and when it is not sufficiently purified by the fire; and partly in not being deceived by a cheap brass penny if it is fabricated to glitter like gold. They have to recognize coins stamped with the heads of usurpers; and in spite of the greater difficulty, to determine which coins bear the head of the legal emperor and yet have been illegally minted: and finally, they have to use scales to discover whether the legal coins have lost anything of their proper weight.

The Gospel text, by using this simile, tells us what we ought to do in the life of the spirit.

First, whatever doctrine enters the heart, we have to examine it to see whether it is of God and purified in the Holy Spirit's fire, or whether it belongs to the false religion of the Jews or arises from the intellectual pride of a secular philosophy and is making a mere outward show of piety. We must fulfil the precept of the apostle: 'Believe not every spirit, but prove the spirits whether they are of God.' [30]

This first test is failed by men who become monks and then are drawn by the grace of style, or by philosophical teachings which have an apparent meaning consonant with religion and attractive to religious men, like cheap brass coins manufactured to resemble gold and so impoverishing their cheated owners for ever: they entice them away again to the world's clangour or to the bombast of heretical thought. We read in the book of Joshua that this happened to Achor, who coveted and stole a golden weight from the camp of the Philistines, and was smitten with a curse and condemned to suffer an eternal death.

mind the years of old, and I meditated, by night I exercised myself with my heart, and searched out my spirit' (Ps. 77:6–7, LXX). Again, 'The Lord knoweth the thoughts of man, that they are but vain.' (Ps. 94:11): and 'the thoughts of the righteous are judgements' (Prov. 12:5). In the Gospel the Lord said to the Pharisees: 'Why do you think evil in your hearts?' (Matt. 9:4)."

[29] A saying found nowhere in the Gospels, but commonly reported among the early Fathers.

[30] I John 4:1.

Secondly, we should take care that no faulty interpretation, mixed with the pure gold of Scripture, should delude us about the value of the money. Wily Satan tried to impose thus upon our Lord and Saviour like any ordinary man. With an evil motive, he interpreted a text about the guardian angels, which applies generally to all men, as though it possessed a special application to him who needed no guardian angels: 'For he shall give his angels charge concerning thee, to keep thee in all thy ways: and in their hands they shall bear thee up, lest at any time thou dash thy foot against a stone.'[31] By some skilful assumption he twists and turns the precious text of Scripture into a meaning harmful and contrary to the true meaning, like a coin which seems to be gold but is stamped with the usurper's head.

Sometimes he tries to cheat us with counterfeits, by suggesting that we ought to undertake some good work—a work which apparently leads towards virtue, but which would not be approved by our elders and in fact leads to sin. Sometimes he suggests excessive or impossible fasts, too long vigils, too many prayers, unsuitable reading, and so brings us to a bad end. Sometimes he persuades us to go visiting for good and religious purposes, and so extracts us from our spirit-filled cloisters and our quiet and friendly retirement. Or he persuades us to undertake the charge of nuns or of pauper women, and so entangles us in the anxieties which destroy a spiritual life. Sometimes on a plea of building the faith of many and winning souls for religion, he incites us to want to be ordained, and so snatches us from the humility and the discipline of our way of life.

All these courses of action deceive the unwary by appearing to be merciful and pious; they are contrary to our salvation and our profession. They are like coins which imitate the coins of the true emperor, but have not been coined by the legal mint. Though at first they seem full of piety, they have not been coined by approved and Catholic Fathers, but have been manufactured in secret and bring loss to the ignoramuses who accept them unawares. However useful and needful they seem to be at the moment, later they begin to undermine the solidity of our religious profession and to weaken (so to say) the whole body of our purpose. Then it is best that they be amputated like a right hand or foot, which we need, yet which causes us to stumble. Better it is to leave behind one limb if by so doing we may keep the other parts of the body healthy and active, and so be able to limp into the kingdom of heaven, than to try to take

[31] Matt. 4:6.

the whole body with us and stumble on the way. To be parted from our strict rule may lead to a loss which can never be compensated by future results and which would cause all the best fruits of our labour to be destroyed in hell-fire.[32]

21. Not long ago we heard that Abba John, who lives at Lycopolis, was deluded in this way. He had put off taking food for two days and had exhausted his body. And when at last he sat down to eat, the devil came to him in the shape of a hideous negro, and fell at his feet saying: 'Forgive me for making you undertake this labour.' John, who possessed a perfect judgement, understood that on the pretext of an abstinence unsuitably practised, the devil had cheated him and forced him into a useless fatigue of body, and worse, a fatigue which would harm the spirit. Here he was cheated by a forged coin: he respected the face of the true emperor imprinted upon it, but failed to examine carefully enough whether it was legally struck.

The final duty of a good money-changer is to check the weight. Whenever we find a particular course of action suggested, we weigh it, with a judgement as careful and as balanced as possible, to determine whether it is a course of common honesty, whether it can be done soberly and in the fear of God, whether it is the course of integrity; or whether it is short weight like a dud coin, a trivial piece of ostentation or conceit or love of novelty. We weigh it in the public scales, that is, test it by the acts and teachings of the apostles and prophets: and then either keep it as true and genuine and authorized by those authorities, or else carefully throw it away as debased and of an inadequate and unauthorized weight.

22. We need, then, the power of discrimination for four purposes:

First, to know whether the metal is genuine or painted.

Secondly, to reject as forgeries (because bearing the illegally stamped head of the legal emperor) ideas which falsely suggest works of piety.

Thirdly, to detect the coins which are stamped with the usurper's head, the perversion of the precious gold of Scripture by untrue and heretical interpretations.

[32] "*Proverbs* expresses this sort of illusion powerfully: 'There are ways which seem to be right to a man, but their latter end will come into the depths of hell,' and 'An evil man is harmful when he attaches himself to a good man'—which means that the devil deceives when he puts on a cloak of sanctity. 'But he hates the sound of the watchman,' which means the power of discretion which comes from the advice of the Elders. (Prov. 16:25, LXX; 11:15, LXX.)"

Fourthly, to reject the coins which are light-weight, corroded by vanity, coins which cannot pass the test when weighed in the scales of the fathers.

Without this discrimination we might lose the reward of all our labour, by disobeying the command which our Lord warned us to do all we could to observe—'Lay not up for yourselves treasure on the earth, where rust and moth corrupt, and where thieves break through and steal.' [33] To do anything with the aim of increasing our reputation is to lay up treasure on earth; to hide it, and bury it where demons will eat it, vanity will corrode it like rust, pride will ruin it like moths: and the man who hid it will gain nothing from it.

We should ever examine the inner sanctuary of the heart, and track down whatever comes into it—perhaps a snake or lion has crept into the mental fastness through the undergrowth and has left a spoor which other beasts could follow, if we were heedless. It is as though we were always to be ploughing up the ground of the heart. The plough is the constant recollection of the Lord's cross: and by its means we shall exterminate the rats and vipers which have made their habitations in our field."

23. Seeing our surprise and earnestness at his words, he stopped his discourse out of respect and was silent for a little. Then he added: "Your eagerness has provoked me to talk at length, my sons; it struck a spark which kindled me into flame. I see that you thirst for the teaching which leads to a perfect life. I still want to say a little more about the virtue of a balanced judgement, 'discretion,' a grace which guards the keep in the Castle of All Virtues, and to give you practical examples of its value and the opinions of the old fathers about it. I remember how often people have importuned me, even to tears, to talk on this subject, and how although I longed to satisfy them, I could not—I felt nothing, had nothing to say, and could not even send them away with a little word of comfort. This is a clear sign that the Lord gives a man grace of speech in proportion to the sincerity with which his audience wishes to hear him.

Only a little of the night remains, not enough to finish the subject. Let us therefore go to rest. If we do not take a little rest now we shall later have to sleep all night long. Let us keep the remainder of our talk for another day or night. The best counsellors on the subject of 'discretion,' ought to start by displaying the virtue in their own conduct and not fall into its

[33] Matt. 6:19.

opposite by talking too long, and so contradicting what they preach by their practice. Though I still mean to talk about the virtue of 'discretion,' so far as the Lord gives me power, it will be a fundamental advantage if I am not so busy praising the excellence of moderation that I go on talking immoderately."

*   *   *   *

So Moses put an end to the Conference, though we were still greedy for more. He encouraged us to sleep for a short time, suggesting that we should lie down on the mats on which we were sitting and use our bundles for pillows. These bundles are made of thick papyrus leaves evenly tied together into long, slender bales six feet in length. Sometimes the brothers use them at the daily service instead of a low stool, sometimes as pillows, for they are quite soft and comfortable. They are thought particularly suitable for use by the monks because, though they are reasonably soft, they are cheap and easy to make: papyrus grows everywhere on the banks of the Nile, and the material is flexible and easily utilized.

We obeyed the old man's command to go to sleep though we thought it tiresome, for we were still excited and delighted by his conference, and were looking forward to continue the talk.

*   *   *   *

[The next morning Moses resumed his talk. He described "discretion" as the greatest gift of God's grace. St Antony had taught that it was the mistress of virtues because without it the virtues could end in ruin. Discretion teaches the monk to avoid excess on either hand and ever to walk the king's highway. Herein lies the wisdom without which the inward house cannot be built. Discretion is the mother of virtues, as well as their guardian and regulator.

Moses gave examples of destruction through lack of discretion—too rigorous solitude, too rigorous abstinence, too much faith in visions.

Germanus asked how to gain discretion, and so become good "money-changers."

Moses replied that true discretion is gained by true humility. And the first proof of humility is to reserve everything (even the thoughts) to the judgement of the elders. A wrong thought is enfeebled the moment it is confessed. There is nothing so liable to cause a fall as leaving the advice of the elders and experimenting with untried methods.

Discretion is to be found, not in all old men, but in those old men known to have lived a religious life when young.

Practically, Moses insisted upon (1) the importance of disclosing thoughts to the Elders and receiving discretion from them, and (2) the need for moderation in fasting and vigils, excessive abstinence being as weakening to the soul as no abstinence.]

CONFERENCE 9

The First Conference of Abba Isaac

ON PRAYER

1. If the Lord gives his blessing, these Conferences of Abba Isaac will keep the promise to write about unceasing prayer, which I made in the second book of the Institutes. When I have completed these, I believe I shall have fulfilled the duty which Bishop Castor of blessed memory laid upon me, as well as your request, Bishop Leontius and brother Helladius. First, you will forgive the length of the book. I tried to compress and to omit much, but still it is longer than I planned. That is why I leave out much of blessed Isaac's talk about various monastic teachings and proceed to the latter part of his discourse.

2. Isaac: "Every monk (who looks for the perfect way) aims at uninterrupted prayerfulness. As far as is possible to a frail man, he struggles for imperturbable peace and purity of mind. This is the reason why we try so unwearyingly to practise the different disciplines of the body and the spirit. The discipline of the body and spirit on the one side, and unceasing prayerfulness on the other, cannot help having a mutual effect upon each other. The keystone in the arch of all virtues is perfect prayer, and without this keystone the archway becomes rickety and insecure. Conversely, without the virtues no one can attain the continual serenity of prayerfulness which I am discussing. Therefore, I cannot rightly and shortly treat of the effect and chief object of prayer (which is perfected in the truly virtuous life), unless first I treat systematically the way of avoiding sin and attaining goodness. As the Gospel parable teaches, the man who is going to build a tower first takes care to estimate and assemble his materials. But it is impossible to build a fine tower upon this prepared material unless the ground is cleared of rotten or dead rubbish and the foundations are built in firm (or 'lively' as they say) soil or on rock. So it is in the realm of the spirit. To build a tower of the spirit, you must clear the soul of its sins and passions, and build firm foundations of simplicity

and humility upon the Gospel: this is the only way the tower can rise unshakable, as high as heaven. Then, though the tempests of passion be poured down upon it, though the floods of persecution beat upon it like battering-rams, though the storm of hostile spirits blows upon it, it shall still stand, and stand undamaged.

3. No one can offer prayer of a proper intensity and sincerity, unless he is seeking to live thus: first, there must be no anxiety about the bodily needs—not only no worry about a piece of business, but not even the recollection of it: no detraction: no gossip: above all, no anger nor wrongful sorrow, for these cannot but disturb the spirit: no lust of the flesh: no love of money.

By clearing the ground—weeding out these and other public sins—a man makes his life pure, and attains the state of simplicity and innocence. Then he must lay a foundation deep enough to support a tower that will reach to heaven: and the only foundation deep and strong enough is humility.

The lower storeys of the building are the other virtues. The soul should be kept from wandering abroad, and then, little by little, will begin to lift its eyes to contemplate God.

Whatever the mind has been thinking about before it prays will certainly come to it while it is praying. Therefore, before we begin to pray, we ought to be trying to be the kind of people whom we wish God to find when we pray. The mind is conditioned by its recent state. In prayer, the mind remembers recent acts or thoughts or experiences, sees them dancing before it like ghosts. And this annoys us, or depresses us, or reminds us of past lust or past worry, or makes us (I am ashamed to say) laugh like fools at some absurd joke or circumstance, or go over again some recent conversation. Whatever we do *not* want to creep into our time of prayer, we must try to keep out of the heart when we are not praying.

St Paul's words were: 'Pray without ceasing,' and 'In every place lifting up pure hands without wrath or controversy.' [34] To obey this is impossible, unless the mind is purified from sin, is given to virtue as its natural good, and is continually nourished by the contemplation of God.

4. There is a good comparison between the soul and a delicate little feather. If a feather has not been touched by damp, it is so light that the slightest breath of wind can puff it high into the air. But if even a little damp has weighed it down, it cannot float, and falls straight to the ground. In the same way the

[34] I Thess. 5:17; I Tim. 2:8.

mind, if not burdened by sin and the cares of daily life and evil passion, has a natural purity which lifts it from earth to heaven at the least breath of a meditation upon the invisible things of the spirit. The Lord's command is sufficient warning—'Take heed that your hearts be not *weighed down* by surfeiting and drunkenness and the cares of this world.'[35] So if we want our prayers to reach the sky and beyond the sky, we must make sure that the mind is so unburdened by the weights of sin and passion as to be restored to its natural buoyancy. Then the prayer will rise to God.

5. Yet we should notice the weights of the mind which the Lord selected. He did not mention adultery, fornication, murder, blasphemy, theft, which everyone knows to be damnable sins. He mentioned 'surfeiting and drunkenness and the cares of this world': faults which worldly men do not take trouble to avoid, nor consider damnable, and which (shameful though it is) some people who call themselves monks think harmless or profitable.

Though these three sins, literally committed, weigh down the soul to the earthy, and separate it from God, they are easily avoidable: especially by people like ourselves who are a long way from ordinary life and have absolutely no opportunity to engage in literal overeating or drunkenness or worldly business. But even though we have given away all our property; even though we have not feasted, have not drunk wine; even though we have been living in a hermit's cell—there is another kind of overeating and drinking and anxiety about the world, a spiritual kind which is just as dangerous, is harder to avoid, and which frequently traps us.[36] The heart soiled with sin and passion will be a heart weighted by this drunkenness of the spirit. And anxieties can still afflict us, even though we are not engaged in worldly business. That is proved by the elders' rule that any food which is more than 'unavoidable, necessary, and ordinary' diet must be regarded as 'worldly anxiety.'

For example: suppose that a job with a wage of a shilling

---

[35] Luke 21:34.
[36] "Cf. the prophet (Joel 1:5, LXX) 'Awake, ye that are drunk, but not with wine': and another, 'Be astonished and wonder and stagger: be drunk, and not with wine: be moved, and not with drunkenness' (Isa. 29:9): so the wine of this 'drunkenness' must be what the prophet calls 'the fury of dragons': see the roots from which this vine is growing. 'From the vineyard of Sodom is their vine, and their branches of Gomorrah': for the fruit and seed, of the text 'their grape is a grape of gall, theirs is a cluster of bitterness' (Deut. 32:33 and 32, LXX)."

would satisfy our needs, and we try to work longer hours for two or three shillings: or suppose that two tunics are sufficient, one for the night and one for the day, yet we become owners of three or four; or suppose a hut of one or two rooms would be adequate, yet we build four or five rooms, and these larger and better decorated than we need—then we are moved by secular pleasure and desire, and are letting worldly passion reign, so far as is possible for people in our situation.

6. We have practical proof that this happens by the prompting of devils. One day an elder of repute was passing by the cell of a brother who was suffering from this disease of the soul and used to sweat to build and repair buildings which he did not need. From a distance the elder watched him breaking up a rock with a heavy hammer. And he saw a negro standing beside him, putting his hands on the hammer and inciting him to work harder. For a long time the elder stood there, marvelling at the terrible appearances of the demon, astonished that the monk could thus be deceived. For when the monk was exceeding weary and wanted to stop work and rest, he was incited by the demon to pick up his hammer again and go on. And he was so buoyed up that he did not feel the harm which this overwork was doing him. In the end the elder, disturbed by this horrible, satanic, jest, turned aside to the monk's cell, greeted him, and asked: 'What are you doing, my brother?' He replied: 'We are working at this exceedingly hard rock, which we can hardly break at all.' The elder said: 'You are right in saying *we* can't. You were not alone when you hit it, but an unseen person was standing by you, driving you on to hit harder.'

In this way it is no proof that our hearts are not plagued with ambition, if we abstain from worldly occupations in which we could not engage even if we wanted; nor if we despise what would, if we achieved them, render us notorious among worldly men as well as religious men: but only if we eschew everything which ministers to our own power, even when it seems to be clothed in a garment of right.

Truly these things which seem trivial, or which we see other monks allow without a qualm, weigh the mind down more in proportion than the bigger things which normally and in their measure intoxicate the senses of worldly men. For they prevent the monk from leaving the earthly mind behind and concentrating his due attention upon God: and even a little parting from that supreme good must be regarded as an approach to destruction.

When the mind is freed from lust, established in tranquillity, and does not waver in its intention towards the one supreme good, the monk will fulfil the precept of St Paul, Pray without ceasing,' and 'In every place lifting up holy hands without wrath and controversy.'[37] By purity of heart (so to say) the mind is abstracted from earthly feelings and is re-formed in the likeness of an angelic spirit. Then, whatever thought the mind receives, whatever it considers, whatever it does, will be a prayer of true purity and sincerity."

7. Germanus: "I would I could keep the thoughts of the things of the spirit as easily as I can conceive their first beginnings! I conceive them in my heart through remembering the Scripture or through recollecting spiritual acts or through an intuition of the heavenly mysteries; and then they vanish all too soon; though how, I do not know. And when the mind has found some other opportunity of spiritual experience, other thoughts crowd in upon us and scatter the thoughts we had grasped. The mind has no perseverance, no stable control of its thoughts; even when it does seem to retain them for a while, I believe it happens unintentionally. And if the retention of a thought is not in my power, why should I think the origin of that thought to be so?

But this is a digression. We ought to keep to the plan of your discourse, in order not to delay any further your exposition of the nature of prayer. Leaving this question to its proper place, I ask you to tell us at once the nature of prayer, particularly in the light of St Paul's command to 'pray without ceasing.' By 'nature of prayer,' I would like first to know what sort of prayer it is that ought *always* to be offered: and secondly, how we can offer this prayer whatever it is. Your explanation confirms our ordinary experience that this cannot be done by any light purpose of heart. For you have defined the goal of the monks, the summit of his moral ascent, to consist in perfect prayer."

8. Isaac: "I imagine that no variety of prayer can be apprehended fully without great purity of heart and soul, and the illumination of the Holy Spirit. There are as many kinds of prayer as there are different states of soul, as many kinds of prayer as there are souls. Although I know that my dull heart prevents me from experiencing all kinds of prayer, yet so far as my slender experience allows, I shall try to go through them in order.

According to the progress of the mind in purity, the state in

37 I Thess. 5:17; I Tim. 2:8.

which its response to circumstance and its own effort have placed it, its prayers will vary from moment to moment. It is therefore certain that no one can go on sending up a prayer which never changes. A man prays in one way when he is lively; in another when he is weighed down with melancholy or despair; another when he is heartened by success; another when he seeks absolution; another when he asks for increase of grace or a special virtue or the removal of a special sin; another when he is stricken with fear at the prospect of hell and the judgement to come; another when he is longing for the future good; another in need and danger; another in peace and serenity; another when he is enlightened by some revelation of heavenly mysteries; another when he is oppressed by sensations of dryness and barrenness.

9. I have spoken on the states of prayer, not as much as the subject needs, but as much as the time and my scant abilities warrant. Now I am faced with a greater difficulty: to expound the four kinds of prayer which St Paul mentioned: 'I exhort therefore first of all that supplications, prayers, intercessions, thanksgivings, be made.' [38] We cannot suppose that St Paul made this fourfold distinction without good reason.

First we must investigate what he meant by the different words he used, *supplication, prayer, intercession, thanksgiving*. Then we must ask, are they to be used simultaneously? Do they enter into every prayer which is offered, or are they to be offered in turn? If in turn, are they to be offered by the same man at different times, or should one man offer supplications, another prayers, another intercessions, another thanksgivings, in accordance with his state of life and spiritual progress?

10. First, then, I must consider the meaning of the words, and the difference between them: secondly, whether they are to be offered separately or simultaneously: thirdly, whether St Paul arranged this order with a view to teaching the hearer something further, or whether he put them in this order without a particular reason. This last suggestion seems to me obviously absurd. I cannot believe that the Holy Spirit uttered anything through the apostle without meaning something by it.

So I begin in the order I have said, and trust in the Lord's help.

11. 'I exhort therefore first of all that supplications be made.' 'Supplication' is a beseeching or petition for sins. In it a person, repentant for his present or past sins, asks for pardon.

[38] I Tim. 2:1.

12. 'Prayers' are those by which we offer a vow to God. In Greek it is called *Euche*, which is the synonym of *vow*.[39]

We pray in this way, when we renounce the world and vow to mortify every act and earthly relation and to serve God with the whole heart. We pray, when we promise to despise secular honours and wealth, and follow the Lord with contrite heart and poverty of spirit. We pray, when we promise to be chaste in body, and to suffer unwearyingly; or when we vow to tear from the heart the roots of anger or the sorrow that brings spiritual death. If we are guilty of sloth, if we fall again to our old sins, we shall be before the judgement seat about our prayers and vows, and it will be said of us 'It is better not to vow, than to vow and not to pay': or, as it is in Greek 'It is better for thee not to pray, than to pray and not to pay.'

13. The third kind, intercession, is customarily offered, in moments of fervour, for other men and women—our family, the peace of the world. To use St Paul's words, we pray 'for all men, for kings, and all in authority.'[40]

14. The fourth kind, thanksgiving, is when the mind recollects what God has done or is doing, or looks forward to the good which he has prepared for them that love him, and so offers its gratitude in an indescribable transport of spirit. Sometimes it offers still deeper prayers of this sort; when the soul contemplates in singleness of heart the reward of the saints and so is moved in its happiness to pour forth a wordless thanksgiving.

15. From each of these four kinds rise other opportunities of richer prayer. Whether the prayer is expressing repentance, or is pledging the heart in the confident trust of a pure conscience, or is expressing the intercessions which spring from a charitable heart, or is rendering thanks in the sight of the great and loving gifts of God—we have known prayers dart up like sparks from a fire. It is therefore clear that all men need to use all four kinds. The same person according to his diversity of affective states will use prayers of repentance or offering or intercession or thanksgiving.

Nevertheless, the first kind seems particularly suitable to beginners, who are still smarting under the recollection of their sins. The second kind seems particularly suitable to people who

39 "Where we read in Greek *Tas euchas mou Toi Kyrioi apodoso*; in Latin we read: 'I will pay my vows unto the Lord.' Cf. the text of Eccl. 5:3–4, 'If thou vowest a vow unto the Lord, do not delay to pay it'—which is written in Greek, 'if thou prayest a prayer unto the Lord, do not delay to pay it.' "

40 I Tim. 2:1–2.

have already attained a certain progress towards goodness. Intercession seems particularly suitable to people who are ful-filling the pledges of self-offering which they made, see the frailty of others, and are moved by charity to intercede for them. Thanksgiving seems particularly suitable for those who have torn out of their hearts the sins which pricked their con-science and are at last free from fear of falling again: and then, recollecting the generosity and the mercy of the Lord, past or present or future, are rapt away into that spark-like prayer which no mortal can understand or describe.

Yet sometimes the mind which is advancing to the true state of purity and has begun to be rooted in it, can conceive all these kinds of prayer in a single action; it cannot be understood, but may be compared to the leaping of a flame. It consists of a powerful and wordless pouring forth of prayer to God, which the spirit, with groanings that cannot be uttered, sends up though not conscious of its content. In that moment it conceives and puts forth what no one can describe, and which the mind apart from that moment cannot remember.

So it happens that, whatever state of life a man has reached, he sometimes can offer pure and devout prayer. Even in the lowliest place where a man is repenting from fear of punishment and the judgement to come, his 'supplications' can enrich him with the same ardour of spirit as the man who has attained to purity of heart, gazes upon God's blessing, and is filled with an ineffable happiness. As the Lord said, he begins to love the more, who knows he has been forgiven the more.[41]

16. Yet, in progress towards goodness, we ought to aim at those kinds of prayer which are offered from the vision of future good or from charity—or at least (to speak in a way more appropriate for beginners) which are directed to acquiring a virtue or eradicating a sin. We cannot attain the higher kinds of prayer unless our mind has little by little been elevated by an advance in the sort of petition which it offers.

17. The Lord himself deigned to be the author, by his example, of these four kinds of prayer—in this, too, is fulfilled the text: 'the things which Jesus began both to do and teach.' He used *supplication* when he said: 'Father, if it be possible, let this cup pass from me': or, as is sung in his person by the Psalmist: 'My God my God look upon me; why hast thou for-saken me?' and texts like these. He used *prayer* when he said: 'I have magnified thee upon the earth, I have finished the work

41 Cf. Luke 7:47.

which thou gavest me to do': and 'For their sakes I sanctify myself, that they also may be sanctified in the truth.' He used *intercession* when he said: 'Father, those whom thou hast given me, I will that they also may be with me, that they may see my glory which thou hast given me': and 'Father, forgive them, for they know not what they do.' He used *thanksgiving* when he said: 'I confess to thee, Father, Lord of heaven and earth, that thou hast hid these things from the wise and prudent, and hast revealed them unto babes. Even so, Father: for so it seemed good in thy sight': and 'Father, I thank thee that thou hast heard me. But I knew that thou hearest me always.' [42]

Although he used these four kinds separately and at different times, accommodating himself to the measure that we understand, he showed that in a perfect prayer they can be offered simultaneously; in the long prayer which he offered and which we read at the end of St John's Gospel. The text is too long to insert here: but the careful reader will find this to be so. St Paul in the Epistle to the Philippians said the same, though slightly changing the arrangement, and showed that they ought sometimes to be offered altogether in one ardent offering—'In everything by prayer and supplication with thanksgiving, let your requests be made known to God.' [43] Here he particularly wanted to teach us that even in prayers of penitence and self-offering, thanksgiving should not be absent.

18. Out of these four kinds of prayer rises the loftier state of prayer, formed by the contemplation of God alone and by a charity that burns like fire. Here the mind throws itself into love for God and converses familiarly with him as with its own Father. The first words of the Lord's Prayer, 'Our Father' teach us to strive for this state. When we confess the God and Lord of all Creation to be our Father, we confess that we have been called from a state of slavery to the state of adopted sons.

'Who art in heaven': we pray that we may shrink from the earthly life, in which we live as pilgrims, and which divides us so far from our Father, and may long for that country where we know him to dwell; that we may avoid everything unworthy of our sonship, everything that might deprive us of our inheritance and make us liable to his severity. In this loving state of sonship, we shall direct our minds to our Father's glory instead of our own interests; thus:

42 Acts 1:1; Matt. 26:39; Ps. 22:1; John 17:4, 19 and 24; Luke 23:34; Matt. 11:25–6; John 11:41–2.
43 Phil. 4:6.

'Hallowed be thy name': we declare that our desire and our joy is his glory: and in this we imitate our Lord who said: 'He who speaketh for himself, seeketh his own glory. But he who seeketh the glory of him who sent him, the same is true and there is no unrighteousness in him.'[44] This was St Paul the chosen vessel's feeling when he wished that he could be accursed of Christ if only Christ's family might be multiplied, and the people of Israel be saved to God's glory. The man who knows that death is not the end is confident in his wish to die for Christ. Again, 'We rejoice when we are weak but ye are strong.'[45] It is no wonder if St Paul, for the glory of Christ and the conversion of his brother-Jews and of the Gentiles, should want to be accursed of Christ, when even the prophet Micah wanted to be a liar and to lose the inspiration of the Holy Spirit if the Jews could escape the punishment and destruction which he had prophesied—'Would that I were not a man that hath the Spirit, and that I rather spoke a lie.' And there was the case of the lawgiver, Moses, who did not refuse to perish with his brothers who were doomed to die, but said: 'I beseech thee, O Lord, this people hath sinned a heinous sin; either forgive them this trespass, or, if thou do not, blot me out of thy book which thou hast written.'[46]

'Hallowed be thy name' may appropriately be taken thus: the hallowing of God is our own sanctity. So when we pray this prayer, we are saying: 'Make me the kind of person worthy to understand and take thy great holiness to myself; make my spiritual life such that in it thou canst be seen to be hallowed.' This is what happens when men 'see our good works and glorify our Father who is in heaven.'[47]

19. 'Thy kingdom come'—the second petition of a pure heart, that the Father's kingdom may come at once. There is a present kingdom, where now Christ reigns with his saints: and in us this comes to pass when we eradicate wickedness and cast the devil's rule from our hearts, and God begins to rule in us, in fragrant goodness, in chastity instead of adultery, in serenity instead of rage, in humility instead of pride. And there is a future kingdom, which is promised in due time to all the perfect, to all the children of God, when Christ shall tell them: 'Come, ye blessed of my Father, inherit the kingdom prepared for you from the beginning of the world.' To this kingdom the soul turns its gaze and its desires, and prays 'Thy kingdom come.' By the

[44] John 7:18.
[46] Micah 2:11; Ex. 32:31-2.
[45] II Cor. 13:9.
[47] Matt. 5:16.

witness of its conscience, the soul knows that when he shall appear, it will share his glory. No guilty person would dare to want or pray 'Thy kingdom come': for no guilty person would want to face the tribunal of the Judge, knowing that at his coming he would receive prompt and condign punishment instead of reward.

20. 'Thy will be done on earth, as it is in heaven': a petition of sons. There can be no greater prayer than the prayer that earth may be like heaven. To pray 'Thy will be done in earth, as it is in heaven' is to pray that men may be like angels, that as angels fulfil God's will in heaven, men may fulfil his will, instead of their own, on earth. No one can say this sincerely except one who believes that every circumstance, favourable or unfavourable, is designed by God's providence for his good, and that he thinks and cares more for the good of his people and their salvation than we do for ourselves. It may be understood thus: the will of God is the salvation of all men, according to that text of St Paul: 'who willeth all men to be saved and to come to the knowledge of the truth.' [48] It is of this saving will that Isaiah speaks in the name of God the Father, 'And all my will shall be done.' When we pray: 'Thy will be done in earth, as it is in heaven,' we are praying in other words that all the dwellers upon earth may be saved, like the citizens of heaven, through the knowledge of thee, our Father.

21. 'Give us this day our bread,' which is ἐπιούσιος, which means 'supersubstantial': bread which another evangelist calls 'daily.' [49] *Supersubstantial* means that its quality is noble beyond other substances, that its magnificence and holiness exceed that

---

[48] I Tim. 2:4.

[49] Jerome inconsistently translated ἐπιούσιος by *supersubstantialis* in Matthew and by *quotidianus* in Luke. This piece of inconsistency was due no doubt to the same spiritualizing tendency which made Origen deny that the bread intended could be material bread: and it led to surprising consequences in the West, when the identity of the Greek word was forgotten and people believed the difference represented a real difference between the evangelists. Thus there was a discrepancy throughout the Middle Ages between the fact that in the offices the Lord's Prayer was said according to the Matthaean version, but with the apparently Lucan word *quotidianus* (for the offices preserved the wording existing before St Jerome), and the fact that the Vulgate text of Matthew had *supersubstantialis*. Nevertheless, the mistaken word of Jerome was never inserted into the offices, except by the logically minded Peter Abelard, who ordered Héloise and her convent to use the whole Matthaean form and not mix Matthew's text with the apparently "Lucan" word. St Bernard objected to these proceedings.

of other creatures. *Daily* means that without it we cannot live a spiritual life for a single day.

The word 'this day' shows that we must receive it daily, that yesterday's supply is inadequate: the word suggests that we should offer this prayer at all times. There is no day on which we do not need to strengthen the heart of the inner man.

Perhaps the word 'this day' can be understood of 'this life': while we are mortal men, give us this bread. Though we know that it is given to those who shall hereafter deserve it from thee, we ask thee to grant it to us 'this day'—unless a man has deserved to receive it in this life, he shall never partake of it in the life to come.

22. 'Forgive us our debts, as we also forgive our debtors.'

Unspeakable mercy of God! He has given us a form of prayer, has taught us a way of moral life acceptable to himself: has given with the form the command to pray always, and so is eradicating the roots of anger and sorrow: and, above all this, to men who pray he has provided an opportunity, and revealed a way by which they may move God to pronounce a merciful judgement upon them. You might say that he has given a power to make the judge's sentence lenient, because by forgiving others their offences we can draw him to forgive ours— 'Forgive us, as we also have forgiven.' [50] And so with the confidence of faith a man may ask pardon with this prayer—if he has been merciful to his own debtors rather than the debtors of his Lord.

Some of us, regrettably, are inclined to be serene and merciful about sins, however grave, committed by others against God, and inexorable debt-collectors when others commit trifling wrongs against ourselves. The man who from his heart forgives not his brother who has offended, by this prayer calls down, not forgiveness, but judgement, and out of his own mouth asks to incur severer punishment: saying: 'Forgive me as I also have forgiven.' If his request is answered, surely he will be treated after his example, with an implacable sentence. If we want to be judged with mercy, we must be merciful to those who have sinned against us. Only so much will be forgiven to us, as we have forgiven those who have injured us, however wickedly they have injured us.

There are some people who are so dreadfully aware of this that they silently omit the clause whenever the Lord's Prayer is recited congregationally in church: afraid that they are binding

50 Reading *dimisimus* rather than the *dimittimus* of several MSS. and Gibson.

instead of excusing themselves. They do not understand how fruitless is the attempt, with quibbles like these, to make the Judge of all men lenient. He has willed to reveal to men who pray to him the way in which he will judge. Because he wills not to be harsh and inexorable towards them, he has declared his plan of judgement, that we must judge our brother, if he sins against us, in just the way in which we wish him to judge us. 'He shall have judgement without mercy on him who hath shown no mercy.' [51]

23. 'And lead us not into temptation.' About the meaning of this clause there is much discussion. If we pray not to be allowed to be tempted, how shall we have any power of resistance? There is a text: 'Everyone who is not tempted is not proved': and 'Blessed is the man that endureth temptation.' [52] The clause 'Lead us not into temptation,' therefore does not mean 'Do not allow us to be tempted,' but, 'do not allow us to fall when we are tempted.' Job was tempted, but was not 'led into temptation': for he did not call God foolish, nor did he consent to the blasphemy to which the devil sought to lure him. Abraham was tempted, Joseph was tempted, but neither was 'led into temptation' because neither gave way to the tempter.

So finally, 'deliver us from the evil one': let us not be tempted of the devil above our capacity, but with the temptation make 'a way of escape that we may be able to bear it.' [53]

24. You see the method and pattern of prayer put before us by the judge to whom we pray. It contains no request for riches, no thought of honours, no petition for power, no mention of physical health or length of life. The author of eternity would have us ask nothing ephemeral, nothing paltry, nothing transient. He who neglects these petitions for eternity and prefers to ask for the evanescent, insults the generous majesty of God; meanness in prayer offends the judge instead of propitiating him.

25. The Lord's Prayer, given to us with his authority, seems to include the very pattern of a perfect prayer. Yet it carries those who use it to the higher state of prayer which I mentioned before, to that spark-like and ineffable prayer which very few men know by experience. It transcends the senses; is marked by no vocal expression, whether silent or aloud; but the mind, illuminated by an outflowing of light from heaven, does not define it in the narrow limit of human language. With the senses unified, it pours forth prayers, almost with violence, as a spring

51 James 2:13.   52 Ecclesiasticus 34:10; James 1:12.   53 I Cor. 10:13.

pours forth fresh water, and in a second's time darts up a prayer of such richness that afterwards the mind, returned to normality, cannot easily describe it. This state of prayer our Lord typified in those pattern prayers which he is said to have offered in silent retreat upon the mountain, and when (though here he gave an example impossible to imitate) in an agony of prayer he let drops of blood fall upon the ground.

26. Can anyone, however experienced, explain adequately the origins and causes and diversities of compunction in spirit, which strikes the spark in the mind and elevates it to prayer of fervent purity? I will now give a few examples of these occasions of compunction, so far as I can by God's aid remember them at the moment.

Sometimes the verse of a psalm which we are singing sets off the spark. Sometimes the beauty of the cantor's voice rouses the dull mind to a concentrated prayer. I know that the clarity and solemnity of the reader of the psalms can contribute to the fervour of the congregation. Often the address or conference of some holy man has been fruitful in stirring the affections of the hearers. I have known myself snatched away into true compunction of spirit by the death of a brother monk or of a dear friend or relative. Sometimes the memory of my own half-heartedness and carelessness has elevated my soul. No doubt there are countless occasions of this sort, which can rouse the mind, through God's grace, from its drowsiness and half-heartedness.

27. It is just as difficult to describe how these compunctions arise from the inner sanctuary of the soul. Sometimes it happens because the soul is filled with an indescribable joy and cannot help breaking out into ejaculations, and even the occupant of the next cell feels the power of the happiness in the heart. Sometimes the mind withdraws into a kind of secret abyss of silence, sudden illumination leaves it speechless, the awe-struck spirit locks its feelings within or loses feeling altogether, and pours out its longings to God in groanings that cannot be uttered. Sometimes a compunction of grief overwhelms it, and the only way to express it is by a release of tears."

28. Germanus: "I have very little experience, but even I have experienced something of this compunction of spirit. Sometimes tears will rise when I remember my sins, and then I am visited by the Lord and refreshed by the unspeakable joy which you have described: and the joy, by its very power, has given me the assurance not to despair of forgiveness. I believe there is no loftier state of prayer than this. But the trouble is that

it cannot be created when we choose. Sometimes, when I am struggling as hard as I can to excite a compunction of penitence, and I have decided to imagine my sins, I fail altogether in the effort: my eyes remain as dry as a flint and I cannot squeeze a drop of moisture out of them. When I am granted tears, I am happy. But when I cannot call them at will, I am cast down."

29. Isaac: "Not all varieties of weeping are evoked by the same feeling. There is a weeping because the heart is pricked by sin.[54] There is a weeping which springs from contemplating eternal good and longing for future light, and tears of joy and desire cannot help but break out; as the soul is athirst for the mighty living God, saying: 'When shall I come to appear before the presence of God? My tears have been my meat day and night.'[55] There is a weeping which rises, not from the consciousness of mortal sin, but still from the fear of hell and the terrible judgement; and the soul makes its own the prophetic prayer: 'Enter not into judgement with thy servant: for in thy sight shall no man living be justified.' There is a weeping caused, not by self-knowledge, but by awareness of others' sins and their lack of repentance. So Samuel is said to have wept for Saul; and the Lord in the Gospel, and Jeremiah before him, are described as weeping for the city of Jerusalem, 'O that my head were water and mine eyes a fountain of tears! And I will weep day and night for the slain of the daughter of my people.' And then there are the tears of the 101st psalm: 'I have eaten ashes for my bread and mingled my cup with weeping.' This was not caused by the same feelings as those of the penitent in Psalm 6, but arose from the anxieties, poverty and suffering of this life, the common lot of the righteous in the world.[56]

30. You can squeeze tears out of dry eyes and with a hard heart, but this is quite a different kind of weeping. I do not believe that this sort of weeping is altogether without profit, for the intention is good, especially in people who have not yet been

---

[54] "As in the texts: 'I have laboured in my groanings, every night I will wash my bed; I will water my couch with my tears' (Ps. 6:6); and 'let tears run down like a torrent day and night: give thyself no rest, and let not the apple of thine eye cease' (Lam. 2:18)."

[55] "And 'Woe is me that my sojourning is prolonged': 'Too long hath my soul been a sojourner' (Ps. 42:3-4; 120:5, LXX; 143:2)."

[56] "This is shown by the title as well as the text, for the title reads: 'A prayer of the poor, when he was in distress, and poured forth his prayer to God.' It is clear that the psalm is placed in the mouth of one of those poor men of whom the Gospel speaks: 'Blessed are the poor in spirit: for theirs is the kingdom of heaven' (Matt. 5:3; cf. Jer. 9:1; Ps. 102:9)."

able to reach perfect knowledge or to be thoroughly purified of past and present sin. But in people who have already progressed so far that they love goodness, this kind of weeping never ought to be extracted unnaturally. Even if it succeeds, it cannot rival spontaneous weeping as an occasion of elevated prayer. It is more likely by the failure of the effort to depress the soul and drive it away from that intention towards heaven in which the prayerful and reverent mind ought to be stable. It will force the soul to relax its concentration and instead go feebly after a weeping which is forced and futile.

31. To teach you the feeling of true prayer, I will give you, not my opinion, but that of St Antony. I have known him sometimes so long at his prayers that the sun rose before he had finished. And I would hear him, still in a rapture of spirit, cry out to the sun: 'Why do you hinder me? The rising of your light draws my mind away from the true light.' And St Antony also uttered this heavenly, inspired, saying on the end of prayer: 'That prayer is not perfect in which the monk understands himself and the words which he is praying.'

I hardly dare to add anything from my own slender experience. But so far as I can I will now point out how you can tell whether a prayer is one which the Lord hears.

32. If we pray unhesitatingly, without any touch of hopelessness to weaken the confident faith of the petitioner—if in the act of earnest prayer we feel ourselves to have obtained our request—we should not doubt that our prayers have effectively reached God. A man will deserve to be heard in proportion as he believes that God is looking upon him and that God can grant his prayer. It is impossible to minimize the Lord's declaration—'Whatsoever ye ask when ye pray, believe that ye shall receive, and it shall come to you.'" [57]

33. Germanus: "I am sure that this confident faith in being heard springs from a clear conscience. But sin yet pricks my heart; I have no merit to plead for me. How can I have this faith so confident as to presume that my prayers will be heard?"

34. Isaac: "The Gospels and the prophets teach us that prayers are heard for different reasons according to the different condition of the praying souls.

The Lord declares first, that if two agree, their prayer will be heard: 'If two of you shall agree upon earth touching anything for which they shall ask, it shall be done for them of my Father which is in heaven.'

[57] Mark 11:24.

He declares, secondly, that prayer in fulness of faith (which he compared to a grain of mustard seed) is heard. 'If ye have faith as a grain of mustard seed, ye shall say unto this mountain, Be thou removed, and it shall be removed; and nothing shall be impossible to you.'

Again, persevering prayers, which the Lord called importunity, will be heard. 'Verily I say unto you, that if not because of his friendship, yet because of his importunity he will rise and give him as much as he needs.'

Again, almsgiving will be heard. 'Shut up alms in the heart of the poor, and it shall pray for thee in the time of tribulation.'

A reformed life, or works of mercy, will be heard. 'Loose the bands of wickedness, undo the bundles that weigh down,' and (after a few words which castigate the uselessness of a sterile fast) 'Then thou shalt call and the Lord shall hear thee; thou shalt cry, and he shall say, Here am I.'

Sometimes, the sufferer's prayer of agony is heard. 'When I was in trouble I called unto the Lord, and he heard me,' and 'Afflict not the stranger, for if he crieth unto me, I will hear him, for I am merciful.' [58]

You see how many different ways prayer may be made so that it is heard. A hopeless conscience should make no one despair of being granted requests for a good which is saving to eternity. And as I look at our plight I grant that we possess none of the virtues—the right agreement between two people, faith like a grain of mustard seed, the works of charity which the prophet deserves—yet cannot we have that importunity which he supplies to all who want it? And to mere importunity he has promised that he will answer.

We must pray, then, without faithlessness and believe that merely by keeping at our prayer we shall be granted what we have asked in accordance with God's will. Wanting to grant us the everlasting good of heaven, the Lord encourages us to constrain him by our importunity. He does not scorn nor reject the importunate, but welcomes and praises them, and with his generosity promises to give them what they hopefully persevere to win. 'Ask, and ye shall receive: seek, and ye shall find: knock, and it shall be opened unto you. For everyone that asketh receiveth, and he that seeketh findeth, and to him that knocketh it shall be opened.' And 'all things, whatsoever ye shall ask in prayer, believing, ye shall receive,' and 'nothing shall be impos-

58 Matt. 18:19 and 17:20; Luke 11:8; Ecclesiasticus 29:15; Isa. 58:6 and 9; Ps. 120:1; Ex. 22:21 and 27.

sible to you.' [59] So even if all the other grounds for confidence are lacking, at least we can rouse our importunities; for anyone, without either merit or difficulty, can do this.

The man who prays must not doubt that he will certainly not be heard so long as he doubts whether he is heard. The example of blessed Daniel, whose prayer was answered twenty-one days after he began to pray, teaches us how unwearyingly we must petition the Lord. If we think the answer is slow in coming, we should not cease from the intention with which we began. It is possible that the Lord is postponing his gracious reply for some useful reason, or that the angel who was bringing us God's gift was delayed by the devil's resistance after he left the Almighty's presence. Certainly the angel cannot bring the gift if he finds that we have stopped wanting it. This could surely have happened to Daniel unless he had persevered so courageously to the twenty-first day.

A sense of hopelessness must not weaken our confident faith, even when we imagine that our request has been refused. Let us wholeheartedly accept the Lord's promise: 'All things, whatsoever ye shall ask in prayer, believing, ye shall receive.' We should consider the text of the evangelist, St John, where he removes all doubt about the matter: 'This is the confidence which we have in him, that whatsoever we ask according to his will, he heareth us.' [60] He commands us to have this full unhesitating confidence in requests which suit not our own convenience and comfort, but the Lord's will. The Lord's Prayer teaches us to include this in our prayers—'Thy will be done'— Thy will, not our will.

Remember the words of St Paul: 'We know not what to pray for as we ought.' [61] Hence we understand that sometimes we ask for a thing which would militate against our salvation; and that our request is refused by one who perceives our good more accurately and truly than we do ourselves. This was clearly what happened to St Paul when he prayed to be freed from Satan's messenger, who was permitted by the Lord to buffet him for his good: 'For which I besought the Lord thrice that he might depart from me. And he said unto me, My grace is sufficient for thee, for strength is made perfect in weakness.' [62] Even our Lord felt this in his human person (here giving us an example in prayer as in all else) when he prayed, 'Father, if it be possible, let this cup pass from me: nevertheless, not as I will

[59] Luke 11:9–10; Matt. 21:22; 17:20. [60] I John 5:14.
[61] Rom. 8:26. [62] II Cor. 12:8–9.

but as thou wilt' [63]—though his will was certainly not discordant with his Father's will. 'For he had come to save what was lost, and to give his life a ransom for many,' and 'No man taketh my life from me, but I lay it down of myself. I have power to lay it down, and I have power to take it again.' [64] The will of the Father and the will of the Son is everywhere one.

Instructed by this example of our Lord, we ought to end every prayer with the proviso: 'Nevertheless, not as I will, but as thou wilt.'

*   *   *   *

Everyone is aware that the person who is praying with concentration cannot observe the three profound inclinations which are usual at the end of the office in monastic congregations. [65]

35. Above all we ought to observe the teaching of the Gospel, to enter into our closet, and shut the door, and then pray to our Father. This has a spiritual meaning. We pray 'in the closet' when we have driven from the heart the turmoil of thoughts and cares, and are offering our prayers like friends whispering intimately. 'The shut door' means that we are praying silently, to him who searches the heart and not the lips. 'In secret' means that with a concentrated heart and mind we display our petition to God alone, and no devilish enemy can discover what we are asking.

So we ought to pray in deep silence. This is partly to avoid disturbing monks, praying nearby, with murmur or noise; but partly to prevent the demons, who are especially alert to pounce on people at their prayers, from knowing our intention. In this

[63] Matt. 26:39. For the Christology, see Gibson's note *ad loc.*
[64] "He speaks again in Psalm 38 (40:8) through the mouth of the blessed David, of the absolute unity between his Father's will and his own: 'To do thy will, O my God, I have willed.' We read of the Father, 'God so loved the world that he gave his only-begotten Son': and we read of the Son, 'Who spared not his own Son, but gave him for our sins': we read of the one 'Who spared not his Son, but gave him for us all.' and of the other, 'He was offered because he willed it himself.' (Matt. 18:11 and 20:28; John 10:18; John 3:16; Gal. 1:4; Rom. 8:32; Isa. 53:7, Latin.) Even in the mystery of the Lord's resurrection we are taught of the harmony in God's working. St Paul declares that the Father raised his body from the dead; the Son prophesied that he would raise the temple of his body, 'Destroy this temple, and in three days I will raise it up' (Gal. 1:1; John 2:19)."
[65] This tailpiece is so curious that the Roman edition of 1588 added an extra negative to provide the contrary sense. None of the best manuscripts supports the extra negative, and it is worse sense than the original.

way we shall obey the command: 'Keep the doors of thy mouth from her who sleepeth in thy bosom.' [66]

36. Hence we should pray often but shortly. If we dawdle about our prayers, the subtle enemy might be able to sow a seed in our heart.

The true sacrifice to God is a contrite spirit: the saving offerings and libations are the sacrifices of righteousness and praise. The true, acceptable, victims and burnt offerings are those offered by a contrite and humble heart. And if we practise this discipline and concentration of spirit which I have described, we shall be able effectually to sing: 'Let my prayer be set forth in thy sight as the incense: let the lifting up of my hands be an evening sacrifice.' [67]

*   *   *   *

Dusk reminds me that we ought to join in our evening devotions. In spite of my meagre experience I seem to have discoursed for a long time, however brief it has been in proportion to the profundity and difficulty of the material."

He ended. We felt awe and wanted him to continue. But after we had celebrated Vespers, we received his promise that at dawn he would treat the subject further; and so in happiness at what we had learnt and at his promise of more, we returned to our cells to lie down for a little sleep. We felt that we had been shown the excellence of prayer, but that we had yet to learn fully the method and the power by which we could acquire or preserve the state of unceasing prayerfulness.

CONFERENCE 10

The Second Conference of Abba Isaac

ON PRAYER

1. I have tried, however unskilfully, to describe with God's help the sublime customs of the hermits. The order of my discourse now forces me to insert a passage which may seem like a pimple on a lovely body. Yet I have no doubt that less educated readers will learn much from it about the image of Almighty God which Genesis describes. So I insert it with a view to a better understanding of a great doctrine which cannot be misapprehended without blasphemy and heresy.

2. The clergy of Egypt observe the feast of Epiphany as the time of our Lord's birth as well as the time of his baptism, and,

[66] Micah 7:5. [67] Ps. 141:2.

unlike the western Church with its two separate festivals, keep both commemorations upon the same day. They keep a custom of immemorial antiquity that after Epiphany the Bishop of Alexandria sends a letter to every church and monastery in Egypt declaring the dates for the beginning of Lent and Easter Day.

A few days after the first conference with Abba Isaac, arrived the customary festal letter from Bishop Theophilus of Alexandria.[68] Besides declaring the date of Easter, he included in the letter a long refutation of the absurd heresy of the Anthropomorphites. Nearly all the monks in Egypt, being uneducated and therefore holding wrong ideas, received this with bitterness and hostility: and a large majority of elders from all the ascetic brotherhood decreed that the bishop was guilty of a grave and hateful heresy, because (by denying that Almighty God was formed in the fashion of a man, when Scripture bears clear witness that Adam was created in his image) he seemed to be attacking the text of Holy Scripture. Even the hermits in the desert of Scete, who were more educated and more spiritually advanced than any other Egyptian monks, rejected the letter of Theophilus. The priests who were presiding over three of the four churches in Scete would not allow the letter to be read at their meetings: and the only exception was Abba Paphnutius, who was the priest of my own congregation.

3. Among those caught by the error was a monk named Sarapion, who had for many years lived a life of strict discipline and had achieved the leading of a truly good life. Almost first among monks in merit and in years in the desert, equally he was almost first in his ignorant prejudice against orthodox believers. The saintly priest, Paphnutius, used many exhortations to bring him back to the true belief, but unsuccessfully. To Sarapion the view seemed a novelty, not found in tradition.

It chanced that a deacon of great learning, named Photinus, arrived from Cappadocia with the object of visiting the brothers in Scete. Paphnutius gave him a warm welcome. And to support the doctrine contained in the letter of Bishop Theophilus, he led Photinus into the middle of the congregation, and in the presence of all the brothers, asked how the Catholic Churches of the East understood the text in Genesis: "Let us make man after our image and likeness."[69] Photinus explained how all the leaders of the churches understood the text spiritually, not literally nor crudely, and made a long speech adducing numer-

68 In the year 399.   69 Gen. 1:26.

ous proofs from Scripture. "That unmeasurable, incomprehensible, invisible majesty cannot be limited by a human frame
or likeness. His nature is incorporeal, uncompounded, simple,
and cannot be seen by human eyes nor conceived adequately by
a human mind."

At last old Sarapion was moved by the numerous and convincing assertions of this learned man, and consented to the
traditional faith of Catholics. Abba Paphnutius and the rest of
us felt great joy at his assent; joy that the Lord had not allowed
a man of such age and goodness, who had erred in simple
ignorance, to end his days unorthodox in the faith.

When we stood up to give thanks to the Lord in prayer, the
old man felt mentally bewildered at having to pray, because he
could no longer sense in his heart the anthropomorphic image
of God which he had always before his mind's eye when praying.
Suddenly he broke into bitter weeping and sobbing, and throwing himself prostrate on the ground with groans, cried: "Woe is
me! They have taken my God away from me, and I have none
to grasp, and I know not whom to adore or to address."

Germanus and I were deeply moved by this scene. And with
the effect of the last Conference still in our hearts, we returned
to Abba Isaac. When we reached his presence we addressed him
thus:

4. "Your last Conference on prayer stirred our desire to put
aside all else and return to you. But this new incident has
strengthened the desire still further. Abba Sarapion, misled by
skilful demons as we believe, fell into grave error. And this
has cast us down into a state of hopelessness. We are thinking
how for fifty years he has so admirably lived as a great ascetic
in this desert, and yet through ignorance not only lost the merit
of that life but incurred a risk of eternal death. So, first, we
want to know how and why this grave error crept upon him.

Secondly, we ask you to teach us how we can reach the state
of prayer of which earlier you taught us at length, and so finely.
Your earlier conference made us admire that state, but did not
show us how to achieve or secure it."

5. Isaac: "It is not surprising that a very simple man who
had never received any instruction on the being and nature of
God could be caught and deceived, even until now, by an error
which he mis-learnt a long time ago. This error is not, as you
suppose, a modern illusion of demons, but an inheritance from
the ignorance of the old heathen. They used customarily and
erroneously to worship demons fashioned in the likeness of men,

and even now they think to worship God in his majesty—the incomprehensible and indescribable—in the limited form of some statue. And they suppose they have nothing to worship unless they have in front of them a statue, which they can continually address in their devotions, can mentally conceive, and can keep in front of their eyes. Against this error is directed the text: 'And they changed the glory of the incorruptible God into the likeness of the image of corruptible man.' And Jeremiah says: 'My people have changed their glory for an idol.' [70]

This is the way in which this error has been implanted in some men. Nevertheless, in people whose souls have never been polluted by heathenism, the error is contracted by ignorance, under cover of this text: 'Let us make man in our image and likeness.' Hence the so-called Anthropomorphite heresy has risen out of the detestable interpretation of this text, a heresy which maintains obstinately and perversely that the limitless and simple nature of God is fashioned in human form and features. Anyone well-instructed in Catholic doctrine will detest the idea as heathen blasphemy: and in detesting it he will come to that pure state of prayer where the person will allow (I need not say) no effigy of God to be mingled in his prayers, and will not even admit the recollection of a saying or an action, or the outline of a character.

6. I said in my first Conference that every soul attains the kind of prayer proportionate to its purity: for it can abandon the contemplation of the earthy and material only in proportion as its state of purity carries it upwards to see Jesus in the mind's eye—Jesus still in the humility of his incarnate life, or Jesus glorified and coming in majesty. Jesus coming in his kingdom shall not be seen by men who are restrained by a weakness like that of the Jews and therefore cannot say with St Paul: 'And if we have known Christ after the flesh, yet now we know him so no more.' [71] Only those of purest sight look upon his divinity, men who have climbed up from earthly acts and thoughts and have gone apart with him into a high and lonely mountain. Jesus, untroubled by any earthly thought and passion and sin, exalted in the purity of his faith and goodness, discloses the brightness of his face and likeness to men who can look upon him because their souls are pure.

Inhabitants of cities and villages and hamlets, men engaged in the ordinary and virtuous pursuits of life, sometimes see Jesus; but they cannot see him with the distinctness possible to

[70] Rom. 1:23; Jer. 2:11.   [71] II Cor. 5:16.

those who can climb up with him upon the mount of saintliness, as did Peter, James and John. So in the wilderness he appeared to Moses, and spoke with Elijah. He wanted to teach us this and leave us an example of perfect purity. As the source of holiness, a source unpolluted like a spring of fresh water, he did not need to go apart in the wilderness to attain that perfect purity. No dirt, no stain from the crowds of human society could lessen the fulness of his purity of heart, for he it is who cleanses and purges all pollution.

Yet he went apart alone to the mountain to pray. He gave an example of withdrawal, to teach us that if we want to address God with a heart of integrity we should go apart from all crowd and tumult that disturbs our peace; and there, though still mortal men, we may in part succeed in attaining at least the shadow of the bliss promised to the saints in the future, and God may be to us all in all. [72]

7. Then our Saviour's prayer, wherein he prayed the Father for his disciples, will be truly fulfilled in us: 'that the love wherein thou lovedst me may be in them, and they in us': and 'that they all may be one, as thou, Father, art in me and I in thee, that they also may be one in us.' This unity will be when that perfect love of God, wherewith 'he first loved us' [73] has passed into the affections of our own hearts. So his prayer will be fulfilled, and we believe that that prayer cannot fail of its effect.

Then God shall be all our love, all we desire and seek and follow, all we think, all our life and speech and breath. The unity which now is between Father and Son shall be poured into our feelings and our minds: and as he loves us with a pure, sincere, unbreakable charity we on our side shall be linked to him by a lasting affection that nothing can spoil. In that union, whatever we breathe or think or speak is God. So the end of his prayer is attained in us—'that they all may be one as we are one: I in them, and thou in me, that they also may be made perfect in one': and 'Father, those whom thou hast given me, I will that where I am, they may also be with me.'

This should be the aim and purpose of the solitary: to seek to possess in some measure, even while mortal man, the first bridal gifts from the heavenly country and its glory. I repeat: this is the end of all true goodness, that the mind may every day be lifted beyond the material sphere to the realm of spirit, until the whole life and every little stirring of the heart becomes one continuous prayer."

[72] I Cor. 15:28.   [73] John 17:21–6; I John 4:10.

8. Germanus: "We were bewildered by the first conference and returned to you for further explanation. But now our bewilderment has grown. Certainly this doctrine stirs us to long for the bliss of heaven; but the more we yearn, the more we despair. For we still do not know how to achieve the sort of disciplined life which can enable us to reach this lofty goal. I beg you to be patient and allow me to explain (perhaps at some length) what we had begun to consider during our daily meditations in our cell. I know that you are unused to being troubled by the silly questions of weak brothers like ourselves. Yet it is worth bringing these silly questions into the open, so that the absurdity in them may be corrected.

We think that every art or science must begin with rudiments easy and suitable for the uninitiated. A man must be trained, so to speak, on the milk of the intellect, and thereby may grow, step by step, from ignorance to education. First he acquires the more obvious principles, passes the gateway to his subject, and thereby can climb without difficulty to the pinnacles of knowledge. A boy cannot frame sentences until he has learnt the alphabet properly. He cannot become a quick reader unless he can first read short and simple nouns. The man ignorant of grammar will never be able to write elegant prose or to become a sound philosopher.

This higher discipline in which we learn to cleave to God continually, must doubtless have first principles, foundations on which a man may build to raise the lofty tower. I think, though hesitantly, that its first principles consist in learning by what meditations God may be grasped and conceived; and then, how to preserve this thought, whatever it is, uninterruptedly: and I am sure that this uninterrupted preservation is the true perfection of the discipline.

We want you to show us material for this recollectedness by which God is conceived in the mind and the conception is retained permanently. Thereby we may keep it in front of us; and, when we feel we have fallen away, may at once be able to return, without any delay or ignorant meandering of the thoughts.

Sometimes, when my mind has wandered away from contemplating God, I wake up as if from a sleep as sound as death; I look round like a drowsy man just out of bed, for the subject-matter to recreate recollectedness. The process of finding the material distracts and delays me: before I find the vision again, my purpose of heart is beginning to fade. I am sure it happens because I do not keep before my eyes some special intention in the way of a formula to which the wandering mind could be recalled from its travels—so to say, a quiet harbour after a long and stormy voyage. Thus the mind, constantly hampered by this ignorance, teeters to and fro like a drunkard and does not even grasp the spiritual thought which comes to it, unasked and unsought. As it goes on receiving one sensation after another, it is unconscious of their arrival, their origin, or their departure."

9. Isaac: "Your question is intricate: and the fact that you have asked it proves you to have made headway towards purity of mind. To ask questions, still more to use a delicate introspection in this matter, is only possible to a person who by mental zeal and alertness has reached a stage where he can understand the complications of the problem; to a person whose constant attempts at a disciplined life have given him the experience whereby he may knock at the gates of mental purity. I see that you are no longer standing at the outer gate of true prayer, but are knocking at its inner door, and have already pushed it half open. A visitor who has reached the main hall of a house can easily be shown its inner rooms: and with God's guidance I think it will be easy to bring you to the heart of true prayer. I believe you will allow no obstacle to hinder your self-examination. The man who knows what questions to ask is on the verge of understanding: the man who is beginning to understand what he does not know is not far from knowledge.

So I am not afraid of the charge of speaking irreverently or betraying secrets if I now disclose what I omitted from my earlier Conference. I think that by God's grace your own study would have taught you the way even if you had no words of mine to help you.

10. You made an admirable comparison between spiritual discipline and the education of children. A child cannot recognize or make letters before he has become used to seeing them every day in wax copies. I must give you the formula for contemplation. If you carefully keep this formula in front of you, and learn to recollect it all the time, you can use it to mount to the contemplation of high truth. Every monk who looks for continual recollection of God uses this formula for meditation, and with the object of driving every other sort of thought from his heart. You cannot keep the formula before you unless you are free from all bodily care.

The formula was given us by a few of the oldest fathers who remained. They did not communicate it except to a very few who were athirst for the true way. To maintain an unceasing recollection of God it is to be ever set before you.

The formula is: 'O God, make speed to save me: O Lord, make haste to help me.' [74]

This verse has rightly been selected from the whole Bible for this purpose. It fits every mood and temper of human nature, every temptation, every circumstance. It contains an invocation of God, a humble confession of faith, a reverent watchfulness, a meditation upon our frailty, a confidence in God's answer, an assurance of his ever-present support. The man who continually invokes God as his guardian, is aware that he is always at hand. The formula contains a fervent charity, a fearful contemplation of the devil's power, a regard for the defender's succour which alone can relieve the beleaguered soul from the devil's siege by day and night. The verse is an impregnable battlement, a shield and coat of mail which no spear can pierce. Souls sunk in accidie or worry or melancholy thoughts of any kind find the cure of despair in this verse, which shows them God's watch over their struggles and their prayers. Souls happy in their spiritual progress, it warns against a bubble-like complacency, assuring them that only with God's protection can they keep what they have won; teaching them not merely to ask his help, but to ask it speedily.

I repeat; each of us, whatever his condition of spiritual life, needs to use this verse. The man who wants to be helped in all circumstances and at all times, shows that he needs God to help him in prosperity and happiness as much as in suffering and sorrow. He needs to be delivered from the one, and maintained in the other. For he knows that frail human nature cannot remain unimpaired in either state without God's help.

Suppose I feel gluttonous; I look round for food unknown among hermits; in the middle of the desert I scent the cooking of a dish fit for kings, and against my better will I cannot help hungering for it. Then I must say immediately: 'O God, make speed to save me, O Lord, make haste to help me.' Or I am tempted to eat supper too early, or am struggling to eat no more than the right and customary quantity, I must cry out: 'O God, make speed to save me; O Lord, make haste to help me.' I need severe fasts to quench lust, yet I dare not undertake them through the delicacy or dryness of my stomach. And so to quieten the lust without severe fasting, I must pray: 'O God, make speed to save me: O Lord, make haste to help me.' I go to

[74] Ps. 70:1.

supper at the correct time and shudder at the food and cannot eat what I must eat to live, then I must sigh: 'O God, make speed to save me: O Lord, make haste to help me.'

Perhaps I want to keep my heart stable by forcing myself to read the Bible. But a headache stops me, by nine o'clock in the morning I have fallen asleep with my head on the page—and I am driven to go to bed before the appointed hour, and so fail to say the full office and the proper series of psalms—again I must say: 'O God, make speed to save me: O Lord, make haste to help me.' Perhaps night after night I suffer some devilish insomnia and am exhausted from lack of sleep, gain no refreshment from my night's rest. I must breathe: 'O God, make speed to save me: O Lord, make haste to help me.'

Perhaps, if I have not yet tamed the flesh, some sudden temptation against chastity comes upon me softly at night: and I must prevent this invading fire from burning up the fragrant flowers of chastity. So I must call: 'O God, make speed to save me: O Lord, make haste to help me.' Perhaps I feel the heat of passion to have cooled. Then this virtue—nay, this grace, for it is a gift of God—I must keep within me by saying carefully: 'O God, make speed to save me: O Lord, make haste to help me.'

Perhaps temptations to anger, or avarice, or melancholy afflict me and force me to disturb my calm state, so pleasant to me. I must prevent myself being bitter by crying aloud: 'O God, make speed to save me: O Lord, make haste to help me.' Perhaps some temptation to accidie, or vanity, or pride, or to despise the half-heartedness of other monks, creeps upon the mind. To stop this devilish suggestion, I must pray with deep contrition: 'O God, make speed to save me: O Lord, make haste to help me.'

Perhaps I have repented long and so have pricked the bubble of pride and gained the grace of humility and simplicity. So that 'the foot of pride' may not again 'come against me,' and 'the hand of the sinner disturb me.' [75] and that satisfaction at my success may not cause still worse moral damage, I must call with my whole heart: 'O God, make speed to save me: O Lord, make haste to help me.'

Perhaps wandering thoughts career about the soul like boiling water, and I cannot contest them, nor can I offer prayer without silly mental images interrupting it; I feel so dry that I seem incapable of spiritual feeling, and many sighs and groans cannot

[75] Ps. 36:11.

save me from dreariness—I must needs say: 'O God, make speed
to save me: O Lord, make haste to help me.'

Perhaps by some joyous rapture I feel that the Holy Spirit
has visited me, and I have gained a re-directed purpose, a
concentration of mind, a liveliness of heart. And through these
overflowing sensations I discern a sudden disclosure by the
Lord of sacred truths hidden from me till now. To dwell upon
these truths for more than a moment, I must be careful to keep
praying: 'O God, make speed to save me: O Lord, make haste
to help me.'

Perhaps in the night I am encompassed by appearances of
unclean spirits and in my turn am thrown into a despair even of
life and salvation. I shall find in the whole-hearted praying of
that verse a safe fortress for the fugitive: 'O God, make speed to
save me: O Lord, make haste to help me.' Then the Lord
restores and consoles me, and I feel that he is garrisoning me
with his countless hosts of angels, and suddenly I can dare to go
out to face the enemy and provoke them to fight, when a
moment before I was trembling with fear of death and shudder-
ing in mind and body at their touch or proximity. To abide by
God's grace in this strength and courage, I must say with my
whole heart: 'O God, make speed to save me: O Lord, make
haste to help me.'

Continuously and ceaselessly, in adversity that we may be
delivered, in prosperity that we may be preserved but not puffed
up, we ought to send up this prayer. Meditate on it, never stop
turning it over within your breast. Whatever work or ministry
or journey you are undertaking, go on praying it. While you are
going to sleep, or eating, or in the last necessities of nature, think
on it. It will be a saving formula in your heart, will guard you
from the attacks of demons, will cleanse you from the stains of
earthly life, lead you to contemplate the unseen things of heaven,
and carry you up to the ineffable glow of prayer which very few
have experienced. Sleep ought to catch you thinking about this
verse, until you are so moulded by its use that you pray it when
asleep. When you wake it should be your first thought, it should
force you from your bed to your knees, and thence send you out
to your daily work, there to be always with you. You should
think on it, in Moses' words, [76] at home or on a journey, going to
bed or rising from bed. You should write it on the doors of your
lips, the walls of your house, the sanctuary of your breast.
Whether you kneel down to pray or whether you rise up from

[76] Deut. 6:7.

praying and turn to the needs of your daily life, this should be your prayer.

11. This formula the mind should go on grasping until it can cast away the wealth and multiplicity of other thoughts, and restrict itself to the poverty of this single verse. So you will attain with ease that Gospel beatitude which holds first place among the other beatitudes: 'Blessed are the poor in spirit: for theirs is the kingdom of heaven.' This noble poverty will fulfil the prophet's saying: 'The poor and needy shall praise the name of the Lord.' [77] Truly, what higher or holier poverty can there be than this, that a man knowing he is defenceless of his own, asks help for daily life from another's generosity, and realizes his life and being to depend every moment on God's help. Such a one truly confesses himself 'the beggar of the Lord,' like the Psalmist who said: 'I am a beggar and a poor man: and God helps me.' [78]

So by God's light he mounts to the manifold knowledge of God and thereafter to feed on mysteries loftier and more sacred: the prophet said: 'The high hills are a refuge for the stags, and the rocks for the hedgehogs.' [79] I think this meaning of the text is appropriate for this reason. A man who perseveres in simplicity and innocence, is aggressive to none and content to defend himself from being spoiled by his enemies; like the hedgehog hiding under a rock, he is protected, by his continual recollection of the Lord's passion and meditation upon this verse of the psalms. With the same spiritual intention the book of Proverbs speaks about hedgehogs—'The hedgehogs are a feeble folk, who have made their homes in the rocks.' [80] Nothing is feebler than a Christian; nothing weaker than a monk, who for wrong may take no vengeance nor even indulge mild feelings of annoyance, however concealed within his breast.

The man who in his moral ascent possesses simple innocence and yet the gift of wisdom has Satan crushed like a poisonous viper beneath his feet. And, as a stag browsing upon high pastures, his quick intelligence feeds upon the lofty mysteries revealed by the prophets and apostles.

There, with deep compunction, he will make the thoughts of the psalms his own. He will sing them no longer as verses composed by a prophet, but as born of his own prayers. At least he should use them as intended for his own mouth, and know that they were not fulfilled temporarily in the prophet's age and circumstances, but are being fulfilled in his daily life. There are

[77] Matt. 5:3; Ps. 74:21.   [78] Ps. 40:17, LXX.
[79] Ps. 104:18.   [80] Prov. 30:26, LXX.

times when a man understands God's Scriptures with the clarity
with which a surgeon understands the body when he opens up
the marrow and the veins. These are the times when our experience seems to show us the meaning by practical proof before we
understand it intellectually.

For example, if we have the same attitudes of heart wherein
the Psalmist wrote or sang his psalms, we shall become like the
authors and be aware of the meaning before we have thought it
out instead of after. The force of the words strikes us before we
have rationally examined them. And when we use the words, we
remember, by a kind of meditative association, our own circumstances and struggles, the results of our negligence or earnestness, the mercies of God's providence or the temptations of the
devil, the subtle and slippery sins of forgetfulness or human
frailty or unthinking ignorance. All these feelings we find expressed in the psalms. We see their texts reflected in the clear
glass of our own moral experience. And with that experience to
teach us, we do not hear the words so much as discern the
meaning intuitively. We will not merely recite them like texts
committed to memory, but bring them out from the depths of
the heart as an expression of moral reality.

So the mind shall attain that purest of pure prayers to which
our earlier Conference led, so far as the Lord deigned to grant
us; the prayer which looks to see no visual image, uses no mind
nor words; the prayer wherein, like a spark leaping from a fire,
the mind is rapt upward; and, destitute of the aid of the senses
or of anything visible or material, pours forth its prayer to
God with groanings and sighs that cannot be uttered."

12. Germanus: "You have most clearly explained the system
of spiritual discipline for which I asked, and perfect prayer
itself. There can be nothing more sublime than to fold the recollection of God into the little space of a meditation upon a single
verse, to summarize all the prayerful feelings in one sentence.

Now, we beg you to expound our one remaining problem.
You have given us this verse as a kind of formula. How can we
keep it permanently before us? By God's grace we have been
liberated from the stupidities of secular thoughts—how may we
grasp spiritual thoughts and never let them go?

13. When the mind has begun to take the meaning of a
psalm, it passes on unawares and unintentionally to some other
text of Scripture. When it has just begun to meditate upon that
text and has half considered it, its attention is caught by another
passage and it forgets all about the earlier matter for meditation.

And so it goes on, hopping from text to text, from psalm to psalm, from Gospel to Epistle and thence to a prophetic book and thence to a narrative in the historical books of the Old Testament; meandering vaguely through the Bible, choosing nothing and grasping nothing on purpose, considering no text to its depth; the mind becomes a dilettante, a taster of spiritual meanings, not a creator or owner of them. At the time of the office it totters about like a drunkard, its worship ever inadequate. During the prayers it is thinking about a psalm or lesson. During the singing of the psalter, it is thinking about something quite outside the text of the psalm. During the lesson, it is thinking about something that has to be done, or remembering something that has been done. So it receives or rejects nothing in a disciplined and orderly manner, but seems to be knocked about by haphazard assaults, powerless to keep or to linger over the text which pleases it.

We therefore need to know how to worship adequately by these means, and how permanently to hold this verse which you gave us as a formula. Then our feelings would not rise and fall hither and thither under their own impetus, but would respond to the control of the will."

14. Isaac: "I think that enough was said on this subject in our earlier discussion. But because you want me to repeat it, I will give a brief summary on how to make the heart stable.

Three things make the wandering mind stop wandering: watching, meditation, prayer, when used purposefully and assiduously. This is only possible if the anxieties and worries of this life are first put away, through tirelessly engaging in work undertaken not for monetary gain, but for the religious needs of the coenobium. This is the only way to obey St Paul's command, 'Pray without ceasing.'

He prays too little, who only prays when he is on his knees.

But he never prays, who while on his knees is in his heart roaming far afield.

Therefore what we wish to be while praying, we ought to be before we begin to pray. The praying mind cannot help being fashioned by its earlier condition, cannot help its earlier thoughts lifting it upward to heaven or pulling it downward to earth."

* * * *

Thus far Abba Isaac, to our wonder, gave his second Conference on the nature of prayer. He gave his teaching about meditating on that one little verse, as an outline for beginners.

Germanus and I admired the teaching and wanted to follow it, for we believed it to be a short and easy way. But when we tried it, we found it harder to observe than our previous method of wandering haphazardly through the Bible and meditating on a variety of different texts.

*   *   *   *

However, it is certain that a man is not incapable of perfection or purity of heart because he cannot read. Perfection and purity are available for anyone who uses one brief text—if he uses it with a purpose of heart strong and unwavering towards God.

CONFERENCE 11

First conference of Abba Chaeremon

ON PERFECTION

1. After I first learnt the faith, I lived in a monastery in Syria. And there, after making a certain amount of progress, I began to look for that higher grace which leads to a perfect life. I therefore resolved to go to Egypt at once, and travel through it to the furthest fastnesses of the Thebaid, with the object of visiting the many holy people whose fame had resounded through the earth. If I could not imitate them, I might at least learn from them.

After a long voyage, I came with Germanus to an Egyptian city named Thennesus. It is a town surrounded by the sea on one side and salt marshes on the other: and since the inhabitants are so short of land, they devote themselves to earning a living by seafaring and trade. When they want to build a house, they have to lay its foundations by bringing soil by sea from a distance.

2. On our arrival God blessed us, for he had brought to the town a saintly and eminent bishop named Archebius. Archebius had been plucked out of a society of hermits and made Bishop of Panephysis, but he had maintained as a bishop the rigorous discipline of the hermitage, altered nothing of his humble manners and did not flatter himself on his high office. On the contrary, he said that he had been made a bishop, not because he deserved it, but because he had been expelled from his hermit's way as unworthy to remain, inasmuch as he had tried for thirty-seven years to reach purity of heart, and had failed.

He had come to Thennesus on the business of electing a bishop, and welcomed us warmly like a father. When he heard that we wanted to visit the fathers in the distant parts of Egypt, he said to us: "First of all, come and see the old men who live near our monastery. They are crippled with age, but you have only to look at them to see that they are holy men and even to learn a great deal from them. A saintly life is more educative than a sermon: and by their lives you can learn the lesson which, I am sorry to say, I can no longer teach you because I have lost it. If I cannot produce for you the pearl of great price, I can at least show you where you may best find it: and I think that this may partly make amends for my own inability to help you."

3. So he took his staff and his scrip, like all Egyptian monks starting a journey, and guided us to his own city of Panephysis. The land round here used to be very rich, and rumour says that it used to supply the emperor's court with food. But in an earthquake the sea flooded in, destroyed the villages, and turned its fertile lands into salt-marshes. Some people there apply literally to the country the verse of the Psalms which was intended allegorically, "He hath turned rivers into a wilderness: and the springs of waters into a thirsty land: a fruitful land into salt, for the wickedness of them that dwell therein."[81] The flood-waters had turned the hillocks of higher ground, on which villages had been built, into islands: and since the inhabitants had fled, these places were suitable for holy men wanting to live alone.

Among the hermits of the region, three old men named Chaeremon, Nesteros, and Joseph, had lived there for the longest time.

4. Archebius chose to take us to see Chaeremon first, because his cell was nearest to Archebius's own cell, and because he was the eldest of all, being over a hundred years old. Though mentally he was still vigorous, his back was so crippled by age and by constant kneeling in prayer, that he could only move by crawling on hands and knees like an infant. His limbs were useless, defunct, yet he still kept the rigour of his rule. We gazed at his face, which was wonderful, and then at his method of moving.

We humbly asked him to teach us, and said that we had come simply to learn the rules of the spiritual life.

He sighed deeply and said: "What can I teach you? In my old age I have become so weak that I have softened my earlier austerities and consequently destroyed my confidence that I could teach. How can I presume to preach what I do not practise,

[81] Ps. 107:33-4.

or tell someone else to do something which I myself do half-heartedly or not at all? That is why I have refused to allow any younger man to live with me in my old age, because I am afraid that his discipline would be weakened by my example. A teacher will never exercise an effective authority unless he drives it into the heart of his pupil by his actions."

5. At this we felt very embarrassed, and replied: "The conditions of life here, and of living as a hermit to this age, are conditions which a robust young man would find difficulty in enduring, and ought to teach us all we need even if you tell us nothing. We have already learnt a lesson from you. Still, we beg you to put aside your silence for a short time, and tell us how to grasp at the goodness we see in you—how to reverence it, at least, since we cannot copy it. As perhaps you know, we are spiritually backward and do not deserve to have our request granted. But at least the trouble of this long journey from the monastery, at Bethlehem, trouble caused by our wish to learn your ways and to make spiritual progress, ought to persuade you to answer."

6. Then the blessed Chaeremon said:

"Three things enable men to control their sins: fear of hell or the law of the land; hope for the kingdom of heaven: and the love of goodness for its own sake.

We read that fear hates the touch of evil: 'the fear of the Lord hateth evil.' And hope repels the onslaught of every sin—'All those who hope in him shall not fail.' And love does not fear downfall into sin, for 'charity never faileth,' and 'charity covereth a multitude of sins.' [82] That is why St Paul summarized all salvation in those three virtues, 'Now abideth faith, hope, charity, these three.'

Faith is what makes us shun sin from fear of its punishment in the future judgement; hope calls our mind away from the present life and the pleasures of the body to seek our reward in heaven; charity kindles the mind to love Christ and the goodness of the spirit, and so to hate whatever is contrary to them.

These three virtues, which call us to stop sinning, seem all to aim at the same goal, but they differ widely in excellence. Properly speaking faith and hope are qualities of men who are on the way towards goodness but as yet do not love it: charity is a quality of God, and of men who have received into their beings the image and likeness of God. God, alone, acts from love of goodness for its own sake, without being moved by fear, or

[82] Prov. 8:13; Ps. 34:22; I Cor. 13:8; I Peter 4:8.

hope of reward. 'The Lord,' said Solomon, 'has done all things for his own sake.' [83] Out of pure goodness he bestows his abounding good on saint and sinner. Wrong cannot weary him nor sinfulness provoke him, for he ever abides the same, pure and unchanging goodness.

7. A man who is aiming at the perfect life will climb up from the first rung, the fear which is rightly called *servile*—as it was said: 'When ye have done all things, say "we are unprofitable servants." '[84]—and will mount to the rung of hope. The man who hopes is like a paid servant, not a slave; for he is secure in his status and exemption from servile punishment, looks for a wage in return for his labour, is conscious of his services, and expects payment under contract—and therefore cannot be like a son who loves his father, trusts his father's generosity, and never doubts that all his father's goods are his own.

The prodigal who had lost his father's goods and the name of son, did not dare to aspire to this state of sonship—'I am no more worthy to be called thy son.'[85] He fed upon the husks that the swine did eat and was not filled (it means, the squalid food of sin), and then he returned to his right mind, was stricken with repentance, and began to loathe the filth of the sty and to fear starvation. So, like a slave, he began to want to be a paid servant, and said: 'How many hired servants of my father have bread enough and to spare, while I perish with hunger. I will arise, and go to my father, and will say unto him, Father, I have sinned against heaven and before thee, and am no more worthy to be called thy son: make me as one of thy hired servants.' But his father ran out to meet him, and listened to his humble and penitent words with a family affection deeper than his son's, and lifted him above the state of a hired servant and restored him to his sonship.

We likewise ought to mount quickly upward, in the strength of a love that cannot be broken, to be sons who believe that all their father's goods are their own, who are made in the image and likeness of their father, and who like his true Son can say: 'All things that the Father hath, are mine.' St Paul says it of us: 'All things are yours, whether Paul, or Apollos, or Cephas, or the world, or life, or death, or things present, or things to come—all are yours.' Our Saviour commanded and called us to this likeness: 'Be ye perfect, even as your father in heaven is perfect.'[86]

83 Prov. 16:4. 84 Luke 17:10.
85 Luke 15:19. 86 John 16:15; I Cor. 3:22; Matt. 5:48.

In people on the way to the perfect life, there can come moments when the love of goodness is interrupted: the mind, through half-heartedness or happiness or some passing pleasure, relaxes its tautness, loses its fear of hell and hope of future reward. Sometimes fear and hope can each be stages leading to an advance; one who has begun by avoiding sin out of fear of hell or hope of heaven, can pass to the rung of charity. 'Fear is not in love, but perfect love casteth out fear: for fear hath torment, but he who feareth is not perfect in love. Let us therefore love, because God first loved us.' [87]

Therefore we can only ascend to the truly perfect way if, as he first loved us simply to save us, we love him simply because he has loved us. We must strive earnestly to pass from fear to hope, from hope to the love of God and of goodness for its own sake; and as we reach this last stage, we shall grasp goodness immovably, so far as that is possible for human nature.

8. There is a lot of difference between the man who eradicates sin by fear of hell or hope of God's reward, and the man who loves God and therefore shrinks from wickedness, possesses purity simply because he loves purity, and acts out of a pleasure in present virtue. The reason is that, in this second state, the man acts in just the same way when there are no observers: he prevents secret thoughts of evil entering the heart simply because the heart loves goodness: whatever is contrary to goodness is not received into the heart, indeed is abhorred. To hate sin from a love of present good is different from avoiding illicit passion for the sake of future gain: the one is afraid of loss in the present, the other of punishment in the future. It is better not to want to leave the good because you like the good, than not to consent to evil because you are afraid of evil. In one the good act is voluntary, in the other it is extracted by a kind of compulsion based on punishment or reward.

The man who abstains from sin out of fear, will return to what he likes when the fear evaporates. Therefore he will never achieve a stable character of goodness; will not secure a tranquil chastity, will always be liable to onslaughts. Wherever there is war, there will be risk of wounds. A soldier in a battle, however bravely he fights, however many mortal wounds he inflicts on the enemy, cannot help sometimes being hurt by the enemy's sword. But a conqueror of sin, who has won through to peace, will keep the character which is now all his own, be-

[87] I John 4:18–19.

cause he believes no loss to be worse than the loss of his inmost chastity. He regards any grave fall from virtue as a severe punishment, and therefore thinks nothing more precious than his present purity.

So the presence or absence of other people will make no difference to his conduct. Everywhere he bears round with him his conscience as the judge of his actions and inner thoughts; listening intently to hear its voice, knowing that it cannot be avoided, or cheated, or escaped.

9. A man can only live according to his conscience if he relies upon God's help and not upon his own endeavours. But if he does live according to his conscience, he will then begin to pass from the states of servile fear and hireling hope to the state of an adopted son, moved by neither fear nor greed but by never-failing charity. The Lord administered a rebuke in which he taught where fear and charity were each appropriate: 'A son knoweth his own father, and a servant feareth his lord: and if I be a Father, where is my honour: and if I be a Lord, where is my fear?' The slave must fear his master, because 'if knowing his lord's will he has done things worthy of stripes, he shall be beaten with many stripes.'[88]

In charity, then, man attains the image and likeness of God, and delights in goodness for its own sake. He possesses a measure of God's patience and gentleness. He refrains from anger at the faults of others, sympathizes with their weaknesses and intercedes for their pardon. He remembers that for many years he suffered from the same passions until the Lord's mercy saved him. Seeing that it is grace and not works which delivered him from concupiscence, he will know how to show mercy instead of wrath to the erring. In serenity of heart he will sing to God the verse of the Psalms, 'Thou hast broken my chains: I will offer to thee the sacrifice of praise' and 'Except the Lord had helped me, my soul had almost dwelt in hell.' In this humble spirit he will be able to obey even that Gospel command of perfection, 'Love your enemies, do good to them that hate you, and pray for them which persecute and slander you.'

So God will grant us the reward, to be made in the image and likeness of God and to be called his sons: 'that ye may be sons of your Father which is in heaven, who maketh his sun to rise upon the good and the evil, his rain to fall upon the just and unjust.' This was the feeling in which St John said: 'that we may have confidence in the day of judgement, because as he is,

[88] Mal. 1:6; Luke 12:47.

so are we also in this world.' The only way in which our weak
and frail human nature can resemble his nature is by pouring
out the loving heart in tranquillity, to good and bad, just and
unjust; by doing good because it is good. So we come to the
true state of adopted sons of God, of which St John wrote:
'Everyone that is born of God doth not sin, for his seed is in him,
and he cannot sin, because he is born of God'; and 'We know
that everyone who is born of God sinneth not, but his birth
from God preserveth him, and the wicked one toucheth him
not.' [89]

This last text, 'he cannot sin,' must only be understood of
deadly sin, not of all sin. In another text St John says that we
should not even pray for a man who does not want to be rid of
deadly sin: 'If a man knows his brother to be sinning a sin not
unto death, let him ask, and he will give him life for them
that sin not unto death. There is a sin unto death: I do not say
that he should pray for that.' From sins not unto death the
most faithful servants of Christ, however vigilantly they live,
cannot altogether keep themselves free: and of them St John
says: 'If we say that we have no sin, we deceive ourselves, and
the truth is not in us': and: 'If we say that we have not sinned,
we make him a liar, and his word is not in us.' [90] No holy man
can prevent himself falling into the little sins, sins of speech and
thought, of ignorance and forgetfulness, sins which we do not
will and sins that we do will, sins which take us by surprise.
They are far from being deadly sins; still, they bring guilt.

10. When a man has come to love goodness and to imitate
God, then he will be clothed in the Lord's spirit of compassion,
and pray for his enemies: 'Father, forgive them, they know not
what they do.' [91] Not to be merciful and sympathetic with
others' faults, but to be rigid and censorious, is clear proof of a
soul sunk down in sin. No one like this can obtain perfection of
heart because he is without that instrument which enables the
full requirements of the law to be obeyed: as St Paul said: 'bear
ye one another's burdens, and so fulfil the law of Christ.' Nor
does he possess charity which 'is not grieved, is not puffed up,
thinketh no evil, endureth all things, beareth all things.' 'A
righteous heart pitieth the life of his beasts; but the heart of the
ungodly is without pity.' A monk is certain to fall into the same
sins which he mercilessly condemns when he finds them in
another. 'A rigid king shall fall into evil,' and 'one who stops

[89] Ps. 116:16–17; Matt. 5:44–5; I John 4:17; 3:9; and 5:18.
[90] I John 5:16; 1:8 and 10.   [91] Luke 23:34.

his ears so as not to hear the weak, shall himself cry, and there shall be none to hear him.' " [92]

11. Germanus: "You have spoken with power and grandeur about the perfect charity of God. But we are troubled for this reason. While you were so much exalting charity, you said that the fear of God and the hope of eternal reward were imperfect. But the prophet seems to have disagreed with you. 'Fear the Lord, all ye his saints: for they that fear him lack nothing.' Again, he avowed that in acting righteously his motive was the vision of the reward from God. 'I have inclined my heart to do thy righteous acts always, for the reward.' And St Paul said: 'By faith, Moses, when he was grown up, denied himself to be the son of Pharaoh's daughter; choosing rather to be afflicted with the people of God than to have the pleasure of sin for a season, esteeming the reproach of Christ greater riches than the treasure of the Egyptians; for he looked unto the reward.' [93]

Then how can we believe fear and hope to be imperfect? David gloried that he did righteous deeds with an eye on the reward. Moses refused to become a member of a royal family out of hope for future reward, and preferred suffering to the treasures of Egypt."

12. Chaeremon: "God's Scriptures call us, who have free will, to the different rungs in the ladder of perfection, but call one in one way, another in another, according to the mental condition of each person. The perfection of each person is not the same; the crown of each head is not of the same uniform pattern. Not everyone possesses the same power or earnestness of will. God's word has offered different measures of perfection to different kinds of people.

This is obvious, from the variety of beatitudes in the Gospel. The people whose is the kingdom of heaven are called blessed; and the people who shall inherit the earth are called blessed. The people who shall be comforted are called blessed, and so are those whose hunger after righteousness has been filled. Yet we believe that there is a vast difference between living in the kingdom of heaven, and possessing as much as you like on earth, a vast difference between receiving comfort and being filled with righteousness, a vast difference between the merciful who shall obtain mercy, and the pure in heart who shall be deemed worthy to enjoy the glorious vision of God.

'For there is one glory of the sun, and another of the moon,

---

[92] Gal. 6:2; I Cor. 13:4–7; Prov. 12:10, LXX; 13:17, LXX; 21:13, LXX.
[93] Ps. 34:9; 119:112; Heb. 11:24–6.

and another glory of the stars; for star differeth from star in glory, so also is the resurrection from the dead.' It is in accord with this rule that God's Scripture praises those who fear him: 'Blessed are all they that fear the Lord,' and it even promises them a beatitude full and entire. Yet Scripture also says: 'There is no fear in love: but perfect love casteth out fear: for fear hath torment. But he that feareth is not yet made perfect in love.' Again: on the one side Scripture says that it is a grand thing to serve the Lord, and 'serve the Lord in fear,' and: 'It is a great thing for thee to be called my servant,' and: 'Blessed is that servant whom his Lord, when he cometh, shall find so doing.' Yet on the other side, the Lord said to the apostles: 'I no longer call you servants, for the servant knoweth not what his Lord doeth: but I call you friends, for all things whatsoever I have heard from my Father, I have made known unto you.' And 'Ye are my friends, if ye do whatsoever I command you.' [94]

You see how there are different rungs in the ladder of perfection, and that the Lord calls us upward from what is high to what is higher. You can be perfect in the fear of God. Then you go, as it is written 'from strength to strength,' from one kind of perfection to another kind of perfection, from fear to hope. In this new stage you are called onward to a still higher blessedness, charity. He who was a faithful and wise servant, becomes a friend and an adopted son.

In this light you must understand what I said. I do not assert that the continual contemplation of eternal punishment or of the blessed reward promised to the saints, is worthless. I assert that they are useful and introduce their possessors to the beginning of the life of bliss: and yet, that charity, with its fuller confidence and joy, will take them out of servile fear or hope of payment, to love God and be adopted as his sons: so to say, from being perfect to being more perfect.

Our Saviour said: 'In my Father's house are many mansions.' And although everything shines which is in the sky, the sun and the moon and the morning star and the rest do not all shine with the same light. St Paul puts charity not only above fear and hope, but above every other sort of gift of God, however great and wonderful, and sets out to show us 'a more excellent way.' When he had finished his catalogue of God's gifts, and wanted to describe them more in detail, he first wrote: 'And yet I show unto you a still more excellent way. Though I

94 I Cor. 15:41–2; Ps. 128:1; I John 4:18; Ps. 2:11; Isa. 49:6, LXX; Matt. 24:46; John 15:14–15.

speak with the tongues of men and of angels, and though I have the gift of prophecy and understand all mysteries and all knowledge, and though I have all faith so that I can remove mountains, and though I give all my goods to feed the poor, and give my body to be burned—and have not charity, it profiteth me nothing.' You see that there is nothing more precious, more perfect, more sublime, more lasting, than charity. 'Whether there be prophecies, they shall fail: whether there be tongues, they shall cease: whether there be knowledge, it shall vanish away. But charity shall never fail.' Without it the most transcendent and excellent kinds of spiritual gift—even the glory of martyrdom itself—is made nothing.

13. The man who is rooted in this perfect charity must climb one more step to a higher fear. This fear arises not from terror of punishment or greed for a reward, but from love. A son fears a generous father, brother fears brother, friend fears friend, husband fears wife—fears not blows nor abuse, but the least offence against the loving relationship. In deed and word he acts with a reverence, in fear that the love of the other towards himself may begin to grow cooler. One of the prophets has finely described the grandeur of this kind of fear: 'Wisdom and knowledge are the riches of salvation: the fear of the Lord is its treasure.' He could not have expressed more clearly the value of this fear, than by saying that the riches of our salvation (which are true wisdom and knowledge of God) cannot be preserved without it. The Psalmist invited saints, not sinners, to this fear of the Lord: 'Fear the Lord, all his saints: for they that fear him lack nothing.' The man who fears the Lord like this, will lack nothing for his perfection.

St John was obviously talking about fear of punishment when he wrote: 'he that feareth is not made perfect in love, because fear hath punishment.' There is a lot of difference, then, between the fear which lacks nothing, which is the treasure of wisdom and knowledge, and the imperfect fear which is called 'the beginning of wisdom,' which carries its own punishment with it, and so is expelled from the hearts of the truly charitable. For 'there is no fear in love: but perfect love casteth out fear.' If fear is the beginning of wisdom, what will the end of wisdom be but in Christ's charity, a charity which includes the fear of true love, and so is called the treasure of wisdom and knowledge?

Thus there are two fears. A beginners' fear, the fear of men who are still slaves and afraid—'The servant shall fear his Lord,' and the Gospel text, 'I no longer call you servants, for the servant knoweth not what his Lord doeth'; and therefore, he said: 'The servant abideth not in the house for ever, but the son abideth for ever.' He grants us to pass from fear of punishment to the fullest liberty of charity and the confidence of the friends and sons of God. St Paul, who had himself been brought by the Lord's love out of servile fear, laid aside the lower and affirmed that the Lord had enriched him with a higher good. 'God hath not given us the spirit of fear, but of power and of love and of a sound mind.' And St Paul thus addressed men who truly loved their heavenly Father, and whom God had already adopted and transformed from slaves into sons: 'You have not received the spirit of bondage again to fear, but you have received the spirit of adoption, whereby we cry Abba, Father.'

The other fear appears in the text where the prophet is describing the sevenfold gift of the Spirit which according to the mystery of the incarnation full surely descended upon our Lord's manhood. 'And there shall rest upon him the spirit of the Lord: the spirit of wisdom and understanding, the spirit of counsel and strength, the spirit of knowledge and of true godliness,' and lastly and emphatically 'the spirit of fear shall fill him.' [95] About this text you should first take care to observe that he does not say, as of the others, that 'the spirit of fear *shall rest upon him*,' but '*shall fill him*.' The power of it is so abundant that if once it possesses a man in its strength, it possesses his mind to the exclusion of all else. Linked with the charity which never fails, it fills and permanently possesses the soul whom it has seized, and cannot be lessened by the temptations of any this-worldly happiness. This is the perfect fear, which is said to have filled the Lord's humanity, who came to redeem mankind and give them their example and pattern of goodness. The true Son of God, who did no sin, neither was guile found in his mouth, could not feel the servile fear of punishment."

14. Germanus: "Now that you have finished your description of perfect charity, I should like to ask a further question, on the aim of chastity. I am sure that the pinnacle of charity, whereby we reach up to the image and likeness of God, cannot exist without perfect chastity. But we should like you to teach us whether chastity so stable that no allurement ever interrupts the heart's integrity is a possibility in this life."

15. Chaeremon: "It is a mark of holiness to be always learn-

95 Mal. 1:6, LXX; John 15:15 and 8:35; II Tim. 1:7; Rom. 8:15; Isa. 11:2.

ing or teaching how to cleave to the Lord. Day and night, as the Psalmist said, we ought to meditate on him all our lives, and thereby nourish the mind in its hunger and thirst after righteousness, a hunger and thirst which can never be satisfied.

But the Saviour in his loving-kindness wishes us to look after our servant the body: and we ought to look after its needs so that it may not grow too tired. 'The spirit is willing but the flesh is weak.' [96] It is time to eat a little, and afterwards we shall be able to discuss your enquiry more attentively."

[Chaeremon went on in his second conference to the theme of chastity as a possible state of life, distinguished from, and higher than, continence, but only possible by God's grace and long patience. In the third conference of Chaeremon (Conference 13) Cassian took the opportunity, since he had been led to the subject of grace, to write a tract against St Augustine's views on predestination and irresistible grace. He was ever anxious to preserve the sense of moral responsibility and initiative and effort, which he feared that the Augustinian doctrines must undermine.

Conference 14 is the first conference of Abba Nesteros, and on "spiritual knowledge," i.e., the way to understand and interpret the Scriptures, and the moral qualities and religious insight necessary for rightly understanding them.]

CONFERENCE 15

The Second Conference of Abba Nesteros

ON MIRACULOUS GIFTS

1. After evening service, we sat down as usual on the mats, ready to listen to the talk which he had promised. For some little time we kept a respectful silence: and he it was who spoke first.

"In the course of our previous talk we have come naturally to the subject of spiritual gifts.

The traditions of the elders teach that there are three reasons for these gifts. One is for purposes of healing, a grace which sometimes accompanies holy and chosen men because of their sanctity. We read that the apostles and many of the saints did signs and wonders by the Lord's authority: 'heal the sick, raise the dead, cleanse the lepers, cast out devils: freely ye have received, freely give.' [97]

[96] Ps. 1:2; Matt. 15:32 and 26:41. [97] Matt. 10:8.

The second reason is to edify the church, to build up the faith of the people who bring their sick, or who are themselves in need of healing. Here the power of healing proceeds even from men who are sinners unworthy of it. The Saviour says in the Gospel: 'Many shall say to me in that day, Lord, Lord, have we not prophesied in thy name, and in thy name cast out devils, and in thy name done many mighty works? And then I will confess to them, I never knew you: Depart from me, ye workers of iniquity.' But if the patients, or those who bring them, lack faith, this prevents the men who possess the gift of healing from exercising it. So the evangelist Luke wrote: 'Jesus could not there do any mighty work because of their unbelief': and the Lord himself said: 'Many lepers were in Israel in the days of Elisha the prophet, and none of them was cleansed but Naaman the Syrian.' [98]

The third is healing worked by the deceitful power of demons. It happens when a man who is obviously a sinner is regarded as a saint and friend of God because he works miracles, others are led to copy his sins, scandal arises, and religion is defamed: or sometimes the demons do it to lift into pride the man who believes himself to possess the miraculous gift, and so prepare him for a more disastrous fall. They pretend that they are being burnt up and driven out from the bodies where they were dwelling through the holiness of people whom truly they know to be unholy.[99]

2. Then we ought not to admire people, who possess these powers, on account of these powers. We should see whether they are morally reformed. God's grace gives this to a man, not for miscellaneous reasons like the faith of someone else, but in proportion to his own earnestness. This is the knowledge of true goodness, which St Paul calls charity, and is more excellent than all the tongues of men and of angels, the faith which moves mountains, all knowledge, the sacrifice of one's property,

---

[98] Matt. 7:22-3; Mark 6:5-6; Matt. 13:58; Luke 4:27.

[99] "Deuteronomy refers to this: 'If there rise up in the midst of thee a prophet, or one who says that he has seen a dream, and declare a sign and wonder, and that which he hath spoken cometh to pass, and he say to thee: Let us go and follow after other gods whom thou knowest not, and let us serve them: thou shalt not hear the words of that prophet or of that dreamer, for the Lord thy God is tempting thee, that it may appear whether thou lovest him or not, with all thy heart and with all thy soul.' And in the Gospel we read: 'There shall arise false Christs and false prophets, and shall give great signs and wonders, so that, if it were possible, even the elect should be led astray' (Deut. 13:1-3; Matt. 24:24)."

even than the ultimate glory of martyrdom. First he gave a list of the different sorts of spiritual gifts—'to one is given by the spirit the word of wisdom, to another the word of knowledge, to another faith, to another the gift of healing, to another the working of miracles' and the rest. And then he laconically puts charity above them all, 'and yet show I unto you a more excellent way.' The text is plain: the summit of perfection and blessedness consists not in working miracles but in pure charity. All else will pass away, charity will abide.

That is why I never saw my teachers set any store by miracles. Even when they possessed this particular grace of the Holy Spirit, they would never use it except in some extreme and compelling necessity.

3. I remember how Abba Macarius, who was the first to live alone in the desert of Scete, raised a dead man to life. It happened like this.

A heretic, a disciple of Eunomius, was trying to pervert the catholic faith by skilful argument, and had succeeded in capturing a good number of followers. Disturbed by these losses, catholic men asked blessed Macarius to come and save the simple faith of all Egypt from this shipwreck. When Macarius came, the heretic used subtle syllogisms to attack him, and tried to drag him into the prickly jungle of Aristotle, about whom Macarius knew nothing. But Macarius replied to his lengthy arguments by a short text of St Paul. 'The kingdom of God is not in word, but in power.'[1] Let us go to the cemetery, and invoke the name of the Lord upon the first corpse we find. Let us prove our faith by our works, as the Scripture says. Let the Lord's testimony decide upon the orthodox faith, and not a futile debate. This is the judgement which is infallible.''

The heretic was very embarrassed at hearing this in the middle of the crowd, but for the moment he pretended to agree and promised to appear there next day. When the next day came, all the people assembled expecting a great spectacle. But the heretic, stricken by the consciousness of his infidelity, fled away and escaped from Egypt. Macarius and the people waited for him until 3 o'clock. But seeing that he had refused the contest, Macarius gathered the people whose faith had been perverted and led them to the cemetery.

The river Nile overflows and covers the whole country for no small part of the year, turning it into what looks like a sea, and making boats the only means of communication. Hence the

[1] I Cor. 4:20.

Egyptians have the custom of embalming the dead and then burying them in tombs lifted above ground level. The soil is too damp to make normal interment possible. If you bury a body in it, the successive floods bring it to the surface.

Macarius stood by a very old corpse, and said: 'Man, tell me this. If that damnable heretic had come here with me and I had invoked in his presence the name of Christ my God, would you have risen from the dead in front of these people, who were almost led away by his false teaching?' The man rose and said that he would. Then Abba Macarius asked him what he had been during his life, when he lived and whether he had known Christ's name. He said that he lived under the ancient kings of Egypt and had not in those days heard of Christ's name. So Abba Macarius replied: 'Sleep in peace with the rest of your fellows, waiting for Christ to raise you at the last.'

Perhaps this power of grace in Macarius would always have remained hidden unless he had been driven to work the miracle by the danger into which the province was running, and by his true love for Christ. He did it not for the sake of ostentation, but was forced to do it for the love of Christ and the good of the people. This is what Elijah did, as we read in the Book of Kings, when he called down fire from heaven upon the sacrifice ready on the pyre, so as to free his people's faith from being endangered by the wonder-working of the false prophets.

4. Perhaps I should say a little of the deeds of Abba Abraham, who was nicknamed the Simple because of his innocence and the simplicity of his manners. In Eastertide he had gone from his hermitage into Egypt with the aim of harvesting. A woman besieged him, weeping and praying, for her baby who was already weak and half-dead from lack of milk. Abraham gave her a cup of water, signed with the sign of the cross: and as soon as she drank it, her dry breasts began marvellously to flow with milk.

5. Once when he went to a village, a mocking crowd surrounded him and jeered at him. They showed him a man who for many years had had a crippled knee and was forced to crawl, and tempted him saying: 'Abba Abraham, give us a sign if you are a servant of God, and restore this cripple to health—or we shall believe that the name of Christ whom you worship is powerless.' He at once invoked Christ's name, stooped down, and pulled the man's withered foot out. And at his touch the bent and withered knee was straightened, and he happily walked away on his legs, which he had forgotten how to use through so many years of weakness.

6. These men felt no pride in their power to do miracles of this sort. They said that the miracles were wrought by them, not because they were good men, but because the Lord was merciful. They rejected the admiration which comes from popular regard for miracles, using the words of the apostle: 'Men and brothers, why marvel ye at this, or why look ye on us as though by our own power or holiness we had caused this man to walk?' They thought that a man should never be cried up for the wonderful gifts of God, but only if he was a good man doing good intentionally. Men of corrupted minds, heretics, cast out devils and work miracles in the name of the Lord. It is true that when the apostles complained: 'Master, we saw one casting out devils in thy name, and we forbade him because he followeth not with us,' Christ at the time replied: 'Forbid him not, for he that is not against you is for you.' But when in the judgement these wonder-workers say: 'Lord, Lord, have we not in thy name prophesied, and in thy name cast out devils, and in thy name done many mighty works?', Christ proclaimed that he would answer: 'I never knew you: depart from me, ye workers of iniquity.'

He himself warns people to whom he gives this power of miracles because of their holiness, that they are not to be proud of it: 'Rejoice not because the devils are subject to you, but rejoice rather because your names are written in heaven.' [2]

7. He who is the author of all miracles and wonder-working called his true and chosen disciples to hear his teaching, and showed them what they were most particularly to learn. 'Come, and learn of me'—not to cast out devils by heaven's power, not to heal lepers, not to raise the dead. Though I do these things by some of my servants, man cannot ascribe to himself the praise due to God, cannot snatch for himself any part of the glory due to God alone: man is but the agent, the minister. Instead, he said: 'Learn of me, for I am meek and lowly in heart.' [3] Everyone can learn this lesson and obey it. Wonders and powers are not always necessary, for some are harmful, and are not granted to everyone.

Humility, then, is the queen of all the virtues, she is the stable foundation of the house of heaven, she is the peculiar and marvellous gift of the Saviour. The only person who can without risk of pride work the miracles which Christ wrought, is the man who follows our gentle Lord not in working miracles

[2] Acts 3:12; Luke 9:49–50; Matt. 7:22–3; Luke 10:20.
[3] Matt. 11:28–9.

but in patience and humility. He whose motive is ostentation in commanding unclean spirits or healing the sick or showing some wonderful sign to the people, is a stranger to Christ though he invokes Christ's name: for he is proud, and follows not his master's humility.

When the Lord was returning to his Father, he wrote, so to say, his will, and left it to his disciples thus: 'A new commandment give I unto you that ye love one another; as I have loved you, so do ye also love one another': and immediately afterwards, 'By this shall all men know that ye are my disciples, if ye have love to one another.' He did not say: 'If ye do signs and miracles like me,' but 'if ye love one another.' Surely none but the humble and the meek can obey this commandment.

That is why our elders never counted as true monks men who boasted of their exorcising powers and spread the grace which they possessed (or alleged they possessed) in front of crowds of admirers. And the ostentation was futile. 'He who trusteth in lies feedeth the winds: and the same runneth after birds that fly away.' We find their retribution in the Book of Proverbs, 'Whoso boasteth himself of a false gift is as easy to see as the wind and the clouds and the rain.' [4]

So, if we are present when someone works a miracle, we are not to admire him because of the act, but only for his moral life. We are not to ask whether the devils are subject to him, but whether he possesses the charity which St Paul described.

8. It is a bigger miracle to eject passion from your own body than it is to eject an evil spirit from another's body. It is a bigger miracle to be patient and refrain from anger than it is to control the demons which fly through the air. It is better to rid your own heart of the melancholy which corrodes it, than it is to rid someone else of bodily disease. The power which heals your own soul is finer and loftier than the power which heals another's body. The soul is more important than the body, its salvation more urgent. The more precious the material, the more destructive is the fall.

9. Of bodily healing, the Lord said to his apostles: 'Rejoice not that the devils are subject to you.' [5] They did it not in their own strength, but in the power of his name which they invoked. So they are warned against the presumption of claiming any glory on this score, for God did it by his power. They are warned to claim glory on the ground of the inner purity of life and

[4] John 13:34–5; Prov. 10:4; Prov. 25:14, LXX.
[5] Luke 10:20.

heart, for thereby it was granted that their names should be written in heaven.

10. I will prove what I have said by ancient evidence and God's oracles. Here are the very words of the blessed Paphnutius, when giving his opinion about admiration of miracles and the grace of purity: words which he learnt from the mouth of an angel. In his old age Paphnutius still kept a strictly disciplined rule of life. He believed that he was absolutely immune from temptations to his chastity, for he knew that in the long struggles with demons he had always emerged the victor.

One day some monks were visiting him; and while he was preparing for them the lentil porridge which they call *athera*, a flame darted out and burnt his hand while it was in the oven—it easily happens. But Paphnutius was deeply depressed, and began to consider silently in his mind thus: 'Why is there not peace between me and the fire? The fiercer fighting with the demons has ceased: yet this little ephemeral fire has attacked me. What of the eternal fire on the dreadful day of judgement which searches out the good and the bad? Will it pass me over?' His mind was still chasing these melancholy thoughts when sleep suddenly came over him. And in his sleep, an angel of the Lord came, and said: 'Why are you sad, Paphnutius? Are you sad that you are not yet at peace with the fire from the oven, while you have not fully purified the lusts of your body? So long as the roots of that lust dwell within you, they will not let the material fire be at peace with you. You will not feel it at peace with you unless you make the following experiment to prove that all lust is extinct. Go, lay hold upon a fair maiden. And if your heart remains tranquil, and your bodily senses serene, this fire in the oven will be as harmless and gentle to you as it was to the three children in the burning fiery furnace at Babylon.'

Old Paphnutius was struck by the vision, and did not risk the experiment which God had suggested, he guessed that his chastity might not stand the test. Instead, he examined his conscience, and investigated the purity of his heart. 'It is not then surprising,' he said, 'that I feel the fire to be still hostile to me though I have conquered unclean devils and believe the fire's onslaught to be far more trivial than those of the demons. It is a greater gift to kill lust within than to drive the devils without by the Lord's high power and invocation of his name.' "

So Abba Nesteros ended his account of the true working of the miraculous gifts of God. Moved by his teaching we were eager to hear the elder, Joseph, whose cell was some six miles away: and Abba Nesteros conducted us thither.

[The two Conferences of Joseph were delivered upon friendship and on making promises, the second because Cassian or his friends were worried by his breaking of his word to the community at Bethlehem of an early return. These two Conferences ended the second division of Cassian's work. But he was also sending seven other Conferences to the monks living in the Stoechades islands, and these are at present Conferences 18–24, a group miscellaneous in character. Here are translated the eighteenth, on the three kinds of monks: and the nineteenth, on the aims of the coenobite and hermit.]

CONFERENCE 18

Conference of Abba Piamun

ON THE THREE SORTS OF MONKS

1. After we had visited and talked with those three old men, whose conferences I have tried to describe at the request of our brother Eucherius, Germanus and I were still eager to visit the remoter parts of Egypt where most of the holy men were living. We came to Diolcos, a village near one of the seven mouths of the Nile. It was off our route, but we wanted to see the ascetics there. The moment we heard of a celebrated monastery founded by the old fathers, we started out thither not knowing what we should find—like money-making merchants, risking the journey but hoping for greater profits.

At Diolcos we wandered round for a long time from cell to cell. We were like travellers surveying a high range of mountains, who in the end found the highest—Abba Piamun, towering over the others in his sanctity, the oldest of the ascetics there and their priest. The others directed us to him because they looked towards him as navigators guide their course by a lighthouse. Like the city set on the hill in the Gospel, shining its light upon the country, Piamun enlightened us. God's grace testified to his goodness, for in our presence he worked miracles. But them I must omit, if I am to keep to the proper plan of this book. I did not promise to write about God's miracles, but about the discipline and rules of the holy men as far as I can remember them. My intention is to show people how to lead the good life, not to give the reader idle stories which are useless for reforming his character.

When Piamun understood that we were strangers, he welcomed us warmly and hospitably. He first asked where we had come from, and why we had come. And when he heard that we had come to Egypt from a community in Syria with the aim of finding the way of perfection, he began to talk.

2. "My sons, anyone who wants to be skilful at an art will fail unless he takes the utmost pains to study the system and observe the rules of the best masters. It is silly to think you can become like people whose industry you are refusing to imitate, simply by wishing to become like them. I have met people who have come here from your country simply to travel round the monasteries without any intention of starting to keep the rules of the monks or of retiring into cells and putting into practice what they have seen or heard. They retained their native character and manners: and some allege that they really changed their country not with any purpose of spiritual profit, but simply because they were poor and in want in their own country. They were so obstinate that they could learn nothing, and could not even stay any length of time here. And if they came here and yet changed nothing, not fasting, nor psalmody, nor clothes, we naturally thought their only reason for coming here was to find food.

3. I believe that you have come here because God has drawn you to follow our way to knowledge. And if so, you must altogether abandon the rules which you were taught in Syria during the early days of your vocation, and humbly follow whatever you see our elders do or teach. You must not be troubled or stop imitating us because at the moment you do not see the reason of something. If men are (in the right sense) simple enough to think well of everything, if they are careful to copy whatever the elders have taught or practised, and not to argue about it—then through experience they come to know the reason why. The man who learns by argument will never find the true reason: for the enemy, seeing him trust to his own judgement rather than that of the fathers, easily pushes him into thinking valuable and saving practices to be harmful or futile. The enemy can cleverly play on his presumption: and so he clings obstinately to his unreasonable opinions, and decides that only to be holy which his stubborn judgement regards as right.

4. First, you should know how our way of life arose, and who founded it. A man can only be trained effectively in some art and be led to practise it earnestly, when he recognizes the eminence of its authors.

In Egypt there are three kinds of monks. Two are excellent, the third is half-hearted and at all costs to be avoided.

The first kind is the coenobites. These are monks living in a community under the government of a single elder. Most of the Egyptian monks are coenobites.

The second kind is the hermits. These are men who have first been trained in communities to the life of virtue and have then chosen to live a completely hidden and solitary life. This is the life which I wish to follow.

The third, and culpable, kind is the Sarabaites.

I shall talk about each of these three kinds in turn. First, as I said, you ought to know the founders of each kind. From this knowledge alone may arise a dislike of the sort which is to be shunned, and a desire for the sort which is to be followed. Each way will carry the man who follows it to the destination which its founder reached.

5. The system of the coenobites arose at the time when the apostles were preaching. The crowd of believers in Jerusalem was of this sort, as it is described in the Acts of the Apostles: 'The multitude of believers was of one heart and one soul, neither said any of them that any of the things which he possessed was his own, but they had all things in common. They sold their possessions and property and divided them to all, as any man had need.' And, 'For neither was there any among them that lacked; for as many as possessed fields or houses, sold them and brought the price of the things that they sold and laid them before the apostles' feet: and distribution was made to every man as he had need.'

The whole Church, I assert, lived then as the coenobites live, now so few that it is difficult to find them.

But after the death of the apostles, crowds of strangers and men of different races flowed into the Church; the apostles had judged that since they were new converts and had grown accustomed to pagan habits, nothing more should be asked of them than that they should 'abstain from things sacrificed to idols, and from fornication, and from things strangled, and from blood.'[6] Their faith was cooler than the faith of the first Christians: and so the faith of the whole Christian body began to grow cold. The liberty, conceded to the Gentiles because they were neophytes and therefore weak in faith, began little by little to infect the whole Church at Jerusalem and diminish its per-

6 Acts 4:32–5; 2:45; 15:29.

fect life. And as day by day the number of converts at home and abroad grew, and the primitive Christians lost their fervour, the leaders of the Church as well as the new converts began to lose something of their strict discipline. There were some who thought they might lawfully do what was allowed to the Gentiles, and follow Christ though they kept all their property and money.

And so the Christians who were still fervent as the Christians of apostolic days, and remembered the original and perfect way of life, left their cities and the company of those who thought they could live negligently and comfortably in God's Church, and dwelt in places outside the cities, or in even more remote haunts. They began to keep privately and as individuals the rules which they remembered were given by the apostles to the whole Church.

The coenobites' discipline grew up from the disciples who separated themselves in order not to be infected by lax Christians. After a short time, marked out from most of the faithful by their celibacy and their separation from their relatives and society, they came to be known as *monks* or *monazontes*, because they lived a disciplined life alone. When they joined together they were known as coenobites, and their cells and habitations were called coenobia. This was the earliest kind of monk; first in time and in the grace of God; and for many years, until the time of Abba Paul and Antony, it remained the only kind. We still see the traces of it in strict coenobia.

6. These coenobites, men of perfect life, were, if I may say so, a stem from which grew many flowers and fruit—the hermits. Everyone knows the founders of this way, whom I mentioned just now, Abba Paul and Antony. Their motive for choosing the solitary life was not cowardice nor intolerance of community living, but a wish to advance further in the contemplation of God (though Paul is said to have been driven into the desert to escape arrest during the persecution). So this second way of perfection sprang out of the first. Its followers are called anchorites, that is *withdrawers*. They have not remained satisfied with defeating the attacks which the devils secretly plan in human society, but have been ready to meet them in open war. That is why they have penetrated courageously into the fastnesses of the desert, like John the Baptist who remained in the desert all his life, or Elijah and Elisha and the others whom St Paul mentioned: 'They wandered about in sheepskins and goatskins, being in want, distressed, afflicted, of

whom the world was not worthy: wandering in deserts, in mountains and caves of the earth.'[7]

7. While the Christian religion was happy in these two ways for monks (though by degrees the system of the hermits also began to deteriorate) there appeared, or rather reappeared, a faithless variety of monk: the kind which was represented by Ananias and Sapphira, at the beginning of the Church's history, and which the apostle, Peter, had so severely forbidden. The apostle did not allow the inventors of this sinful way to be restored after repentance and satisfaction, but destroyed them as you would a noxious weed. As long as the memory of Peter's severity remained impressed upon the faithful, this kind of monk was regarded as hateful by everyone and no one tried that way of life. But when the memory of the dread sentence on Ananias and Sapphira had faded, gradually there appeared the Sarabaites. This is an Egyptian word, meaning persons who have deserted their communities and live each to himself. They are descended from Ananias and Sapphira. They do not follow the perfect way: they prefer to pretend to follow it. No doubt they want to be rivals of, and to gain the kind of credit given to, people who choose Christ's utter poverty above all the riches of the world.

They pursue true goodness feebly. They must needs become monks in order to gain the repute of monks, but they make no effort to follow their discipline, disregard the rules of the communities, are outside all control from the elders, fail to use the elders' traditions to conquer their self-will. They make a public profession of renunciation, and acquire the credit of the title,

---

[7] "The Lord's words to Job refer to them figuratively: 'But who hath sent out the wild ass free, and who hath loosed his bands? To them I have given the wilderness for a house, and a barren land for his dwelling. He scorneth the multitude of the city and heareth not the cry of the tax-collector. He looketh round about the mountains of his pasture, and seeketh for every green thing.' So in the Psalms: 'Let now the redeemed of the Lord speak, those whom he hath redeemed from the hand of the enemy. . . . They wandered in a wilderness, in a place without water. They found not the way of an inhabited city. They were hungry and thirsty: their soul fainted in them. And they cried unto the Lord in their trouble, and he delivered them out of their distress.' So Jeremiah: 'Blessed is the man that hath borne the yoke from his youth. He shall sit solitary and keep silent, because he hath taken it up upon himself.' It is the hermits who with love and in earnest sing the words of the Psalmist: 'I am become like a pelican in the wilderness. I watched, and am become like a sparrow alone upon the house-top' (Heb. 11:37–8; Job 39:5–8, LXX; Ps. 107:2–6; Lam. 3:27–8; Ps. 102:7–8)."

and then go on living in their homes just as before, carrying on the same work; or they build cells for themselves, call them 'monasteries' and live in them as they please. They disobey the Gospel commands not to be anxious about our daily bread or our everyday affairs. It is only possible to obey these commands if you abandon all your property, and so subject yourself to the superiors of a community that you cannot say you are your own master in anything.

Shirking the austere rule of a community: living two or three together in a cell; under no direction: aiming above all else at having freedom from the elders, of going where they like, and of satisfying whatever passion they like—they are more busied about the necessities of life day and night than are coenobites. But their intentions and faith are quite different from those of coenobites. They toil, not to offer their produce or earnings to the steward of the community, but to save money for themselves. See what a gulf lies between them. The coenobite takes no thought for the morrow, and offers God the most acceptable fruits of his labour. The Sarabaite is faithlessly anxious, not only about the morrow, but about years ahead: he believes God false or impotent, because he has promised to give sufficient food and clothing and yet cannot or will not. The coenobite prayerfully seeks absolute poverty for ever, the Sarabaite seeks wealth. The coenobite struggles to fulfil more than the regular task in his daily work, so that if the monastery has more than it needs, the extra money may be given away by the abbot in prisons or in the guestchamber or in the infirmary or to the poor: the Sarabaite works so that whatever is extra above his daily but greedy needs, may be spent extravagantly or saved for his future use. Even granting that their ill-gotten earnings are sometimes distributed in better ways than these, it is still true that they are not aspiring after goodness. The coenobite, in his humility and obedience, accounts to the monastery daily for what he has earned, and surrenders it with the same self-sacrifice with which he originally devoted himself to poverty; he re-dedicates himself daily to a life of renunciation. The Sarabaite every day rushes headlong into sin by being complacent about his generosity to the poor. The coenobite, patient under his discipline, continuing steadfastly in his chosen way, never to obey self-will, becomes crucified daily to the world, a martyr while he is still on earth. The Sarabaite is dragged down to hell by his half-heartedness.

In Egypt there are almost equal numbers of coenobites and

Sarabaites. But in other provinces, where the needs of the Catholic faith have forced me to travel, I have found this third kind, the Sarabaites, to be abundant, and almost the only sort of monk.

In the time of Lucius, who was an Arian bishop during the reign of Valens, I ministered to the brethren from Egypt and the Thebaid who had been exiled to the mines of Pontus and Armenia because they stood firm in their orthodoxy. And on this journey, I very occasionally found disciplined coenobites in a number of cities, but I discovered that no one had even heard of the way of the hermits.

8. There is also a fourth kind of monk, which lately I have observed appearing among people who look and behave like hermits. At first they are fervent and for a short time seek the true coenobite's life. But they quickly grow lukewarm, because they are too complacent to put aside their old sins, will not bear the yoke of humility and patience for long, disdain the control of the elders: and therefore they look out for separate cells and want to live alone. Since no one will then trouble them, they will be able to be reputed patient, gentle and humble.

This half-hearted scheme prevents anyone whom it infects from approaching the way of perfection. So far from being eradicated, sins strike deeper roots. It is like a fatal poison in the stomach—the more deep-seated in the body, the more it creeps onward and generates incurable disease. Out of reverence for the solitary, no one dares to criticize his faults: and so he has chosen rather to know nothing about his own faults than to get rid of them. Goodness is begotten, not by forgetting about sin, but by destroying it."

9. Germanus: "Is there any difference between the *coenobium* and the *monastery*, or are they two names for the same thing?"

10. Piamun: "Some people use the two words as synonyms. But there is this much difference. Monastery means the spot, the place where the monks live. Coenobium means not only where they live but how they live, the kind of rule they adopt. And monastery can be used to mean a hermit's cell, coenobium cannot be used except where a number of brothers are dwelling together in unity. Monastery is also used to describe the groups of Sarabaites.

11. I see that you have learnt the principles of this way of life from the best kind of monks. You are aiming at the heights of the hermit's way after being rightly trained in the coenobium. I am sure that you there learnt humility and patience and are

still following them—and truly following them from the heart, not merely putting on an appearance by humble-sounding words and humble-seeming postures.

Once Abba Sarapion finely mocked this sham humility. A man arrived at his cell, making a great show of lowliness in his dress and speech. Sarapion, as is usual, asked him to offer a collect. The visitor refused, and said that he was guilty of such crimes that he did not deserve even to breathe the same air: refusing the mat, he sat on the ground: still less would he allow Sarapion to wash his feet. After supper it is usual to have a religious conference. So Sarapion began, with kindness and gentleness, to warn him against being an idle and haphazard wanderer, especially as he was young and strong. He told him that he ought to settle in a cell, subject himself to the rules of the elders, and maintain himself by his own work instead of living on the hospitality of others. Since St Paul was working for the spread of the Gospel, he might reasonably have lived on others. Yet he preferred to work day and night to get daily bread for himself and those who were ministering to him and could not work themselves.[8]

At this speech the visitor fell into grief and vexation, and could not keep the bitterness of his heart out of his face. So Sarapion said: 'My son, you have accused yourself of bearing the burden of crime, and you were not afraid to lower your reputation by confessing wicked sins. How is it, then, that I see you moved with indignation, so that you cannot even pretend to keep a serene countenance, at my simple little piece of advice? There was nothing abusive in what I said, its motives were edification and friendship. Is it possible that in humiliating yourself you were hoping to hear me say: "The righteous man is his own accuser when he begins to speak"?[9] You must keep true humility of heart: and true humility comes, not from affectation of posture or speech but from an interior humbling of the mind. Humility and patience will shine out, not when a man accuses himself of crimes which no one will believe, but when he bears arrogant and unjust abuse with a gentle peaceableness.' "

12. Germanus: "We should like to know how to get and keep that tranquillity. If we are told to be silent, it is easy to say nothing. But we sometimes lose interior gentleness of heart even

[8] Cf. II Thess. 3:8; Acts 20:34.
[9] Prov. 18:17, LXX. For this story, cf. *Apophthegmata*, Serapion, G.4: *Verba Seniorum* VIII, 9: and these translations, p. 98.

when we succeed in being silent. So I think that no one can be stable in gentleness unless he is living alone in a hermit's cell."

13. Piamun: "The only source of true patience and tranquillity is deep humility of heart. If it flows from this source, you do not need the solitary's cell to gain it. If it is nourished internally, by its mother and guardian humility, it needs no external support.

But if criticism annoys us, it is certain that humility has no firm foundation, for even a mild breeze can ruinously shake our house. The patience which is admirable does not consist in a peace of mind which is retained because it is never assailed: it consists in the peace which remains amid tempestuous temptations to lose it. Troubles which the world thinks will overthrow it are its strengthening: blows which the world thinks will blunt it, are its sharpening.

Everyone knows that *patience* is derived from *passion* and *endurance*: and therefore that you cannot call anyone patient unless he endures indignities without annoyance. So Solomon rightly praised the patient man: 'Better is the patient man than the strong, and he who restrains his anger more than he that taketh a city'; and 'A long-suffering man is mighty in prudence, but a faint-hearted man is very foolish.' [10] Therefore, if a wronged man flares up in anger, the wrongful abuse should not be thought the *cause* of his sin, but the *manifestation* of a hidden weakness.

Our Lord and Saviour taught a parable about two houses, one founded on a rock and the other on sand. On both houses fell the rain and the floods and the storms. But the one built on the rock sustained the violence unharmed: the one built on shifting sand straightway collapsed. It is obvious that it did not collapse because the rains and the floods beat upon it, but because it had been built foolishly on sand. The saint does not differ from the sinner in not being tempted so strongly. The saint is not conquered by a great onslaught, the sinner falls to a trivial temptation. As I said, we should not praise the courage of a man who had won a fight without opposition. No conflict with an enemy—no victory.

'Blessed is the man that endureth temptation, for when he has been proved, he shall receive the crown of life which God hath promised to them that love him.' St Paul said that 'strength is made perfect' not in ease and comfort, but 'in weakness.' 'For behold, I have made thee this day a fortified

[10] Prov. 16:32, LXX; 14:29, LXX.

city, and a pillar of iron, and a wall of brass, over all the land, to the kings of Judah, and to the princes thereof, and to the priests thereof, and to the people of the land. And they shall fight against thee, and shall not prevail: for I am with thee, saith the Lord, to deliver thee.' [11]

14. I want to give you two examples of true patience.

A religious woman was once so ardent in pursuing patience that she sought out temptation instead of avoiding it. She wanted to test herself and teach herself not to yield. She was of aristocratic ancestry, and lived at Alexandria, serving the Lord faithfully in the house left to her by her parents. She went to Bishop Athanasius of blessed memory, and asked him to allow her to support one of the widows at present being maintained by the Church's treasury. Her actual words were: 'Give me one of the sisters to look after.' The bishop praised her intention and saw that she was generous in her almsgiving. So he ordered that one of the widows should be selected who was outstanding in integrity and seriousness and self-discipline. Otherwise, if the recipient of the charity were a sinner or wicked woman, he was afraid the donor's generosity would be diminished or that in disgust she might even take some harm to her own faith.

Taking the widow home, the lady rendered her every service. She soon discovered her modesty and gentleness, and found that she was given thanks for everything which she did. So after a few days she returned to Bishop Athanasius and said: 'I asked you to give me someone to refresh, someone whom I could try to please by my services.' Athanasius did not yet understand what she wanted, and thought that the head of his treasury must have neglected to obey his command. Enquiring with some heat the cause of the delay, he discovered that she had been given the most honourable widow on the Church's list. So he gave secret orders that she should be given the worst of the widows, the one who bawled and brawled and drank and gossiped more than any other widow guilty of these vices. It was all too easy to find the woman. The lady received her, began to keep her at home, serve her as carefully as she had served the first. Now the only thanks she got was reviling and wrong-doing and cursing; the woman complained continually that she had been asked from the bishop with no intention of doing her good but solely with the object of torturing and scorning her: she said that instead of passing from labour to rest, she had passed from rest to labour. Her wanton abuse culminated in

[11] James 1:12; II Cor. 12:9; Jer. 1:18–19.

blows. But the lady meekly redoubled her efforts to serve her. She learnt to overcome the harridan by obeying her quietly, and to soften her abusive rage by humanity and gentleness.

By these exercises she was strengthened and obtained the true patience for which she was looking. And she went to Bishop Athanasius and thanked him for the good his selection had done to her. She said that he had (at last) given her what she wanted, a most wonderful teacher of patience, whose constant abuse, like the oil with which a man smears himself when about to wrestle, had trained her patience to be perfect. 'At last you have given me someone to look after, for the first rather honoured and refreshed me by her services.'

It is enough that this story should be told about a member of the female sex, to edify us and even confound us. We cannot keep our patience if we shut ourselves up in cells as wild beasts retire to their lairs.

15. Here is another example, one of Abba Paphnutius.

Paphnutius lived a strict life in the fastnesses of the celebrated desert of Scete, where he is now presbyter. The other hermits called him the Buffalo, because he seemed to have a kind of innate love of solitude. Even as a youth he was eminent in goodness and grace; the chief ascetics of that time marvelled at his seriousness and stability of purpose, and in spite of his age elected him into the number of the elders on the ground of his character.

But one of the monks, like the patriarch Joseph's brothers, was inflamed by jealousy against him. Wanting to spoil the reputation of Paphnutius, he hit on a devilish plot. He seized the moment on Sunday when Paphnutius was away from his cell at church. He stole into the cell, and there hid his own book among the plaits which Paphnutius was in the habit of weaving from palm-leaves. Confident in his plan, he went to church like a man with a clear conscience. At the end of the service he lodged a public complaint to the holy Isidore (who was Paphnutius' predecessor as priest of this hermit brotherhood), alleging that his book had been stolen from his cell. The complaint disturbed the brothers and above all their priest, because they knew not what to suspect or what to decide, and were extremely astonished inasmuch as no one remembered a similar crime being perpetrated in that desert before (and it has never happened since). The plaintiff then urged that they should all be confined to the church while searchers were chosen to examine every hermit's cell. The priest entrusted the task to three of the elders. They ransacked the bedding in each cell, and at last found the book where the plotter had hidden it, in Paphnutius' cell, among the plaits. The searchers immediately carried it back to church and displayed it.

The conscience of Paphnutius was perfectly clear. Yet he offered to make satisfaction like a man who admits he is a thief, asked and prayed to be put in the penitents' seat. In his shame and modesty, he was afraid that if he tried to plead not guilty, he would merely be believed to be a liar as well as a thief, since everyone accepted the evidence. He straightway left the church, his mind not really cast down but trusting in God's judgement. He poured out prayer and lamentations, trebled his fasting, and was seen by everyone to be prostrating himself in humility. For nearly a fortnight he thus bruised his flesh and spirit: and then on Saturday and Sunday came early in the morning to church, not to receive Holy Communion, but to lie prone in the church porch and beg for pardon.

Then God, who knows all secrets, did not allow him to be further buffeted by providence, nor further slandered by his fellows. The wicked and guilty monk, who had 'stolen' his own property, and had skilfully ruined the reputation of another, had perpetrated his crime unseen. But the devil who had egged him on caused it after all to be known. The monk, seized by some terrible demon, blabbed about his whole plan, and betrayed himself. For a long time he was so troubled by an unclean spirit that he could not even be cleansed by the prayers of the holy men in Scete who possessed the miraculous gift of exorcising demons. Not even the special grace of the priest, Isidore, could expel this savage spirit: though Isidore was richly endowed by the Lord with this power, so that he could sometimes heal the possessed even at a distance. Christ was reserving this glory for the young Paphnutius. And thus the sinner was healed by the prayers of him against whom he had sinned, and the name whose reputation he had tried to blast was the name which brought him pardon and relief from his suffering.

Paphnutius in early days already showed the signs of his future character, already planned the way to the perfection which was to be matured as he grew in years. And we too—if we want to be as saintly as he was—must lay the foundations of that saintliness in the same way.

16. I had two reasons for telling this story. Knowing that our temptations are less than his, we shall seek better for

patience and tranquillity when we contemplate the rock-like stability of Paphnutius. Secondly, we must resolve that we can never be safe from violent and devilish temptations if to protect our patience we put our trust in something outside us instead of inside us—in the cell or the solitude or our association with holy men or anything else external. In the Gospel our Lord said: 'The kingdom of God is within you.' [12] And unless the same Lord strengthen and protect our minds, we are wrong if we think we can defeat the attacks of the enemies which fly through the air merely by living with other men, or a long way off, or inside walls to keep them out. Paphnutius had all these things: yet the tempter found a way to attack him, and was not repelled by a hermitage, or a desert, or holiness in the men of that society. He was not moved by an assault like that because he had fixed his heart's hope not on anything external, but on the judge of all secrets; and, conversely, did not the envious and guilty monk enjoy the protection of a solitary life and a distant cell and the company of St Isidore his abba and priest, and of other holy men? The satanic hurricane fell against a house built on sand, and destroyed it.

Then let us not seek our peace outside ourselves. Let us not think to cover our own impatience with someone else's patience. As 'the kingdom of God is within you,' so 'a man's foes are they of his own household.' No one is more my enemy than my own heart, the inmost indweller of my household. If we are careful, we can prevent ourselves being injured by internal enemies. If our own household is not assailing us, there is the kingdom of God and peace of mind. Look carefully, and you will see that I cannot be injured even by a villain, if I am not at war against myself within my own heart. If I am injured, the sin is not due to the assault from outside: it is due to my own lack of patience. Strong meat is healthy to the healthy, but it kills a sick man. It cannot hurt the eater unless his own illness makes the food harmful to him.

If ever a temptation like that of Paphnutius arise among the brothers, we need never be shaken from the path of peace, need never allow an opening to the blasphemy and slander of worldly men, need never be surprised that wicked men are to be found secretly among the holy societies. This world is a threshing floor which sifts us, and tares destined for everlasting fire are mixed with the richest wheat. Remember that Satan was chosen to be an angel, Judas an apostle, the heresiarch

[12] Luke 17:21.

Nicolas a deacon. It is no wonder that wicked men are to be found among the ranks of the saints. (Some say that the heresiarch Nicolas was not the man appointed to the diaconate by the apostles, but they cannot deny that he was one of the disciples at a time when all the disciples were as perfect as the very few whom you now find with some difficulty in coenobia.)

Then let us forget the sad fall of the brother in that desert; forget the horrible stain which he afterwards blotted out by his tears of penitence; forget the ancient sin of envy which was made the worse because he was a religious. Let us remember the example of St Paphnutius, follow his humility with all our power, a humility which was no sudden offspring of the hermitage but had first been acquired in human society and then perfected in the solitary life.

Envy,[13] you should know, is a disease more difficult to cure than any other sin. I would almost say that once a man is poisoned by it there is no antidote. It is the plague of which the prophet spoke in an allegory: 'Behold, I will send among you serpents, basilisks, against which there is no charm: and they shall bite you.' It is a good comparison between envy and the poisonous bite of the basilisk, for by envy Satan, the source of all poison, perished. By envy he first slew himself and then the Lord whom he envied: he poured deadly poison into himself before he poured it into man. 'By the envy of the devil death entered into the world: they therefore who are on his side follow him.'[14] The first person to be corrupted by it allowed no antidote by repentance; and so the envious put themselves outside the help of him who can cure the bite. Tormented not by the faults of the people they envy, but by their prosperity, they cannot admit the truth about others and are always on the watch for trivial and silly causes of offence. These imaginary causes of offence cannot be overcome so long as the deadly virus is in them and they will not bring it to the surface. The wise man has said: 'If a serpent bite without hissing, the charmer can do nothing.' It is only the silent bites which wise men cannot cure.

---

[13] This little conclusion on the sin of envy is given a separate chapter heading by some important manuscripts. Unlike the later list of "seven deadly sins" envy had found no place in the "eight capital sins" which Cassian had treated in the *Institutes*. I have suspicions about its Cassianic authorship, on grounds of Latin style and mode of handling the subject-matter, but these suspicions can claim no support in the manuscripts.

[14] Jer. 8:17; Wisdom 2:24.

The disease is so incurable, that it is made worse by treatment; the sore is inflamed by ointments. Solomon says: 'Envy endures nothing.'[15] The more progress another has made in humility or patience or generosity, the more a man envies him, and wants his ruin or death. The eleven patriarchs could not be diverted from their envy by any submission on the part of their brother who had done no harm: and Scripture relates of them: 'His brothers envied him because his father loved him, and they could not speak peaceably unto him': and in the end they were so jealous that they would listen to no entreaties, plotted his death, and were scarcely satisfied with the sin of selling him into slavery.

Thus it is sure that envy is more destructive than the other faults, more difficult to eradicate: for it is kindled by the remedies which cure other sins. For example: The man who grieves for an injury done to him, is cured by a generous compensation. Though he was indignant at the wrong, he can be placated if satisfaction is rendered humbly. But what will you do for a man who is more offended the more kind and humble you are to him? He is not irritated by his own greed, which a bribe can heal, nor by his desire to injure, or love of revenge, which gentleness could overcome. He is irritated by another's happiness. Where shall we find a man who, to satisfy another's envy, will want to lose his own prosperity or wish a disaster to happen to him?

Therefore, in order not to lose the moral life within us, the part of us indwelt and quickened by the Holy Spirit, by a single bite from the basilisk, let us continually ask the help of God to whom nothing is impossible. The other snake-poisons are the carnal sins: and though frail human nature easily falls into these, it is as easily cleansed. These other bites show marks on the body; and however dangerous the swelling, a skilful doctor can apply the healing remedy and the poison shall not reach the heart—the wise guide to God's Scriptures can apply the saving words and prevent the moral poison from killing the soul for eternity. But envy is like the basilisk's poison—it leaves no mark and penetrates to the very life of religion and faith before the person is aware that he is wounded. The jealous man is not raising himself up against man but blaspheming against God, for he is scandalized by nothing in his brother except his happiness, and is therefore attacking, not man's guilt, but the judgements of God.

15 Eccl. 10:11, LXX; Prov. 27:4, LXX.

This then is that 'root of bitterness springing up': it raises itself to heaven, scorning God who gives his good to mankind.

No one should be worried because God threatens to send 'basilisks' to bite men whose sins offend him. It is certain that God cannot be the author of envy. Yet it is fair, and worthy of God's justice, that in bestowing good gifts on the humble and refusing them to the proud and the wicked, he should smite and consume with envy those who deserve to be given over to a reprobate mind, as St Paul says. This is what is meant by another text, 'They have provoked me to jealousy by them that are no gods: and I will provoke them to jealousy by them that are no nation.' " [16]

*   *   *   *

By this conference Piamun stirred our desire to proceed further in our step from the primary school of the coenobium to the secondary grade of the hermitage. It was under his guidance that Germanus and I learnt the elements of the hermits' way, and began to acquire that knowledge which we afterwards extended in Scete.

CONFERENCE 19

Conference of Abba John

ON THE AIMS OF THE COENOBITE AND HERMIT

1. Only a few days afterwards, we went to the coenobium of Abba Paul, in order to find further instruction. There were more than two hundred resident monks. But in honour of a feast, the anniversary of the death of an earlier abbot of the monastery, a vast crowd of monks from other coenobia was visiting the place. I mention this meeting because I want shortly to describe the patience of one monk, his imperturbable gentleness in the presence of the whole crowd. It is true that this conference is concerned with the words of Abba John, who left the desert and in humility became again a monk in a coenobium. Yet I do not think it absurd to digress briefly if, as I believe, the story is edifying to earnest men.

When the crowd of monks was seated by parties of twelve in the huge open-air court, one of them was slow in bringing in a dish. Abba Paul was walking round and carefully supervising the monks who were serving. When he saw the delay, he publicly gave the monk such a smack with his hand that the

[16] Heb. 12:15; Jer. 8:17; Rom. 1:28; Deut. 32:21, LXX.

sound was heard even by people sitting a long way off and with their backs turned. The young man took the blow serenely, said nothing, gave no sign even of a murmur, did not move his lips, indeed did not change for a moment his modesty and serenity and colour of countenance: a remarkable instance of patience. We had lately come from our monastery in Syria and had not been given such clear examples in how to be patient. Everyone, and not only our two selves, but the men familiar with these practices, marvelled, and even the most advanced learnt a particular lesson. For it was not only that his father's correction did not disturb his patience. It was the fact that although he was made a spectacle to such a great crowd, his face showed not even a blush.[17]

2. We found in this coenobium a very old man named John. I have thought it right to include what he said, because he was a man of such humility. Humility, though it is the mother of all goodness and the foundation of the whole house of the spirit, is banished out of our own system. So it is not surprising that we cannot climb to their moral level. So far from being able to bear the discipline of the coenobium until old age, we are scarcely ready to endure its yoke for two years and dare to run out to a liberty which does our soul harm. And even for that short time we seem to submit to the elders not as the rule directs but as and how we like.

When we first saw old Abba John in Abba Paul's coenobium, we were struck by his age and natural grace. With downcast eyes we began to pray him to show us, ignorant though we were, why he had left the free and noble life of the hermit, wherein he had won a fame beyond the fame of other men, and had chosen to enter the coenobium and bear its yoke.

John replied that he had been unequal to the hermit's discipline, and incapable of following that way to perfection: he had therefore gone back to school, to see if he could rightly keep the rules of the coenobium.

We refused to accept this humble reply, and went on importuning. At last he began to talk.

3. "You are surprised that I have left the hermit life. It is not at all that I reject it or disapprove of it, I regard it with the utmost veneration. First I passed thirty years in a community

[17] Some medieval copyists struggled with interpolations either to defend Abba Paul's action (as Caroliruhensis 92 from Reichenau) or to make it clear that the action was bad and that Cassian disapproved of it (as Parisinus nov. acq. 2170).

and then another twenty as a hermit. And I am very glad of those twenty years: at least half-hearted hermits will not be able to accuse me of being slothful. But though I found the purity of the life, I also found that it was not unmixed with bodily anxieties. It seemed better to return to the coenobium to aim at a lower target and hit it more easily, and to avoid the risk of failing at the effort after a loftier way. It is better to make a little promise and keep it than to make a big promise and break it.

If I put forward anything too freely or proudly, please do not think it a form of boasting, but out of charity and a care for your edification. I think I ought to keep back nothing of the truth because you have importuned me so earnestly. It is possible you will learn something if I lay aside my humility for a little and simply tell you what I am aiming at. I hope you will not have to blame me on grounds of vanity: and I hope I shall not have to blame myself for failing to tell you the truth.

4. If there is anyone who delights in the desert loneliness and the separation from society; if there is anyone who can say with Jeremiah: 'I have not desired the day of man, thou knowest'; [18] I confess that with God's help I was that man, or was on the way to being that man. I remember how often the Lord granted me to be taken up into a kind of rapture, so that I forgot my frail body and my mind lost its sense of material reality, my eyes could not see and my ears could not hear. My mind was full of meditation and contemplation upon God, so that often in the evening I did not know I had eaten food and next morning had no idea whether I had broken my fast last night. So on Saturday I used to lay out food for seven days: seven pairs of rolls of bread in a sort of basket, so that I should know whether or not I had eaten. By this method I could not forget when the week was ended and the services of the church had come round. Even if the raptures of which I spoke should interfere with this plan, still the order of work from day to day prevented me making this mistake.

But I pass over the merits of the desert. My subject is not the manifold good things to be found there, but the respective aims of the coenobite and hermit. I will briefly answer your request to explain why I chose to leave the desert, and expound the high advantages of the common life which I preferred to all the fruits of the desert.

5. At first there were few hermits in the desert. We had

[18] Jer. 17:16.

plenty of room and freedom. At first we lived far in the fastnesses of the desert and were often taken up into heavenly
visions. In those days there was no crowd of visiting monks, no
need to undertake the distracting burden of hospitality. In those
days my spirit burned within me, I hungered for the peace of
solitude and the life filled with a bliss like the angels.

But soon a large number of monks began to live in the
desert. There was less room, less freedom. And I found that my
ardour for the contemplation of God began to cool, and my
mind had to busy itself with all kinds of earthly matters. I therefore determined to fulfil my ascetic purpose in the coenobium,
rather than become a half-hearted solitary by constantly having
to look after my bodily needs. I no longer have freedom, I am
no longer taken up into ecstasies of spirit. But I have this consolation, that I can obey the Gospel in taking no thought for the
morrow. If I lose the purity of contemplation, I gain by
having to obey a rule.

It is a wretched thing for anyone to undertake some art or
study and never become perfect at it.

6. Now I will shortly explain the great benefits I enjoy here.
I leave it to you, after you have heard my evidence, to judge
whether the profit to be found in the desert can compensate
for the advantages here: and you will be able to decide whether
I chose to be shut up in these walls because I disliked the solitary's purity or because I was aiming at it.

In this monastery, I do not have to arrange my day's work.
I am not bothered with buying or selling, I do not have to think
about storing food. I am not anxious about preparing to receive
the numerous visitors as well as look after the residents—and
above all I am not subject to popularity nor therefore to the
temptation to arrogance, which is the worst thing in the desert
life, and which has been known to do away in God's sight with
the merit of desert austerities. But passing over the risks of
spiritual pride and vanity which afflict hermits, I lay the stress
on a burden which troubles them all, the provision of food. The
present hermits are not content, like the stricter ancients, to do
without oil: they are even beginning to be dissatisfied with the
lax rule of the present generation which enacts that for all
visitors during the year it shall be enough to provide a pint of
oil and a measure of lentils. At the moment two or three times
that amount is believed to be almost too little. Our predecessors,
though more austere than we in following the rules of the
desert, were accustomed, when mixing vinegar and pickle, to

add a single drop of oil to repel the temptation of vanity. The present generation are grown so lax that they break an Egyptian cheese to give it taste, pour in more oil than it needs, mix into a single flavour two kinds of food each with its proper taste and each of which could by themselves be refreshing at different meals. They are now beginning to own so much that on the excuse of 'hospitality' they keep a blanket in their cells—I can hardly say it without shame.

I pass over the things which specially afflict the worshipping and contemplative mind—the frequent meetings with the brothers, the duties of receiving guests and bidding them farewell, visits to each other, various interminable discussions and pieces of business; even when you are at leisure, the mind seems taut with expectation of some bother ahead. The result of all this is that the hermit loses his freedom, is shackled in the heavy chain of worry, never finds that ineffable eagerness in his heart, and so loses the profit of his way of life.

Living in a community and among a crowd of men I am likewise deprived of this contemplative profit, but at least I have peace of soul and freedom from business. If hermits have not this quiet, which is indispensable, they will have the austerities of the desert without the benefit of it. Possibly there might be in the coenobium some little loss in purity of heart. But I shall be satisfied with the compensation of the Gospel text, a compensation which surely cannot be worth less than all the fruits of the desert, that I should take no thought for the morrow. And if to the end of my life I am the obedient disciple of an abbot, I may in some measure imitate him of whom it is said: 'He humbled himself, and became obedient unto death': and so I may humbly be able to use his words: 'I came not to do mine own will, but the will of the Father which sent me.' " [19]

7. Germanus: "It is obvious that, unlike the many ascetics content with the foothills of the two ways of life, you have climbed the heights. We would know then, what are the respective goals of the coenobite and the hermit? I suppose that this can only be discussed adequately by a man who has long experience in following both ways of perfection, and so can show us their value and their aim."

8. John: "I should have defended the absolute assertion that the same person cannot be perfect in both ways of life, but I know some few exceptions to the rule. If it is difficult enough to find a man who is perfect in one of them, how difficult, almost

[19] Phil. 2:8; John 6:38.

impossible, to find someone perfect in both. If this has ever happened, it cannot be put under any general rule. You cannot get a universal rule out of a very few instances, out of the experience of a very few. What if a few people have attained a saintliness beyond the common capacity of most men and the frailty of normal human nature; we must not draw conclusions valid for everyone, and must regard it rather by way of miracle than by way of an example to follow.

As far as I am able, I will now answer your question.

The coenobite aims at mortifying and crucifying all his selfwill, at taking no thought for the morrow as the Gospel says. It is plain that only a coenobite can reach this perfection: like the man whom the prophet Isaiah blesses and praises in these words: 'If thou turn thy foot away from the sabbath, from doing thy own will in my holy day, and glorify him, while thou dost not thine own ways, and thine own will is not found to speak a word: then shalt thou be delighted in the Lord, and I will lift thee up above the high places of the earth, and will feed thee with the inheritance of Jacob thy father. For the mouth of the Lord hath spoken it.'

The hermit aims at freeing his mind from all earthly thoughts, and to unite it with Christ so far as his human weakness allows: like the man of whom the prophet, Jeremiah, spoke: 'Blessed is the man who hath borne the yoke from his youth. He shall sit solitary and hold his peace, because he hath taken it upon himself.' The Psalmist said: 'I am become like a pelican in the desert. I watched and became like a sparrow alone upon the housetop.' [20]

These are the two different aims. Unless the follower of each way attains his aim, he will gain no good from his hermitage or his coenobium.

9. Each perfection then is partial, not complete. Perfection in the full sense is a gift of God, and it is rare indeed. The truly perfect man is he who can endure with an equal peace of mind the austerities and loneliness of the desert, and the weaknesses of his brethren in the community. In neither mode of life is it easy to find a complete person. The hermit cannot achieve contempt for material possessions, the coenobite cannot achieve the pure prayer of the contemplative.

I know that Abba Moses and Paphnutius and the two Macarii possessed both in completeness. They went out beyond the other inhabitants of the desert to lonelier places, so far as

[20] Isa. 58:13-14; Lam. 3:27-8; Ps. 102:7-8.

possible they never sought for company; and yet they put up with the frailties of all the people who came to see them and profit by them, an almost incessant bother accepted with an imperturbable patience. And men supposed that they had spent all their lives in learning how to show the usual hospitality to their visitors. No one could decide at which kind of life they had progressed further. They were great-hearted men, wonderfully fitted for either kind of life.

10. Others begin to become rather like animals, owing to the long silence and loneliness, and slink away from man's approach. When they are brought out of retirement for a short time by visiting brethren, they shy away with obvious signs of fright. This usually happens to people who have become hermits prematurely and without a good previous training in the community life. Their faults are not eradicated, they are as poor hermits as they are coenobites, and are blown about here and there by puffs from every troublesome breeze. On the one side they are annoyed and impatient at meeting other monks. On the other side they dislike the loneliness and silence which they have chosen, because they do not even know the true reason for choosing it, but think its supreme merit to be a way of avoiding human company or of seeing human faces."

11. Germanus: "What remedy is there for people like ourselves whose weakness consists precisely in this, that we had too little instruction in the coenobium and entered the desert life before we had eradicated our faults? How can we attain the stable and imperturbable and patient mind? We left school too young, before we had fully learnt our lessons, when we went away from our coenobium. Now we are living in the desert. How shall we acquire long-suffering and patience? Living alone, we do not meet men who cause us annoyance. How shall conscience, in exploring our inward motives, decide whether or not we are right in thinking we possess true peace of mind?"

12. John: "God, who truly heals souls, will certainly offer a remedy to those who truly seek it: especially to repentant men who are not hopeless or neglectful of their faults nor conceal them, nor wantonly refuse the healing of penitence when the opportunity is offered; and to men who fly humbly and prudently to God to heal the sins they have contracted from ignorance or error or necessity.

If we go into the desert with our faults still hidden within us, they no longer hurt others, but our love of them remains. Of every sin not eradicated, the root is still growing secretly within.

We can decide whether it is alive by certain tests. For example: if we receive visitors even for a short stay with the slightest trouble of mind, it proves that we still have in us the source from which the tumbling stream of impatience flows. Or if we are expecting a monk and for some reason he is a little late, and our mind is silently indignant with him or annoyed that we have so inconveniently to wait for him, it will prove to our conscience that the seeds of anger and grievance are still within. If a monk asks us to lend him a book or some other loan, and we are saddened by the request, or even refuse it, that will prove that we are still entangled in the sins of avarice and covetousness. If, through reading Holy Scripture or a sudden memory, we think of a woman and feel the least lust towards her, it shows that lust is not yet extinguished in our body. If we compare our own strict discipline with the lax practices of another and feel the slightest temptation to puff ourselves, it proves that the terrible plague of pride is still infecting us.

If we see these signs within, we know that it is not the desire to sin, but the opportunity to sin, which has vanished. If ever we started mixing in society again, these passions would creep out of their caves and show that they were not new; visible at last, they had been in us all the time.

In this way even a hermit can discern whether the roots of sins are eradicated or not—if he tries not to show off his purity before other men, but only in the sight of him to whom all hearts lie open."

13. Germanus: "We see how to discover the signs of weakness. All our daily experience confirms what you have said. You have shown us the evidence and causes of the disease, now we would know the cure. The man who will best talk about the cure of ill-health is the man who, by the evidence of the patients, is most accurate in diagnosis. You have so clearly diagnosed the cause of our disease that we have some faint hope of a cure. Yet your words have driven us into a despair which will destroy our spiritual life. You say that in communities men acquire the first stages in salvation and none can be healthy in solitude unless he has first cured his faults in a coenobium. We are afraid that perhaps, as we were imperfect when we left our own community, it is now impossible for us to be perfect in the desert."

14. John: "People who really want to cure their illness are sure to find a remedy. We ought to look for the cure of each sin in the same way that we looked for its evidence. Just as I said

the faults of ordinary life persist in the solitary's life, so I affirm that all the instruments for pursuing virtue and healing are available in the desert. If a man discovers, by the signs I mentioned, that he is liable to impatience and anger, he ought ever to be training himself in the virtues opposite to these faults. He ought to imagine various injuries being offered to himself by some hypothetical person, and so accustom his mind to be perfectly humble and submissive in the face of everything that wickedness can do to him. He ought to imagine roughness, conduct unbearable against himself, and penitently meditate on the gentleness with which he should receive it. If he looks at the sufferings of the saints or the Passion of the Lord, he will see that these wrongs and punishments are less than he deserves, and will be readier to bear all sorrow. And at those times, inevitable even in the strictest desert life, when he is for some reason summoned to the meeting of the monks, he should censor his inner feelings, if he finds that he is silently troubled about trivialities, and should accuse himself of all those bitter wrongs which his daily meditation has been training him to bear. And in self-reproach he should say: 'My good man, are you the same fellow who set yourself up to overcome all evil while you were at training-school in the desert? Are you the man who lately imagined bitter abuse and unbearable punishments against yourself and fancied that you were strong enough to bear them without the mind being disturbed? Is it not remarkable that this unconquerable patience has slipped before an idle word? How is it that a mild breeze is rocking the house which you thought to be built on solid rock? What has happened to that silly longing of yours for war when you were at peace? You used to say: "I am ready, and am not troubled," and with the prophet: "Prove me, O Lord, and try me: search out my reins and my heart": and: "Prove me, O Lord, and know my heart: question me and know my paths; and see if there be any way of wickedness in me." [21] Have you prepared for war and yet been frightened by a little ghost of an enemy?'

With these penitential reproaches a man should condemn himself and not let the disturbing temptation go unpunished. He should fast the more rigorously, watch longer in the night, restrain his appetites, and so crucify by exercises the inconstancy of mind which ought to have been repressed while he was a coenobite. One thing we must hold tightly, to keep a true and lasting patience. It is never lawful for us to be angry because of

[21] Ps. 119:60; 26:2; 139:23-4.

material loss or mental conflict, since God's law forbids us to remember a wrong, just as it forbids us to revenge ourselves.

What worse fate can befall the soul than the loss, through a sudden blinding flare of bad temper, of the clear vision of the true and eternal Light, the loss of the contemplation of him who is 'meek and lowly of heart'? [22] What should twist a man away from his true nature more than the loss of the ability to discern between good and evil, to use a sober and disciplined and wise judgement? Is it not deplorable that a sane and sober man should do what would not be pardoned in a man so tipsy that he was partly out of his senses?

Whoever considers this damage to the soul, will bear every variety of loss or injury or punishment of cruel men. He will think nothing more damaging than anger, nothing more precious than peace of mind and stable purity of heart. To find these we ought to lose even spiritual benefits, if those spiritual benefits cannot be won without troubling the peace of mind."

15. Germanus: "You have shown that the cure for diseases like anger, gloom, and impatience, consists in setting the opposite qualities against them. I should like to know what kind of remedy it is possible to bring against the spirit of lust. Surely the fire cannot here be quenched by imagining temptations? I believe that even to glance at the temptation with the mind, let alone increasing the incentive, is fatal to chastity."

16. John: "The question is a wise one: and even if you had not asked it, I was being led naturally to it. I am sure that the answer is easy for you, since you have acutely gone ahead of what I was going to say. The puzzle of a question is easily unravelled when the question itself is put in such a way as to imply the right answer.

For curing the faults which I have been talking about, human society, so far from being a hindrance, is beneficial. The more often men see they are impatient, the more thoroughly they do penitence and the more rapidly do they achieve a sound mind. And since there are no incentives to impatience and irritation in the desert, we ought to imagine temptations to it so as to have a struggle and find a cure more rapidly. But against lust, a different method is needed. Not only has the body to be deprived of the opportunities, the mind has to be brought to forget all about it. For weak spirits it is bad enough to admit even a little recollection of it, the sort that arises from remembering a holy woman or reading a passage of Holy Scripture. And

[22] Matt. 11:29.

this was why our elders used wisely to omit passages of this kind when younger monks were present.

To monks who have won through to perfect chastity, there are plenty of tests to determine whether their conscience may judge the heart to be incorrupt. To a chaste man there is a test of the same kind. If he is sure that the roots of the disease have been eradicated, he may explore the grace of his chastity by making some mental fantasy of temptation. To men who are still weak this imaginative exploration is more destructive than useful, and must be avoided. If the perfect man can stand unharmed by this kind of fantasy, if his mind and body remain unperturbed, he will have a proof of purity. And in this purity he will train his mind, and will even think it harmful if some necessity forces him into the presence of a woman."

Here Abba John ended his conference, seeing it was 3 o'clock and time for our meal.

III

The Rule of Saint Benedict

INTRODUCTION

FOR THE PLACE OF THE RULE IN EARLY monasticism, see the general introduction.

The best manuscript of the Rule appears to be that of Saint Gall 914. Indeed it was argued by Ludwig Traube that a copy of the autograph of the Rule was sent from Monte Cassino to Charlemagne in the year 787, and that the Saint-Gall manuscript is a copy of this copy. This hypothesis has been shown to be speculative: and it is no longer possible to rule out of account the evidence of a different manuscript tradition, represented in particular by the earliest extant manuscript (Hatton 48 in the Bodleian Library) which cannot have been copied much later than 700.

It is possible that the Rule was in part a copy of an earlier Rule, of which we have either the representative, or the descendant by a different line, in the *Regula Magistri*: of this rule the known manuscripts go back to the sixth century. The matter is still under examination: materials for following the debate will be found in the select bibliography.

In this translation I took as a basis the Douai translation of 1700. But I have revised it very freely indeed, and have sought to bring it into line with modern knowledge about the text of the Rule.

The Rule of Saint Benedict

THE TEXT

Prologue

Son, listen to the precepts of your master; take them to your heart willingly. If you follow the advice of a tender father and travel the hard road of obedience, you will return to God, from whom by disobedience you have gone astray.

I address my discourse to all of you who will renounce your own will, enter the lists under the banner of obedience, and fight under the lead of your lawful sovereign, Christ the Lord.

First, I advise that you should implore the help of God to accomplish every good work you undertake; that he, who has now vouchsafed to rank us in the number of his children, may be no more grieved at our doing amiss. For we ought always to use his grace so faithfully in his service, as to give him no occasion to disinherit his children like an angry parent, or to punish for eternity his servants, like a master incensed at their crimes—servants who have refused to follow him in the way to glory.

Let us then exert ourselves now. The Scripture awakens us, saying: "Now it is the hour to arise from sleep"; and with eyes wide open to the light of heaven, and ears receptive to the word of God, let us hear what his voice repeats to us every day. "Today if you will hear his voice, harden not your hearts." And again, "He who hath ears to hear, let him hear what the Spirit saith unto the churches." What does he say? "Come, my children, hearken unto me and I will teach you the fear of the Lord." "Run while ye have the light of life, that the darkness of death overtake you not." [1]

The Lord, seeking to draw from the crowd one faithful servant, asks: "What man is he that desireth life and would fain see good days?" [2] If you reply: "It is I," God answers: "If

[1] Rom. 13:11; Ps. 95:8; Matt. 11:15; Rev. 2:7; Ps. 34:11; John 12:35.
[2] Ps. 34:12–15.

you will possess the true and everlasting life, keep your tongue from evil and your lips from speaking guile. Depart from evil and do good: seek peace and pursue it. And when you have done this, then my eyes shall be open upon you, and my ears shall listen to your prayers, and even before you call upon me I will say: 'Behold, I am here.'" Dearest brethren, can we imagine anything more tender than this invitation of our Lord? See, in his goodness, he points out to us the way of life.

Let us then gird up our loins; let us walk by faith and try to serve him with good works; and thereby let us advance in his ways with the Gospel as our guide, that we may deserve to behold him who has called us to his kingdom. If we want to fix our dwelling there, we cannot arrive thereto without running in the ways of virtue. But let us enquire of the Lord with the prophet: "Lord who shall dwell in thy tabernacle, or who shall rest upon thy holy hill?" Brethren, let us hear the Lord's answer to the question, an answer which shows the way to the heavenly tabernacle: "He that walketh without blame and does right: he that speaketh truth in his heart; he that hath kept his tongue from guile, hath done no evil to his neighbour, and hath not believed slander of his neighbour." [3] He who drives the tempter and his temptations far from his heart, defeats his malice, and dashes his rising thoughts against the Rock Christ. He who fears the Lord without growing proud of his virtue and humbly acknowledges that what is good in him does not proceed from himself. He who gives God his due, and with the prophet blesses the work of God in himself: "Not unto us, O Lord, not unto us, but unto thy name give the glory." The apostle Paul found nothing of his own to boast of in his preaching: "By the grace of God (says he) I am what I am," and again, "He that glories, let him glory in the Lord." On this account our Lord in the Gospel tells us: "He that heareth these words of mine and doeth them, I will make him like the wise man who hath built his house upon a rock. The floods came and the winds blew, and they beat upon that house, and it fell not, for it was founded upon a rock." [4]

Our Lord expects that our works should ever correspond with these declarations of Scripture. Therefore, in consideration of the evils which we have to redress, he has given us the days of our life, and prolongs them to afford us an opportunity of making peace with him. "Dost thou not know," says the

[3] Ps. 15:1–3.
[4] Ps. 115:1; I Cor. 15:10; II Cor. 10:17; Matt. 7:24–5.

Apostle, "that the patience of God inviteth thee to repentance?" For our tender Lord assures us: "I will not the death of a sinner, but that he should be converted and live." [5]

When we enquired of the Lord about the person who should dwell in his tabernacle, we were informed what conditions were necessary for it; and it is now ours to perform those conditions. [6] Therefore our hearts and bodies are to be prepared to fight under his command; and we must beseech God to supply with his grace what it is impossible for nature to effect alone. Moreover, if we desire to avoid the pains of hell, and to compass eternal life, we must, while we have time in the body and ability to use the opportunity of a religious life, make haste and practise now the virtues which will serve us for all eternity.

To conclude: I am to erect a school for beginners in the service of the Lord: which I hope to establish on laws not too difficult or grievous. But if, for reasonable cause, for the retrenchment of vice or preservation of charity, I require some things which may seem too austere, you are not thereupon to be frightened from the ways of salvation. Those ways are always strait and narrow at the beginning. But as we advance in the practices of religion and in faith, the heart insensibly opens and enlarges through the wonderful sweetness of his love, and we run in the way of God's commandments. If then we keep close to our school and the doctrine we learn in it, and persevere in the monastery till death, we shall here share by patience in the passion of Christ and hereafter deserve to be united with him in his kingdom. Amen.

1. Of the several sorts of monks

It is well-known that there are four sorts of monks.

The first is of coenobites, who dwell in convents under the direction of a rule and an abbot.

The second is of anchorites, or hermits. These are not men who have hurried away into solitary cells with the indiscreet zeal of beginners, but have served a mature probation in monasteries, and there learnt by the example and help of their fellow-monks how to fight the devil; and thereafter are sufficiently appointed, without any other help than that of God, to

---

[5] Rom. 2:4; Ezek. 33:11.

[6] The Oxford manuscript of the Rule ends the Prologue here with: "and if we perform that duty, we doubtless shall become the heirs of heaven." But the evidence of *Regula Magistri* is now to be added to the evidence from other manuscripts of the Rule (especially Sangallensis) that this shorter version of the Prologue was not original.

enter the wilderness and fight a single combat against the sins
of the flesh and the ill thoughts of the mind.

The third kind of monks, a pernicious kind, is that of the
Sarabaites. These, without any probation of rule or experience
(which test men as a furnace tests gold), live up to the practice
of the world. Like lead in a furnace, they live softly and pliably:
and by their very tonsure they are reproached of their infidelity
to God. They dwell two or three together, or one alone;
shepherdless, in no other fold but that of their own will, have
no other law but what is agreeable and pleasing; they measure
the proportion of holiness by their own choice and ideas, and
call unlawful what they dislike.

The last sort is of those called Gyrovagi or Wanderers, whose
whole life is a ramble from province to province, staying three
or four days in each place; ever in motion and never settled,
slaves to their pleasures, mere epicures, worse even than the
Sarabaites.

The wretched ways of all these are fitter to be buried in
oblivion than to be the subject of our discourse, and I pass them
over. My aim is with God's help to give rules to the most
vigorous kind, that of the Coenobites.

2. *What qualifications are required for an abbot?*

An abbot qualified to govern a monastery, ought always to
remember the name he bears, and to maintain by his good life
the title of superior: for he is esteemed to supply the place of
Christ in the monastery, being called by his name; according
to the apostle: "Ye have received the spirit of the adoption of
sons, whereby we cry Abba, Father"; [7] and therefore the abbot
ought not to teach, establish, or command anything contrary to
the law of the Lord, but so to deliver his ordinances and teaching
that they may work on the minds of his disciples like a leaven or
seasoning of divine justice.

Let the abbot always remember that at the dreadful day of
judgement he is accountable for the obedience of his disciples
as for his own teaching. He is to remember that whatever the
Father of the family finds ill in the flock, shall lie at the shepherd's door. He shall not be declared guiltless in the Lord's
judgement unless he has taken all the pains he can for a disobedient and turbulent flock. If he has used his utmost care to
cut out their sins, he may say to the Lord with the prophet: "I
have not hid thy justice within my heart: I have declared thy

7 Rom. 8:15.

truth and thy salvation: but they have despised and rejected me." [8] And eternal death shall be the punishment of them that have been disobedient to his care.

When anyone takes upon him the office of abbot, he is to instruct his disciples in two ways. That is: he is to lay before them what is good and holy, more by example than by words: to teach the law of the Lord by word of mouth to such as are of a quicker comprehension, and by example to those of harder hearts and meaner capacities. He ought to create by his conduct an aversion from the thing which he condemns in his discourse; then he will not himself prove a castaway while he preaches to others, and will avoid God's reproach: "Wherefore dost thou declare my righteousness and take my testament into thy mouth? For thou hatest discipline, yea and hast rejected my exhortation"; and, "thou hast seen a mote in thy brother's eye, and hast not seen the beam in thine own." [9]

He is not to be partial, or to love one more than another, unless upon consideration of greater virtue or obedience. He is not to prefer the freeborn monk above the slave, except some other reasonable cause intervene. In such case it is allowable that the abbot should dispose of persons as he judges expedient and fair. Otherwise everyone is to keep his proper place; because, whether slaves or freeborn, we are all one in Christ, and we have all enlisted in the same service under one common Lord who is no respecter of persons. The only reason why God puts one man above another is because the one lives a better life and is humble. Therefore the abbot's charity must extend equally to all, and his discipline be impartial, to each according to his merits.

In his teaching the abbot is ever to observe this rule of the apostle: "Reprove, beseech, correct": [10] which consists in a judicious timing: to mix gentleness with sternness: at one time to show the severity of a master, at another the tenderness of a father: to use rigour with the irregular and the turbulent, but win to better things the obedient, mild, and patient. I warn him to reprove and chastise the careless or contemptuous.

Nor is he to dissemble the faults of those that go amiss, but to do his utmost to root them out as they begin to grow; always mindful of the danger of Eli the priest of Shiloh. Those who are of nobler character and are more capable of understanding, he is to admonish twice. But mere profligates, stubborn, proud, or

[8] Ps. 40:10; Isa. 1:2.   [9] Ps. 50:16–17; Matt. 7:3.
[10] II Tim. 4:2.

disobedient, the moment they begin to do amiss, must be reclaimed by the rod. The abbot must know what is written:
"The fool is not corrected by words": and, "strike thy son with
the rod, and thou shalt deliver his soul from death." [11]

The abbot ought ever to remember what he is and what is
meant by the name he bears, and to know that more is required
of him to whose charge more is committed. Let him reflect how
difficult and perplexing a business he undertakes, at once to
govern many souls and to be subject to as many humours: to
suit himself to everyone with regard to their capacity and condition; to win some by fair means, others by reprimands, others
by dint of reason: that he may not suffer damage to his flock,
but rather rejoice at the increase and improvement of it.

Above all, he is not to dissemble or undervalue the care of
souls committed to his charge, for the sake of temporal concerns,
which are earthly, transitory, and fleeting; but ever to reflect
that the government of souls is his business, and that he is
accountable for them. And if perhaps the monastery have too
little money, he is not to be disturbed thereat; but to remember
how it is written: "Seek ye first the kingdom of God and his
righteousness, and all these things shall be added unto you";
and again, "Nothing is wanting to them that fear him." [12]

Let him further reflect that he has undertaken the care of
souls, and is to prepare his accounts: let him be sure that at the
day of judgement he will be answerable for as many souls as
he has brothers, as well as for his own. If he is ever in dread of
the severe examination which he is to undergo for the sheep committed to him, he will be as careful about himself as he is about
his charges: and so he will together cure the sins of others by
his government, and amend the faults in his own life.

3. *The manner of assembling the community in council*

Whenever any matter of moment is to be debated in the
monastery, the abbot is to assemble the whole community, and
to lay open the business before them: and after having heard
their opinions, and maturely debated with himself, he may
resolve on what he judges most profitable.

We have for this reason ordained that the whole community
shall be assembled, because God often reveals what is best to
the young. The brothers shall give their opinion with humility
and submission, and not maintain their judgement with
vehemence, but leave all to the disposal of the abbot, and jointly

[11] Prov. 18:2; 29:19; 23:13–14.   [12] Matt. 6:33; Ps. 34:10.

assent to what he decides fit. Yet, as it is the duty of the disciple to obey his master, so it is no less the part of the master to decide according to the rules of equity and prudence.

All are to observe the Rule as their guide, and no one is rashly to deviate from it. No one in the monastery is to be biased by his self-will, nor may anyone argue with his abbot with heat when at home, or at all when abroad. If he does, he shall be liable to regular chastisement. Nevertheless the abbot himself is to act in everything with a regard to the Rule and in fear of God; knowing that in all his proceedings he is to give an account before the truly impartial Judge.

If any matter of lesser consequence is to be decided for the advantage of the house, he is only to consult the elders: according as it is written: "Do thou nothing without counsel, and thou shalt not repent when thou hast done." [13]

4. *Of the instruments of good works*

First, to love the Lord God with all the heart, with all the soul, and with all the strength.

Next, to love the neighbour as oneself.

Next, not to kill.

Not to commit adultery.

Not to steal.

Not to covet.

Not to bear false witness.

To honour all men.

Not to do to another what we would not have done to ourselves.

To renounce oneself, in order to follow Christ.

To chastise the body.

Not to seek after pleasure.

To love fasting.

To relieve the poor.

To clothe the naked.

To visit the sick.

To bury the dead.

To help those that are in trouble.

To comfort the afflicted.

To eschew the ways of the world.

To prefer nothing before the love of Christ.

Not to give way to anger.

Not to lay up revenge.

[13] Ecclesiasticus 32 : 19.

Not to cover deceit in the heart.

Not to make a pretended peace.

Not to forsake charity.

Not to swear, for fear of being perjured.

To speak truth from the heart as well as the mouth.

Not to return evil for evil.

Not to do an injury: but to bear one with patience.

To love our enemies.

Not to return curse for curse, but rather a blessing for it.

To suffer persecution for righteousness' sake.

Not to be proud.

Not given to wine.

Not given to too much eating.

Not to sleepiness.

Not to laziness.

Not to complaining.

Not to detraction.

To repose all trust in God.

To attribute all the good we have in us to God, and not to ourselves.

To acknowledge all evil to be our own, and to impute it to ourselves.

To fear the day of judgement.

To dread hell.

To long in the spirit for eternal life.

To keep death every day before our eyes.

To keep a continual watch over our actions.

To be convinced that God sees us wherever we are.

To dash evil thoughts, as soon as they arise in the heart, against the Rock Christ; and to discover them to our spiritual father.

To preserve the tongue from evil and wicked talk.

Not to love much talk.

Not to love vain talk, or such as occasions laughter.

Not to love much or raucous laughter.

To listen willingly to the reading of holy books.

To use frequent prayer.

To confess to God every day in prayer, with tears and sighs, our past offences.

To amend those sins for the future.

Not to accomplish the desires of the flesh.

To hate our own will.

In all things to obey the abbot's command, although (which

God forbid) he act contrary himself: being mindful of the precept of the Lord which bids us: "Do what they say, not what they do." [14]

Not to want to be called a saint before we are, but first to be so, that it may be said of us with greater truth.

Every day to live up to the commandments of God.

To love chastity.

To hate nobody.

Not to be addicted to jealousy.

Not to be envious.

Not to love contention.

To avoid ambition.

To venerate the elders.

To love the younger.

To pray for our enemies, for the love of Christ.

To be reconciled to those who have quarrelled with us, before the sun go down.

And never to despair of God's mercy.

These are the instruments of spiritual progress. If day and night we employ them, and at the day of judgement commend them into the hands of God, we shall be crowned with the reward he has promised "which neither eye hath seen nor ear hath heard, nor hath it entered into the heart of man what things God hath prepared for them that love him." [15]

The best place to practise these things is the monastery with its seclusion—provided that we remain steadily in the community and do not leave it.

5. *Of obedience*

The first degree of humility is a prompt and ready obedience. This is fitting for them who love Christ above all else. By reason of the holy duty they have undertaken, or for fear of hell, or for eternal glory, they make no more delay to comply, the very instant anything is appointed them, than if God himself had given the command. Of these the Lord said: "At the very sound of my voice he hath obeyed me." And again he declared to them that teach: "He that heareth you, heareth me." [16]

They who are of this temper abandon all, even to their very will; instantly clear their hands and leave unfinished what they had begun; so that the command is carried out in the moment it is uttered. Master and disciple are lent wings by the fear of

[14] Matt. 23:3.   [15] I Cor. 2:9.   [16] Ps. 18:44; Luke 10:16.

God and the longing for eternal life, and so the command is obeyed in a flash.

It is for the sake of obedience that they enter into the narrow way of which the Lord said: "Narrow is the way that leadeth unto life." [17] The "narrowness" of the way is opposite to the broad way suggested by self-will and desire and pleasure: and they follow it by delighting to dwell in a community, to be subject to their abbot, and to follow the judgement of another. Such men live up to the practice of our Lord, who tells us: "I came not to do mine own will, but the will of him that sent me." [18]

This obedience will be pleasing to God and man, when it is performed with no fear, no delay, no coldness, no complaint, no reply. The obedience we pay to superiors is paid to God: for he tells us: "He that heareth you, heareth me." And it is to be done with willing heart, "because God loveth a cheerful giver." [19] When the disciple obeys unwillingly, with a grudge in heart or mouth, though he does the thing, yet he is so far from being pleasing to God, who sees reluctance in the heart, that he acquires no merit, but only incurs the penalty of those that murmur, till he has made a due atonement.

6. *Of silence*

Let us do as the prophet says: "I said, I will take heed unto my ways, that I offend not with my tongue. I have set a guard upon my mouth. I held my tongue, and was humbled, and kept silence from good words." [20] Here the prophet shows that if, for the sake of silence, we ought sometimes not to speak what is good; much more are we obliged to avoid all evil talk, for fear of the punishment due to sin. Therefore, frequent leave to talk is not to be granted to those who are advanced in perfection, although the subject be good and holy and edifying. Because it is written: "In much talk you shall not avoid sin"; and elsewhere, "Life and death are in the power of the tongue." [21] It belongs to the master to speak and teach, it is the duty of the disciple to hear and obey.

And therefore, if anything is to be asked from the superior, it must be with humility and submission. As for scurrility, idle jests or silly talk, I order that they be never heard in the monastery.

[17] Matt. 7:14.   [18] John 6:38.   [19] II Cor. 9:7.
[20] Ps. 39:1–2.   [21] Prov. 10:19 and 18:21.

7. *Of humility*

Brethren, the Scripture asserts that "everyone that exalteth himself shall be humbled, and he that humbleth himself shall be exalted." It shows us thereby that all exaltation is in some measure the pride which the prophet tells us he took care to shun: "O Lord, my heart is not exalted, nor mine eyes lifted up: I have not aspired to great things, nor wonders above myself." And his reason for it is: because (says he): "If I had not thought humbly of myself but had exalted my soul, thou wouldst have driven away my soul like an infant weaned from the breast of its mother." [22]

Therefore, brethren, if we want to attain true humility, and come quickly to the top of that heavenly ascent to which we can only mount by lowliness in this present life, we must ascend by good works, and erect the mystical ladder of Jacob, where angels ascending and descending appeared to him. That ascent and descent means that we go downward when we exalt ourselves, and rise when we are humbled. The ladder represents our life in this world, which our Lord erects to heaven when our heart is humbled. And the sides of the ladder represent our soul and body, sides between which God has placed several rungs of humility and discipline, whereby we are to ascend if we would answer his call.

The first degree, then, of humility is, to have the fear of God ever before our eyes: never to forget what is his due, and always to remember his commands: to revolve in the mind how hell burns those who have contemned God, and how God has prepared eternal life for them that fear him: to preserve ourselves from the sins and vices of thought, of the tongue, the eyes, hands, feet, self-will and fleshly desires. Man ought to think that God always looks down from heaven upon him, and that all he does lies open to his sight, is daily told him by the angels. The prophet shows this truth, when he describes God as present in our thoughts, "searching the heart and reins"; and, "Our Lord knows the thoughts of men"; and again, "Thou hast understood my thoughts a great way off": and, "The thought of man shall confess to thee." That he may ever watch the perverseness of his thoughts, let the right-minded brother continually repeat in the language of his heart: "Then I shall be without blemish before him, if I keep myself from mine iniquity." [23]

[22] Luke 14:11; Ps. 131:1–2.
[23] Ps. 7:9; 94:11 (*Regula Magistri* and a few MSS. add the second half of the versicle); 139:1; 76:10; 18:23.

As for our own will, we are forbidden to pursue it by these words of the Scripture: "Turn away from thine own will": and we are required to ask of God in prayer, that his will may be done in us. We have reason to be convinced that we ought not to be guided by our own will, when we take account of what the Scripture tells us: "There are ways which to men appear to be right, whose endings nevertheless plunge us into the very depth of hell." And again, when we reflect fearfully upon the character given to the negligent: "They are corrupt and become abominable in their own pleasures."

As regards our sensual desires, we must remember that God is ever present; as the prophet says to the Lord: "All my desire lies open before thee."[24] So unlawful desires are to be carefully avoided, because death lurks behind the door at the very entrance to pleasure: whence the Scripture forbids us to "pursue our lusts." [25]

If then the eyes of the Lord observe both the good and the wicked, and God looks down from heaven upon the sons of men, to see if there be any that understand or seek after God; and again, if night and day our guardian angels give an account of what we do to the Lord; we must, every moment, be on our guard, lest God, at any time, should surprise us, as the Psalmist terms it, "leaning towards evil and rendered unprofitable"; and sparing us in this life (because he is good and waits for our becoming better) should reproach us in the next: "These things didst thou do, and I kept silence." [26]

The second degree of humility is, if anyone, not wedded to his own will, finds no pleasure in the compassing of his desires; but fulfils with his practice the word of our Lord: "I came not to do mine own will, but the will of him that sent me." The Scripture also says: "Pleasure hath its penalty, but need winneth a crown." [27]

The third degree of humility is, when anyone submits himself with obedience to his superior for the sake of the love of God, after the example of the Lord, of whom the apostle says: "He was made obedient even unto death."

The fourth degree of humility is, when anyone, in the practice of obedience, meets with hardships, contradictions, or affronts,

24 Ecclesiasticus 18:30; Prov. 16:25; Ps. 14:1; 38:9.
25 Ecclesiasticus 18:30.
26 Prov. 15:3; Ps. 14:3; 53:2-3; 50:21.
27 John 6:38. The second text is not from the Bible but from (e.g.) *Acta Martyrum*.

and yet bears them all with a quiet conscience and with patience, and continues to persevere. The Scripture says: "He who perseveres to the end, the same shall be saved," and again: "Let your heart be strengthened, and wait for our Lord." And to show that the faithful servant ought to suffer every trial for God, the Scripture speaks in the person of those that suffer: "For thy sake we are killed all the day long: we are accounted as sheep for the slaughter." And afterwards, in full assurance of their reward, they say with happiness, "But in all these things we are conquerors through him that loved us." In another place the Scripture tells us: "Thou, O God, hast proved us: thou hast tried us with fire, as silver is tried. Thou hast led us into the snare, and loaded us with afflictions." And to show that we ought to live under a superior, it goes on, "Thou hast set men over our heads." [28]

So these sufferers live up to the command of God, bearing injuries and adversity with patience. But more: Struck on one cheek they offer the other. They give away their coat to him that takes away their cloak. Forced to walk one mile, they go two. They bear with false brethren, like Paul the apostle. They bless them that curse them.

The fifth degree of humility is, humbly to confess to the abbot every unlawful thought as it arises in the heart, and the hidden sins we have committed. The Scripture advises this, saying: "Reveal your way to God and hope in him": and again: "Confess to God because he is good: for his mercy endureth for ever." [29] And in the prophet: "I have made known my sin to thee, and have not covered my iniquities. I have said, I will declare to God my own iniquities against myself: and thou hast forgiven the wickedness of my heart." [30]

The sixth degree of humility is, if a monk be content with anything though never so vile and contemptible; and to think himself inadequate, and unworthy to succeed in whatever he is commanded to do; saying with the prophet: "I was brought to nothing and knew nothing. I am become like a brute beast before thee, yet I am always with thee." [31]

The seventh degree of humility is, when one does not merely call oneself the least and most abject of all mankind, but believes it, with sincerity of heart: humbling oneself and saying with the prophet: "I am a worm and no man: a scorn of men, and the outcast of the people." "I have been exalted, humbled, and

[28] Matt. 10:22; Ps. 27:14; Rom. 8:36-7; Ps. 66:10-12.
[29] Ps. 37:5; 106:1.   [30] Ps. 32:5.   [31] Ps. 73:21-2.

confounded." And again: "It is good for me that thou hast humbled me, that I may learn to keep thy commandments." [32]

The eighth degree of humility is, when a monk does nothing but what is countenanced by the constitutions of the monastery, or the example of the elders.

The ninth degree of humility is, when a monk controls his tongue and keeps silence till a question be asked. For the Scripture teaches that "in much talk you will not avoid sinning"; and "the talkative man shall live out his life haphazardly." [33]

The tenth degree of humility is, not easily to lay hold on occasions of laughing. For it is written: "He who laughs loud is a fool." [34]

The eleventh degree of humility is, when a monk discourses with moderation and composure, mixing humility with gravity; speaking few words, but home, and to the purpose; not raising the voice. "The wise man is known because he speaks little." [35]

The twelfth degree of humility is, when the monk's inward humility appears outwardly in his comportment. And wherever he be, in the divine office, in the oratory, in the monastery, in the garden, on a journey, in the fields—wherever he is sitting, walking or standing, he is to look down with bowed head conscious of his guilt, imagining himself ready to be called to give account at the dread judgement: repeating in his heart what the publican in the Gospel said with eyes downcast: "Lord, I am not worthy, sinner that I am, to lift up my eyes to heaven"; and with the prophet "I am bowed down and humbled on every side." [36]

After he has climbed all these degrees of humility, the monk will quickly arrive at the top, the charity that is perfect and casts out all fear. And then, the virtues which first he practised with anxiety, shall begin to be easy for him, almost natural, being grown habitual. He will no more be afraid of hell, but will advance by the love of Christ, by good habits, and by taking pleasure in goodness. Our Lord, by the Holy Spirit, will deign to show this in the servant who has been cleansed from sin.

8. *Of the divine office during the night*

In the winter time, that is from the first day of November until Easter, having regard to different circumstances, they shall

[32] Ps. 22:6; 88:15; 119:71.   [33] Prov. 10:19; Ps. 140:11.
[34] Ecclesiasticus 21:20.
[35] From the *Sentences of Sixtus*, a book of proverbs and moral sayings.
[36] Luke 18:13; Ps. 119:107.

rise at 2 o'clock in the morning, that they may have time to rest till after midnight, and the time of digestion be past. What time remains after the office is done, they may use in studying the psalms and lessons if they do not yet know them thoroughly.

From Easter to the first of November, they shall so arrange the night office as to leave a very short interval after it (so that the brothers may go out for the needs of nature) and then begin Lauds at break of day.

9. *How many psalms are to be said at the night office?*

In the winter, they shall first say three times the versicle: "O Lord, open thou my lips, and my mouth shall show forth thy praise": then recite Psalm 3 and the *Gloria*. Afterwards Psalm 94 is to be sung with an antiphon, or at least sung: then the hymn of St Ambrose: then six psalms with antiphons. Then, after the versicle, the abbot is to give the blessing. And when all are in their seats the brothers shall read by turns three lessons out of the book upon the lectern: after each they shall chant three responsories. Two of the responsories shall be said without the *Gloria*. After the third lesson, the cantor shall say the *Gloria*. As soon as he begins to say it, all shall rise from their seats out of honour and reverence to the Holy Trinity. At the night office they shall read the inspired books of the Old or New Testaments, and also the commentaries written upon them by those fathers who are celebrated, Catholic and orthodox. After these three lessons with their responsories, six other psalms are to be sung with *Alleluia*: then a lesson out of the apostle, to be said by heart: afterwards the versicle, and the litany, that is, *Kyrie Eleison*. And so shall end the night office.

10. *The manner of the night office during summer*

From Easter to the first of November the same distribution of psalms is to be observed as aforesaid: except that the lessons out of the book shall be omitted by reason of the shortness of the nights in summer, and one lesson of the Old Testament shall be said by heart in place of the other three, and a short responsory follow. The rest must remain as before, so that there be never fewer than twelve psalms said in the night office, besides the third and the ninety-fourth psalms.

11. *The manner of the night office on Sundays*

On Sundays they shall rise earlier to the night office, and shall observe this order. After six psalms as above, and the versicle, everyone shall sit, each in his place, and they shall read from the book (in the manner we have already mentioned) four lessons with their responsories, so that the *Gloria* be only sung by the cantor at the fourth responsory. And as soon as the *Gloria* begins, everyone shall rise from his seat out of reverence. After these four lessons, six other psalms shall follow in order, with their antiphons and versicle like the earlier psalms. Then they shall read four more lessons with their responsories, in the same way as before. Next they shall say three canticles from the prophets, as the abbot shall appoint: these shall be sung with *Alleluia*. Then, when the versicle has been said and the abbot has given the blessing, they shall read four lessons more of the New Testament, according to the same order. After the fourth responsory the abbot shall begin the hymn *Te Deum laudamus*. After that the abbot shall read the lesson from the Gospel, everyone standing in reverence, and at the end of it they shall all answer *Amen*. Then the abbot shall add the hymn *Te decet laus*: and after the blessing they shall begin Lauds.

This order for the night office on Sundays shall be observed throughout the year, summer and winter: unless (though God forbid) they should chance to rise late, and so be forced to omit something of the lessons or responsories—this is carefully to be avoided. But if it should happen notwithstanding, he whose negligence caused it shall make due satisfaction to God in the oratory.

12. *The manner of saying the office of Lauds*

At Lauds on Sundays they shall recite, first, Psalm 66 without an antiphon; next Psalm 50 with *Alleluia*. Then Psalms 117 and 62; then the Canticle *Benedicite*: and the *Laudate* Psalms: then the lesson from the Apocalypse, to be said by heart: the responsory, the hymn of St Ambrose, the versicle, the canticle from the Gospel, the *Kyrie Eleison*, and so end.

13. On *ferias* the office of Lauds shall be in the manner following. Psalm 66 shall be said, without an antiphon as on Sundays, and leisurely, that all may be present at Psalm 50, which must be said with an antiphon. Then they shall say two other psalms in this order—On Mondays, Psalms 5 and 35: Tuesdays, Psalms 42 and 56: Wednesdays, Psalms 63 and 64: Thursdays, Psalms 87 and 89: on Fridays, Psalms 75 and 91: on Saturdays, Psalm 142, and the Canticle of Deuteronomy divided into two *Glorias*. On other days they shall say one canticle out of the prophets, one on each day, according to the custom of the church at Rome.

After this shall follow the *Laudate* Psalms: a lesson of the apostle, to be said by heart: responsory: hymn of St Ambrose: canticle of the Gospel: *Kyrie Eleison*, and so end. At the hours of Lauds and Vespers they shall always end with the Our Father, to be said aloud by the president so that all may hear. This is because of the animosities and scandals which are wont to arise in monasteries. By the promise they make to God when they say in the prayer: "Forgive us as we forgive," the religious may abolish this vice amongst themselves. At the other hours only the last clause of the prayer shall be said aloud, and all shall answer: "but deliver us from evil."

14. *The order of the night office on the festivals of saints*

On the festivals of saints, or other solemnities, they shall observe the same order as on Sundays: except that they shall say the psalms, antiphons, and lessons proper for the day. But the number shall be kept as before.

15. *At what times Alleluia is to be said*

From the holy feast of Easter till Whitsuntide, Alleluia is to be said with both the psalms and the responsories; but from Whitsuntide to the beginning of Lent, only with the second six psalms at the night office. Every Sunday, except in Lent, the Alleluia shall be said with the Canticles and the psalms of Lauds, Prime, Terce, Sext, and None: and Vespers with an antiphon. The responsories are never to be said with Alleluia except from Easter to Whitsuntide.

16. *How the divine office is to be performed through the day*

"Seven times a day have I praised thee," said the prophet. We shall perform this consecrated number of seven if we offer prayer (the duty of our profession) at the hours of Lauds, Prime, Terce, Sext, None, Vespers, and Compline. It was of these day hours that he said: "Seven times a day have I praised thee." Elsewhere the same prophet makes mention of the night office, "at midnight I rose to confess to thee." At these times, therefore, let us render praise to our creator "for the judgements of his justice" [37]—that is, Lauds, Prime, Terce, Sext, None, Vespers, Compline: and let us rise at night to confess to him.

17. *How many psalms are to be said at these hours?*

The Psalms of the night office and of Lauds are appointed: we now proceed to the other hours. At Prime they shall say

[37] Ps. 119:164 and 62.

three psalms with a *Gloria* after each. The hymn of this hour shall be said after the versicle, "O God make speed to save me," before the psalms begin. Then, at the end of the three psalms, they shall say one lesson, versicle, *Kyrie eleison*, and so end.

The same order shall be observed at Terce, Sext, and None: beginning with the versicle, "O God make speed to save me," the respective hymn of the hour, three psalms, lesson, versicle, *Kyrie Eleison* and so end. If the community be numerous, they shall be sung with antiphons. Otherwise, not.

At Vespers they shall say four psalms with their antiphons. After these psalms, a lesson, with its responsory: the hymn of St Ambrose: a versicle: the Canticle of the Gospel, *Kyrie Eleison*, Our Father, and so end.

At Compline they shall recite three psalms only, without antiphon and plainly. Afterwards the proper hymn: lesson: versicle: *Kyrie Eleison*, and the blessing to end.

18. *After what order the psalms are to be said*

First, shall be said the versicle, "O God, make speed to save me: O Lord, make haste to help me," and *Gloria*: afterwards a hymn proper to each hour.

For Sunday Prime they shall say four divisions of Psalm 118. At the three other hours, Terce, Sext, and None, three other divisions of the same Psalm 118.

For Prime on Mondays, they shall say three psalms (1, 2 and 6): and so every day until Sunday, they shall continue to say at Prime three psalms, choosing them in order till Psalm 19 is reached, but always dividing Psalm 9 and Psalm 17 into two. By this means they shall always begin the night office of Sunday with Psalm 20.

For Terce, Sext, and None on Mondays, they shall employ the nine remaining divisions of Psalm 118, three at each hour. The whole of Psalm 118 being thus said in the two days Sunday and Monday; on Tuesday, for Terce, Sext, and None, they shall say three psalms at each hour, chosen from Psalm 119 to Psalm 127—which makes nine psalms. These are to be repeated every day till Sunday at the same hours. The order for the hymns, lessons, and versicles, shall not vary on any day.

So shall they always begin Psalm 118 on Sunday.

Vespers shall be sung every day with four psalms, taken from the psalms numbered 109 to 147, except those which are taken up for the other hours, namely Psalms 117 to 127, 133 and 142: apart from these exceptions all these psalms are to be said at vespers. And because there are three less than there should be, they shall divide the longer psalms into two, namely Psalms 138, 143 and 144. But because Psalm 116 is very short, it shall be joined with Psalm 115. Apart from psalms, the rest of the Vesper office—lessons, responsories, hymns, versicles, and canticles, shall be as I have said.

At Compline they shall always repeat the same psalms: 4, 90, 133.

These are the arrangements for the psalmody at the day offices. The remaining psalms are to be distributed equally among the seven night offices, dividing the longer psalms and always assigning twelve for each night.

Notwithstanding, we hereby declare that if anyone does not approve of the present distribution of psalms, he may appoint otherwise, if he thinks better: provided he takes care that the whole psalter, of a hundred and fifty psalms, be sung every week, and that they begin it again at the night office each Sunday. It is a mean devotion if monks should in a week sing less than the whole Psalter with the usual canticles. We read that our holy fathers bravely recited the Psalter in a single day; God grant that we, their degenerate sons, may do the like in seven.

19. *How we ought to sing*

We believe God is everywhere, and his eye beholds the good and wicked wherever they are: so we ought to be particularly assured of his special presence when we assist at the divine office. Therefore we must always remember the advice of the prophet, "To serve God in fear": "to sing wisely": and that "the angels are witnesses of what we sing." [38] Let us then reflect what behaviour is proper for appearing in the presence of God and the angels, and so sing our psalms that the mind may echo in harmony with the voice.

20. *What reverence is needed for prayer?*

If we want to ask a favour of any person of power, we presume not to approach but with humility and respect. How much more ought we to address ourselves to the Lord and God of all things with a humble and entire devotion? We are not to imagine that our prayers shall be heard because we use many words, but because the heart is pure and the spirit penitent. Therefore prayer must be short and pure, unless it be prolonged

38 Prov. 15:3; Ps. 2:11; 47:7; 138:1.

by a feeling of divine inspiration. Prayer in common ought always to be short, and when the sign is given by the superior, all should rise together.

21. *Of the deans of the monastery*

If the community be numerous, they shall make choice of religious persons of good reputation and exemplary lives, and appoint them deans. They shall govern their respective charges, according to the laws of God and the commands of their abbot. They are to be so qualified that the abbot may safely entrust part of his duty to their hands.

They shall not be elected according to their seniority, but with regard to their conduct and their wisdom in teaching. And if perhaps one of them be found blamable for pride, and does not make amends even after three rebukes, he shall be removed from office: and another, worthy, shall be substituted in his place.

As regards the prior, we ordain the same.

22. *How the monks are to sleep*

Each monk shall sleep in a separate bed. In arranging the dormitory the abbot shall take account of seniority and spiritual progress. If possible, everyone shall sleep in the same room. But if their numbers do not permit; then they shall sleep by tens or twenties, with their seniors among them to take care of them. A lamp shall burn in the room throughout the night.

They shall sleep in their habits, and girt with their girdles or cords: not with knives at their side, or they might hurt themselves in their sleep. Thus they will be ready to rise the instant the bell rings and hurry to be first at the divine office, yet with all gravity and composure. The younger brothers shall not have their beds near each other, but split up among the seniors. As they rise for the office, they shall softly exhort each other, to take away the excuses of those who are sleepy.

23. *Of excommunication imposed for faults*

If any of the community prove rebellious, disobedient, proud, or murmuring, or contemptuously disobey the holy Rule or the commands of his elders, he shall be admonished, according to the precept of our Lord, once and then twice by the seniors in private. If notwithstanding he does not mend his ways, he shall be publicly rebuked. If then he remains incorrigible, and understands how great the penalty is, he shall be excommunicated. If he be obstinate, he shall be liable to corporal punishment.

24. *The measure of excommunication*

The excommunication or correction ought to be in proportion to the fault committed, and the judgement of it shall depend on the abbot's discretion. If anyone be found guilty of lesser faults, he shall be deprived of the common task: in the following way. Persons thus deprived shall not conduct psalm or antiphon in the oratory, or read any lesson until satisfaction is made. They shall eat their meal alone, after the community has done. For example, if the community dines at noon, the delinquent shall eat at 3 o'clock: if they at three, he shall not eat till the evening, and this until he has deserved his pardon by a due atonement.

25. *Of greater faults*

The brother who is convicted of greater faults shall be suspended both from the table and from the oratory. None of the community shall keep company or converse with him. He shall pursue alone the work enjoined to him, in tears of penance, meditating the terrible saying of the apostle "Such a person is made over to Satan, for the destruction of the body, to the end the soul may be saved at the day of the Lord." [39] He shall eat alone, when and what the abbot thinks fit. He shall not receive the blessing from anyone that passes by; nor shall the meat be blessed that is given to him.

26. *Of them who company without leave with excommunicated persons*

If any brother, without the abbot's order, presume to converse at all with an excommunicated person, or send a message to him, he shall incur the same punishment.

27. *What care the abbot is to take of those that lie under excommunication*

Let the abbot use his utmost care on behalf of those that do amiss: for "they that be whole need not a physician, but they that are sick." And therefore he ought to employ his whole address, like an experienced physician, and dexterously convey experienced elders to them, who know how to encourage the wavering brother and win him insensibly to humble himself and make amends; and to give him comfort, that he may not "be overpowered with excess of grief." As the apostle says: "Let charity be redoubled towards him," [40] and the prayers of all be offered for him.

[39] I Cor. 5:5.   [40] Matt. 9:12; II Cor. 2:7–8.

For the abbot is to be solicitous about delinquents; he is to take all pains and use all his wisdom to prevent any of his flock from perishing. He must know that he has taken his office not to tyrannize over souls that are well, but to take care of souls that are sick. Let him stand in awe of the reproach which God menaces by the mouth of the prophet: "You chose what seemed thriving and likely: and you cast away what was weak and infirm." [41] And he should imitate the example of the good shepherd who left ninety and nine of his flock in the mountains, and went to seek the one which was gone astray, and took so much compassion on its weakness that he deigned to lay it on his sacred shoulders and bring it back to the flock.

28. *Of those who will not amend after frequent correction*

If a brother, after frequent corrections for any fault, or even after excommunication, does not amend his ways, he shall be punished with more severity, that is, with the rod. And if still he remains incorrigible, or if (God forbid) he grow proud and takes upon him to justify his proceedings, then the abbot must do what the prudent physician does.

If he has endeavoured to soothe his distemper with the healing balm of good counsel, and the remedy of holy Scripture, and if he has applied the more violent medicines of excommunication and the rod; and still he sees that all his efforts are of no avail; let him try his greatest means, prayer by himself and his community, that God, who can do all things, may vouchsafe to work the cure.

But if this also has no effect, then let the abbot use the surgeon's knife, and sever the infected member from the community. As the apostle says: "Drive away the evil man from among you": and again: "If the unfaithful man goes away, let him go" [42]—and then one diseased sheep will not infect the flock.

29. *Whether they who leave the monastery are to be received again?*

The brother who by his own fault goes out of the monastery, and desires to return, shall first give caution for his sincere amendment of the fault for which he left the place, and then be received into the lowest rank, to make trial of his humility. And if he does the same again, he shall be admitted to the third

[41] Ezek. 34:3–4.   [42] I Cor. 5:13 and 7:15.

time; but after that, he must know that all further entrance shall be refused.[43]

30. *What correction is proper for children?*

Government ought to be suited to everyone's age and capacity: and therefore the faults of children or younger people, who do not understand how great is the penalty of excommunication, are to be corrected with severe fasts or whipping.

31. *What qualities are required in the cellarer of the monastery?*

The cellarer of the monastery shall be chosen out of the community, discreet, mature in his behaviour, and sober: no glutton; not proud, factious, truculent, slow, or prodigal; but one who fears God, and who can act like a father to the whole community. He is to take care of everything: to do nothing but what the abbot commands: to observe orders: and not to irritate the brethren. If a brother chance to demand anything unreasonable of him, he is not to be contemptuous in his refusal, but to refuse reasonably and humbly. He is to be careful of his own soul, and remember that St Paul says: "He that has done his duty well, gains for himself a good degree." [44] He is to show a particular concern for the sick, children, strangers and the poor, as being accountable for them at the day of judgement.

He is to regard the movables and estate of the monastery as sacred like the vessels on the altar: to undervalue nothing: to observe a middle way between meanness and prodigality: not to waste the property of the monastery, but to act with moderation, and with regard to the abbot's command.

In particular he is to be humble: so that when he has not the wherewithal to grant what is asked, at least he may afford good words; remembering that the Scripture said: "A good word is above the greatest gift." [45]

He shall have under his care whatever the abbot appoints, and not meddle with anything he forbids. He shall give the

---

[43] There is a difficulty of interpretation here, complicated by a textual crux among the manuscripts as the scribes and commentators struggled to make clear what was meant, or what they thought was meant. Was the monk who was driven out for a fault allowed three chances of returning, or was it simply three chances for the monk who left the monastery voluntarily? Many modern commentators think the second. Many early scribes thought that the first is what was meant.

[44] I Tim. 3:13.   [45] Ecclesiasticus 18:17.

brothers their usual allowance without any grudging or reluctance; for fear of giving offence, and of what the Word of God threatens to those who "scandalize any of the little ones." [46]

If the community be numerous, he may be allowed assistants, to render the duty of his employment easy and less perplexing. Whatever is to be asked or given, shall be done at appointed times, so that no one in the household of God shall be troubled or irritated.

32. *Of the tools and property of the monastery*

The abbot shall choose some of the brothers, on whose life and conduct he can rely, and make them responsible for the goods of the monastery—tools, clothing and the rest, any of the property that he thinks right.

He shall keep an inventory of these things himself: so that when the brothers succeed one another in these places, he may know what he is giving and what he receives back. And if anyone is found to have impaired the goods of the monastery by being slovenly or neglectful, he shall be corrected: and if he does not amend, he shall incur punishment in accordance with the rule.

33. *Whether monks ought to have any property?*

The vice of possessing property is particularly to be banished from the monastery. No one may presume to give or receive anything without the abbot's leave, or to possess anything whatever, not even book or tablets or pen. The monks' bodies and their wills are not at their own disposal. They must look to all their needs to be supplied by the common father of the monastery. No one may have anything which the abbot does not give or permit. "Everything shall be in common" as the Scripture says: "nor shall they presume to call anything their own." [47] And if anyone be found inclined to this especial vice, he shall be told of it once and twice: and if he do not make amends he shall be liable to punishment.

34. *Whether everyone ought to have the same?*

The Scripture tells us: "It was divided to every man severally, as he had need." We distinguish partiality (which may God forbid) from a consideration of infirmities. He that needs less, should give God thanks and not be vexed. He that needs more, has an occasion to humble himself for his own infirmity and no

46 Matt. 18:6.   47 Acts 4:32 and 35.

reason to grow proud for being an object of pity. And by this means every member may live in peace.

Above all there must be no grumbling, for any reason, by word or sign. The grumbler is to be severely punished.

35. *Of the weekly officers in the kitchen*

The brothers are to serve by turns; and no one is exempt from duty in the kitchen, unless he be hindered by ill-health or employed on some business for the good of the monastery. From this service a monk learns charity and gains a greater degree of merit. Notwithstanding they shall provide assistance for the weak, to take away all occasion for grievance; and in general, everyone shall have help, with regard to the circumstances of the community and the situation of the place.

If the community be numerous, the cellarer shall be exempt from the kitchen, as well as those (aforesaid) who are more profitably employed. The others shall serve each other in charity.

He who has finished his week, on Saturday, shall clean everything, and wash the towels which the brothers have used to dry their hands and feet: and, with his incoming successor of the next week, he shall wash the feet of the whole community. He shall restore to the cellarer the vessels which belong to his office, and restore them clean and undamaged: and the cellarer shall deliver them to the next man, so that he may keep a weekly check upon them.

An hour before meals the weekly officer may be allowed to take a drink and a piece of bread above the usual allowance, and so be able to serve his brothers at meals without complaint or too great hardship. But on great festivals he shall abstain until the end of the office.

On Sundays after Lauds, the weekly officers—ending and beginning—shall kneel down before the whole community in the oratory and ask their prayers. The officer who has ended his week shall say this verse: "Blessed art thou, O Lord, who hast helped me and comforted me"; [48] and after this has been said three times, he shall receive a blessing. Then the officer who is beginning his week shall say the verse: "O God, make speed to save me, O Lord, make haste to help me": and after everyone has repeated this three times, he shall receive his blessing and enter upon his duties.

[48] Ps. 86:17.

36. *Of the sick brothers*

The care of the sick is to be put before everything else. They are to be tended as Christ himself, who tells us: "I was sick and you visited me," and "Inasmuch as you have done it unto one of the least of these, you have done it unto me." [49]

The sick on their side are to reflect that the attention paid to them is for the honour of God, and they are not to be a grievance to those that tend them, by demanding too much. Yet even, if they ask too much, they are to be borne with, for thereby they are a means to a greater reward.

The abbot is to take great care that they do not suffer by the negligence of those who look after them. An infirmary, apart, is to be appointed for their care, and one to look after it who fears God and is diligent and solicitous.

The use of baths may be allowed to the sick as often as may be fitting; but for those who are well, and, particularly, young people, only seldom.

The sick who are very weakly are to be allowed to eat meat to help their recovery. But as soon as their health is re-established, they are to abstain like the rest.

The abbot is to take great care that the sick be not neglected by the cellarer or those that look after them. The fault of his disciples is, in some measure, his own fault.

37. *Of old men and children*

Although nature of its own accord is inclined to take pity on old men and children, yet it is better they should be provided for by the authority of the Rule. Their weakness is always to be considered, and the rigour of the rule about eating is not to be enforced. They shall be shown tenderness, and given leave to eat before the proper times.

38. *Of the weekly reader*

There shall be reading during meals. The reader shall not be anyone, whoever happens to pick up the book: one person shall read for a week, beginning on Sunday. As he enters on his week, after the office and the Communion, he shall ask everyone for their prayers that God may preserve him from the spirit of vanity. In the oratory he shall begin the verse: "O Lord, open thou my lips, and my mouth shall show forth thy praise" and everyone shall repeat it three times. Then he shall receive the blessing, and so enter upon his office.

[49] Matt. 25:36–40.

Complete silence shall be kept during meals. There shall be no whispering: no one is to say anything except the reader. The brothers are to supply each other with what they need in the way of food and drink, so that no one needs to ask for anything. If anything is lacking, they are to ask for it by a sign, not by speaking.

No one is to ask questions about what is read or about any other subject, so that no one will have to answer. The one exception is if the superior wishes to say a few words that are edifying.

The weekly reader may take a little food before he begins to read, so that he may share in the meal with sanctification, and so that he does not find difficulty in fasting a long time. He can eat after the community meal, with the brothers who during that week are serving in the kitchen.

Not all the brothers in turn are to read or to sing; only those whose reading or singing edifies the listener.

39. *Of the quantity of food*

I am of the opinion that for normal nourishment, whether they are eating at noon or 3 o'clock, two dishes will be sufficient at each meal. This is to provide for the weakness of different people, so that the brother who cannot eat one dish may perhaps be able to eat the other. All the brethren are to be content with these two hot dishes: and if fruit or young vegetables can conveniently be had, they may be allowed a third.

A full pound of bread shall suffice for a whole day, whether they dine and sup, or have only one meal. If they sup as well as dine, the cellarer shall keep a third part of the bread for the evening.

Notwithstanding, it shall be in the abbot's power to increase the allowance, if he thinks fit, for those with heavier work. Yet he must take care to avoid excess or sudden temptation to gluttony. For nothing is so contrary to the life of a Christian as overeating: as our Lord said: "Take heed lest at any time your hearts be charged with surfeiting." [50]

The same quantity is not to be given to the younger children: they should be given less than the others, and always be frugal.

Except the very weak, no one shall eat meat at any time.

40. *Of the quantity of drink*

"Every man hath his proper gift from God, the one after this manner, and another after that." [51] So it is a nice point to

[50] Luke 21:34.   [51] I Cor. 7:7.

prescribe a certain measure of food and drink for others. Notwithstanding, having regard to the weakness of the sick, I am of opinion that a hemina [52] of wine every day will suffice. Yet be it known to those whom God has granted the gift of abstinence, that they shall have an especial reward.

If the necessity of the place, or the hard work, or the heat of the summer, makes them need more, it shall be in the power of the superior to add to the allowance: yet always with caution, that they may not fall to the temptations of satiety and drunkenness. Although we read [53] that wine is never for monks, it is hard to persuade modern monks of this. At least we must all agree that we are not to drink to satiety, but with moderation. "For wine makes even wise men to fall into apostasy." [54]

Where the poverty of the place prevents this measure being available, but much less, or even none at all; the monks there are to bless God, and not complain.

I give this especial instruction, that no one shall complain.

41. *What hours are most convenient for meals?*

From Easter to Whitsuntide the community shall dine at noon and sup in the evening. But from Whitsuntide to the end of the summer, if they are not working in the fields or troubled by an excessively hot summer, they shall fast on Wednesdays and Fridays until three in the afternoon. On other days they shall dine at noon. When working in the fields or oppressed by heat, they shall dine at noon every day, if the abbot thinks fit. But he must so moderate and dispose everything that souls may be saved and that the brothers may do their work without having good reason to complain.

From September 14th until the beginning of Lent, the community shall always eat at three in the afternoon. In Lent, and until Easter, they are to eat in the evening, but at such a time that they do not need lamps, and the meal may be finished in daylight. At all times, they must so manage the hour of the meal, whether they dine or sup, that it is in daylight.

42. *Of silence after Compline*

Monks at all times ought to study silence, but most of all during the night. Throughout the year, whether they are having supper or fasting, a similar rule shall apply. In the time of year

---

52 Quantity unknown. Probably between a pint and half a pint.
53 In *Vitae Patrum* V. 4.31: see page 53 above.
54 Ecclesiasticus 19:2.

when they are having suppers, as soon as they rise from the table, they shall assemble in one place, and one of them shall read the *Conferences* or *The Lives of the Fathers*; or at least some book which will edify the listeners. They are not to read the first seven books of the Bible or the book of Kings, because that part of Scripture is not profitable to weak understandings at such a time: these books are to be read at other times.

If it is a time of year when they are fasting, they are to leave a short interval after Vespers, and assemble as before for the reading of the *Conferences*. The reader shall read four or five pages, or as much as time allows. During this interval, anyone who has been occupied on special duties has time to join the assembled brothers.

When they are all present, they shall say Compline. And after Compline, no one shall be allowed to speak. If any be discovered to break this rule of silence, he shall be gravely punished: unless it be on account of guests and their needs; and even then it must be done with composure and moderation and gentleness.

43. *Of those who come late to the divine office or to table*

As soon as the bell rings, everyone shall leave the work he has upon his hands and hasten to the office, as quickly as he can, though without rudeness and so that there is no place for jesting. Nothing shall be put before the work of God.

If anyone comes to the night office after the *Gloria* of Psalm 94 (a Psalm which, with this in mind, we wish to be recited very slowly), he shall not take his place in the choir, but stand lowest of all, or in a place apart appointed by the abbot for the negligent: so that he may be seen by the abbot and the community, until he do public penance at the end of the divine office.

I have thought it right that they should stand in the lowest place or in a place apart, so that the very shame of being seen by everybody may reform them. For if they remain outside the oratory they may be inclined to return to bed again and sleep or at least to sit down outside and trifle away the time, and so give the evil spirit his opportunity. Therefore they are to enter the oratory, so that they are present for part of the office, and may amend for the future.

He who comes late to the hours of the day office, after the versicle and the *Gloria* of the first psalm, which is said after the versicle, shall stand in the lowest place, as above, and not presume to join in choir till he has made satisfaction; unless the abbot gives him absolution and leave to join in—even so, on condition that he makes amends for his fault.

He who does not come to meals before grace is ended (for all shall say grace together and pray together and all sit down together to table) shall be rebuked twice for his negligence: and if he does not amend, he shall not be admitted to the common table, but shall eat apart from the rest, and his allowance of wine shall be taken from him till he has made satisfaction and mended his ways. The same penalty shall be inflicted on him who is not present at the grace which is said after meals.

Nor shall anyone presume to eat or drink, but at the hour appointed. But if the superior offers him something and he refuses it, he shall receive nothing whatever at the time when he does want what he first refused, or indeed anything else; until he has made atonement.

44. *How excommunicated persons are to make satisfaction*

He who for a great fault is suspended from oratory and table, shall lie prostrate at the door of the oratory during the divine office; saying nothing, but lying there, with his head touching the ground, at the feet of everyone as they come out. This he shall repeat until the abbot declares that he has made satisfaction for his fault. And when he is allowed by the abbot to come into the oratory, he shall throw himself at the feet of the abbot and the whole community, to ask their prayers. Then, if the abbot commands, he shall be received into the choir in a place appointed him; but he is not to lead a psalm or read a lesson or take any other individual part in the office, until further order from the abbot.

At the end of every office, he shall prostrate himself where he stands, until again the abbot judges him to have made satisfaction and bids him desist.

They who for lesser faults are only deprived of the table, shall make satisfaction in the oratory till the abbot commands otherwise. They shall do it until he gives them the blessing and says: "It is enough."

45. *Of those who make mistakes in the oratory*

If anyone, while reciting a psalm, responsory, antiphon, or lesson, make a mistake, unless he humble himself by making reparation before all, he shall incur a greater punishment. For he would not retrieve by humility what he did amiss by neglect.

Boys for this fault shall be chastised.

46. *Of those who fail in any other matters*

If anyone, being employed in the kitchen, store, refectory, bakehouse, garden, or anywhere else, commits a fault, breaks or loses anything, or in any way fails in his duty, and does not immediately declare his fault and offer himself of his own accord to make amends before the abbot and the community; when it is discovered by another, he shall be more severely punished.

But if the fault be a hidden matter concerning the soul, he shall only reveal it to his abbot or spiritual elders, who know how to heal their own wounds as well as the wounds of others, and will not disclose and publish them abroad.

47. *Of the duty of ringing for offices*

The abbot ought to undertake the charge of ringing to the divine office night and day, or to entrust it to a brother who is punctual, so that everything may be done at the proper times.

The leading of the psalms and antiphons shall be done by those appointed thereto, in their order after the abbot. No one shall presume to sing or read who has not skill enough to do it with edification. It is to be done with humility and composure, and in the fear of God, and by the persons whom the abbot appoints.

48. *Of daily labour*

Idleness is the enemy of the soul. Therefore the brothers must spend a fixed part of their time in sacred reading, and another fixed part in manual labour.

From Easter to September 14th they shall go out and work, at any necessary task, from 7 a.m. until 10 a.m. or thereabouts. From 10 a.m. until about noon, they shall employ their time in reading.

After dinner at noon, they may rest on their beds in silence. If anyone would rather read a book, he may, provided he does not disturb others.

The hour of None is to be advanced, and said about 2.30 p.m. and afterwards they shall return to their work until Vespers. If the circumstances or the poverty of the place require that the monks cut their corn themselves, they must not look upon it as a grievance. For they are truly monks if they live by the work of their hands, as our forefathers and the apostles have done before them. Yet all is to be done with moderation, by reason of weak constitutions.

From September 14th to the beginning of Lent they are to read quietly until 8 o'clock: then Terce shall be said: and from Terce to None they shall work at their appointed tasks. As soon as the first bell for None goes, they are to stop work and get themselves ready in time for the second bell. After the meal they are to apply themselves to reading and to learning the psalms.

In Lent, they are to read from break of day until 9 a.m., and then work at their different tasks until 4 p.m. During Lent they are each to take one book of the Bible,[55] and read the whole of it from beginning to end: these books are to be distributed at the beginning of Lent. Particular care should be taken that one or two of the elders be deputed to go round the monastery, and oversee the monks at the times appointed for reading, to discover if any of them be bored, or idle, or trifling away his time with frivolous talk instead of serious reading, unprofitable to himself and an interruption to others. If (though God forbid) any such person be found, let him be rebuked, twice if necessary; and if he then does not amend, he shall be punished in accordance with the Rule, severely enough to make the others afraid. No one shall converse with another brother at improper times.

On Sundays all shall employ their time in reading, except those who have been given special duties. If there be anyone so negligent and slothful that he neither can nor will meditate or read, he must be employed about some other work which he can do, and must not be idle. Those brothers who are sick or of tender constitutions must receive consideration from the abbot, and be employed in a craft or work suitable to their strength, that they may not be altogether idle, nor burdened with labour beyond their powers and so driven away from the monastery.

49. Of the observance of Lent

The whole life of a monk ought to be a continual Lent. But because this perfection is so uncommon, at least I advise everyone, during the holy season of Lent, to practise particular purity of life, and redeem their negligences of other times. This will be rightly performed if we control our faults, and betake ourselves to prayer with tears, to reading, to compunction of heart and to abstinence.

---

[55] The older translations said: "one book from the library," the Latin being de bibliotheca. But there is now strong evidence that bibliotheca means Bible, divided into various codices. Cf. A. Olivar in Rev. Arch. Bibl. y Museos, 55 (1949), pp. 513–22: Mundo in Revue Bénédictine, 1950, pp. 65–92.

Therefore, in Lent, everyone must of his own accord add something above his usual practice; for example by offering more prayer in private, by taking less than usual in food and drink, so that everyone may, with comfort in the Holy Ghost, make a voluntary sacrifice to God of something beyond what is normally appointed him. This means that each shall deprive his body of something in eating, drinking, sleeping, talking and the little liberties of merriment and discourse; and he is to look forward, with a pure joy of spirit, to the holy feast of Easter.

Each shall make known to the abbot what he is offering up, and so it is to be done with the abbot's prayers and approval. For what is done without the consent of him who is their spiritual father, shall be looked upon as presumption and vanity, and not regarded as gaining merit. Everything must be done with the abbot's approval.

50. *Of brothers who work far from the oratory, or who are on journeys*

The brothers who, with the abbot's knowledge, are employed a great way from the oratory and cannot return at the usual time for offices, shall say the office at their place where they labour, in the fear of God and on their knees. In the same way those who are travelling shall keep the proper times for the office, and discharge their duty to God as well as they can by themselves.

51. *Of those who make short journeys*

The brothers who go out on any account whatever, with the intention of returning the same day, shall not, under pain of excommunication, presume to eat away from the monastery, though invited to do so, unless they have the abbot's leave.

52. *Of the oratory of the monastery*

The oratory must be a place suited to its name, and not used for any other business or purpose. When the divine office is ended, everyone is to go out in complete silence, and reverently before God, so that if a brother wants to remain for private prayer, he may not be disturbed by the ill-conduct of another. If at any other time anyone wants to pray by himself, he is to enter quietly and say his prayers: not in a loud voice, but in penitence and sincerity of heart. Except for the purpose of private prayer, no one shall remain in the oratory at the end of the office, lest he should, as we said, be a hindrance to another.

53. *The manner of entertaining guests*

All guests coming to the monastery shall be received as Christ himself: for he will one day say: "I was a stranger, and you took me in." [56] And everyone shall receive due honour, especially clerics [57] and pilgrims.

As soon as he hears that a guest has arrived, the superior, or some of the brothers, shall meet him with all the kindness that charity suggests. They shall pray together, and then salute each other with the kiss of peace. They shall not give the kiss of peace until they have prayed, to make sure that the visitor is not one of the devil's devices.

The salutation shall be given with deep humility, whether the guests are arriving or departing. It shall be with a bow or with a prostration on the ground, for Christ is to be adored in them and is being received as the guest.

After their welcome, the guests are to be led to the oratory. Then the superior, or a monk appointed by him, shall sit with them. He shall cause the Scripture to be read before the guest, for the sake of edification, and afterwards shall entertain them kindly.

The superior shall be dispensed from fasting out of regard to the guest, unless it be a particularly important fast which cannot be broken. But the brother shall continue to fast as usual.

The abbot shall pour the water over the guest's hands; and he, and the community, wash the feet of all the guests. After they have washed them they shall say the verse: "Lord, we have received thy mercy, in the midst of thy temple." [58]

They shall take particular care to entertain the poor and the pilgrims with more than common kindness, because Christ is most of all received in their persons. The awe which we have of the rich makes it natural for us to honour them.

The kitchen that serves the abbot and the guests shall be separate from the other. In this way guests, who are always coming to the monastery, cannot disturb the community when they arrive at irregular hours. This kitchen shall be served by two brothers, who take office for a year at a time, and understand the duty well. They shall have assistance when they need

[56] Matt. 25:35.
[57] *Domestici fidei.* Some older translations wrote "Catholics," but this is probably meaningless in the context. "Monks" is another possible meaning.
[58] Ps. 48:9.

it, so that they may serve contentedly. When they have little to do, they shall go out to work elsewhere, as they are ordered. And in all other offices of the house, the same consideration must be shown, to furnish assistants when need requires; and when there is nothing to do in their own work, they shall do what is appointed elsewhere.

The guest-room shall be entrusted to the care of a brother whose soul is possessed with the fear of God. It shall contain sufficient beds decently furnished. In all things the house of God is to be administered by wise men in a wise way.

Without leave, no one shall company or converse with guests. But if he chances to meet and see a guest, he shall salute him humbly, as I said, and after asking his blessing, shall pass by, saying only that he is not allowed to talk with a guest.

54. *Whether monks ought to receive letters or anything else?*

It is not allowable for any monk, without the abbot's leave, to send or receive letters, or presents, or any little tokens from their relations or from anyone else whatsoever, not even from each other. And if he is sent anything by his relatives, he shall not presume to accept it, till he has given notice to the abbot. If the abbot orders him to accept it, the abbot may dispose of the thing afterwards to whom he pleases: and the brother, to whom it was sent, shall not take it amiss, or he might expose himself to the temptations of the devil.

Whoever disobeys these regulations, shall be liable to punishment in accordance with the Rule.

55. *Of the clothes and shoes of the brethren*

The brothers shall be furnished with clothes suitable to the situation and climate of the place where they live. More is required in cold countries and less in hot. This is left to the abbot's discretion.

For temperate climates we are of the opinion that it is enough for each monk to have a cowl (the cowl for winter shall be of thicker stuff, that for the summer thin and worn) a tunic, a belt [59] for their work, shoes and stockings.

The monks are not to be disturbed at the colour or coarseness of these clothes, but to be content with what the country produces and can be had cheaply.

The abbot shall take care that their habits be not too short, but of the right size.

[59] The Latin is *Scapulare*. For its meaning, see the convincing note by Dom Justin McCann, pp. 192-3.

When new clothes are given out, they shall there and then restore the old ones, to be laid up in the wardrobe for the poor. It is enough for each to have two cowls and two tunics, for change at night and for the convenience of washing. More than two would be superfluous: if anyone has more than two, the extra should be taken away. And they are to return their stockings, or anything else that is old, when they are given new ones.

Those who are to make a journey shall be allowed clean drawers from the wardrobe, and shall restore them, washed, when they return home. Their clothes for journeys shall be somewhat better than ordinary; furnished from the wardrobe, and to be restored on their return.

For bedding, this shall be enough: a mattress, blanket, coverlet and pillow. The beds shall be frequently inspected by the abbot, to see that they contain no private property. If he finds anything for which he has not given leave, the culprit shall be subjected to severe punishment.

To root this vice of private property entirely out of the monastery, the abbot shall allow everything that is necessary: cowl, tunic, stockings, shoes, belt, knife, pen, needle, handkerchief, tablets. Thus there will be no pretence of need. Yet the abbot is always to remember what is said in the Acts of the Apostles: "distribution was made to everyone according as he had need."[60] And in the same way he is to consider the infirmities of the needy, without having regard to the ill-will or the envy of others. But he must be mindful that God will deal with him according to his works.

56. *Of the abbot's table*

The abbot shall always eat with guests and pilgrims. When there are only a few guests, he may invite whom he pleases of the brothers, provided he take care to leave one or two of the elders with the community, for the maintenance of discipline.

57. *Of the craftsmen of the monastery*

If there are monks in the community skilled at any craft, they shall work at it with humility, if the abbot allows them. But if anyone grows proud, and values himself upon his skill, and thinks himself profitable to the monastery, he must be taken off his work and not allowed to practise it; unless perhaps

[60] Acts 4:35.

he humble himself and the abbot may think good to employ him again.

If any of their handiwork is to be sold, let those who make the bargain take care to get no unfair advantage, and remember the example of Ananias and Sapphira: for they, or any others, who try to turn the common goods of the monastery to a dishonest profit, would incur the death of the soul as Ananias and Sapphira did of the body.

In the price of goods, they must take care to avoid avarice, and must sell at a little cheaper rate than men of the world sell, "that in all things God may be glorified." [61]

58. *The manner of receiving men into the monastery*

When anyone presents himself to be admitted as a monk, they shall not easily give him entrance; but, as the apostle advises: "Make trial of the spirits, to see if they are of God." [62] If he is importunate and goes on knocking at the door, for four or five days, and patiently bears insults and rebuffs and still persists, he shall be allowed to enter. He shall stay in the guest-room for a few days. Thence he shall go to the cell where the novices study and eat and sleep.

An elder, who has the address of winning souls to God, shall be appointed as the director of the novices. He is to watch over them carefully, and thoroughly examine whether they truly seek God, whether they are sincere in the worship of God, in obedience, in bearing trials. The novice shall be warned of all the hardships and difficulties on the road which leads to God.

If he promises to persevere in his resolution, at the end of two months they shall read this Rule to him, from beginning to end, and say to him: "Here is the Law under which you wish to be Christ's soldier. If you can observe it, enter: if you cannot, freely depart." If he remains firm, he shall be led back to the novices' cell, and his patience shall be further tried.

At the end of six months, the Rule shall be read to him that he may know what he is undertaking. And if he persists, after four months the Rule shall be read a third time. And if, upon mature deliberation, he promises to observe the whole Rule and to obey whatever commands he is given, he shall be admitted as a member of the community, and he shall know that by the Law of the Rule it shall not thenceforth be in his power to quit the monastery, nor to shake off the yoke of the Rule, which he

[61] I Peter 4:11.   [62] I John 4:1.

might have accepted or refused during so long a time for deliberation.

The person to be received shall make public profession in the oratory, of his stability, amendment of life, and obedience. The promise is to be made before God and his saints, so that if at any time he breaks his promise, he may know that he will surely be damned by God whom he is mocking.

He shall write down this promise in the form of a petition in the name of the saints whose relics are there, and of his own abbot. He shall write it with his own hand: or, if he cannot write, another shall do it at his instance, and he shall add his mark and with his own hand lay it upon the altar. As he places it on the altar, he shall say this verse: "Receive me, O Lord, according to thy word, and I shall live: and let me not be disappointed of my hope." [63] The whole community shall repeat this three times, and end with the *Gloria*. Then the novice shall throw himself at the feet of all, to ask their prayers; and afterwards he shall be looked upon as a member of the community.

If he has any property, he shall first distribute it to the poor, or make it over to the monastery by a formal donation, without any reservation for himself. He knows that for the future he is not even master of his own body.

While he is still in the oratory, his own clothes shall be removed, and he shall be clad in the clothes of the monastery. But his clothes shall be kept in the wardrobe; so that if ever (God forbid) he should be enticed by the devil and consent to leave the monastery, he can be stripped of his habit and turned out.

His petition, which the abbot took from off the altar, is not to be returned to him, but preserved in the monastery.

59. *Of the sons of rich and poor, offered to God in the monastery*

If a nobleman makes an offer of his son to God in the monastery, and the boy is young, his parents shall write the petition (as before); and, making a gift to the monastery,[64] they shall wrap the child's hand and their petition in the altar-cloth, and so deliver him to God.

[63] Ps. 119:116.

[64] *Cum oblatione.* The difficulty of this interpretation is the final sentence of the chapter, where the destitute are also supposed to make a gift. Nevertheless it still seems the most probable meaning in the context. Another suggestion is "at the offertory" in the mass.

As regards their property, they must promise under oath in their petition, that neither they, nor their agent, nor any other person, will ever give any piece of private property to him, or even give him the opportunity of acquiring it.

But if they want to give alms to the monastery for their own merit before God, they may make a conveyance of what they please to the monastery, and (if they wish) reserve the income to themselves. In this way there will be no breach open whereby the boy (which God forbid) may look forward to owning property and so be drawn into ruin—as I have known happen.

The poorer shall do the same. Those who have nothing at all shall simply make the petition, and with an offering tender their boy, in the presence of witnesses.

60. *Of priests who may wish to live in the monastery*

If a priest asks to be received into the monastery his request shall not be allowed without due consideration. But if he persists in his petition, he is to know that he must keep the whole Rule. He shall be exempted in nothing, and so will better answer the question: "Friend, why camest thou hither?" [65]

Notwithstanding, he may take place after the abbot, give blessings, conduct services, if the abbot so ordains. Otherwise he is not to undertake anything whatever. He is to remember that he is bound to observe discipline according to the Rule, and is particularly to give a good example of humility.

If there is a question of order, or any other matter, to be settled in the monastery, he must expect to be in the place which is his due according to the time when he entered the monastery, and not the place which is granted him out of respect to his priestly office.

If any other ecclesiastic has the same desire to join the community, he shall be allowed a moderate place; provided that he makes a promise to keep the Rule and to persevere.

61. *How pilgrim monks are to be received?*

If a pilgrim monk arrives from a distant country, and wants to live as a guest in the monastery, and is content to submit to the ways of the place as he finds them, without troubling the house by demanding more than is customary; he may be admitted for as long as he pleases.

If he reasonably and humbly and charitably represents that something is wrong and should be redressed; the abbot shall

[65] Matt. 26:50.

maturely deliberate upon it, and consider whether God did not send him there for that intent.

If afterwards he wishes to remain there, he is not to be refused. For while he was a guest, they have had an opportunity of seeing his way of living. But if they have remarked anything disorderly or vicious, so far from admitting him to the community, they shall politely desire him to depart, for fear that others will be misled by his bad example.

If on the contrary he does not deserve to be sent away, not only shall he be admitted to the community if he requests it: they shall invite him to stay and teach the others by his example. Wherever we are, we serve one Lord, fight under one sovereign.

If the abbot finds that he deserves to be advanced, he may give him a higher place in the community. The abbot may also do this with priests and ecclesiastics, as above, provided he sees that their good life deserves that consideration.

But the abbot is to take care that he does not admit to his monastery any monk of a known monastery without the consent of his abbot or credentials from him. For it is written: "Do not to another, as you would not have done to yourself." [66]

62. *Of the priests of the monastery*

If an abbot wants to advance any of his monks to the order of priest or deacon, he shall make choice of persons worthy of the office. The person ordained must be careful to avoid vanity or arrogance, and not to take upon him anything that the abbot does not command. He is to remember that he has only a greater obligation to keep discipline according to the Rule. Because he is a priest, he is not to forget obedience to the Rule and good order, but is to advance more and more on the way to God.

He must always expect to have his seniority from the day of his entry into the monastery, and not that which belongs to the service of the altar; even if the community and the abbot want to promote him in consideration of his good life. He is nevertheless to understand that he must keep the Rule appointed for deans and priors. If he acts otherwise, he shall not be looked upon as a priest but as a rebel.

If after frequent rebukes he does not amend, the bishop shall be brought in to see his faults. If not even then does he amend, and his faults are manifest, he shall be dismissed from the

[66] Tobit 4:15.

monastery. Yet his disobedience must be refusal to obey the Rule.

63. *The order of precedence in the community*

Their places in the monastery shall be determined by their time of entry, the goodness of their life, and the decision of the abbot. The abbot is not to disturb his flock, which is a trust, by using an arbitrary power to do anyone an injury, but must ever remember that he is to give account to God of his decisions and actions.

According to the precedence which he has determined, or which they observe amongst themselves, they shall go to the kiss of peace, receive the Holy Communion, lead the Psalms, and take their place in the choir. Wherever they are, age shall be neither here nor there in determining precedences; for Samuel and Daniel, though but children, were made judges of elders.

All, except those whom for particular reasons the abbot has degraded or advanced, shall take their place according to their date of entry into the community. For example, he who comes to the monastery at 8 o'clock shall know that he is junior to him who came at 7 o'clock, whatever his age and rank.

But boys are to be kept under discipline to everyone.

The junior monks are to honour the seniors, and the seniors to love the juniors. In talking to one another, no one may call another by his own name. But the seniors shall call the juniors "brothers," and the juniors shall call the seniors "Reverend fathers." And because the abbot is esteemed to be in the place of Christ, he shall be called "Lord and abbot," not as his own due, but out of honour and love to Christ. The abbot ought to reflect, and behave in a manner worthy of so great an honour.

Wherever the brothers meet, the junior shall ask the senior's blessing. When the senior passes by, the younger shall rise to give up his seat; and he shall not presume to sit down again till he is bidden by the senior: according to the words of Scripture "in honour preferring one another." [67]

Little children and boys shall keep their regular places in the oratory or at meals. Elsewhere they shall be supervised and under discipline, until they come to years of discretion.

64. *Of the abbot's election*

In the election of the abbot, they shall observe this method, That person shall be constituted and received abbot, whom the whole community has unanimously elected in the fear of

[67] Rom. 12:10.

God: or whom a part of the community, though a minority, has chosen with greater prudence.

The person to be appointed is to be chosen for the goodness of his life and the excellence of his wisdom, even though he be the last in the house according to seniority.

If it should happen (God forbid) that the whole congregation should unanimously conspire to elect a person to support them in their ill practices, and their disorder grow notorious to the bishop of that diocese, or to the abbots or other Christians of the neighbourhood, they are to prevent the success of the conspiracy and appoint an abbot who will be a faithful steward over the house of God. They shall be assured of a good reward if they do it with pure motives and zeal for God: and that they will be guilty of sin, if they neglect to interfere in these circumstances.

The person elected must reflect how weighty a burden he undertakes, and who will demand an account of his administration. He must remember that he is more obliged to profit his flock than to preside over them.

He is to be well-versed in Holy Scripture, so as to know how to bring forth from his treasure things new and old. He is to be chaste, sober and merciful. He is ever to put mercy above justice [68] that he may himself deserve mercy at the hand of God.

He must hate sin, and love the brothers. And when he is forced to punish them, he must use all discretion and moderation, and so will not shatter the vessel by trying to scour it too clean. He must be aware of his own frailty, and remember that it is forbidden to break the already bruised reed. [69] We do not mean that he should countenance the growth of vice; but that he use discretion and tenderness as he sees it expedient for the different characters of his brothers. He is to endeavour much more to be loved than feared.

He must observe a calmness in his ways, and not be uneasy, nor overmuch wedded to his own notions: not jealous nor too suspicious, for then he will never be free of worry. He must be cautious and circumspect in his commands; and he is to examine his commands to see whether they are in accordance with God's will or arise from worldly motives, and is to use restraint, remembering the discretion of Jacob: "If I make my flocks go further, they will all die in one day." [70] Discretion is the mother of virtues. He must follow the example of Jacob and others, and

[68] Cf. James 2:13.　　　　[69] Cf. Isa. 42:3; Matt. 12:20.
[70] Gen. 33:13. It is possible that the sentence means "he is to use discretion,

so adjust his measures, that the strong may be led to press onward, and the weak may not be disheartened. Above all he is
to observe this Rule in every point: so that when he has faithfully discharged his duty, he may hear from the mouth of the
Lord the words said to the good servant who gave his fellow-
servants wheat in due season: "Verily I say unto you, he will
set him over all his goods." [71]

65. *Of the prior of the monastery*

The appointment of the prior frequently causes great dis-
orders in monasteries. There are some people who succumb to a
wicked spirit of ambition, look upon themselves as a second
abbot, and usurp a dictatorial authority: hence breed scandals
and factions in a community. This happens especially in communities where the prior is appointed by the same bishop, or
the same neighbouring abbots, who appoint the abbot. It is
easy to see how absurd this system is, for the method of his
appointment gives him occasion to grow proud from the
moment he takes office, since it suggests to him, temptingly, that
he is exempt from the abbot's authority: for, he says to himself:
"you and the abbot derived your authority from the same
people." So arise animosities, quarrels, detraction, jealousy,
dissension, disorder. While the abbot and the prior are at vari-
ance, their souls must needs be exposed to danger. And the
monks, who become partisans, and flatterers of the one side or
the other, promote their own ruin. But the originators of the
faction are chiefly responsible for the danger into which
everyone is running.

Therefore I have thought it expedient, for the keeping of
peace and charity, that the abbot should control the appointment to every office in his monastery. If possible, he shall make
use of deans to administer the monastery as he shall direct. If
there are many commanders, no one will grow arrogant.

But if the circumstances of the place require it, or the

whether his commands concern spiritual matters or temporal matters."
But I think this is an improbable use of the phrase *secundum saeculum*.
Saeculum is used with a bad meaning in the *Rule*, chapters 1 (*servantes
saeculo fidem*), 4 ("*Saeculi actibus se facere alienum*"). The use in 7 ("*scala . . .
est vita in saeculo*") is probably, but not quite certainly, neutral. I do not
think Benedict would have conceived of "secular actions" in the monastery as opposed to "spiritual actions." See especially his instructions
that all the common goods of the monastery are to be treated like the
vessels upon the altar.

[71] Matt. 24:47.

community requests, humbly and reasonably, that a prior be appointed, and if the abbot judges it to be expedient; then the abbot is himself to appoint a prior, choosing the person himself after taking the advice of brothers who fear God.

The prior shall respectfully perform whatever the abbot commands, and do nothing against his wish and arrangement. The higher his office, the more exact he ought to be in observing the Rule.

If the prior be found to have grave faults, or is puffed up with pride, or is proved to be contemptuous of the holy Rule; he is to be admonished, up to four times. If he does not amend, he shall be liable to punishment in accordance with the Rule. If he does not then amend his ways, he shall be deposed from his office, and another, who is worthy, shall be chosen in his place. If afterwards he disturbs the quiet of the house and prove disobedient, he shall be turned out of the monastery.

Yet the abbot must not forget that he must give God an account of all his decisions; he must not let himself be influenced by jealousy, which can consume the soul like a fire.

66. *Of the porters of the monastery*

At the gate of the monastery they shall place an old man of sense, who understands to take messages and to deliver them, and has maturity enough to make him mind his business. He must have a cell by the gate, that he may be always nearby to answer knocks. As soon as he hears a knock, or the voice of a beggar, he shall say: "Thanks be to God" or "Bless ye the Lord": and then answer the business quickly, in the fear of God, in charity, and with perfect civility. If he needs help, he may be allowed one of the younger monks.

The monastery ought to be so arranged that, if possible, it may have all necessaries within its precincts—water, a mill, a garden, and the wherewithal to work at several trades. Then the monks will have no occasion for rambling abroad, which is not good for their souls.

I wish this Rule to be read often in the community. Then no brother can excuse himself upon the score of ignorance.[72]

67. *Of brethren sent on journeys*

Monks who are to be sent on a journey shall commend themselves to the prayers of the community and of the abbot.

[72] This was almost certainly the end of an earlier draft of the Rule. The succeeding chapters have nothing to correspond with them in *Regula Magistri*.

Absent monks shall be always commemorated at the end of the divine office.

The day they return home, they shall lie prostrate on the floor of the oratory at the end of all the offices, and ask the community's prayers that God will please to forgive the faults which they may have been surprised into committing on their journey, through sight or hearing of evil, or through idle talk. No one shall presume, under pain of punishment according to the Rule, to relate what has happened to him outside the monastery, for this may occasion many evil consequences. The same penalty shall be incurred by him who presumes to leave the cloister and go anywhere at all, or do anything however unimportant, without the abbot's leave.

68. *If a brother be ordered to do something impossible*

If a brother is ordered to do something difficult or impossible he shall receive the order with good temper and submission. If he sees that it is altogether beyond his power, he may patiently wait an opportunity to show his superior why it is impossible, provided he do it in a humble and not in a rebellious spirit. If, notwithstanding his plea, the superior persists in the order, the brother is to be persuaded that it is for his good, and in charity, trusting in God's help, shall obey.

69. *That no one in the community ought to defend another*

Great care is to be taken that no monk presume to defend or protect another, even though they be kinsmen. Great scandals can ensue. If any be found guilty on this point, he shall be severely punished.

70. *That no one shall strike another irregularly*

To take away all occasion of presumption in the monastery, we order that no one at any time shall presume to excommunicate or strike another, unless he have the abbot's authority. "Let offenders be publicly rebuked, as a fearful example to others." [73]

But everyone shall have a hand in the education and discipline of children up to the age of fifteen: yet they are to be dealt with reasonably and with restraint. Anyone who exercises discipline upon those older than fifteen, without the abbot's leave; and anyone who is heated with the children and does not

[73] I Tim. 5:20.

control himself, shall be punished according to the Rule. It is written: "Do not to another what you would not have done to yourself." [74]

71. *That the brothers are to be obedient to each other*

Obedience of its own nature is a thing so good, that they are to pay it to each other as well as the abbot; being assured that by this way of obedience they will come to God. Leaving aside the commands of the abbot or the priors appointed by him (which take precedence of all private instructions), we declare that the junior are to obey the senior, with readiness and charity. If anyone makes trouble, he is to be corrected.

If a brother, for whatever reason trivial though it be, is rebuked by the abbot or by one of his seniors—even if he is conscious that his senior is offended or moved at him, however mildly—he shall on the spot throw himself at the feet of the senior and remain there, by way of satisfaction, until the vexation be gone and he receive the senior's blessing. If anyone scorns to do this, he shall be liable to corporal punishment. If he is obstinate, he shall be expelled from the monastery.

72. *Of the right jealousy which monks ought to have*

There is a bitter and wicked jealousy which separates from God and leads towards hell. But there is a rightful jealousy which separates from sin and leads towards heaven and eternal life. This is the jealousy monks ought to practise from motives of charity: namely, "to prefer one another in honour." [75] They are to bear with patience the weaknesses of others, whether of body or behaviour: and strive with each other in being obedient. They shall not follow their own good, but rather the good of their brothers. They shall be charitable, with a pure heart, towards their brothers. They shall fear God. They shall love their abbot with a sincere and humble affection. They are to put nothing at all before Christ; whom we pray to lead us together to eternal life.

73. *That this Rule does not contain the whole law of righteousness*

I have written this Rule with the object of showing that monks who keep it have at least something of virtuous charac- ter, and must have begun to live a truly good life. But men aspire to the perfect life; and for them there are the teachings of the holy fathers, which will lead those who follow them to

[74] Tobit 4:15.   [75] Rom. 12:10.

true perfection. What page—even sentence—of the inspired Old and New Testaments is there that is not an excellent rule of life? What book of the holy Catholic fathers is there that does not point out the nearest way to come to our Creator? The *Conferences* of the fathers, their *Institutes* and *Lives*; the *Rule* of our father, Saint Basil—these are instruments to help the monk, who follows them, to lead a good life; to us, idle and neglectful sinners, they are a reproach and shame.

Whoever you are, who desire to advance apace to the heavenly country, practise first, through Christ's help, this little Rule for beginners. And in the end, under God's protection, you will climb those greater heights of knowledge and virtue to which the holy fathers beckon you.

APPENDIX

Notes to The Sayings of the Fathers

The Text

As is explained in the introduction, this is not intended to be a full apparatus: but is intended to secure, so far as is possible in the present state of knowledge, that the translation represents the text as it was in the sixth and seventh centuries and not the text as it became established in later medieval tradition.

The following manuscripts, with their abbreviations here used, have been of service:

B   Brussels, Bibliothèque Royale 1221 (9850–2), fol. 5–107: this manuscript came, almost certainly, from the house of St Médard at Soissons and can be dated by a remarkable frontispiece to the years 695 to 711. It contains I.1 to XV, 39: and was the best manuscript to be consulted by Rosweyde. The volume was at one time in the library of the Bollandists.

C   Cologne Chapter Library 165. The manuscript is a semiuncial which has been dated in the sixth or seventh century. I incline to think that this dating is too early, and that the early eighth century is more probable: but the manuscript is in any case an early authority of importance. In some scribbling on the last folio occurs the name Hilduinus episcopus: Hilduin was Bishop of Cologne in 842–9. The manuscript ends at X.68. It stands in close relationship with B above.

D   Brussels, Bibliothèque Royale 8126–8, fol. 62–148, of the ninth century. Its affinities are not with B but with M. It was seen, though not used carefully, by Rosweyde, and ends at XV.16.

M   Milan, Biblioteca Ambrosiana F.84 sup. The manuscript was from Bobbio and appears to be of the eighth century. With many omissions it contains extracts from almost every part, and is therefore of particular importance for the later parts (after XV.39) which no other pre-Carolingian manuscript (unless W be pre-Carolingian) reaches.

P   Paris, Bibliothèque Nationale Lat. 5387, a MS. of Colbert: dating from the end of the ninth century. This is the latest of the group of manuscripts here consulted, apart from those at

Monte Cassino and in the Bodleian. But it is important as a good manuscript which has preserved nearly all the original text apart from the first few folios which have been lost (it begins at III.3).

R   Rosweyde's text, editions of 1615, 1617, 1628 and reprinted with a few slips by Migne in PL 73. The edition was a great advance on all its predecessors, because Rosweyde had consulted two good manuscripts, B and D above. But the curious thing is how little he allowed the good readings to affect his text at crucial points. The B manuscript's readings would have made several passages intelligible to him, and the evidence of the other early manuscripts proves that these more intelligible meanings were not subsequent corrections but were the original text. Yet it must be remembered that R represents a good tradition. R alone is almost certainly wrong: R in support is not to be despised.

S   London, British Museum, Additional MSS. 15350. This is a cartulary of the Priory of St Swithin at Winchester, originally in the Chapter Library at Winchester. At each end are pasted fragments of parts XIII and XIV in an uncial hand, not later than the eighth century.

W   Würzburg, University Library Mp.th.qu.30, an Anglo-Saxon minuscule said commonly to be of the eighth century, though I incline to the view that it may well be ninth century. This manuscript has a very long lacuna in the middle, and is in some ways the least reliable of the early manuscripts, that is if I may judge only by the internal evidence of the quality of readings which it provides.

I have also examined six manuscripts of later date, useful mainly for detecting how ancient are the divergencies of the Textus Receptus from the early manuscripts: three from Monte Cassino (143, 400, 463: here abbreviated as A^1, A^2, A^3), all of the eleventh century and closely akin: and three from the Bodleian Library, all of the twelfth century—Hatton 84 fol. 27–112, probably from France (O^1): Douce 351 fol. 6–153 (O^2) and Bodleian 386 fol. 58–162 (O^3).

Syr   Parallels in the Syriac texts translated by Wallis Budge, *The Paradise of the Fathers*, volume ii (1904).

G   Parallels in the Greek *Apophthegmata*, in the version printed by Cotelier in *Ecclesiae Graecae Monumenta*, 1677–86 and reprinted by Migne, *Patrologia Graeca*, volume 65.

There are also certain parallels, not without importance, in the Coptic fragments printed by G. Zoega, *Catalogus Codicum Copticorum* (Rome 1810), pp. 288–341.

For a further list of manuscripts see A. Siegmund, *Die Überlieferung der griech. christl. Literatur in der lat. Kirche* (1949), pp. 136–8.

Part I

The titles to the different parts, though early, are not original.
The correct title of the whole is *Adhortationes Patrum in profectu monachorum*, as the uncial MSS. show.

For Part I:

BMCRD are complete.
P does not begin until the middle of III.3.
W contains 1–4, 8–10, 12, 14–16, 19, 22–3.

2. M has an odd reading for R's *neque poeniteris* etc: neque poeniteat
    de re peritura et contine linguam tuam et ventrem.
    Continens R   Conterens W
3. exigit RM   requirit BC
    virtute, linguae continentiam, et castitatem corporis R
    vertutem de lingua et castitatem de corpore BC
    vertutem linguae continentia et castitatem corporis W
    veritatem, linguae continentiam M
6. quoniam quicumque semetipsum necessitatibus subjecerit atque
        coegerit R
    qui per omnia sibi ipsi violentus est adversum desideria sua B
        (and probably C, but illegible)
    quicumque semetipsum necessitatibus, artioris vitae sumpserit
        M
7. BC om. abstinendi, homines fugiendi. M = R
8. Johannes Nanus RBCW   Johannes pusille stature M
    in castitate linguae BC
    in puritate et munditia linguae RMD
    in jejunio in patientia R
    in jejunio in poenitentia BCWA¹A²O¹O³G
    M goes straight from non irascens to includens te in sepulchro
        and omits the long section.
9. in subjectione et praeceptis RM
    in subjectione BC
10. proposito mentis RM   intentione mentis BC
    prius RMD   primus BC
11. hoc fac, et custodi cor tuum RBC
    hoc faciat cor tuum M
12. B has here and in a few other places (e.g. I.15) Dixit abbas
        Pemen pastor
14. paupertas, tribulatio, et discretio RMD
    paupertas et tribulatio BCW
16. in ipsa hora R   veniens in ipsa hora BCMW
19. in hominem R   in animam BCWD
21. tibi male loquitur RBMD   de te male loquitur C
    facias alicui calumniam RM   calumnieris BCD
    te in calumniam ducit R   contemptum BCM

22. neque curiose agere RM om. BC
Superbire corde RBC superbe sapere corde M
his est monachus RBC his est omnibus monachus M

Part II

M omits altogether.
P does not begin until III.3.
BCR are complete.
W has cc. 1–3, 7–8, 12–14, 16.

1. revolvuntur R resolvuntur BCW
5. habentes sonum R non habentes sonum BC
7. una matrona virgo R una virgo BC
Canopo [Canopo RGSyrA¹O¹O³] campo B cf. VP iii.65.
facias mare R fiat mare BC
Oro Deum RBCW G Syr A¹O¹O³. The less ferocious *Ora* is a
fault of the Migne edition.
12. posito a lacu BC posito a puteo R
14. Sit . . . agat . . . sit BCWA¹ sis . . . agas . . . sis R
15. semper R om. BCD
16. in solitudine discesserat BC in eremo RW
diceret BCWD dissereret R

Part III

BCR are complete.
P begins in the middle of III.3.
M has III.4–18 tucked surprisingly between IV.30 and IV.31
(ff. 12–15).
W has III 1–4, 7, 15–16, 20, 22, 24, 26.

1. suarum RD om. BC
2. Abbatem Antonium W
3. mundi istius vanitas BRW cf. DG suavitas C
dolore sine mitigatione et infinitas lacrimas animae BC
dolore et sine mitigatione infinitas lacrymas habentes animae R
incurras BP curras W corruas R
5. ante oculos BPC
6. in charitate om. M agapem MPD
9. Macharium maiorem MPC Macharium RBDG
lacrimae nostrae corpora nostra MBPCDG
11. M omits the last sentence.
voluptates P voluntates al.
14. turpibus om. M
15. capitio RWBD cucullo P collo (corr. cocollo) M
16. In all the early MSS. R's Syncletica is spelt Syncletice, Sincletice, Sincleticen, Sinclitice.
inprimis MPCWD impium (*corr.* impiorum) B impiorum R
17. Coelitus MBPCD celerius R

18. In the middle of III.18 M goes straight on with IV.31. It is therefore clear that M was already copying a manuscript with its folios out of order, for the first words of IV.31 are not missing in M: they are to be found before III.4.

20. hunc condemnatus es venire BC
hunc condemnatus venisti P
condemnatus est venire W
hunc condemnatus jussus es venire R
huiusmodi visitationem BCP   visionem RD

21. Simul BPR   sibi C

22. veniat ei timor BC   venit et timor RD

23. coram coelo et terram BCP   coram coeli et terrae Domino R

25. is omitted by PW

27. tribulatur anima mea BCP   tribulant animam meam R

Part IV

BC are complete.

P is complete except for 9, 31A, 39.

M has IV.8, 10, 15–17, 20, 22–3, 25–8, 30, 31, 31B, 31D–3.

R complete except for 31A, 31B, 31C, 31D, 31E.

W omits 2–6, 8, 10, 12, 15–24, 26, 29, 31, 31A, 31B, 34–7, 52–4, 57, 59–60, 64–6, 69.

1. comitatum DPCG   comitem R

8. parvissimum MBCPD   parvum RO[1]

9. The omission of 9 from MPW is possibly due to the similarity in the beginning of 9 and 10. Venit aliquando.

12. adplicuissent . . . voluissent . . . eis . . . attulistis . . . posuistis BCP (but P has accessissent for adplicuissent).

15. venisset gavisi sunt adinvicem MPCDG
venissent gavisi sunt adinvicem B
venisset adinvicem R

16. This is one of the sharp divergences of readings:
Cellia . . . tectum ecclesiae PMSyr
cella . . . tectum ejus DBCRO[1]O[2]O[3]
M's support for the later P, and the Syriac, show the high quality of P.

22. valde MP   fortiter RCD

24. Esium R   Aesium BC   Paesium P   Cassian

26. vocaretur MPD   vacavit BCRG

31. vinum omnino monachorum non est BP   Rule of St Benedict (ch. xlv)
vinum monachorum omnino non est RO[1]O[2]O[3]
vinum monachorum non est MD
The phrase is important, because the dating of the Rule of St Benedict in part depends on it.
After R's 31, some of the early manuscripts contain a group

of sayings which must have dropped out of R. The Latin text is as follows:

31A. Dixit iterum abbas Pastor: Abominatio est domino omnis corporea quies. BCD

31B. Dixit iterum abbas Pastor: Anima nullo alio humiliatur nisi sibi subtraxerit panem. [nisi si sibi BC nisi sibi PMD]

31C. Iterum dixit quia si recordetur homo verbi quod scriptum est, ex ore tuo justificaveris et ex ore tuo condemnaveris eligit magis magisque tacere. [magis unusquisque tacere P justificaveris et ex ore tuo PWSyr (om. B)]

31D. Dixit iterum senex quia frater interrogavit abbatem Pambo si bonum est laudare proximum. Et respondit ei bonum est magis tacere. [Pastorem M Pambo DPWCBG tacere MPWCD facere B]

31E. Frater interrogavit abbatem Pastorem, dicens quomodo debeo esse in communi conversatione fratrum. Dixit ei senex, Qui sedet inter fratres debet omnes fratres tamquam unum inspicere; et custodire os suum et oculos suos; et sic poterat requiescere. [So PMBC in communi omni conversatione W]

34. superfluum CR superfluo B transitorium P

36. celebratio BCR sacrificium P
onidium P cf. G enidium C in idtum B modicum R

42. animalia alia acriora medicamenta a se expellunt C
animalia medicamentis acrioribus expelluntur P
animalia acriora medicamenta a se expellunt CWD

44. After *os suum*, P adds: et vivificat animum suum

46. repperitur PBCW rapitur R

48. in coelis coram excelso coronabitur PC
in coelis corona ab excelso coronabitur BRWO[1]

54. cripta BCR chameram P

59. farinis lenticulae pulmentum BC
farina lenticulae pulmentum P
farinula lenticulam et zippulas R
rafanelaeum R trafaneleon C oleum de radicum semine P

63. copadium BCRW particulam P
[Here is an instance of the tendency of P to modernize language which the copyist did not fully understand (similar cases in IV 59, 67, 68). This instance is clearly wrong because the change makes the story unintelligible.]

64. manducassent singuli binos paximates BCP
manducassent singulos paximates R
alios binos paximates PC alios duos B alios denos DRSyr (!)
P ends: Ecce igitur quantum victu suo propter Dominum vere monachi subtrahebant

67. sirisculam BC surisculam RW vasculum P
Consequar BCP consequatur W consequi merear R

68. iam senem BCRW iam vetulam P

70. Convocati BCRW   congregati P

Part V

[The Brussels Manuscript has a separate division for IV 66–70 and henceforth numbers the parts one more than the textus receptus.]

BP give a long title for V. Incipit relationis diversae pro cautela quae adhibendo nobis est contra insurgentia in nobis fornicationum bella. After V.4, in addition to the first words of the apophthegm, P has a heading De cogitatione fornicationis.

PC are complete.

B has three folios missing: one from the middle of V.18 (eam quae corruerat) to near the end of V.23 (de hoc ipso et dixit ei); one from the middle of V.37 (in inferioribus partibus Aegypti) to the middle of V.38 (veniens sacerdos dixit) and one from the middle of V.40 (patres ut potentes) to the middle of V.41 (omnibus et nisi quia).

R has all but 2A.

W has 1–5, 7–14, 16–28, 29–41: a surprisingly complete collection for W.

M begins in the middle of V.4 (inferis converte bellum), and has 4–7, 9–14, 16, 18–20, 28 (part), 30–33, 35–40.

2A. Dixit abbas Johannis formae brevis quia satiatus si vel cum infante loquatur iam fornicatus est in cogitatione sua BCPW

4. cum valde a fornicationis daemone BCPW   male R
   Ubi vadis MBCP   quo R

5. Cyrus MBPW   Cirus C

6. pictores BRCP   pectoris M
   consensum et opere ipso peccatum BPC
   cursum et opere M
   consensum et opera peccati R

8. Continuo semper paratus PC
   continue semper paratus BW
   semper paratus R

10. A fornicationis daemone BCW
    a fornicationibus daemonum R
    a fornicatione vitio demonum M

11. tectulum MBCPD   lectum RW

13. veni ad me et increpa eum et ita increpatus abscedit BPW
    veni ad me et ita proditus abscedit M
    veni ad me et prode eum et ita proditus abscedit P
    omnino corruebas deorsum MW
    omnino corrueres deorsum RP
    domino corruebas deorsum BC
    denuo corrueres deorsum B corr.

16. in platea per tabernam MPBWC
    in platea aut per tabernam R

17. numquam alienum vas BC
    non igitur alienum vas W
    non atque alienum vas P
    non alienum vas R
    rumpatur BPCW   rumpetur R
19. dilectaretur C   delectabatur WR
    voluptate cuperet in P
    voluntarius caderet in M
20. etsi laboro tamen ponderis hujus laboris fructificare me sentio.
    Sed huc magis roga MP
    etsi laboro video tamen pondere laboris hujus fructificare me.
    Sed hoc magis roga C (and W, but quasi for etsi, and ex
    pondere) cf. D
    quia si laboro, tamen ex pondere laboris hujus considero
    fructificare me. Sed hoc roga R
21. isti . . . qui PC   istae . . . quae R (unintelligently)   istas . . . qui
    W
22. dispensationem CWP   dispositionem R
23. attulit R   accepit PW   habens secum C
    innotuit PC   innotui WR
24. fundebatur BPCW   reversabatur R
26. carnalis BD   carnales C   curialis PWR
    incurrit diaconus ille BPWR   diabolus C
28. consulendo BR   consolando PCW
    in temptationem fornicationis M
    in cogitationem fornicationis BC
    in fornicationem PWR
    Ecce puto MRW   Ecce puta BPCD
29. Dei sancti BPC   Dei magni et sancti R
30. ablactare MBC   segregare PWR
31. M omits Et scandalizatus est . . . dico tibi vale discedens, and
    still has a coherent narrative.
32. The manuscripts show R's text to be faulty here. See
    DBPCWMO¹O²Syr. tamen non extorquent. Tuum ergo est
    et suscipere et non suscipere [BC tuum ergo est cum dei
    adjutorio hujusmodi a te repellere cogitatum]. Scis autem
    quid fecerint Madianitae? Qui ornaverunt filias suas, et
    statuerunt eas in conspectu Israhelitarum. Non tamen alicui
    extorserunt ut miscerentur cum eis sed qui voluerint incur-
    rerunt in eis. Alii autem indignantes comminati sunt, et cum
    interitu eorum qui praesumpserant, ulti sunt fornicationem.
        Ita agendum est de fornicatione, quae in cogitatione
    ascendit. Respondens autem frater dixit sene, Et quid faciam?
    Quia fragilis sum, et superat me passio haec. Ille autem dixit
    ei, Intentus esto ad hujusmodi demones, et quando initium
    faciunt loquendi in corde suo . . . , etc. as R
        (M ends at suscipere et non suscipere. It is clear that R's

Respondens autem frater . . . esto ad hujusmodi . . . has been misplaced.)

33. Si ergo jactetur in nobis et non adquiescentes deo nostro adjuvante proiciamus illam a nobis facile rumpitur. Si autem jactatam super nos cum dulcedine susciperemus adquiescentes ei conversa fit fortis ut ferrum et difficile rumpitur. Necessarium igitur est . . .

[MBPCWD: deo nostro adjuvante *om.* MPR, probably primitive.]
projiciamus MBPCR proficiamus W dulcedine P
cum dulcedine MBCW fit BP sit CW *om.* M
Necessarium . . . spes salutis, *om.* M
corona BPCWR coronam perpetuam M

34. completum RPW *om.* BC

35. infirmanti dependere MBPCW infirmanti deferre R
inoboedientiae meae MR inoboedientiae BPCW

36. pessime a demone fornicationibus. Quattuor enim demones in specie MBPCWD
pessime a daemonibus. In specie R

37. solus in cella MPCWD solus in ecclesia R
velut lapidea MPCWD velut lapis R

39. Magnam rem fortiter egisti BC
Magnam rem implere potuisti P
Magnam rem fortiter gessisti R
ordo monachorum. Et ita placuit deo donare mihi salutem et egressus sum et factus sanctus monachus. DMBCPSyr (sanctus MBC sum PD)

40. admirans MBPCW adjurans R

41. admirandus, inexpertus tamen hujusmodi insidiantes astutiae, CD
admirandus, cum experientiam calliditates diabolicas non haberet P
admirandus ignotus tamen hujusmodi insidiantis astutiae W
admirandus, ignotus tamen habere hujusmodi insidias astutiae R
totum annum intente PWR unum annum intente C
exsultans spe PWR exultans ipse BC
revelatum est de transitu suo BPCW relatum est de transitu suo R

Part VI

The title in B is:

Incipit capitulum de non possidendo in quod oportet et cupiditate vitare.
P De non possidendum in quo oportet.
M Incipit de non possidendo in quo oportet cupiditate calcari.
C has no break as usual.
W has a space but no title.

BPR are complete.

C is (for C) surprisingly incomplete: it contains 1, 5–6, 8–11, 13–14, 16, 20–22.

M has the major part of VI.1, and then the rest of the book is lost in a lacuna until VII.5.

W contains 1, 5–7, 11–12, 15–17, 20–22.

6. maius omnibus BCW   magis omnibus P   melius omnibus R
7. praedica invicino PW cf. SyrG   praedica invico BD   praedica jejunium R   et praedicant abbas per tres dies P   da eum illi fratri B
8. sectabat BCDG   insequebatur P   spectabat R
10. destitisti BC   perdidisti P   desiisti R
11. Pistamoni BCP   Pisteramoni R
    turbela BP   turbule C   turbatione R
19. magnus de longinquo C   magnus ignotus BR
20. Obtulit BPCW   Attulit R
21. pedem tuum, totum corpus tuum putrefiet PCW
    pedem tuum, corpus tuum putrefiet B
    pedem tuum, putrefiet R
    constituerunt ut BPCW
    constituerunt diem ut R

Part VII

Title in BP:

Incipit narrationes diversae ad patientiam et fortitudinem nos aptantes

R is complete.

BP are complete except for R's 24.

C contains 1, 3–6, 8–9, 11–23, 25–47.

M beginning after its lacuna in the middle of 5, has 6–9, 15–16A, 19, 22–3A, 25, 28, 30–4, 36–9, 41–3A, and then there is another lacuna from VII 43A to near the end of VIII.17.

W contains 1, 3, 5–6A, 8B, 10, 12, 15–17, 25, 27, 30–3, 35–45.

It will be noticed that R's 24 is absent from all the early MSS

8. Video me quietum MCW   vide hominem quietum R
9. ostium MBPRD   hospicium C
   fessus R   om. MBCP
   ingrediens mane MBCP   egrediens mane R
   de manibus istis egreditur MP
11. quam grave et quod BC   quam grave quod PR
12. inveniretur, cunctis occiderent BPCW   om. cunctis R (G shows the original to have been contis)
    Adoro Iesum Christum filium Dei vivi BPCW   adoro filium Dei vivi R
    Crucifixit peccatum et qui occidit mortem BPCWG
    crucifixit et occidit mortem R

13. signum monachi BPC   virtus monachi R
15. mutes MBPCWR (muta appears to be a Migne miscopying)
16. Dixit iterum: multi stimuli sunt diaboli. Cum paupertate PG
    M ends the chapter at visitavit te Deus.
      Si per salutem corporis non vincitur, inegritudinem mittit, et
        cum delectationibus seducere MBPCW (cf. G)
      Sin autem satietatem corporis immittit, et cum delectationibus
        seducere R
      residuum quod sequitur mereatur ut inducamur BPCW
        (mereamur, B. *corr.*) (residuum est W)
      residuum est quod sequitur, ut inducamur R (induamur C)
      Perfectus enim eris per hujusmodi tribulationes trinitatis BC
      Perfectus enim reddens per trifurium hunc tribulationem P
      Perfectus enim eris per hujusmodi tribulationes WR (tribula-
       tionem R)
17. Omnia nobis proficiebant ad destruendam corporis desideria
    quoniam jejunia BPCW
    Omnia nobis pro destruendo corporis desiderio necessaria sunt
    quoniam jejunia R
    Non cogitemus quia BCW
    Nunc cognovimus quia P
    Non contristemur, quia R
19. Sexaginta annos BPCRSyr   xl annos M
20. Supervenientium tibi. Instruere manifesto viatoris exemplo
    quem cantandi intentio nec sarcine molestiam nec laborem
    sentire permittit itineris P
BC=R but praegravatus qui flatando et C
      praegravatus qui flando et B
22. M omits the introduction to the anecdote:
    Frater quidam erat in cella BPCR
    Frater quidam erat in loco qui dicitur cellas M
    nemo eum . . . invitabat BPCR
    nemo eum in eclesia . . . pro caritatem invitabat M
24. R only
27. The appearance of the name Arsenius (when the last proper
    name was Hyperichius) suggests that this was intended by the
    compiler as the beginning of a new little collection; and from
    the subject matter of the next few apophthegms, the collection
    was evidently upon the subject of accidie. But there is no
    manuscript evidence in support of this possibility.
28. extaediaris BCWR   taedium pateris M   taedium patereris P
30. gestiat MP   stringatur C   striniatur B cf. D   strinuatur W   vaga-
    tur R
31. ab aqua illa milia quinque MBPCWSyr   ab aqua illa R
32. tempore tentationis MBPWR   tempore tribulationis C
33. laboris et patientiae opus BCW   labor et patientia opus PR
35. ita et monachus vel qui R   monachus vel *om.* BC

37. quod vult BPCW   quantum vult R
39. omnem temptationem MBPCW   tentationem R
40. regulam monachi MBPCW   regulam monachilem R
    invenit eum nihil operantem BC
    invenit eum nihil operatum PWR
42. adjudicavit MBPWR   adjuvavit C
    exegerimus R   exigerimus M   exierimus BCW   sciremus P
43. instruens MBPW   instituens R   *om.* C
47. mittit gratiam suam et ipse tibi est consolatio, si in caritate BC
    mittit gratiam suam et satisfaciet tibi si in veritate PD
    mittit angelum et gratiam suam, et ipse tibi est consolatio, si in
    caritate R

Part VIII

BPCR are complete: remarkable for C.
M begins after its lacuna at the end of VIII.17 and contains 19–23.
W contains 1–4, 9, 11–14: and then the long lacuna of W, from
  VIII.14 to XVI. 16.

1. Venite ambulate PC   venite et videte B   venite ambulate B
   corr.   Ambulate R
2. spoliata PCW   despoliata R   spoliatur B
4. presbyter nihil nisi panem BPCW   presbyter nisi panem R
   Frater aliquid mihi opus est BC   frater aliquis factus est P
   Frater aliquis mortuus est W   frater aliquis motus est R
   miscuit BPCWR   miscui B *corr.*
6. in alienis verbis BPC   alienis verbis R
8. indignus sis etiam vivere BPC [sit C]   indignum jam vivere R
12. habui effugere spiritum PWR   habui spiritum BC
13. plorare BPCW   flere R
15. in montem Abbatis Antonii BPC   in montem R
    quando discessurus BPC   quia discessurus R
16. et dicendi sermonem BPC   edicendi sermonem R
18. ingressu BPR   egressum C
19. manifestatus MBPC   manifestus R
20. semen BPR   germen C
    Dixit iterum sicut impossibile est ut saecularem gloriam
        habentes caelestem fructum faciant, sic etiam qui veram
        humilitatem habent celestem gratiam merentur M
21. edebant BPCR   aedificabant M
22. surrexissent BPR   surrexisset MC
    vitae in id quodcumque fratribus invenisset BC
    vitae in id quod cum fratribus invenisset R
    vitae in adventu fratrum MP
23. Providentia CR   prudentia MBD
    Humana prudentia omnem vigorem interioris hominis amputat
        et relinquid eum aridum MD

Part IX

Title:

De eo quod non oporteat judicare quemquam MBCR　indagare P
BP are complete.
CR are complete except for 12A.
MD contain 1, 3, 5, 8–9, 11–12.
W is in the long lacuna.

1. pertulit MBPC　tulit R
2. Surgit autem abbas bisarion BC　surgens enim abbas besarion P
   surrexit autem Besarion R
3. addixisti BPR　adduxisti C　judicasti M
4. Moysem, ut veniret BPC
   Moysem, dicentes ut veniret R
   vetustam BPC　vetustissimam R
   portant BC　portavit secum et venit P　post se portavit R
6. prodiderimus BPR　prodegerimus C
7. in ipsis locis BPC　in ipsius locis R
   fossatum BR　fossata C　caretam P
   videns eum senex afflictum BPR　afflictum *om.* C
   videre desidero BPC　videre volui R
   sursum sursum in coelo, ego autem deorsum deorsum BPCG
   Sursum in coelo, ego autem deorsum R
8. quietem MBPC　requiem R
9. Pior MPRD　prior BC
11. bibere et non bibebat MBPC
    bibere et non poterat R
12. mane manducantem MBPC　comedentem R
    facta est celebratio missarum MBPR　facta est missarum C
    sermonem otiosum BC　sermonem odiosum R
12A. Vir quidam sanctus cum vidisset quemdam peccantem flevit
     amare, et dixit, iste hodie ego crastina. Verumtamen quali-
     tervis peccet aliquis ante te non judices eum sed judica te
     magis esse peccatorem quam illum BP [B vidisset　P audisset
     B quam illum　P quam eam]

Part X

R omits 71A, 71B, 71C, 103A, 103B, 103C.
C is complete from 1–68 and then ends altogether. The ending of C
   at X.68 is probably not fortuitous for M begins X.69 with a big
   initial.
P, surprisingly, omits 3 and 51A.
B has lacunas between 19 and 25, 76 and 78, 85 and 96.
W is in its long lacuna.
M contains 1–2, 6, 8, 10–11, 13, 15–16, 19, 27, 31, 35, 38, 44, 47,
   50, 51B, 53–61, 64–7, 69, 74–6, 80, 85–8, 90–2, 94, 96–8, 102–3,
   103B, 103C, 109–11, 113–14.

1. conterentes MBPR   continentes C
2. relaxare rigorem PR   relaxare vigorem BC
5. ex tanta eruditione et scientia BPC
   excitati eruditione et scientia R (probably thinking of excitati
      in 4)
7. parvam holoscellam BC   parvum holosculum P
   parvum holus in cella R B *corr.*
8. discipulus *om.* B
   aestus nimis candens BC   aestus grandis MPR
   operario monacho MBPC   operatio monacho R
11. sunt corporalis labor BPC
    corporalis laboris M
    labor corporis R
    intentus etiam et assiduus in labore MBC
    intentus et jam assiduus in labore P
    intentus etiam assidue ad laborem R
12. Agatho cum factus fuisset BPC   Agatho cum fuisset R
13. mortuum BPC   mortuos R
    non placet Deo BPCR   non placet alicui MD
14. noluit mihi facere sagenam BP
    noluit mihi facere C   noluit facere sagenam R
15. potes mente tua aurum quod videris velut lapides reputare
       MBPCD
    aurum quod videris potes velut lapides reputare R
16. comede parum cotidie MBPR
    comede panem cotidie parum C
    Salvus MPR   sanus BC
18. habens de infirmitate corporis aliquid, oportet sustinere R
    habens de infirmitate corpus aliquam culpam oportet ope
       sustinere C
    habens de infirmitate corpus aliquam culpam oportet sustinere
       B
    incurrens per infirmitatem carnis oportet sustinere P
    fuerit et ammonitus BC   furatus et ammonitus PR
20. solitudo PC   sollicitudo R
22. Reliquerunt fratres PC   Reliquerunt homines R
24. opus animae velut in transitu. Et quod erat velut in transitu
       factum est opus PC
    opus animae, velut cum in transitu factum est opus R
27. eum usque mane affligi DMBPCGSyr   eum affligi R
28. surgo PR   surrexero B   aurio C
    contristetur etiam nullo suscipiente BC
    etiam contristetur nullo sumente R
    etiam conturbetur nullo suscipienti P
29. statim BPC   cito R
    expediunt passiones BC   expedit passiones PR

36. corpusculum meum ne infirmarer BP
    corpusculum meum ne infirmaret C
    corpus meum ne infirmarer R
39. Venit de peregrinis BP
    venit ad peregrinis C
    venit ut peregrinus R
    de Scripturis inquirit BPC
    de Scripturis loquitur R
    aperi os meum de his et imple B
    aperi os meum de his et implebo CG
    aperi os meum et imple P
    aperiam os meum de his et implebo R
41. secus BC securus P securis R
    sine PCR senem B
    aut putrefiunt BPC et putrefiunt R
46. non possum non seminare BPC non possum seminare R
    idem ipsum opus BPC istud opus R
48. homo et negaverit, dicens non peccavi BPC
    homo et non negaverit, dicens peccavi R
50. delavat MBPC delet R puteo BPCR canali MD
51. ideo dixit BPR ideo dico C
52. etiam unius BC etiam si unius PR
56. mihi haereditas MBCD mihi omnis haereditas PR
    ecclesiam illic sibi DMBPCSyr
    ecclesiam clerici sibi R
57. corporeis BC corpori PR
    delegaveris BR delectaveris P denegaveris C
60. repercutiens BPC percutiens R
    dicit et ipse BPC dic ei et ipse R
61. iam non sto BC iam non ero PR
    qui erat abbatis Agathonis BC
    qui erat abbatis Agathonis discipulus R [P omits the clause]
63. Qualimodo BPC Qualis homo R
64. conversatio bona B conversationum bonum C
    conversantium bonorum PR
65. prestat BPC praestabit R
    Bonae quidem sunt operationes MPD
    Bonum quidem est operari BC
    Bonum quidem operaris R
66. bonum BPC bona R
    At X 68 the Cologne manuscript ends.
69. operantes MBP laborantes R
70. sensibiles PR insebiles B insatiabiles B. *corr.*
71. taedium quidam appellaverunt B taedium appellaverunt PR
    After BPR's 71, BP have a series of additions.
71A. Dixit iterum bonum est quidem non irasci. Si autem evenerit,
    nec spatium diei huic passioni concessum est.

71B. Dixit enim, non occidat sol super iracundiam vestram. Tu autem expectas donec tempus vitae tuae occidat, nescis dicere sufficit diei malitia sua. Quare odio [Odio B: odium P] habes hominem qui te [tibi P] nocuit? Non est enim ipse qui nocuit sed diabolus. Odire [odisse P] ergo debes aegritudinem non aegrotum.

71C. Dixit iterum: periculosum namque [namque *om.* P] est si ille qui per activam vitam non venit temptet ut doceat. Sicut enim si quis domum habeat fragilem et suscipiat peregrinos, magis nocuit eis de ruina domus; ita et isti nisi prius caute se sub activae vitae exercitatione aedificaverint, etiam audientes se secum pariter perdunt. Quoniam sermonibus quidem vocaverunt ad salutem morum autem malitia potius nocuerunt.

72. diabolica PR   diabolica pericula R

sin dubio P   manifestum est quia BR

per mediocrem abstinentiam. Omni ergo tempore conversationis BP

mediocri tempore conversationis R

74. in me ignorantem, inveni januas M

76. monachus quidam MPR   Symmachus quidam B

Aegyptius mollibus rebus et colligatis virgis habere graticium in quo requiesceret et pellem stratem sub ipso, et modicum capitale sub caput ejus P

Aegyptius vestitum mollibus rebus, et budam de papyro, et pellem stratam sub ipso, et modicum capitale de cartica sub caput ejus R

77. quaeritur B   Deus quaerit R

79. non fecerit opus loci BP   non fecit fructum loci R

80. voluntatem BRD   voluptatem P

scientem P   scitum R   sciolum MD

82. localibus PR   vocalibus B

83. manserit cum operario si sapit proficit: etsi non proficit, non tamen descendit inferius videndo operantem P

manserit cum operario proficit: etsi non tamen descendit inferius, B

manserit cum operario proficit: etsi non proficit, non tamen descendit inferius R

85. tantum cogitantibus de peccato BP

tantum cogitationibus de peccato MD

tantum est de cogitationibus quam de peccato R

egerat RD   aegrotaret M

retulit MP   retuli RD

91. humilitatem et caritatem MPD   humilitatem R

92. mitte in eo oleum, et fluens refunde oleum et pone P cf. MD

mitte in eo oleum, et accende intus stupam, et refunde oleum, et pone R

93. lumina P   lumen R
senex ille seduxit P   senex ille falsator seduxit R
94. expoliasti P   expulisti MRD
95. personam PR   porsonam Migne
est causa culpae P   est causa R
nolumus salvari P   volumus salvari R
96. opus suum R   psalmodiam suam PD
97. de labore MBPD   de labore fatigatos R
opus Dei et postea dixit cessemus MB [B dicens]
opus Dei et posuit ea quae habebat et dixit R
labore estis MBP
labore estis fatigati R
panem siccum et sal MPR   posuit panem siccum B
fugerent occulte BPR   fugerunt M
    After 103, in MBPD apophthegms not in R.

103A. [BP] Dixit senex quia in heremo etsi laborant Sancti sed
acceperunt iam aliquam partem quietis. Hoc autem dicebat
pro eo quod erant liberi a saecularibus curis.

103B. Dixit iterum senex quia [P. qui] si scit monachus esse aliquem
apud quem proficere possit sed [B. *om*. sed] necessarium
[necessaria DM] corporis cum labore habet ac [B. hac]
propterea non vadit [P. audit] ad eum, hujusmodi monachus
non credit esse Deum.

103C. frater quidam interrogavit parvulum [B. infantem] mona-
chum dicens, Bonum est loqui [B. loquere] an tacere? Dicit
ei puer ille, si sunt verba otiosa, dimitte ea [P. eos]. Si autem
bona, fac locum [P. loco] bono et loquere [fac bonum locum
et loquaere bona M cf. D]. Verumtamen vel si bona sunt
verba, non diu protrahas sed cito incide quod loqueris et
quiescis (quiesce DM)

105. seorsum et seorsum R   curri P
107. ore dicere R   ore docere B
108. oportet hominem habere interius operationem suam. Si enim
in opere Dei occupamur . . . P
109. immoderate comedere MPD   impatienter R
jejunassent primo vel secunda die inanis effecti sunt MD
jejunassent primum valde inanes effecti sunt P
jejunassent primo aporiati sunt BR
110. solitarius sum MPD   solitarius volo esse R
111. projice eum in se MPD   projice eum in terram R
112. mori cum ipso MBP   morari cum ipso R
115. sudario B   subhumerale P   superhumerale R

Part XI

B is complete.
P has lacunas from 1–8 (middle), 18 (middle)–21 (middle), and
37h–43a are misplaced in the middle of X.96.

R omits 2A, 14A, 24A, 31A, 42A, 42B, 42C.
M has 1A, 2, 8B, 11–13, 14A, 15, 17–20, 23, 26–31, 35, 38–40, 42,
    42A, 42C, 43, 44, 46–9, 51–2.
W is still in its great lacuna.

2. Custodiam magnam MRD   magnam *om.* B
4. Eseo B   Arsenio R
5. mundo isto B   mundo hoc R
6. divinam B   divinitatis R
11. reputat BMD   imputat R
14A. Dixit qui supra abbas Johannis brevis quia similis sum homini
     sedenti sub arbore magna et adtendenti beluas multas et
     plura serpentia ad se venientia. Et cum se viderit quia non
     potest stare adversus ea festinat ascendere in arborem ut
     salvetur. Ita et ego sedes in cella mea et adtendo malignas
     cogitationes super me. Et cum non praevaleo adversus eas
     confugio per orationem ad deum et ita salvus efficior ab
     insidiis inimici.
     ascendere in arborem ut salvetur BP
     fugire M
     per orationem MPD   ad orationem B
15. ut se invicem lucraretur in bonum MPB (bono B)
    unde invicem lucrarentur bono R
16. octaginta et quinque P   LXXXV B   octoginta R
    sicut egrederis ita ingrediaris B
    sicut egredieris ita ingredi P
    sicut ingrederis ita egrediaris R
18. dormitaret MPR B *corr.* dormiret B
    cum spiritualium rerum sermo fieret MBP
    cum spirituales res faceret R
    somno relicti sunt B   somno reluctati sunt R
    (P's lacuna begins just above, the words being "impugnatorem
    autem.")
20. ad me veniat pro aliquid responsi veremur conloqui invicem B
    venit ad me pro aliqua re necessariam veremur conloqui
    invicem M
    ad me venerit pro aliqua re veremur invicem R
    tacere MRD   agere B
21. nostram et sobrietate diligentiam adhibemus, non inveniemus
    BP (adhibeamus P)
    nostram timore Dei et sobrietate, non invenimus R
22. primo seorsum BP   primus eorum R
24A. Dixit iterum quia si faciat homo coelum novum et terram
     novam non potest (poterat P) esse securus BP
25. Contemptiosus P   contentiosus R   intentiosus B
29. per diem MBPD   per idem R
30. exacerbabat R   exacerbabat deum MPD

31. eum de adversariis malis B
    eum adversarius P
    eum de adversarii malis R
    eum adversarii M
31A. Dixit sancta sincletice: fili omnes salvari novimus, sed propter neglegentiam nostram a salute deficimur. BP
33. deprimitur BP opprimitur R
34. David psalmista BP psalmista R
    in mari quaedam petrosa sunt, quaedam vero bestiis plena quaedam autem et tranquilla BP
    in mari quaedam vero periculis plena, quaedam autem et tranquilla R
    clamando et vigilando PR clamando B
37. custodierit bene cor BP custodierit cor R
    audit B videt P audit et videt R
    oleo et lychneo *om.* P
    convalescunt BP invalescunt R
    nixum B myxum R stuppam P
39. vixit MBRD dixit P
40. MD add (what alone can make sense of the apophthegm) after *perdidit.* Qui autem tempus perdiderit non potest invenire pro eo quod perdidit.
42A. Dixit senex quia oportet hominem custodire opus suum ne pereat. Nam si aliquis operetur multa et non conservet ea non proficiet. Alter vero si parum operetur et conservet hujus opus stabit MBP cf. D.
    Alter vero PD Alterutro M Si autem alter P
42B. Dixit senex a modico usque ad magnum opus quae ago. Ex fructu eorum intellego quid pariunt sive in cogitationibus sive in actibus meis BP
42C. Dixit senex dormiente te aut surgente vel aliud quid faciente si fuerit deus ante oculos tuos in nullo te inimicus poterit deterrere. Etsi talis cogitatio manserit in homine etiam dei virtus manet et in eo. MBPD
42D. Dixit senex surgens mane dic ad teipsum labora corpus ut pascaris sobria esto anima ut adprehendas hereditatem BP
45. Interior homo ... exteriorem BPSyr
    exterior homo ... interiorem R
47. nihil cogites MBP nihil vanum cogites R
    quiescens in lecto MBPD quiescens R
49. inluminati fuerint oculi MBP non fuerint clausi oculi R
50. monachi R nomina BP (cf. note in Migne PG 65, col. 265)
51. didicit versutias MPRD vicit versutias B
54. semper timeat MBP semper teneat R

Part XII

BPR are complete.
M omits only 4. An unusually complete tradition.

2. exalationem MD   exhalationem R   exaltationem BP
3. quattuor dies MD
4. Sicut scriptum est, ora autem BP   ora autem R
8. fieri MBPD   efficiere R
10. Domine adjuva MBPD   adjuva R
14. fugit MB   statim fugit PRD

Part XIII

BPR are complete.
M omits 4, 8, 11.
The fragment of S begins at 9.

3. septies BM   sexies DPR Cassian
4. clericis ecclesiae quid illic est P
   clericis quid illic est B
   clericis ecclesiae quae illic est R cf. G
8. pergentes BP   divertentes R
9. arbor est hic cui curvante genu et orante quo inclinata BPS
   ipsum sequamur et nos BS   ipsum sequamur MPR
11. volens pulsare et intrare BPS   volens pulsare R
   [S has pulsare et, and the remainder is cut off by the binder.
   But the number of missing letters proves that S must have read
   et intrare.]
12. Quando habui dedi MBP   quando habui praebui R
   prima die MBPS   quadam die R
   cum accepisset MBPS   cum accepissent R
14. Praesbiter B   Abba presbyter MP   Abba R
15. ostium MBPS   hospitium R
   abundantia MBPD [S concealed in binding]   Egestate R
   Iam non habet MBSD   Iam non habeo PR
   glorificaverunt BS   glorificavit MPRD

Part XIV

BPR are complete.
A folio of M has fallen out between 5 and 11.
S has only the first few words of 1, as far as Abbas etiam Alexander.
S also has preserved 10 (near end) to 17.

1. lenius et modeste MPRD   lenius B
   custodire sermones B   custodire sermonem MPD
   custodire mandatum R   modo adhuc complevi MBP
   modo complevi RD
3. mane veniret MBP   mane rediret B
4. expecta me B   expecta MPRD
5. scriptor MPD   scriptor antiquar' B
   scriptor antiquarius R
6. mihi illud ultra dicas BP   mihi illud dicas R

8. fieris BP   fies R
13. Dicebant senes BPS   dicebat senex MR
14. mandatis BPMS   mandato R
16. quod iubes MBPSD   quomodo iubes R
    conplexata est eum et coepit BS
    conplexa est eum et coepit MP
    complexa eum coepit R
18. Amplexatus est eum et osculabatur MBP
    amplexatus est eum R

Part XV

P is complete.

R is complete except for 82A; the excellent B manuscript, complete
to 39 except for the omission of 24, unfortunately comes to an
end at 39.

M has a large lacuna from the first lines of 1 to the middle of 14 and
another from the beginning of 31 to the beginning of 66. It then
has 73, 76, 79, 81, 83, 85–6, 88–9.

W is still in its long lacuna.

1. dilatantur BD   ditantur PR
5. soliti erant BP   solebant R
6. usus est BP   utebatur R
7. cogitationibus tuis interrogas P
   cogitationibus suis (*corr.* tuis) interrogas B
   cogitationibus suis R
9. P includes at the end of 8 the first sentence of BR 9
   projecit se etiam senex BPD   projecit se senex R
   loqui me saepe DBPSyr   loqui me semper R
10. longinquo BPD   longaevo R
    fecit et ita dormivit consummans BP
    fecit consummans R
11. quattuor ingressi sunt templi PD
    quatuor ingressus sunt templi B
    quatuor ingressus sunt ad aditum templi R
12. petentes PRD   paenitentes B
14. ut faciant orationem PRDG   ut faciant operationem B
    mandatum . . . expellit BPDG   mandata . . . expellunt R
19. meipsum semper sine cessatione BP
    meipsum sine cessatione R
20. Aliquando MBP   Quando R
    sicut mos est PR   sicut Moyses B
    Dixit autem Abba Theodorus, Perdiderunt monachi ingenui-
        tatem [reverentiam P] et non dicunt, Ignosce MPBG (*om.* R)
21. diaconus MPR   monachus B
    si non vis ministrare B
24. Unexpectedly omitted by B

25. nullam causam in conceptu M
    nullam causam in conspectu BPR
31. contenebant B   contemnebant PR
42. archiepiscopus P   episcopus R
43. Vade, quidquid vides P   quidquid vides R
49. humilitas P   humilitas monachi R
50. duritiam cordis P   summitates cordis R
51. sapientiam habet et non est succensus ignem verborum dei sicut
    et Joseph resolvatur cum acceperit principatum. Multae
    enim horum cum sint temptationes in medio hominum.
    Bonum est enim P
52. perfectioni meae P   perfectio animae R
54. Sed nec tunc ita de te sentias quia si omnia P
    Sed nunc si ita de te sentias quasi omnia R
    dissolvit P   resolvet R
55. et intelligentior R   *om.* P
    scriptum est enim qui se putat stare videat ne cadat sale
    conditus P
    sed esto spirituali sale conditus R
59. sermones P   cogitationes R
    quia nec nos potuimus id custodire ne faciat istud. Inveniamus
    nos postea id ipsud facientes P
62. quousque expoliaret P   quo spoliaret R
64. inventus esset in ecclesia P   tentus esset in ecclesia R
    iactatur P   insectatur R
67. temptamur R   non temptamur P
75. contemnes P   condemnes R
76. te minorem facies MR   cum timorem facis P
    perturbant MP   perturbat R
80. temporum in sordidis cogitationibus ut cum eas adsumere
    aspicimus, nos ipsos P
    modici boni operis R   boni operis P
82. At the end of 82, P has:
    Monachus aliquis vulneratus a quodam tenens manum ad
    vulneris prostravit se ad pedes percutientis se et gratias agens
    deo.
85. notitiam R   fiducia MP
    ex hoc fiduciam sumes et desiderare R
    ex hoc desiderare MP
88. pax magna P   pax maxima R

Part XVI

R is complete.
P has a folio missing between the middle of 16 and the middle of 19.
M has 1, 3–7, 9–10, 12, 17–19.
W's lacuna ends at 16.

None of the early MSS. contains 20. Rosweyde printed it as a separate *Vita*, PL 73, 661–2. F. Nau showed (*Histoire de Thais, Annales du Musée Guimet*), that the hero of the story is not Paphnutius but Sarapion the Sindonite.

1. valet tantum quantum PM   valet pretium quod R
6. onerandum MP   carricandum R
13. cf. Moschus *Pratum Spirituale* 212
14. superveniunt R   superbiunt P
16. libicus genere PSyr   rusticus genere R

Part XVII

WR are complete.
P begins at 3.
M omits 7, 11–12, 15–16, 19, and has a lacuna from the middle of 20 to XVIII 19.

SELECT BIBLIOGRAPHY

The Sayings of the Fathers

A. EDITIONS

Text in *Vitae Patrum* books V–VI, edited by Heribert Rosweyde, 1615, 1617, 1628: reprinted, and most accessible, in Migne *Patrologia Latina*, vol. 73, columns 851–1024.

B. LITERATURE

W. Bousset, *Apophthegmata Patrum*, Tübingen, 1923.

J. Brémond, *Les Pères du désert*, Paris, 1927. (With introduction by Henri Brémond.)

Cuthbert Butler, *The Lausiac History of Palladius*, Texts and Studies series, vol. vi, Cambridge, 1898.

J. C. Guy, "Remarques sur le texte des *Apophtegmata Patrum*," in *Recherches de science religieuse*, 1955, pp. 252–8.

J. O. Hannay, *The Spirit and Origin of Christian Monasticism*, London, 1903.

K. Heussi, *Der Ursprung des Mönchtums*, Tübingen, 1936.

P. Ladeuze, *Le Cénobitisme Pakhomien*, Louvain, 1898.

H. Leclercq, Article "Cénobitisme" in *Dictionnaire d'Archéologie chrétienne et de Liturgie*.

L. Th. Lefort, *Les vies coptes de saint Pachome et de ses premiers successeurs*, Louvain, 1943.

H. Lietzmann, *The Era of the Church Fathers (A History of the Early Church*, vol. iv), English translation, 1951.

W. K. Lowther Clarke (translator), *The Lausiac History of Palladius*, London, 1918.

——*The Ascetic Works of Saint Basil*, London, 1925.

A. Siegmund, *Die Überlieferung der griech. christl. Literatur in der lat. Kirche*, Munich, 1949.

B. Steidle (editor), *Antonius Magnus Eremita*, Studia Anselmiana 38, Rome, 1956.

Helen Waddell, *The Desert Fathers*, 1936.

E. White, *The History of the Monasteries of Nitria and of Scete*, New York, 1932.

F. A. Wilmart, "Le Receuil latin des Apophtegmes" in *Revue Bénédictine*, 1922, pp. 185–98.

H. B. Workman, *The Evolution of the Monastic Ideal*, London, 1913.

Cassian

A. EDITIONS

The best edition is that of M. Petschenig in the Vienna Corpus, vols. 13 and 17 (1886 and 1888). The older edition of A. Gazet (Douai, 1616, reprinted in Migne, *Patrologia Latina*, vols. 49–50) is not to be despised, because of the care and range of its annotations.

E. C. S. Gibson translated most of the works of Cassian in the series of *Nicene and Post-Nicene Fathers*, vol. XI (Oxford, 1894), and gave the translation a valuable preface.

B. LITERATURE

M. Cappuyns, Article "Cassien" in *Dictionnaire d'Histoire et de Géographie ecclésiastiques.*

O. Chadwick, *John Cassian*, Cambridge, 1950.

S. Marsili, *Giovanni Cassiano ed Evagrio Pontico*, Studia Anselmiana, Rome, 1936.

M. Olphe-Galliard, Article "Cassien" in *Dictionnaire de Spiritualité, d'Ascétique et de Mystique.*

Saint Benedict

A. TEXT

The text of the Rule, according to the Sangallensis 914 manuscript, is printed by Ph. Schmitz: the new amended edition (Maredsous, 1955) has a useful introduction by Christine Mohrmann on the language of Saint Benedict. Diplomatic edition of Sangallensis 914 by Morin in 1900. The text by B. Linderbauer (1928) is useful. Two other editions, both by English Benedictines, are important: one by Cuthbert Butler (revised edition 1927 and 1936), an edition with good notes and references: the other by Justin McCann (1951) with excellent introduction and notes.

For the textual history of the Rule, L. Traube's classic *Textgeschichte der Regula S. Benedicti* (1898, second edition 1910) is still worth reading. For the recent attack on it see B. Paringer in *Revue Bénédictine*, 1951, pp. 81 ff. The diplomatic edition of the *Regula Magistri* (ed. H. Vanderhoven and F. Masai; Publications de Scriptorium, vol. iii, Brussels, 1953) is indispensable. For a recent survey, with bibliography, of the argument over the priority of the *Regula Magistri*, see G. Penco "Origine e sviluppi della questione della *Regula Magistri*" in B. Steidle (ed.), *Antonius Magnus Eremita* (Rome, 1956), pp. 283–306.

B. LITERATURE

Cuthbert Butler, *Benedictine Monachism*, 2nd edition, London, 1924.

J. Chapman, *Saint Benedict and the Sixth Century*, London, 1929.

J. McCann, *Saint Benedict*, London, 1937.

Ph. Schmitz, Article "Benoît de Nursie" in *Dictionnaire d'Histoire et de Géographie ecclésiastiques.*

INDEXES

GENERAL INDEX

It is not always possible, particularly in "The Sayings of the Fathers," to determine whether references to the same name are references to a single person or to two or more people of the same name

Biblical References